Building Western Civilization

From the Advent of Writing to the Age of Steam

ALAN I MARCUS

Iowa State University

HARCOURT BRACE COLLEGE PUBLISHERS

Fort Worth Philadelphia San Diego New York Orlando Austin San Antonio
Toronto Montreal London Sydney Tokyo

To Marjorie Marcus Schulz,
for making her big brother's life fuller and better

Publisher	**Christopher P. Klein**
Senior Acquisitions Editor	**David C. Tatom**
Developmental Editor	**Sue A. Lister**
Project Editor	**John Haakenson**
Senior Production Manager	**Kathy Ferguson**
Senior Art Director	**Brian Salisbury**
Photo Research and Permissions	**Cindy Robinson/Carrie Ward**

Cover Image: David Carson/Superstock

Requests for permission to make copies of any part of the work should be mailed to: Permissions Department, Harcourt Brace & Company, 6277 Sea Harbor Drive, Orlando, Florida 32887-6777.

Address for Editorial Correspondence: Harcourt Brace College Publishers, 301 Commerce Street, Suite 3700, Fort Worth, TX 76102.

Address for Orders: Harcourt Brace & Company, 6277 Sea Harbor Drive, Orlando, FL 32887-6777. 1-800-782-4479 (in Florida).

(Copyright Acknowledgments are on page 369, which constitutes a continuation of this copyright page.)

Harcourt Brace College Publishers may provide complimentary instructional aids and supplements of supplement packages to those adopters qualified under our adoption policy. Please contact your sales representative for more information. If as an adopter or potential user you receive supplements you do not need, please return them to your sales representative or send them to:

Attn: Returns Department
Troy Warehouse
465 South Lincoln Drive
Troy, MO 63379

Printed in the United States of America

ISBN: 0-15-500115-9

Library of Congress Catalog Card Number: 96-79890

7 8 9 0 1 2 3 4 5 6   067   9 8 7 6 5 4 3 2 1

Contents

Preface

The title of this book, *Building Western Civilization*, evokes images of bricks and mortar, structural elements, being fashioned to create an edifice. That imagery serves western civilization well. Structures, those long gone as well as those still extant, record its history. Three major types of structures have left indelible marks as western civilization's building blocks. The most obvious structural elements are physical: buildings, machines, devices, those things commonly thought of as technologies. Construction of ziggurats, pyramids, roads, churches, walled cities, monasteries, castles, water-delivery systems and cathedrals as well as the more mundane houses secured a disproportionate percentage of revenues and attention during the nearly 6000-year span covered in this volume. Social structures have also been an inextricable facet of western civilization. Habits, customs, social organizations, institutions and living arrangements constitute social technologies upon which western civilization has been constructed. Last but hardly least are intellectual structures, including architectural, scientific, musical, philosophical and artistic concepts and ideas about the nature of the cosmos and humanity's place within it as well as the relationship of the past to the present and the present to the future.

These three structural types are the focus of *Building Western Civilization*. An extraordinary amount of artifactual evidence documents the centrality of these elements. Account books, censuses, literary and artistic productions, governmental edicts, texts and institutions as well as the more conventional architectural and mechanical monuments and relics testify to their existence. These rich primary sources help provide western civilization's portrait.

But just what is this thing called western civilization? Adolf Hitler and Josef Stalin emerged from it but so too did Wolfgang Amadeus Mozart and Albert Einstein. Its agencies have provided an abundance of consumer goods but persons claiming to be part of it maintain that frustration and anomie characterize contemporary life. Western civilization is marked by unprecedented opulence as well as abject poverty, by widespread democracy and intense ethnic hatreds.

The west is now poised to embark upon a new epoch. It seeks to think globally and broaden its definition of the present's debt to the past. But as contributions of African, Asian and Ancient American cultures are elucidated, embraced and integrated, that civilization that has for so long dominated, even monopolized our thought and perspective, must be explored, confronted and understood. What was this thing western civilization? How did it operate? What were its touchstones? Why did it seem so powerful?

Curiously, western civilization has not been rooted in one single place. At various times its cultural capitals have been located as far east as present day Iraq, as far south as Egypt, as far west as Portugal and as far north as Scandinavia. Absence of a geographic home has not hampered the concept of western civilization for it exists as a state of mind. What has made western civilization a concrete formulation is memory, the desire of persons to establish and connect themselves to a place—the "West"— and to a set of ideas. The Judeo-Christian tradition, Greek democracy and the Roman Empire co-exist neatly as part and parcel of the tradition of western civilization. This identification process has occurred for several thousand years. Persons long have viewed themselves as connected to and descended from a tradition that has extended over centuries. To these men and women, there is and has been a western tradition. It is their collective memory, their self-identification. By cleaving to this tradition, they have been able to root themselves and their posterity.

But just as the "West" has no true geographic location, and even incorporates America today, the idea of a discrete, neat western tradition is also a fiction. No matter how much it has been extolled and revered, western civilization has not unfolded incrementally over time. Nor has western civilization provided a compactly circumscribed standardized template of rules and behaviors that has been met over the course of centuries. That is not to say that there is not and has not been a western civilization, of course, or that it has not been extremely influential. Such a view is absolutely preposterous. Western civilization exists in the realm of ideas. Western civilization is not so much a common heritage but the idea of a common heritage. In that sense western civilization parallels the concept of the West. It is the means of establishing and perpetuating a common heritage.

The history of western civilization is the history of those ideas that have functioned to make western civilization a coherent, useful entity. It is about commonalties, those textures and tissues that have been embraced as unifying points in the past. These commonalties have tremendous repercussions. When translated into action, they become wars, religions, governments, art, architecture, science and more. These commonalties frame public action. They dictate what is acceptable and what is not. They are arbiters of public taste and public probity.

Despite the designation western civilization or the western tradition, these commonalties have not been immutable. Persons have demarcated those aspects of the past—ideas, habits, customs and the like—that they deemed relevant only to have others at different times in the past identify different aspects as critical facets of western civilization and cast aside the beliefs and conventions previously held. The unconditional abandonment of aspects of western civilization demonstrates that it is not and was not a continuous set of inalterable beliefs. Nor was it a linear or developmental process in which ideas become more refined and older, inferior ideas discarded. Ideas once dismissed often reassert themselves as vital. What is terribly exciting and offers more than adequate compensation for the inability to pigeonhole western civilization in some convenient developmental scheme is the apparent fact that persons in the past seemed to hold similar assumptions about what constituted western civilization at the same time: Time, not place, provided the unifying thread.

Locked in time, these fundamental notions provide the common definition of what was at that particular time western civilization. These notions seem not to be held by merely a few but to cut across class and ethnic as well as geographic lines, providing coherence and making a civilization a civilization. Contemporaries agreed in a large sense about how the world worked, how things were divided and what was meaningful. These common notions limited and adjudicated possibilities but did not dictate action. Within these common formulations, diversity of strategy and action reigned.

Historians regularly adopt this perspective whenever they designate an epoch an epoch or an era an era. *Building Western Civilization* extends that sort of analysis. It consciously uses the artifactual material of the past to elucidate what at various times during the 6000 years before creation of the steam engine were those generally held assumptions that made western civilization a civilization. Why did they choose to take the action that they did? What set of beliefs were consonant with pursuit of the course that was taken? At what points in the past were coherent set of notions replaced by different formulations?

Through examination of structural elements—the past's physical, social and intellectual institutions and other monuments—answers exist to these questions. All that remains is to ask them. What are those fundamental notions that extend throughout virtually every sphere of western thought at a particular time? What common assumptions make any single civilization a civilization? How do artistic works, religious beliefs and social structures, for example, reflect that time's common assumptions, that time's attempt to come to grips with its past and its means of identification? Why was an old artifact ignored, discarded, adopted, adapted, reconceptualized or transformed into a new artifact? Done in this fashion, history is like an onion as each layer is distinct in itself yet dependent in some way for its shape on the skin closer to the center, each layer representing a particular epoch. As important, each layer of onion skin, like each layer of western civilization, has its own texture, its own all-encompassing commonality, that unites that layer no matter the location.

The scope of this book and its approach impose some constraints. It begins with the advent of writing, the period in which archaeological material can be correlated with the written word. It ends with the creation of the twin pillars of the modern world, the modern State and the first working steam engine, the social and physical engines upon which the industrial world has been built. Not surprising, the approach dictates an almost exclusive western civilization focus. Other cultures receive mention only with respect to and in the context of western civilization. They appear as military menaces, financiers, repositories of classical literature or of technologies, trading partners or spurs to some act or series of action. In no instance were their fundamental notions explored.

Acknowledgments

When several years ago in a moment of weakness I agreed to write *Building Western Civilization*, I expected to rely on over a decade of teaching similar topics to carry me through. I fortunately had the foresight before I signed the contract to coerce two of my colleagues, Achilles Avraamides and Andrejs Plakans, to promise to read each chapter as it was written, to write comments on those chapters and to discuss those comments with me. They certainly have kept their part of the bargain. I have found those discussions a particular joy as well as an intellectually stimulating experience. I have also learned a lot. I thank them for their time and the use of their minds. Professors Amy Bix and Mark Finlay read the manuscript after its completion and provided numerous insights. I am also in their debt. Two of my colleagues, Kenneth G. Madison and George McJimsey, have patiently responded to what to them must have seemed like a never-ending stream of odd and unusual questions as I blatantly tried to pick their brains in service of this volume. Philip Zaring, Howard Segal and Hamilton Cravens also offered help. Two graduate students, Philip Frana and Robinson Yost, carried on extended discussions with me (and with each other) about some of the material in this volume. Their excitement and fervor were both refreshing and enlightening. Three former graduate students also deserve mention: Andrew J. Butrica; Gregory A. Sanford; and W. Keith Sadler. I have framed many of my courses from *Building Western Civilization* and inflicted the interpretations and information upon undergraduate students, including those in freshman surveys, as well as graduate students. The enthusiastic comments as well as helpful suggestions have been incorporated in this book. I would like to thank the following people at Harcourt: Senior Acquisitions Editor David C. Tatom, Developmental Editor Sue A. Lister, Project Editor John Haakenson, Senior Production Manager Kathy Ferguson, and Senior Art Director Brian Salisbury. The book and I are the better for this experience. Finally, my family, Jean, Gregory and Jocelyn, have taken an avid interest in *Building Western Civilization*. Their discussions with me about topics in the book made its writing a thoroughly enjoyable enterprise.

CHRONOLOGY

Significant Cultural Ideas, Events, and Technologies from the Advent of Writing to the Newcomen Steam Engine

3500 B.C.E.	Advent of writing
3500 B.C.E.	Rise of cities, urban-situated, artisan-based handicrafts and urban-directed irrigation agriculture
2600–2200 B.C.E.	Heyday of the Egyptian pyramids and elaborate mummification
c. 2100 B.C.E.	First appearance of monotheism
c. 1800 B.C.E.	Extensive horse warfare
c. 1550 B.C.E.	Large scale iron use
Mid-7th Century B.C.E.	Popularization of the phalanx as military formation
6th Century B.C.E.	Form, 3-dimensionality, balance and harmony as pervasive Greek themes
550 B.C.E.	Trireme as the predominant naval vessel
5th Century B.C.E.	Justification of laws as expression of community sentiments, values and will rather than divine interaction
300 B.C.E.	Rise of Alexandria as a center of Greek learning
320 B.C.E.	Romans begin creation of a huge system of roads tied to Rome
145 B.C.E.	First above-ground Roman aqueduct and proliferation of fountains and baths
100 B.C.E.	Simple watermills used to mill grains
33	Jesus of Nazareth crucified
50	Emergence of blown glass
70	Vitruvius's *Ten Books on Architecture*
300	Overshot or vertical waterwheel
410	Augustine of Hippo articulates the early medieval Christian doctrine that earthly existence was useful only as a means to learn to achieve heaven
c. 500	Creation of Barbarian kingdoms in place of the western Roman empire
c. 600	Numerology serves as a prominent factor in religious architecture
632	Death of Muhammad, prophet of Islam
650–850	Massive depopulation of European cities and a dearth of trade
c. 710	Introduction into Europe of primitive stirrup
c. 780	Charlemagne brings the western barbarian kingdoms under his personal control
700–900	Height of Islamic interest in Greek and Roman texts
c. 900	Feudal arrangements become hereditary and the social structure rigid
c. 900	Considerable use of the heavy plow in northern Europe
c. 900	Padded horse collar fosters use of horse for agricultural haulage
c. 900	Rebirth of towns and the rebuilding of church facilities reflect reemergence of community-decided standards

CHRONOLOGY	continued

c. 920	Simple motte and bailey castles
c. 925	Proliferation of watermills and a renewed interest in circularity
c. 950	Extensive adoption of three-field agriculture
1050	Introduction of crossbow
1075	Stone keeps replace baileys in castles
1095	Pope Urban calls the first crusade against the Muslims
1100	Introduction of windmills
1120	Camshafts and triphammers expand utility of water and wind power
1130	Renewed emphasis on human reason and use of the senses
Early 12th Century	Institutionalization of the idea of fixed social orders and a society of roles as reflecting the Christian god's order-based universe
12th Century	Greek logic texts and other descriptions of nature assume importance
1144	Consecration of the remodeling of the cathedral church at St. Denis and creation of the first Gothic cathedral
1150	Height of guild regulation of social and craft behavior
c. 1150	First medieval university at Bologna
c. 1175	Paper introduced in Europe
c. 1200	Knighthood and chivalry become measures of nobility
c. 1200	Emergence of papal monarchy, signifying church involvement in contemporary affairs and the idea that earthly action leads to salvation
1220	Introduction of mechanical clocks
1270	Extensive use of plate armor
1350	Idea of humankind replaces the gothic idea of social orders
1360	Humankind acknowledged as the master of its own domain and rekindling of European interest in the humanities as faith and reason become separate
1400	Notion that qualities can be modified or reconfigured and that three dimensional form is an important aspect of culture and technology
1415	Portugal begins an era of European exploration of the physical world
1430	Cannons serve as effective siege weapons
1450	Crystallization of large geopolitical entities
1450	Metallic moveable type printing invented
1470	The Basque construct fully rigged ships capable of long range sea travel
1500	Arquebus, a simple handgun, proliferates across Europe
1517	Martin Luther attacks indulgence selling, ultimately rejects Catholicism

CHRONOLOGY | **continued**

1543	Copernicus offers a heliocentric explanation of heavenly motion
1630s	Creation of the modern state and the beginnings of state-sponsored science and culture
1640	Dutch pioneer convertible agriculture
1650	Colonization emerges as a primary means of achieving state wealth
1712	Thomas Newcomen and John Calley construct the first working steam engine

Western civilization needs points of demarcation. It requires a point or points at which it is said to first exist as well as points from which subsequent generations date or measure themselves. The Ancient Civilizations—Sumerian, Egyptian and Hebraic—function quite well in the first capacity. Each made profound contributions and influenced contemporaries; each left tangible evidence of its genius and so stands as an appropriate place of departure. But each ancient civilization did not persist in the same way. The Sumerians died out but their culture remained vibrant and was adopted by others occupying their lands. The Egyptians continued as a people and place for nearly three millennia. The Hebrews had no persisting geographic locus, yet their people held together because of a series of shared fundamental ideas.

PART ONE

Ancient and Classical Civilizations

The Classical Civilizations—Greece and Rome—serve future generations in the second way, as cultural measuring sticks or referents. Time and again, more modern practitioners of Western civilization have reached back to the intellectual, social and physical products of Greece and Rome for inspiration, solace or wonder. They have viewed Greece and Rome as treasured repositories of human ingenuity and experience. In both the case of departure or of reference, Western civilization has taken its past very seriously.

CHAPTER 1

Ancient Civilizations

The Advent of Writing

The written word enables historians to construct the *story* part of history and differentiates that study from archaeology. Little evidence of writing exists prior to 3500 B.C.E. At about that date writing began to appear in an area between the Tigris and Euphrates rivers in what is now modern Iraq.

Cuneiform Writing. A wedge-shaped tip on a reed stylus enabled Sumerians to impress patterns on clay tablets. These patterns represented words or syllables. Most Sumerian writing dealt with record keeping and business transactions.

In Sumer, the first civilization in which we know writing figured prominently, scribes wrote on clay tablets, using reed styluses with sharpened, wedge-shaped ends to impress the appropriate characters. Their script is known as *cuneiform*, a type of writing that began as pictorial representation. Over the years, the Sumerians, who dominated the area culturally for nearly 2,500 years beginning before 4000 B.C.E., abbreviated their caricatures and abstracted them. These symbols represented words or syllables, not letters.

The sudden appearance of the new technology of writing in Sumer (the area from north of Baghdad to the Persian Gulf) was a tremendous achievement but it begs the question of what social need writing satisfied. Small nomadic or tribal groups in which members were in constant contact would have no apparent need to write nor impetus to develop that complicated technology. They could easily communicate verbally, as could residents of small villages. Written communication would prove most advantageous among individuals joined by some common bond yet separated by significant distance. It could organize relations formally among physically dispersed persons as well as record interactions among them. For example, these functions of keeping records and preserving social order would advance the ambitions of people joined by extensive agricultural or commercial relations. Writing could perpetuate balance and stability, ensuring constancy and continued harmony. In addition to providing a means to adjudicate possible work, property, or other disputes, an agreed-upon writing system could facilitate further integration of diverse peoples. Shared myths provide a group with a sense of commonality. Although most myths are initially passed on orally, writing's precision enables mythholders to pass these treasured bonds to the next generation virtually unaltered.

The Urban Revolution

The social factors that would favor the origin of writing suggest the presence of a large population joined by a complex web of relationships. Perhaps it was no accident that creation of true cities occurred in the alluvial plain between the Tigris and Euphrates shortly before writing began. This first urban revolution provided an environment in Sumer in which writing could flourish. But that leads to the next set of questions: What enables a civilization to support cities, and what benefits to the civilization do cities provide? Surely a civilization needs an agricultural surplus to establish cities. Its farmers must grow more than they and their families can consume. Sumer had such a surplus. But farm workers also must feel that they are accruing benefits in return for their labor. Payment in cash or barter was one type of reciprocity. Cities provided convenient focal points for commerce, facilitating trade among a civilization's people as well as with people from the outside. Yet willingness to sustain urban residents—men and women not growing their own food or raw materials and consequently without currency or material medium of exchange— demands a more compelling explanation. These urban dwellers frequently deliver psychic and political payoffs.

Sumer

Sumer proved no exception. In addition to expediting introduction of diverse and new goods, Sumerian cities housed the civilization's religious institutions—temples, priests, and the like. Religion provided Sumerian society's spiritual basis and, therefore, those close to the gods—priests and other religious officials—merited lavish support. Its cities also were the sites of government, both local and state. Kings and their entourages, princes, and other governmental officials resided there and required the opulence of their station. In some civilizations (though not that of Sumer), government and religion were indistinguishable. The ruling and priestly classes are the same in theocracies, for instance, as divine lineage or endowment provides the rationale for earthly leadership.

Sumer and other civilizations placed their most cherished institutions in these early cities and supported them because these sites could be well defended. Close proximity of peoples made raising an army simple, but a city's tall, thick walls, its primary means of defense, served as the paramount inducement. These difficult-to-scale, dense, stone structures frustrated enemies trying to storm the city and plunder its material and spiritual treasures. Substantial wooden gates, wide enough to permit goods to pass into the city, were the principal weaknesses of these municipal fortresses and were defended by projecting towers and deep trenches. They usually became targets of invading armies, which tried to batter them down or even to scale them to enter the compound. An invader's other offensive option was to stop provisions from reaching besieged cities and starve inhabitants into surrender.

A combination of the nature of warfare and the purpose of cities led to a characteristic urban spatial arrangement. Religious, governmental, and sometimes even commercial institutions rested at a city's center. Temples were situated first, and around them clustered the most influential city residents—priests and governmental and commercial leaders. Safety was a factor in central city desirability but so was the fact that virtually all urban activities revolved around the center. It was the place of "business"—markets, temples, government buildings, and the like. To live near these edifices meant little or no daily travel. And travel was by foot, a considerable hardship during the cool winters and blazing summers. Those who could secure housing nearby did so. Those less fortunate lived progressively farther away. The least fortunate had homes near the walls on the periphery or even beyond them. These peripheral people resided among the noxious trades, those few unseemly activities—tanning was the archetypal example—that produced horrible smells and were relegated to the least desirable city location.

Sumerians lived in a somewhat modified version of this early urban model. There the term *city* referred to an area much larger than a walled enclave. Populated by thousands and later tens of thousands, Sumerian "cities," of which there were about ten, were more closely akin to our idea of a region or even a state. In such cities as Mari, Ur, Erech, and Kish, those people lowest in the social order lived in residences clustered outside the walled space. The city governed the agricultural area surrounding the walls. This city-administered territory was so vast it might take several days to walk across.

What made a Sumerian city a cohesive unit was not simply economic ties or defense arrangements. Each city was united spiritually and administratively. Each had its own special god, who, according to Sumerian tradition, was given the area on the day of creation, and its own government administration. Correspondingly, what made Sumer a civilization was that it had citizens who shared a pantheon of gods and sometimes a Sumer-wide government.

Sumerian Worldview

Sumerians held a rather dour perspective on life. They believed that the universe was fixed and unmovable in a boundless sea. The earth was a flat disk surrounded by a hollow space enclosed at the top by a solid, dome-shaped, tin surface. A windlike substance filled the hollow space and gave rise to the sun, moon, and stars. This arrangement and everything else was created, guided, and regulated by numerous invisible, immortal superbeings called *dingirs*, the Sumerian word for god. Numbering in the thousands, dingirs had created humans of clay for but one purpose, to serve them by supplying food, drink, and shelter, freeing them to pursue their divine activities.

That explanation for humanity meant that the species lacked free will, acting only as the dingirs demanded. Humankind's plasticity guaranteed a particularly combustible situation: Dingirs possessed exceedingly strong personalities, humanlike in temperament. Their very human emotions led dingirs to petty jealousies, fury, even irrationality. Dingirs often expressed their anger through cataclysmic natural phenomena, such as earthquakes. Human life, then, was fundamentally marked by uncertainty and haunted by insecurity; individuals could never know the destiny decreed for them by unpredictable, emotional gods. Moreover, each person was helpless to effect change. Yet earthly life seemed markedly better than the Sumerian notion of what occurred after death. When a Sumerian died, the debilitated spirit descended to a dark, vile nether world. There eternity was spent in a ghastly and wretched reflection of earthly existence.

These notions of humanity also extended to the Sumerian arts. Sumerian literature surely reflected the essential formlessness of humankind: Few human characters even received names and virtually none was provided a personality. Authors usually did not sign their works. Almost always authors wrote of humankind in the process of doing something; motion or movement seemed natural because humanity at rest was nothing more than clay. Much of this literature bemoaned humankind's fate. Here is representative snippet of one lamentation:

> Tears, lament, anguish, and depression are lodged within me,
>
> Suffering overwhelms me like one chosen for nothing but tears,
>
> Evil fate holds me in its hand, carries off my breath of life,
>
> Malignant sickness bathes my body.

By contrast, dingirs in these stories always were mentioned by name and given definite personalities.

Sumerian art demonstrated similar themes. Artists always represented humans or terrestrial things as if in shadows and at a task. They expressed humankind generically, as short and squat, and never painted or drew crisp or sharp images, preferring to portray worldly matters in murky forms.

Yet Sumerian life was not as bleak or without possibilities as it might appear. Each family—Sumerian families were patriarchal and nuclear, not extended—claimed a minor dingir as its personal deity. Family members seized every opportunity to request favors from their deity, to ask it to intercede in personal affairs, and to complain about recent setbacks. One such plaintive wail was this:

> I, the discerning, why am I counted among the ignorant?
>
> Food is all about, yet my food is hunger.
>
> On the day shares were allotted to all, my allotted share was suffering.

Dingirs need not respond favorably, of course. And dingirs were not equal. Sumerians arranged their gods hierarchically. A similar sense of hierarchy carried over to city dingirs. Some were mightier than others but all were less powerful than the several creating dingirs. The relative strength of dingirs explained why some individuals and families fared better than others and justified the social status quo in this markedly heterogeneous society. Material success was equated with divine favor and divine power. Sumerians prized wealth and possessions and measured them in terms of land ownership, well-stocked granaries, and large animal herds. The vast preponderance of written documents in Sumer dealt with financial transactions and record keeping, a sign of just how central matters of personal wealth were in that culture.

Owning slaves also signified wealth, and slavery was common as Sumerian military adventurers often returned with captives.

Architecture: Brick by Brick

The religious beliefs of the people framed Sumerian existence and influenced all facets of life. The diligence with which Sumerians constructed and maintained their religious architecture demonstrated the importance of these beliefs and Sumerian devotion to fulfilling their destinies. The Tigris–Euphrates alluvial plain lacked building stone and minerals and had few trees from which to fashion structures, forcing Sumerians to trade for or import those precious materials. Thus structures were built of mud bricks held in place by gravity and not fixed with mortar or cement.

Each brick was formed by hand in a square mold but, rather than flatten the top, Sumerians consciously rounded it off. Bricks considerably thicker in the middle, tapering toward the ends, resulted. They were then left to bake in the sun or were occasionally fired in a primitive stone kiln.

Sumerian plano-convex brick use is revealing. Bricks of that shape make very awkward building blocks. They fail to sit neatly on one another and leave holes that require filling to complete a structure. Sumerians were certainly able to produce flat bricks; that they did not implies that there existed compelling cultural reasons to do otherwise. It seems likely the form was a depiction of Sumerian cosmology: Sumerians pictured a universe—the heavens joined with the earth—as plano-convex in form. The "word" for *land* in early pictographic cuneiforms is a plano-convex representation. That shape, when made of the same material from which humans stemmed, symbolized the bond between dingirs and humans, just as the ziggurat combined heaven and earth.

Whatever the reason for their use, Sumerians needed to compensate for the deficiencies of plano-convex bricks. To increase stability in large structures, they repeatedly varied the bricks' plane of orientation. A row of bricks perpendicular to the main pattern would be laid every several layers. Sumerians plugged gaps with a mastic to lessen drafts within the building. Any of a number of large marsh reeds could provide the mastic's organic matter as could discarded grain stalks or weeds. Bitumen, a naturally occurring petroleum substance that oozed through cracked rock to form surface pools in Sumer, served as binding for the mastic as well as a waterproofing element. Sumerians proved especially adept at this mastic/plano-convex brick combination. With it they fashioned corbel and true arches and arch vaults for their many structures.

Religious Architecture

Temples abounded. No matter how grand, virtually every Sumerian temple was built of mud brick possessing a characteristic plano-convex shape. The earliest Sumerian temples were rather simple structures. A central nave with aisles on either side dominated these buildings. At one end was a podium, surrounded by statuary, and a small, mud-brick table to hold daily animal and vegetable sacrifices. Granaries and storehouses, which provided dingirs food, drink, and thanks, were located near temples.

By 3000 B.C.E., more elegant efforts had supplanted these modest structures. A series of rooms for priestly use flanked the aisles. Forecourts became regular features

Ziggurats. These priestly temples were the holiest Sumerian places. Generally situated on hills, ziggurats evoked staircases, symbolically leading from earth to the heavens.

of temple architecture as did rough-cut limestone foundations. Regularly spaced mud-brick buttresses, columns, recesses, half columns, and clay nails now adorned the temples' outer mud-brick walls. All of these raised elements were design, not building, features and enhanced temple beauty, not stability. Sumerians colored the leaves of these cone-like nails red, black, and buff and arranged them as mosaics. Triangles and zigzags proved particular favorite geometric motifs.

But the most significant change was to place the temple atop a terraced, multilayered artificial hill. The Sumerian word for *temple* translates into "house of the mountain" and placement of the holy building on top of an artificial mountain apparently evoked the power of a mountain in the Sumerian cause. Symbolically connecting heaven and earth, each level of the mud-brick ziggurat was smaller than the one directly beneath it. Sumerians sometimes built these new religious structures on top of earlier ones, for it was the location that remained sacred. Thus, it was not unusual for an old temple to be filled with mud bricks and buried within the first level of the new ziggurat. Elegantly crafted stairways carried the faithful as much as 40 feet from ground level to the temple shrine.

Even these impressive staged temple towers were dwarfed only a few hundred years later with construction of huge temple complexes—one measured 400 yards by 200 yards—that combined ziggurats, storehouses for provisions and wealth, courtyards, and dwellings for priests and support personnel. The later ziggurats themselves reflected the new emphasis. With a base of 200 feet by 150 feet, these lavishly expensive mud-brick structures were set on natural rises and soared an additional 70 feet. The temple shrine remained on top and three stairways, each with precisely one hundred steps, provided access.

Secular Architecture and Furnishings

The architectural elements and techniques used in temples also appeared in domestic architecture. Houses in this socially stratified culture differed considerably. A modest Sumerian home was a small, single-story, flat-roofed affair with a central room surrounded by other rooms. Small, square, open windows with wooden grills marked these tributary rooms, which often looked out on a courtyard. Wealthy Sumerians lived in much more opulent quarters. Their two-story, mud-brick houses usually contained a dozen rooms. A reception room, kitchen, lavatory, servants' quarters, and even a private chapel comprised the lower level, while the upstairs was reserved for the family's bedrooms. Wooden-framed beds, low tables, and high-backed chairs furnished the dwelling, while plaited reed mats, skin rugs, and woolen hangings covered the walls and floors. Clay, stone, copper, and bronze vessels could be found in these impressive residences as could reed baskets and wooden chests. Sometimes these homes covered family mausoleums where deceased relatives were buried.

Sumerian Kingship: Rewards and Responsibilities

Religious and domestic structures pale when compared to those of princes and, later, the king. The king's status as the first prince, as the military suppresser of rivals based in other cities, was reflected in his palaces. A palace stood in each city, guarded by a small standing army loyal to the king. The retinue included chamberlains, deputies, pages, cupbearers (succession through poisoning was not unknown), craftsmen, smiths, basketmakers, cooks, musicians, and singers. The king owned palace lands as well as additional properties (private as well as temple ownership of land occurred in Sumer). The king also dominated various commercial enterprises.

The Military

Land and wealth had come to the king by force. His victorious armies had defeated those of the pretenders to his throne. But victors had little technological advantage over the vanquished; Sumerian armies were all similarly equipped. Military men in Sumer used four-wheeled, two-man chariots. Woven-basket carriages sat on axles mounted directly to three-piece solid wheels, a design that made chariots cumbersome and difficult to steer. One soldier drove the yoked, four-ass team while the other threw lances from the on-board quiver or used a battle-ax in hand-to-hand combat. The light infantry had long spears, battle-axes, and daggers, while their more heavily armed counterparts wore conical copper helmets, leather kilts, and felt cloaks for protection. These foot soldiers lined up several ranks deep and joined their rectangular shields and overlapped spears to attack in phalanx-like formation. Literally crushing the enemy was their gruesome objective.

Trade and Industry

Victory in battle gave the king significant control of governmental functions; among these, overseeing trade and industry was crucial. Market officials, market cleaners, maintainers of the city gates, and overseers of weights and measures were all government employees.

Clothmaking   Controlling the Wool Office and regulating and guiding clothmaking were particularly important kingly responsibilities. His overseers used slave women as weavers, pressers, millers, and porters of wool and flax. Wool, secured from farmers and herdsmen, was stored in a large, local warehouse. Slaves first washed the fibers in hot water and natural wood-ash soap, then dried them. Next, they beat out much of the remaining dirt and carded the wool to disentangle the fibers. Both linen and wool were graded and bleached. The wool was then spun into a continuous thread. The spinners pulled out thin, parallel fibers and then interlocked the fibers by twisting them together. The twisting operation sometimes was accomplished by rolling drawn fibers between palms but slaves also spun by using a hooked stick. This primitive thread was placed on a wooden or bone spindle, which rotated on a clay whorl and operated like a flywheel.

Slaves used these threads to weave cloth, working in three-woman teams on vertical or horizontal looms. This was called the warp. They took one series of threads and stretched them parallel on the loom. They then took a series of threads perpendicular to the warp threads and passed them over and under the threads fixed to the frame. When weaving of these weft threads was complete, the cloth was brought to the fuller, who finished the cloth by scouring or by "walking on the cloth." Fullers trampled on the cloth in a slightly alkaline bath, which bleached it and further consolidated its fibers.

Fulling was quite similar to felting, the process of beating, rolling, and pressing animal hair into a compact mass of even consistency. Beginning with wool spread layer upon layer on a large mat, firm pressure, generally from the feet, was applied to the rolled-up mass, which was periodically unrolled, rerolled, re-pressed for up to five hours. The resulting cloth was then washed and dried in the sun.

Everyone involved in clothmaking, including farmers, herdsmen, and slaves, received yearly allotments of finished cloth. So did the local nobility and the royal family. Linen was generally reserved for priests. Sumerian men wore skirts, either with long felt cloaks or large fringed shawls. Women wore shawl-like dresses that covered them from head to foot.

Agriculture

To do everything humanly possible to ensure an adequate agricultural harvest also fell to the king and princes. Sumerian agriculture depended on irrigation. Blazing, dry summers provided little rain for crops and Sumerians carried water from the Tigris and Euphrates to fields miles distant. The initial part of this process—raising water from rivers and from the infrequent well—posed no technological obstacle. Shadufs—reed baskets covered with bitumen and joined to a large clay counterpoise by a branch—eased water raising. This apparatus rested over a Y-shaped branch fixed in the soil. Lifting the counterpoise lowered the basket into the water source, while gravity would raise the water when the counterpoise was no longer supported. The device could then be maneuvered to dump the water nearby.

Irrigation   Bringing raised water to tilled fields proved more complicated; it required construction of miles of irrigation canals and channels, dikes, weirs, and reservoirs. Canal building itself was no easy task. Builders had to survey routes and effectively use measuring rods and leveling instruments. Once constructed, canals needed frequent repair—baked brick lined some channels—and silt had to be continually removed. A project that massive could hardly be accomplished by individuals working alone. From the start, government helped coordinate the steps involved and required each individual to commit a certain time to canal building and maintenance. Two types of compulsory public service, statewide and local, existed, although well-to-do Sumerians could use their wealth and prestige to purchase substitutes. Each citizen owed the king time to erect and clear the large, main canals. In addition, citizens owed their city another period for the smaller, local feeder canals. Tapping into these feeder canals to transport water to private land remained an individual responsibility.

Sowing and Reaping   Taking advantage of this canal system to grow crops was a purely individual matter. Farmers first flooded their fields and, after saturating the ground, removed standing water. They then let oxen stomp on the wet ground to help kill weeds. The still-damp fields were dressed with pickaxes and dragged. After drying, fields were twice plowed, each time to a different depth, harrowed and thrice raked, and finally pulverized with a clublike mattock. Two oxen hitched together by yoke and pole pulled plows. The ox's unique hump made it the sole animal able to pull heavy loads. A throat and girth harness, which took advantage of the hump to remain fixed without constricting the animal's windpipe, permitted easy breathing even as the animal strained. A seeder, a plow with a tube behind it to drop seeds directly into furrows, was used as a planter and when sprouts appeared, watering began in earnest. During relatively slack periods, farmers built marsh reed–framed huts and barns, which they plastered with mud, to shelter animals.

Sumerians harvested during the dry fall season in three-person teams, reapers, binders, and sheaf arrangers. When the sheaves had been brought to a slightly hilly central place, farmers first used threshing wagons to run over the cereal to separate heads from stalks, and then used threshing sleds (beams with leather-fastened teeth) to disengage the grain from the chaff. The grain–chaff mixture was finally winnowed. Sumerians first stirred the mixture—the grain weighed more than the chaff and presumably would sink to the bottom when moved violently—and then gently tossed it straight up into a slight breeze. Wind winnowing also depended on a weight differential between grain and chaff. The chaff would blow away, while heavier grain would fall straight down, back into the winnowing basket.

Crops   Sumerian farmers grew barley, wheat, and millet for bread and beer—Sumerians had a dingir in charge of beer as well as dingirs for other commodities—and a wide variety of produce. Lentils and chickpeas provided protein; turnips yielded carbohydrates; dates proved a sugar substitute; and onions, garlic, lettuce, leeks, and mustards furnished vitamins and flair. Sumerians also raised animals for food. They ate the meat of cows, sheep, goats, and pigs and drank goat and cow milk. Farmers and their families consumed a portion of these agricultural commodities and set aside an appropriate amount as next year's seeding and breeding stock. The rest went to cities. Oxen pulled the occasional heavy wooden carts and sledges but lighter loads were far more common. Donkeys, loaded down with saddlebag-like satchels, served as primary transport animals.

Fish and birds joined these agricultural commodities in markets. Both fowlers and fishermen used nets to trap their prey and both applied copious quantities of salt to dry and preserve their products. Hooved-animal flesh also was often dried.

Arts and Crafts

The farmers' goods provided sustenance for the dingirs and fed city residents, who were engaged in an impressive variety of tasks. Artisans provided support services for temples and daily life. Sumerian carpenters used saws, chisels, hammers, and braces and bits to build furniture, boats, wagons, and chariots. They employed oak, fir, ebony, willow, cedar, and mulberry but carefully reused scarce wood whenever possible. Coppersmiths burned reeds and operated a foot-powered bellows-like device to refine copper, which they cast, annealed, or hammered. They produced vessels, containers, nails, pins, rings, and tools, such as hoes, axes, chisels, knives, and saws. Coppersmiths also made arms—lance points, arrowheads, swords, daggers, and harpoons.

Potters used wheels to throw pots (some with spouts), fish oil–burning lamps, mortars and pestles, and other pottery. They fired their wares in kilns built into hillsides to create artificial air flow and a hotter fire. Like others in Sumer dependent upon fire, potters became quite adept at using the bow drill. They rapidly bored one piece of wood—the drill stick—into another—the hearth—and the heat produced by friction set aflame wood dust and tinder. Potters used these bow drill–created fires in early times to bake the raw greenware and fuel together in pits. Only later did Sumerians make stone or clay kilns and pits distinct. Potters deliberately left pottery used for refrigeration unfired: Small quantities of liquid would filter through porous pottery walls and evaporate, withdrawing heat from the contents of the vessel and lowering temperatures as much as 10°C. Potters decorated their pottery with colorful, cedar oil–based paint. When ground in a mortar and pestle, cobalt compounds gave a blue pigment, copper salts provided a green hue, and lead antimoniate produced yellow. Black came from powdered charcoal and gypsum yielded white.

Chisel workers and jewelers were most closely identified with the temple. The former sculpted figurines in ivory and the latter worked with gold, silver, and semiprecious stones. Jewelers melted precious metals in their foundries (silver, mixed with galena, a lead ore, was gained through trading) and used three- and four-piece molds to cast small statues. They also annealed the metals, using pins and rivets as well as solder, and made filigrees for temple decorations.

Jewelers derived considerable status from their work. Leathermakers—tanners—suffered because of theirs. The noxious odors arising from preserving animal hides led Sumerians to shun tanners. That ought not to suggest that Sumerians had little regard or need for leather. Their tanners made cattle, pig, goat, and especially sheep hides into leather and used the substance for waterskins, bags, harnesses, skin boats, armor, quivers, scabbards, boots, and sandals. After about 2500 B.C.E., Sumerians also utilized leather, affixed by copper studs, to protect wooden chariot wheels.

Tanners began with animal skin, which they soaked in water for a time and then scoured and pounded to remove the remaining flesh and fat. They next attacked the hair in either of two ways. Tanners would soak the skin in urine to loosen the fibers and then scrape the hide with a knife. Alternatively, they would let it putrefy naturally for some months before scraping and then dip the skin in a strong salt solution to stop the necessary bacterial action. After removing the hair, tanners bated the material by rubbing and pounding animal dung into the skin; enzymes in that distasteful substance reduced swelling and prepared the hide for tanning. Sumerians used three different substances—cedar oil, alum, or tannin, a substance occurring naturally in pomegranate rinds and oak bark—for tanning, the process of manipulating fat into leather to increase suppleness. In each case, they kneaded and stretched a wet skin while it slowly lost moisture and absorbed the tanning agent.

Leftover leather became glue. Tanners placed scraps of hides in a large vat of water and left them to deteriorate for months, sometimes as much as a year. They then placed the putrid, viscous mixture over a fire to boil off the water and concentrate the matter. Sumerians used this glue to bind jewelry and decorate pottery.

Trade

Hides were abundant in Sumer as was pottery clay, but that civilization depended on trade to provide other important materials. Stone, silver, copper, and wood came from outside the realm, possibly from as far as India and Africa. Sumerian merchants exchanged cloth and other woven goods for these precious commodities. Camel caravans brought goods overland. When loads were great, ox-drawn wagons and even wheeless sledges found frequent use. Boats also played a crucial trade role. Skin boats, small reed boats covered with animal skin, and bitumen-waterproofed sailboats carried some small products. Large wooden ships constructed in special shipyards did yeoman service. Powered by oarsmen and poles, these ships were sometimes pulled upstream by people and animals walking on nearby banks.

Medicine

Few medicinal compounds came from trade. Sumerians manufactured their own saltpeter by treating human urine with lime and wood ash and collected salt by evaporating river water. Milk, snakeskin, and turtle shell occurred naturally in Sumer as did cassia, myrtle, thyme, willow, fig, pear, fir, and date. Sumerians made palliatives of the seeds, roots, branches, bark, and gum of these botanic and animal substances. Often these agents were pulverized, mixed with wine, spread as a salve, and sealed with cedar oil. Sumerians used beer to dissolve similar substances for internal use.

Many Sumerian botanic medicines were laxatives, purgatives, or diuretics. Their utility stemmed directly from the then prevalent notion of disease. Sumerians thought fever—severe disease—was the consequence of a dingir-like demon inhabiting the body and attempting to eat its way out. The aforementioned medicines sought to persuade the demon that continued residence in that place would be distasteful. So convinced, the demon would choose to leave of its own volition.

A demon's ability to leave a sick person played a prominent role in two other related therapies. Sumerians often placed a young succulent lamb at the bedside of a diseased person, performed a ritual, and expected the demon to leave the person for the tastier lamb. The lamb was then butchered, which trapped the demon, and its liver was divined for evidence of the transfer. When lambs were not available, a statue could be substituted. When those in the sick person's attendance felt confident that the demon had moved to the statue, they covered the stone sculpture with bitumen to seal in the demon. Bitumen was also used to coat house doors to prevent demons from entering and as a salve for burned or injured hands or feet. In the latter case, Sumerians apparently carried their notion of clay-made humans to its natural conclusion.

Foreign Contact

Sumer did not exist in a vacuum. It traded and fought with other peoples, which diffused Sumerian ideas, techniques, and goods throughout the known world. Sumer seems to have influenced Syria and Palestine, which developed relatively complicated urban civilizations. These places were characterized by contentious city-states and complex social orders, but probably not by writing. Sumer apparently played a more influential role in early Egypt, the civilization that flourished on the banks of the Nile River. Egyptians created pictorial writing, used mud brick for construction, and settled in cities soon after extensive Sumerian contact, although Egyptian municipalities never approached the size of their Sumerian counterparts. Both Sumer and Egypt were polytheistic and hierarchically organized societies. But those similarities can be grossly overstated. Egyptian structures were quite distinct from those of Sumer.

Environmental differences help account for some variation. Egypt was a land of stark contrast. The lush Nile River Valley was the only habitable region. Egyptians engaged in no large-scale irrigation projects but depended instead on the annual flooding of the Nile, which provided the water and fertile silt necessary for farming. Only a small margin existed between catastrophic flooding and famine. The rest of Egypt was desert, rich in copper and stone. These two substances were uncommon in Sumer. Egypt traded with Palestine, Syria, and Sumer but rarely did Egyptians have to fight outside foes. The country was relatively isolated. The Sinai Desert separated it from Palestine, Syria was farther north still, and Sumer was even more distant, 900 miles to the northeast.

Egypt

Environment alone does not explain the differences between these two early literate civilizations. Intellectual constructs played a central role. Egyptians viewed life in terms of opposites. They appreciated geometric parallelism and gravitated to counterposition and dualism, apparently not finding inconsistencies among situations we see as obvious contradictions. Infatuation with juxtaposition and apposition even extended to their conception of themselves. Egyptians spoke of themselves as the People of Two Lands, Lower and Upper Egypt.

The Egyptian inclination to dualism was reflected in their view of an animated universe, including the heavens, and cyclical time. Egyptians commonly used the same names for persons, gods, and events separated by hundreds of years. They perceived the past, present, and future as basically the same, not because nothing ever changed, but because each period would demonstrate the same recurring pattern; Egyptians measured time according to yearly rituals and cycles, only to start over again and repeat. For example, they viewed the annual flooding of the Nile as normal, looked to the stars to predict the day it would occur, and set their calendar around it. Egyptians explained the Nile's annual behavior in terms of a never-ending cycle of life–death–life and talked of the Nile being born in May and dying in November. Similarly, they considered the sun to be born in the east every morning only to die in the west every evening.

Worldview: Maàt

Coincident with cyclical time was the concept of maàt, a central tenet of Egyptian life. Maàt translates into a type of justice and especially order, a stability based on fairness. Maàt ought not be mistaken for equality, however, but rather justification of tradition, of the status quo. Egyptians feared any type of instability, which they identified as fundamental change, and their society had no codified law, which might be consulted to demonstrate that precedent had not been observed. Society's established orderliness was a hierarchy beginning with the king—the pharaoh. As the god who lived among the mortals, the pharaoh guided earthly affairs according to maàt. All authority came from the king, and Egyptians derived their place in the social system by their relationship to the king. Indeed, the dualistic Egyptians viewed each thing, event, or person not as isolated, but only in reference to some other thing, event, or person, often its opposite. Nothing remained alone; things gained definition from that with which they were paired. These stability-maintaining concepts made social mobility—the change in social status of any one person without reference to the rest of the social scale—undesirable and extremely rare. Maàt explained why the present was as it was by noting its similarity to the past. Maàt was normality. The following passage explaining the creation and organization of the human body suggests the Egyptian passion for stability and order:

> It is the heart which causes every completed concept to come forth,
>
> and it is the tongue which announces what the heart thinks. . . .
>
> Thus were made all work and all crafts, the action of the arms, the
>
> movement of the legs, and the activity of every member of the body, in
>
> conformance with the command which the heart thought, which came
>
> forth through the tongue, and which gives the value of everything.

Nationhood

The purported efforts of the legendary Menes, who was said to have unified Upper and Lower Egypt around 3100 B.C.E., exemplified the concept of maàt. Before unification, each land was little more than a series of relatively autonomous, village-centered regions called *nomes*. Menes established "national" administrative districts and at the same time demonstrated his stability-perpetuating fairness by permitting each of the former nomes to serve as a distinct administrative unit under its own royal governor; each nome remained much as it had always been. A similar sensitivity was at work in the transformation of religion, which paralleled Menes' rise. Each nome had long had its own local gods, which were generally represented as combinations of humans and beasts—human-headed animals were especially common—and were celebrated only in that immediate area. "National" gods emerged under Menes. These "new" deities were not new; they incorporated some of the abilities, talents, forms, and names of the local deities, which provided inhabitants of the formerly independent entities continuity and showed them that Menes had an apt sense of fairness—of maàt. Such moves no doubt lessened the shock of unification.

Egyptians gained a national cosmology at the same time that Menes co-opted the human-beasts. It, too, drew heavily on local traditions and the Egyptian affection for apposition. The new cosmology granted deities powers in contradiction to one another, creating inconsistencies and overlapping responsibilities that intrigued the Egyptians. In their creation myth, a hillock arose out of a primordial sea. A living god—Re, the sun god—first revealed himself on that hillock in the form of a phoenix and flew away. The multiformed Re became the creating god and produced the gods of air and moisture on other hillocks as the waters receded, gods who in turn gave birth to the earth and sky gods. Osiris, Isis, and Seth were their children.

Each day Re and his fellow gods traversed the sky in a boat. At night they passed through the underworld only to be reborn each morning. Rebirth also explained how Osiris became god of the underworld. Osiris married Isis but was murdered by their brother Seth in a jealous rage. Isis found her husband's body and brought it to Re, who ordered it embalmed. Isis then waved her hands and Osiris came back to life as king of the underworld, of the dead. They earlier bore a son, Horus, who fought Seth to avenge his father's murder. Horus's triumph installed him as king of the living. It was from Horus that Egyptian pharaohs traced their divinity.

The resurrection of Osiris and continual rebirth of Re were potent Egyptian symbols and reflected a vision far more optimistic than that of Sumer. Egyptians believed in the prospect of eternal life after earthly death. This afterlife was to be similar to earthly existence but could be happier and more pleasant. That possibility provided an important inducement to advance the king since maàt tied both your present and your eternal future to that of the pharaoh. Egyptians felt that in this rigid social hierarchy all who raised the apex raised themselves in equal measure. Put simply, to advance the cause of the pharaoh was to advance the cause of yourself.

Kingship

The king-centered central government controlled every important function. Simple, open-air, wooden or sandstone temples, placed on hallowed ground, served both as the king's palaces and sites for offerings. Priests served both as holy men and as the king's governors. They appointed various civil servants—soldiers, bureaucrats, and craftsmen—to collect crops as taxes, oversee storerooms, and supervise huge public works. The king also granted monopolies on some practices and sponsored trade caravans and mineral expeditions. The king's soldiers always accompanied both types of forays and on occasion established fortresses in the eastern desert to protect Egyptian miners from hostile Palestinians.

Trade and Transport

Egyptians almost always conducted mineral expeditions overland. The eastern desert contained turquoise, gold, iron, and some silver. It also harbored copper, which was in great demand for tools. Egyptians cast and cold- and hot-hammered copper to produce ax heads, adzes, chisels, knives, daggers, spears, implements, basins, saws, bodkins, hoes, harpoons, and plates. They used flint knives to mine ore from surface deposits but needed copper chisels to tap underground veins. Egyptians refined copper ore at the deposit site to reduce the quantity of material they needed to carry back to the Nile Valley. They crushed the ore with hand picks and smelted it with charcoal in a side hill pit, often fortified with a blowpipe blast. The smelted copper was sometimes placed in crucibles and heated again. The slag was then raked off and the metal poured into ingot molds. Workers transported the ingots on pack animals, usually donkeys. As many as 500 animals might accompany a single expedition.

The only overland vehicle used by the Egyptians was the handbarrow, a flat platform held on two or four men's shoulders, generally employed to carry a dignitary. Overland vehicular transport was difficult and therefore not desirable. The annual flooding of the Nile would wipe out improved roads in the valley and wheeled devices would find rough going in desert sands. They would spin their wheels in the sand, while frequent sandstorms would obliterate any desert roadway. Egyptians preferred to travel by water and conducted virtually all trade that way. The smallest boats were mere bundles of papyrus reeds lashed together with ropes; ships to sail the Mediterranean, however, were impressive vehicles. These carvel-built or flush-planked giants were over 150 feet long. The huge cedar timbers necessary to construct these vessels had to be imported from Lebanon. Wooden dowels, mortise and tenon joints, and rope lashings held together timbers. Cabins with column-supported roofs dominated the deck, while low, curved prows and high stem and stern posts gave the ships their distinctive shape. A centrally placed mast held a triangular sail nearly as wide as the ship for sailing; two rows of stern-facing oarsmen (up to 40 total) used curved, broad-bladed oars to propel the ship when rowing was advisable. In both instances, several crewmen manned the steering oars—large primitive rudders—at the stern to keep the ship on course.

Agriculture

Egyptians rarely traded for agricultural products because they devoted themselves to providing food enough for everyone. Ensuring a sufficient quantity of water in desert conditions was the key to successful agriculture. Egyptians preserved the Nile's annual floodwaters by erecting a series of six-foot-high dams and dikes. Water mixed with rich Nile silt would be captured by these barriers and seep into the parched lands for about 100 days. At the end of this period, which the Egyptians called the Season of the Inundation, the pharaoh and his entourage of sandal and fan bearers, foot washers, and others went to the Nile's banks to dig the symbolic first strokes in the soil to guarantee a bountiful harvest. Plowing began immediately after consecration. Pole-yoked oxen pulled a simple stick plow, with one person guiding the team while another leaned on the plow handle to create a deep furrow. A third scattered seeds from a reed basket as soon as the mud furrows were opened and a fourth Egyptian lightly raked over the now full furrow. Prayers to Osiris asked that the crops follow his model and in effect resurrect themselves. During this season, the Season of the Going Out, which referred to the Nile waters, Egyptians mended the dikes and dams and removed silt from the various canals to prepare for the next year's flood. Men used flint knives and sickles to cut off grain heads during the third and final season, the Season of the Harvest, and women collected these valuable commodities in baskets. Baskets were then emptied into sacks, carried to granaries on donkeys or men's shoulders, and beaten with a flail, two sticks lashed together. Wind winnowing separated the grain from the chaff. Farmers saved seeds to be reborn at next year's planting and kiln-dried the remaining grain.

Cereal grains were Egyptian diet staples. Egyptians ate wheat and barley breads and cakes and drank beer. Women used sieves and baskets made of rushes, ground grain on small saddle querns, baked bread in small stone ovens, and served meals on earthenware or alabaster dishes and wheel-thrown pots. Ducks, quail, geese, and fish were plentiful, eaten raw, sun-dried, or salted. Common vegetables and fruits included figs, dates, onions, leeks, and lettuce, but chickpeas and lentils were also known. Egyptians also drank wine, which they made by treading grapes and allowing the juice from the crushed fruit to ferment naturally in large pottery jars. They domesticated cattle, sheep, and goats, and highly prized milk, butter, and cheese.

Hides from domesticated animals were made into leather, which provided sandals and various military equipment. Most clothes in this arid land were made of linen, which came from the flax plant. Egyptians understood that timing of the flax harvest yielded different textured linens. Green-stemmed plants produced a thin thread, while those with yellow stems could make a good substantial linen cloth. The flax fibers were roved (extended and twisted) and spun and hand-woven on a horizontal loom. Linen cloth became simple frocks, robes, and loincloths. Bead necklaces, bracelets, and earrings were frequent accessories as were human-hair wigs, especially among the well-to-do.

Architecture and Furnishings

The structure of social life was reflected in living structures. Prosperous Egyptians owned single-roomed, mud-brick homes surrounded by brick-walled courtyards. Enclosure walls were a characteristic Egyptian architectural feature as were cornices, battered (sloped) walls, and false doors. No matter what the standing of the inhabitants, almost all domestic buildings were of mud brick. Egyptians used stone only for posts and lintels in doorways. Doors were sometimes wood. Roofing was flat, corbeled, or arched and sometimes required structural timbers but even rafters were covered by matting and a thick slab of mud plaster. Ceiling battens also were matted and topped by a thin layer of mud. Floors were mud plaster atop bone-hard gypsum. By 3000 B.C.E., the Egyptians apparently settled on a standard, narrow, rectangular-shaped mud brick. These flat-topped Nile mud bricks differed from those of Sumer in more than shape. The Nile mud contained a higher percentage of clay; Egyptian bricks often needed no mastic.

Furniture in the most elegant Egyptian households testified to the inhabitants' noble station. Demand in this hierarchical society was apparently great enough to support several classes of specialized craftsmen. Jewelers, metalworkers, sculptors, and woodworkers all thrived. Each made furniture to human dimensions. The arm, forearm, finger, and palm were standard Egyptian units of measure. Chair legs were often made of ivory, carved by flint knives, and shaped like animal hooves. The pharaoh's chair legs were crafted to look like the feet of a lion, the imperial beast. Stretched leather thongs served as chair seats and springs for beds. Reed mattresses ensured sleeping comfort and hanging mats guaranteed privacy. Wooden stools, chests, and boxes were held together by miter joints, mortise and tenon cuts, or pegs and decorated with veneer, jewels, or rare wood inlays. Some were even gold sheathed. Colored glass served as an additional decorative element. Egyptians used the plentiful, silicon-rich desert sands to make an opaque glass with a low melting point. Iron and lead salts colored this potted (stirred and melted in a pot) glass, which was beaded, not blown. Craftsmen wrapped the glass around an object to produce a bubble-like shape. Around a thin cord it became jewelry.

Social Life

No matter how well or poorly Egyptians lived and no matter the disparity of wealth among families, they sought to preserve their social structure. Maàt was to govern interactions among people and to sustain the status quo. Egyptians repeatedly articulated their time-honored behavioral code, characteristically in the form of an open letter from father to son. In a world in which fundamental change seemed impossible, certainly not desirable, Egyptians expected sons to replace their fathers and so prepared them to assume that station. Training them to maintain a family unit and behave within a static social system became immensely important. "If a son accepts what a father says," noted one author, "no plan of his miscarries [and he] will stand well in the estimation of the officials." Officials provided only one frame of reference. A husband's relationship to his wife helped determine the strength of the family unit. Sons were advised to marry and "to love thy wife." "Fill her belly," implored one father to his son, and "clothe her back. Make her heart glad as long as thou livest." This injunction to treat wives as partners extended only to what a person justly possessed. Fathers warned their sons not to covet other people's property or position in the social order. To do so violated maàt. Envy of person or property "is a malady, diseaseful, incurable" because it "alienates the trusted one from his master . . . and a man from his wife."

Egyptian art expressed a similar static sense. Sculpture was of persons in rigid positions, generally not engaged in any discernible activity, or of geometric arrangements. Painting was equally flat. Full-faced representations or side views without attempts to portray three-dimensionality characterized the art.

Death and Pyramid Building

Funeral Practices

Growing enough food provided the focus for Egyptian earthly life and agriculture secured a correspondingly large share of resources. Mandatory public service during the growing period kept overflow channels and dams in good repair and demonstrated the notion of interdependence upon which the Egyptian social hierarchy rested. Death was at least as important to maàt-focused social stability, and elaborate funeral arrangements were as central as agriculture. Even before Menes, prominent Egyptians consumed themselves in preparations for life after death. They selected numerous possessions to take with them in the afterlife, which they expected to be very similar to life on earth. Sometimes the early Egyptian nobility even buried their servants alive with them. That we have no evidence that servants considered this an undue burden suggests just how powerful were the ideas of the interdependence of the elements of a stratified social hierarchy and of persisting in the same social role in the afterlife. Early funeral structures also reflected the emphasis placed on death. A monstrous, flat-topped, mud-brick rectangle with sloping sides called a *mastaba* marked the burial site of an eminent deceased Egyptian. Various elaborately connected storerooms under the mastaba housed the body and provisions. This timber-roofed substructure was generally larger than the mastaba itself and usually contained at least one portcullis to seal out jewel-seeking intruders.

Egyptians constructed even more elaborate burial chambers when the national religion of the Menes era reinforced the cyclical nature of existence. Wall paintings, depicting the most mundane activities of Egyptian life, often marked the tombs. Artists used reed-cut brushes to apply the paint and beeswax to seal it. Ships were buried with pharaohs and others so that they could sail across the heavens as part of Re's entourage. Stone sculptures of the deceased, the person's possessions and food, even utensils, frequently lined burial chambers. A chapel was placed at the east and a large gravestone identified the site. Although burial chambers grew more grandiose, mastabas retained their shape until about 2800 B.C.E. when the pharaoh Zoser demanded a structure that would set himself apart from his predecessors. The monument designed by Zoser's vizier, Imhotep, took the mastaba as a model and literally built upon it; to reflect the relative grandeur of his patron, Imhotep piled six mastabas on top of each other, each slightly smaller than the one beneath it, to form a series of heaven-ascending steps. Imhotep used stone, the eternal material, in Zoser's monument, which stood over 200 feet high, but cut the limestone in small rectangles to mimic traditional mud brick.

The Tomb of Tutankhamen. The elaborate wall paintings, death mask, and sarcophagus show the great care given the body of a dead pharaoh and testify to the pharaoh's earthly preeminence.

Imhotep came from Heliopolis, an area that especially celebrated Re. Perhaps his ambition was to create a structure that united the sun god and Zoser. A ray of sunlight symbolically linking heaven and earth or the hillock from which Re first ascended might have provided inspiration for what is now known as the step pyramid. What is clear is that true pyramids, of which there were about 80, followed the step pyramid as subsequent pharaohs demanded even more massive, more complicated burial monuments. Despite the size increase in these stone structures, each pyramid complex had similar constituents. The pyramid itself rested behind a stone wall enclosure. A mortuary temple was placed in front of the pyramid's eastern face. A chapel marked the north, and a small, enclosed ritual pyramid lay immediately to the south. A long causeway heading east connected the pyramid enclosure with the edge of cultivated land. Egyptians located there a magnificent valley temple, complete with statuary and obelisks, which provided entry to the entire complex.

Mummification

The perpetual act of being reborn and dying only to be reborn again meant that the body used in earthly life would be used over and over again. Egyptians believed that the body was composed of several distinct constituents, sometimes with overlapping qualities. Each needed to be preserved in good shape. The *ba* and *ka* were the most important of these appositional elements. The ba was the gross form, the shell. The ka was the personality, the temperament, the life force. It fled the corpse at death. To travel with Re, the ka needed to recognize and be reunited with its vessel, the ba. A stone sculpture of the deceased might serve as an inferior substitute if the ba was destroyed, but Egyptians took great pains to maintain the body through mummification.

Desiccation was the secret of Nile Valley mummification. In fact, in earliest times, bodies of dignitaries were simply buried in the blistering sand, which quickly absorbed body water and dramatically reduced decomposition. By the time of the pharaohs, Egyptians had devised more elaborate means. The body was washed in the valley temple and purified with palm oils and spices. Egyptians sometimes used a piston-powered, syringe-like device to inject the oils. Priests then removed from the body the organs most likely to putrefy—the brain and the thoracic organs—the former drawn by hook through the nose. Natron, a crystalline hygroscopic mixture of sodium bicarbonate and sodium carbonate common in Egypt, was placed inside the organs, which were wrapped in natron-saturated linens and put in four separate vases, which had been hollowed from quartz rock by bow drill. The heart was reinserted in the chest, while the abdomen was packed with linen, natron, sawdust, and aromatic spices, and sewn closed. The body rested in that state for up to 70 days and was finally wrapped in natron and linen.

The crucial opening-of-the-mouth ceremony was the last act prior to interment. This rite supposedly enabled the deceased to partake of food and to speak on his or her daily heavenly journeys. In the case of the pharaoh's mummification, his successor participated in the ritual, a potent reminder to the populace that even pharaohs had social responsibilities. It was also a duty to finish a pyramid complex should a predecessor die before its completion and to administer the royal estates to produce the perpetual temple offerings necessary to sustain the eternal ba.

Pyramid Building

The Egyptian conception of aiding oneself by aiding that particular individual above one in the social hierarchy justified widespread participation in pyramid building. Citizens had an obligation to support the work, either through their labor or property. Construction began immediately after harvest and pharaohs started their tombs soon after their ascension. They selected a site west of the Nile, the land of the setting sun, well above river level but not too distant from the flood plain, and checked to see that rock strata there were free of defects or tendencies to crack. Their overseers, usually royal family members, ordered removal of sand and gravel and leveling and smoothing of the rock bed. They then laid out the pyramid, using palm- or flax-fiber cords to mark distances and the stars to fix the four cardinal points, probably through use of a false horizon, and began to cut the pyramid's descending passages and substructures.

As this preliminary work was going on, quarrymen at distant sites selected and transported rock. Fine limestone, which builders used as an outer casing for the pyramids, was quarried east of the Nile. Granite blocks for columns, doorjambs, lintels, and other structural elements as well as statues and sarcophaguses were mined far to the south. The two types of rock required different quarrying techniques. Copper saws and chisels, wooden mallets, and stone picks were sufficient to detach limestone in either surface or tunnel quarries but granite necessitated a more deliberate process. Quarrymen alternated fire and cold water to crack and crumble inferior stone to reach granite of desired quality. They used ten-pound balls of dolerite, a dark green, naturally occurring igneous rock, as sledgehammers to dig trenches for workmen to get next to and behind the stone. This process also detached the granite block, which might weigh over seven tons, on all sides except the bottom. Egyptians broke the block from its bed using huge levers placed in slots cut for that purpose and levered it out of the pit. They then rough dressed the block, lashed it to reed or palm mats and wooden sledges (some, 30 meters long) and dragged it—ancient Egypt did not use wheeled vehicles—over a log road to prevent it from getting stuck in the sand. Water and perhaps milk were spread on the logs to decrease friction and the likelihood of fire. Laborers deposited the block at the edge of the flooding Nile and prepared to ship it to the building site.

Hauling stones from quarry to pyramid site was a seasonal activity, done only when the Nile reached well beyond flood stage. Rafts carried blocks down the raging river, which sometimes stretched 25 miles beyond its banks. The blocks were levered onto sledges at moorage and pulled by humans and occasionally oxen on log-covered brick and earth rampways to ease the uphill grade. Brick retaining walls often fortified ramps to help them bear the great weight. The pyramid base then was laid without foundation or mortar, although gypsum was sometimes applied throughout the building to help slide blocks into place. Egyptians used no pulleys or cranes in pyramid construction, employing only sledges, levers, ropes, and perhaps cradles. They levered blocks into position by first raising one side of the stone, placing a brace under it, raising the other side, bracing it, and repeating the process until they achieved the desired height and location. To prepare for the next level of construction, a rubble ramp was built to the top of one side of the base. Embankments large enough for workmen to stand on covered the other three sides. Egyptians drew core masonry blocks—generally granite but also some

Burial Complex. Pyramids dominated the desert sky but comprised only one facet of the Egyptian burial complex. Mortuary temples, underground chambers, and subterranean walkways were vital to preparing the pharaoh for eternal life.

poor-quality limestone—up on sledges after they had fitted the stones together and marked them on the ground to ensure that joints, especially bedding joints, would roughly mesh. They continued the process of ramp and embankment building, making sure to keep the same gradient, followed by block lifting and placing until they reached the apex. At that point they made a mortise joint and placed the capstone's tenon in it. The pyramid facing was dressed with fine limestone from the top down as the ramp and embankments were dismantled and the pyramid was uncovered.

These simple methods enabled Egyptians to construct pyramids with as many as 2.25 million blocks. Spatial problems caused by these techniques suggest that relatively few people worked on a pyramid at any time. Each crew may have had as few as 2,500 men. Most were freemen fulfilling obligations to their pharaoh. But even these comparatively small groups required significant support. Workers needed to be housed and fed. Administrators distributed clothing and tools from royal storehouses. Teams cooked for crews and carried water for drinking and washing. Others built barracks, each housing about ten workers.

Pyramid building was quite dangerous. Physicians set simple fractures, binding them with rawhide or encasing them in resin and reed casts, and amputated compound fractures in which bones punctured the skin. Failure to amputate sites of compound fractures meant almost certain death. Physicians trepanned skulls for head injuries, cauterized wounds, and used resin-soaked linen as artificial skin. They also treated disease, generally by manipulation and diet but sometimes by bloodletting, and noted those instances in which their therapies were useless, calling for divine intervention.

Persistence and Change in the Near East

The political and national fortunes of the Egyptians and Sumerians proved markedly different. Egypt managed to survive as a political entity for nearly 2000 years, until about 1300 B.C.E. Sumer proved much less fortunate. Before 2000 B.C.E., the Sumerian people ceased to exist as a succession of invaders had laid claim to that land.

Transformations: Egypt

Egyptian society modified established practices in the millennia after construction of the first pyramid. A marked democratization of funeral arrangements led to less grandiose burial structures as nobles and priests gained power at the king's expense. The divinity of kings was challenged but substitution of military might for religious authority perpetuated the concept of maàt. Even so, civil wars occasionally broke out and, when Egyptians ignored their agricultural infrastructure during these power struggles, famine sometimes resulted. But these changes and disruptions were rather superficial as Egyptian civilization demonstrated a remarkable cultural and intellectual consistency. Egyptians expanded foreign contacts as they shed their isolation-derived security for increased trade and military adventures. A distinct Egyptian presence was found at Crete by 2000 B.C.E., and by 1700 B.C.E. Egypt itself was invaded by by bronze-armored, chariot-riding Hyksos Semites and Indo-Europeans. Egyptians adopted these military practices and drove out the invaders in 1570 B.C.E. They held their own against the fierce Hittites (initially a confederation of Indo-European–speaking peoples from Anatolia), expanded into the Aegean, and conquered the Sudan, Libya, and much of southwestern Asia, extending their conquests as far as the Euphrates River. They remained in control of this vast region until the thirteenth century B.C.E.

Transformations: Sumer

Sumer, in contrast, did not long persist as a national entity. First the Akkadians, then the Amorites (Babylonians) replaced the Sumerians. The Hurrians from the Armenian highlands established the Mitanni empire in northern Mesopotamia around 2000 B.C.E., while the Babylonians remained entrenched in the south. Both were put on the defensive by the Egyptians and the Hittites, who ruled Asia Minor and northern Syria and challenged Egypt for Palestine. The Hittites defeated the Hurrians but were repulsed in the south by the Babylonians, who would lose out in about 1460 B.C.E. to the Kassites. The Kassites themselves were overwhelmed by the Elamites (of what is now western Iran) around 1150 B.C.E.

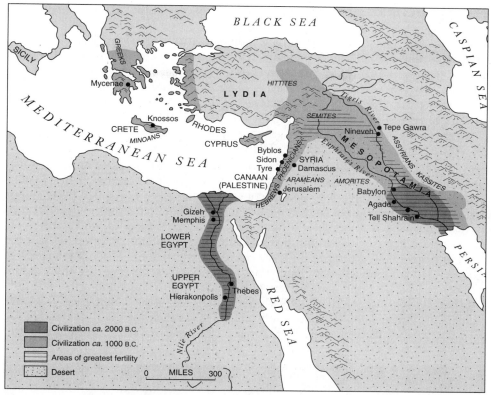

Ancient Near East c. 2500 B.C.E.

Invaders

Several groups invaded the ancient Near East and left their mark there. Each did not leave it in the same way, however. The Hittites introduced new technologies and techniques, for example, while the ancient Hebrews brought new ideas and practices. Yet the vitality of the classic cultures of the ancient Near East, Sumer and Egypt, also persisted. Together with that of the ancient Hebrews, Sumerian and Egyptian cultures provided intellectual structures that extended far beyond the geopolitical importance of these nations.

Hittites

The Hittites were among the most innovative warriors of the period. Mass attacks by light, horse-drawn war chariots enabled them to dominate large areas. The Hittites were among the first—the Hurrians appear to have had extensive horse-breeding knowledge a bit earlier—to employ the horse for warfare and to master lightweight, bentwood construction to make highly maneuverable, spoke-wheeled chariots. Almost as important, three soldiers—a driver, shield bearer, and spearbearer—

manned each Hittite vehicle. The driver drove the chariot directly into enemy lines and the extra soldier provided a numerical advantage over the conventional two-man chariot in the inevitable hand-to-hand combat. Hittite chariots also had quivers attached so that spearbearers could launch distant bow attacks. The Hittites likely led in that area as well. Their composite bows were made up of an ogivally curved wooden bow sandwiched between layers of gut and bone. The gut stretched as the bow was drawn while the bone compressed, which increased range and enabled archers to keep their weapons strung for longer periods without distortion. Regular archers wore bronze and later iron armor as did foot soldiers, who were armed with short curved swords or double-headed battle-axes. The Hittites pioneered large-scale iron use about 1550 B.C.E., first for ceremonial purposes, then for military armaments. It became the standard war material in the Near East by about 1150 B.C.E.

Despite the constant procession of conquerors in the land that had been Sumer, each with its own language and nationality, the essence of Sumerian culture remained virtually unchanged. Conqueror after conqueror adopted the ideas and institutional forms of the people they vanquished and ultimately obliterated. Sumerian writing, legal principles, and artistic and literary conventions persisted. That persistence suggests either the perfection of Sumerian forms or, more likely, that those issues deemed crucial to the Sumerians were of little moment to contemporaries. The Hittites, the group most unlike the Sumerians, help make that point clear. Like the Sumerians, Hittite families claimed individual gods as their own. But it was what the Hittites did after they conquered a foe that set them apart. The Hittites as a matter

Hittite Chariot. The Hittites were master horsemen and woodworkers, two skills they combined in their chariots. In addition, the Hittites added a third charioteer, which gave them numerical superiority in the inevitable hand-to-hand combat that followed chariot battles.

of course absorbed that civilization's gods into their pantheon; the gods of the conquered became Hittite gods. The Hittites also made it a priority to maintain a conquered people's shrines and holy places. But Hittites never accorded religion the geographic and presumably the intellectual prominence that Sumerians did. Hittites placed only walled citadels and palaces in city centers. Temples were relegated to less central positions, a reflection perhaps of the place of religion in Hittite civilization, although the king was the high priest and made several annual pilgrimages throughout his realm to celebrate festivals. Hittites also showed a general disinclination to depend on a deity's arbitrary nature for continued success. Rather than pillage and devastate conquered lands and civilizations as did contemporaries, Hittites achieved stability by entering into covenants with defeated foes in which the vanquished received a measure of freedom—certain rights, obligations, and privileges—as vassals, not serfs, in the Hittite empire.

Covenants bound the Hittite king and the leader of the defeated people. The defeated ruler retained his power and gained the status of a noble in the Hittite kingdom so long as he administered the province in accordance with Hittite-dictated regulations. The form of these agreements also recognized distinctions among past, present, and future. They justified the recently ended war in terms of the vanquished violating or usurping some authority that rightly belonged to the Hittite king; they legalized Hittite action and showed that legality triumphed over illegality. Covenants next established the present relationships—king and vassal and the former land as a territory within the Hittite empire. They then concluded by warning that unless both sides upheld this agreement, the violator would suffer terrible retribution. The parties swore an oath to abide by the covenant's specifics with several curses scheduled to go into effect if either party reneged. The gods, both those the Hittites worshipped prior to this military adventure and those long worshipped by the conquered people, were called upon to witness the agreement and to enforce its penalties should either party violate its clauses.

Hebrews

The Hebrews articulated a similar concept of covenants at about the same time. This people traced its origin to Abraham, who is said to have lived in Mesopotamia around 2100 B.C.E. His seminomadic descendants absorbed many of the features of Sumerian civilization as it was adapted in northern Mesopotamia and organized themselves into clans, populated Palestine, and entered Egypt, where some became enslaved. In the thirteenth century B.C.E., the Hebrews escaped Egyptian slavery to Palestine, which they ultimately conquered, and resumed their tribal existence, uniting only for the common defense. Attacks from the Philistines in the eleventh century B.C.E. resulted in formation of a permanent Hebrew kingdom to repel the invaders.

The omnipotence of their god, Yahweh, was the key Hebraic construct. Nothing preceded him and everything stemmed from him. Unlike the Sumerians and others, who attributed particular acts to whimsy or fate or ascribed causation to relative strengths of gods, the Hebrews' god was sovereign, the master of all, the first and only cause. There existed no place for animated natural phenomena as Yahweh transcended everything. While he certainly did not epitomize human qualities, the Hebrews nonetheless argued that Yahweh created man and woman in his own image;

he granted them autonomy and sovereignty over their own lives. They had the power to choose between good and evil, between righteousness and wickedness. Free will also permitted them to enter into successful agreements. The covenant between Yahweh and the Hebrews was not arbitrary but, like the Hittite covenant, a firm commitment between lord and vassal. It called on the Hebrews to believe only in Yahweh and to follow his rules. In return, they would receive his blessings.

The covenant provided a potent basis for proactive social organization. It bound the good of the individual Hebrew to the collective good through Yahweh. To ensure his or her well-being, each Hebrew needed to make sure that evil and evildoers—people possessed free will to choose evil—must be stopped. And, because no one individual human had the ability to prevent and excise all covenant-violating wrongdoing, that task fell on the community, whose government became the moral and ethical arbiter. Failure to cleave to Yahweh's dicta resulted in misfortune for the Hebrews, a view that marked parts of the past as distinctive, different from other times. It indicated that at times in the past the Hebrews had broken the covenant and indicated that the lessons learned from those past infidelities could be used to fashion a fundamentally different and more successful future. Hebrews saw past, present, and future not as identical but as a continuous story.

King David's Tower and Citadel in Jerusalem. The ancient Hebrews proved adept at stone masonry, often borrowing techniques from the Phoenicians.

The Hebrews wrote down these agreements using a form of writing they learned from the Phoenicians, who occupied cities in the eastern Mediterranean. These great sea traders developed an alphabetic writing system, not a word or syllable-based system, which the Hebrews modified. Phoenicians proved equally adept at building and they oversaw construction of much of the Hebrew-built environment after about 1100 B.C.E. Both the Phoenicians and Hebrews erected a series of large fortified cities to foster and protect trade. Precision marked their construction as builders carefully dressed walls and alternated laying stones widthwise and lengthwise to increase strength. Overlapping gates provided additional security. In Hebrew cities, religious structures dominated the skyline. Limestone walls, free-standing metallic pillars, wood and gold inlays and carvings, and wood-covered stone floors marked the building that housed their written covenant with Yahweh and reflected the emphasis Hebrews placed on that agreement. To build these sites and to pursue military adventures, Hebrews quarried rock and mined ore but relied on Phoenician advisors to smelt copper and Philistine artisans to refine iron; their methods did not differ dramatically from those employed by the Egyptians.

The Hebrews persisted as a people but Assyrians conquered their kingdom in 722 B.C.E. and the Hebrews spread throughout the Assyrian empire. These fierce warriors implemented Hittite-like notions of socio-military organization and controlled all of Mesopotamia, Syria, and Egypt, but their reign was short-lived. Their empire fell to the Chaldeans, yet another Mesopotamian-situated group in the late seventh century B.C.E. Both the Chaldeans and the Assyrians perpetuated Sumerian cultural forms and added to that base rather than replaced it.

Impact of Invasions

Sumerian civilization proved extremely resilient. Sumerians had long been dead yet their beliefs and institutions had been adopted by their conquerors and their conquerors' conquerors. Egyptian civilization also continued as a vital cultural enterprise. The relative geographic isolation of Egypt—despite its later imperial designs—coupled with its emphasis on stability and continuity, helped it persevere for nearly three millennia. The Hebrews, born in Sumer and captive in Egypt, had no geographic identity yet remained a coherent people through their civilization. Their covenant with Yahweh and with one another provided a basis for a union able to withstand the disintegration of their kingdom. The Hebrews, then, jointly held a series of ideas, which made them a definable people, but possessed no geographic unit. The Egyptians had a belief system, a people, and a nation. The Sumerians endured as a series of ideas that continued long after they held no land and no genetic or national identity.

For Further Reading

Aldred, Cedric. *Egypt to the End of the Old Kingdom.* New York: McGraw-Hill, 1965.

Arnold, Dieter. *Building in Egypt: Pharaonic Stone Masonry.* New York: Oxford University Press, 1991.

Bright, John. *A History of Israel.* Philadelphia: Westminster Press, 1959.

David, A. R. *The Pyramid Builders of Ancient Egypt.* London: Routledge and Kegan Paul, 1986.

Edwards, I. E. S. *The Pyramids of Egypt,* 4th ed. New York: Penguin, 1980.

Fakhry, Ahmed. *The Pyramids,* 2d ed. Chicago: University of Chicago Press, 1969.

Harden, Donald B. *The Phoenicians.* New York: Praeger, 1962.

Jacobsen, Thorkild. *Toward the Image of Tammuz and Other Essays on Mesopotamian History and Culture.* Ed. William L. Moran. Cambridge: Harvard University Press, 1970.

Kramer, Samuel Noah. *The Sumerians: Their History, Culture, and Character.* Chicago: University of Chicago Press, 1965.

Lawes, T. G. H. *Pharaoh's People: Scenes from Life in Imperial Egypt.* London: Bodley Head, 1984.

Levey, Martin. *Chemistry and Chemical Technology in Ancient Mesopotamia.* Amsterdam: Elsevier, 1959.

Lucas, Alfred, and J. R. Harris. *Ancient Egyptian Materials and Industries,* 4th ed. London: Edward Arnold, 1962.

Macqueen, J. G. *The Hittites and Their Contemporaries in Asia Minor.* London: Thames and Hudson, 1986.

Mallowan, M. E. L. *Early Mesopotamia and Iran.* London: McGraw-Hill, 1965.

Saggs, H. W. F. *The Greatness That Was Babylon.* New York: Hawthorne, 1962.

———. *Civilization Before Greece and Rome.* New Haven, Conn.: Yale University Press, 1989.

———. *The Might That Was Assyria.* London: Sidgwick & Jackson, 1984.

Senner, Wayne M., ed. *The Origins of Writing.* Lincoln: University of Nebraska Press, 1989.

Trigger, B. G., B. J. Kemp, D. O. O'Connor, and A. B. Lloyd. *Ancient Egypt: A Social History.* Cambridge University Press, 1983.

White, Jon Manchip. *Everyday Life in Ancient Egypt.* New York: Capricorn, 1967.

Wilson, John A. *The Burden of Egypt.* Chicago: University of Chicago Press, 1951.

CHAPTER 2

The Rise of Classical Civilization

Minoan Civilization

Both Egyptian and Mesopotamian civilizations left legacies in Crete, a 150-mile-long island in the Mediterranean Sea, but Minoan civilization, the civilization that emerged on the island, was far different from either. Crete was originally uninhabited; its initial settlers came from Anatolia. But it was the Cretan environment that helped account for the island's distinctive civilization. Violent earthquakes and volcanic eruptions shook the rugged hills of the island and tsunamis engulfed its well-harbored shores. No life-giving river traversed Crete and its mountainous topography, and severe winter storms restricted agricultural activity. Cretans took to the sea in great numbers and established numerous trading routes and partners during the first half of the second millennium B.C.E.

Agriculture

Minoan agriculture reflected environmental factors. Island inhabitants raised cattle, sheep, pigs, and goats, and wheat, barley, vetch, chickpeas, figs, olives, and grapes were staples. Minoans used axes to clear land, wooden plows bound by leather to wooden handles and pulled by pairs of yoked donkeys or oxen to prepare furrows, adzes to weed, and bronze, wooden-handled sickles to harvest. Olives, which Minoans used for olive oil and numerous other products, were beaten from trees with sticks, soaked in water, and crushed in wooden mortars or beam presses. Cretans put the pulp in settling tanks and, when the oil rose to the top, drained the water from the base.

The Glorification of Physical Form

The single most telling facet of Minoan civilization and what set it apart from contemporary civilizations, the glorification of physical form, is not explained by agricultural or environmental differences. Even Minoan dress expressed that virtue. Their woolen clothes set off their bodies. Men wore loincloths or kilts and belt-attached metallic codpieces. Women wore robe-like dresses, deeply slit to the navel, with short, tight sleeves and flounced skirts. Both sexes had long dark curly hair, wore jewelry, and applied rouge and eyeliner. Cloth patterns emphasized symmetry and geometric designs.

Crete and Ancient Greece c. 1600 B.C.E.

The Minoan accentuation of form also was reflected in their highly stylized art and architecture. Minoans gloried in frescoes and landscapes; they painted almost every wall and organized colors in a pleasing manner. Temples were generally L-shaped, with concrete distinctions between rooms and presumably functions. These many-chambered buildings housed priestesses, their families, storerooms, and craftsmen. That Minoans located crafts—gold, copper, shell, and ivory workers as well as potters—in temples further demonstrated the cultural significance of pure form, suggesting that elegance had almost religious connotations. Their thin-walled, kiln-fired pottery highlighted grace, natural forms, and complicated patterns. Minoans regularly portrayed figures in motion, even inanimate objects, but priestesses whirling in religious ecstasy were a particularly popular motif. Even more impressive was the ability of Minoan craftsmen to make art full of life and action. Indeed, it was not simply that their representations showed a religious or technological process—Egyptian tomb painting did that—but that figures were not static and seemed to rise from the surface. According to archeologist Paul M. MacKendrick, Minoan architecture presented the same sense of depth and movement through "variety of line and color, achieved by facades with setbacks, terraces and flat roofs of various heights, the play

Temple at Knossos. Minoans venerated physical form, both in their architecture and in the human body.

of light and shadow on white gypsum stucco, blue-gray local stone, red cypress beams and columns; the alternation of light and darkness in propylons, light wells, peristyles, porticoes, and open courts of various shapes and sizes."[1] That Minoans adopted a form of picture writing as well as abstract representation should not be surprising.

Deities

Minoans venerated sacred symbols—shapes and forms—including the horns of consecration (bulls' horns), pillar, tree, and double ax. A mother goddess, who assumed several guises—fertility; mistress of animals; guardian of cities, households, harvests, and the underworld—and around whom numerous cults emerged, was the dominant figure, but Minoans usually linked her to a year-spirit, a much less powerful god. He would die or be sacrificed at the end of each year and be reborn each spring to be reunited with the goddess. Religious ritual incorporated an almost mythical

[1]Paul MacKendrick, *The Greek Stones Speak: The Story of Archaeology in Greek Lands* (New York W. W. Norton, 1979): 111–12.

transformation of the entranced and whirling priestess into goddess and male youth into year-spirit—Minoans likely engaged in human sacrifice. The year-spirit was sometimes identified as the earthshaker—represented as a bull—who in the sky was the sun god and in the Mediterranean was the sea god. Animal-headed demons existed but they lacked the power of gods, although they could possess humans, who could be freed by exorcism.

Minoans rationally correlated each of their deities' various forms to a specific power or set of powers. For example, they portrayed the goddess of the household with snakes, which presumably lived in crevices near the warm hearth. Shrines to the goddess located in caves were associated with her powers over childbirth and with the underworld as Minoans buried their dead in huge pottery jars in familial caves. Center city temples were much grander. The cedar-timbered Knossos temple covered 24,000 square yards, rose four stories high, and was oriented to the four cardinal points. Its more than 60 rooms flanked a bench- and colonnade-lined sanctuary. In this large center court, ritual bull jumping took place. Minoan men, perhaps as a rite of passage, "danced with the earthshaker"—they put their hands on a bull's horns and leaped over the restrained creature.

Cities, Sailing, and Military

The layout of Minoan cities and towns also emphasized precision and excellence of form. Located near coasts to take advantage of the fine harborage, these population centers were connected with fine stone slab roads, the blocks for which were cut to the appropriate size by bronze saw. Minoans often paved and drained streets within municipalities and provided water and sewerage facilities to some. Clay pipes, each a tapering tube with lugs to tie it to the next, carried drinking water from distant sources to plaster-lined cisterns. Water gathered from roofs flushed stone drains.

The rectangular, elegantly designed Minoan dwellings had flat, tiled roofs and plaster, wooden, or flagstone floors and stood two or three stories high. Minoans constructed lower walls of stone and rubble, and used mud brick for higher elevations and partitions. Vertical and horizontal timbers called tie beams joined the two materials and supported the walls, which were plastered with lime and gypsum and painted with frescoes when still wet. Huge ceiling timbers held up the roof.

Trade and Military Adventures

After about 2000 B.C.E., Minoan single-mast ships with square sails and fixed oars dominated much of the Mediterranean and Aegean seas. These vessels allowed the Minoans to trade with Egypt and the Hittites. Trade became so important that commercially and religiously prominent families became virtually indistinguishable and merged in the social hierarchy.

Minoans also engaged in military adventures. Although Minoan military technology differed little from that of their contemporaries, the beauty of the handles of their bronze daggers and swords far exceeded that of their enemies. Minoans colonized much of the Aegean Sea after about 1700 B.C.E. and began an intense and sustained interaction with an Indo-European group known as the Achaeans.

Mycenaean Civilization

The Achaeans were the Minoans' antithesis. These militaristic agriculturalists yoked draft animals to solid, wood-wheeled wagons and prayed to mighty, mountain-dwelling male gods, contrasting the warm, pleasant sky to the cold, cruel earth where a rather limited earth goddess resided. By the late third millennium, the Achaeans had settled into permanent villages and small walled towns in what is now Greece. After increasing interaction with the Minoans, the Indo-European tribal families began to identify with their new fixed territory and, over centuries, transformed themselves into palace-dwelling princes. A royal house dominated each urban place. And each of these city-states established relationships with each other and with the Minoans, thus facilitating cultural exchange between the two groups.

Culture and Society

By about 1550 B.C.E., Mycenae, situated in the northeast Peloponnesus, emerged as the wealthiest and strongest of the Achaean city-states and for a brief time exerted considerable influence over the others. This empire, if it could in fact be called an empire, was short-lived. But the civilization it brought with it was not. Mycenaean civilization swept the Peloponnesus. It even dominated Crete after about 1400 B.C.E. and replaced Minoan civilization. Mycenaean civilization was a warrior aristocracy that continued numerous Indo-European traditions. A citadel was the focal point of Mycenaean life both in Crete and on the Peloponnesus. Like the Indo-European Hittites, Mycenaeans located this impressive stronghold in a militarily defensible position, such as a hilltop, and protected it with two massive tower-bearing walls as thick as 20 feet. Two-story-high corridors surrounded the central throne room, which was dominated by a raised, circular great hearth and was decorated in frescoes. The top floor provided living space while the ground floor housed workshops and storerooms. Persons affiliated with the citadel/palace lived in kin-based enclaves up to nine miles outside the walls of this castle-like structure. When danger threatened, they retreated behind the citadel's walls.

A king headed Mycenaean administration within each realm. A district governor oversaw each of the king's citadel/palaces. Each governor superintended trade and manufacture, maintained garrisons, raised an army, and collected taxes for his district. Roads, easily traversed by light, wheeled chariots, linked administrative centers of a kingdom together. A considerable degree of social stratification characterized Mycenaean society. Wealthy landowners, bureaucrats, artisans, and slaves were joined with *damos*, generally kin-based groups who worked in common to defend their collective well-being. Damos were typical of militaristic Indo-European societies where substantial numbers of young males were absent on military campaigns and unable to care for their possessions or families. Collective labor protected their property and status. Mycenaeans had diverse occupations: They were goldsmiths, shipwrights, masons, bakers, cooks, woodcutters, messengers, oarsmen, coppersmiths, fullers, saddlers, shepherds, doctors, heralds, potters, foresters, carpenters, bowmakers, carders, spinners, weavers, bath attendants, and unguent-boilers. Each artisan group adopted a deity as its special patron.

Deities and Symbols

A transformed year-spirit was joined with Indo-European tradition to form a patriarchal god known as Zeus. The earthshaker became Poseidon and different aspects of the mother goddess were called Athena, Hera, Rhea, Demeter, and Artemis. These gods received agricultural, precious metal, and human offerings. The pillar, dove, and snake were potent Mycenaean symbols. Bulls and bullhorns were everywhere in evidence. Priestesses and whirling dancers remained religious icons. Human sacrifice persisted but apparently on a more limited basis. As important, the Mycenaeans adopted the Minoan sense of form, even as they expressed martial Indo-European themes. Symmetry, geometrical patterns (especially spirals), and harmony were critical to the Mycenaeans, whose artifacts matched the Minoan perfection of form but expressed much less movement.

Death and Burial

Social stratification even extended to death. Most Mycenaeans were buried in hillsides in beehive tombs. Each family crypt had its own corbel- and post-and-lintel–constructed stone chamber, disguised by a rubble cover. Mycenaeans usually buried daggers and other military equipment with the deceased. Some royal tombs mimicked in form those of more modest circumstances but others were deep underground. A rubble wall marked off the grave circle surrounding these shaft graves. Opulence marked royal burials. The dead wore gold masks, tiaras, pectorals, and breastplates. Bronze doors hid floors carpeted with gold. Mycenaeans placed large quantities of jeweled weaponry in their dead leaders' graves. As was Indo-European

Mycenaean Beehive-Shaped Tomb. Mycenaeans usually placed their tombs in hillsides. Each family had its own stone chamber, and most Mycenaean men were buried with their military regalia.

custom, corpses were buried sitting up. But unlike others of Indo-European descent, some royalty apparently underwent mummification.

Provision of material goods in tombs could imply Egyptian influence—for use in an anticipated afterlife—but it may reflect instead an Indo-European union of individual and property, not severed upon death. Mummification, however, certainly suggests Egypt, perhaps filtered through Crete and the Minoans, a civilization to which the Mycenaeans owed a large intellectual debt.

Invasion and Transformation

The essence of Late Bronze Age Mycenaean culture (but not Mycenae itself, which quickly lost out to numerous small kingdoms) captivated the Aegean until about 1100 B.C.E. when the Dorians, a people from north of the Greek peninsula, and the Sea People, some of whom were likely renegade Mycenaeans who took to pirating, defeated the independent Mycenaean kingdoms. They destroyed carefully nurtured Mycenaean trade routes and sacked many cities. These now impoverished and geographically isolated cities turned inward and, with the decline of trade, markedly cut back public expenditures. Dearth of trade and markets struck skilled crafts particularly hard. Fewer people took up those occupations and over the course of centuries some skills declined and were forgotten. For example, iron, a harder, more durable material, replaced the brittle, more easily broken bronze, especially for weapon manufacture. Replacement of ritual burial by cremation during these static centuries meant that gold death masks, jeweled daggers, and the like would no longer be needed for each deceased king or prince. Skills diminished to such a degree that potters had to use compasses to make circular designs. Literacy disappeared. Cities shrunk in size and scope, their citadels now rising over small, poor hamlets.

Greek Civilization

Although all retained a sense of their Mycenaean roots, each of these citadel-focused hamlet-like cities developed a certain distinctiveness during these cloistered years. When trade resumed in the eighth century B.C.E., these now heterogeneous urban entities welcomed outsiders, and enclaves of foreign merchants appeared in each place. These merchants brought their native ideas and traditions to their adopted cities and a sort of intellectual homogenization occurred. A distinctive, Aegeanwide alphabet, borrowed from the Phoenicians but transformed, marked the union—the emergence of Greek civilization.

By the sixth century B.C.E., the Greeks had rationalized their currencies. Based on the Mesopotamian "talent," these rationalized currencies too followed that land's practice of standardizing each denomination as a specific percentage of the succeeding denomination. Coin size was similarly rationalized throughout the Greek world; size reflected the relative value of the constituent metal.

Development of a common past was part of this homogenization. Songs and epic poetry defined a grand, heroic, collective past and pointed to an even better collective future. Architecture and representation accompanied the new collectivity. A characteristic form of Greek temple crystallized: oblong, pillar-framed buildings with sculpted figures on doorposts and upper walls. Greeks also focused on the harmony and beauty of natural forms, especially the human body, and developed techniques to depict human figures from the front. Like their Minoan ancestors, Greeks gloried in perfect forms in motion.

City-States

Homogenization of place and notions of collectivity spread across the Aegean and beyond in Greek strongholds as the city-state became the unit of government. To be sure, the topography of Greece hampered attempts to unify the entire area politically. Each city controlled the neighboring countryside and governed as if it were a small nation. A sense of cultural homogeneity among its members characterized the city-state. Prior to the rebirth of trade, religion and kinship provided the basis for administration as wealthy, longstanding aristocratic clans governed. Emergence of merchant and landed aristocracies after the eighth century B.C.E. broadened the leadership pool and ended the simple hereditary aristocracy that had characterized the past, even as it reflected an increasingly stratified society.

Social divisions became rigid (although not identical in each city-state) and slavery common, the product in part of successful military engagements. In the leading city-state of Athens, for example, even relatively poor citizens kept a few slaves for household chores. In Sparta the case was somewhat different. The city-state owned slaves and used them to further communal interests, assigning enough to each male citizen to free him to fight full-time in support of the city-state. Other public slaves did the public's work, such as street-cleaning. Wealthier Greeks used slaves for farming or silver mining and as artisans—potters, goldsmiths, fabric makers, cobblers, and spit-makers. These slave artisans passed their craft skills to their children or to apprentices purchased by their owners.

Citizens sometimes paid slaves enough eventually to purchase their freedom, and large-scale iron making provided slaves one avenue to procure considerable income. To make iron, a clay-lined stone cavity, with clay-stoppered holes near the bottom, was positioned on a hilltop to take advantage of the prevailing breezes. Slaves fed this furnace crushed ore, wood charcoal, and limestone and drew off the slag from the bottom. They then cooled the furnace and removed the *bloom*, a tough, spongy iron mass weighing about fifty pounds. The bloom was reheated and hammered to further drive out the slag and consolidate the mass. A relatively malleable wrought iron was the final product.

A large class of alien, permanent residents, *metics*, oversaw commerce and banking and undertook many of government's bureaucratic duties. These metics were taxed, but could not own land. They depended on their patrons, who purchased land in their behalf and otherwise provided amenities.

Citizenship and Military Obligation

Metics and slaves comprised on average roughly half a city-state's population. Citizens and their families made up the other half. The designation "citizen" marked political membership, not family or place. Only males at least 18 years of age could be citizens of Athens, for instance. Their parents had to have been citizens and daughters of citizens and been born in Athens. Only citizens could serve on juries, own land, or hold elective office but they also incurred a series of obligations. Well-to-do citizens supported and commanded naval vessels during wartime, for example. If wealthy, citizens had to lead religious festivals—Greeks had no entrenched clerical cadre—patronize poets, playwrights, and musicians, and sponsor plays and music performances. Citizens had humanistic obligations because the Greeks believed the arts did more than entertain. Poetry, architecture, music, history, and the like educated through use of stereotypes and universal situations and conditions. The Olympic games, remembered for their athleticism and the celebration of form, also provided competitions for poetry, orations, and other humanistic endeavors. But all citizens, no matter how rich or poor, had a mandatory military commitment.

Each citizen served as a *hoplite*, a commitment that embodied the Greek idea of citizenship. It suggested that each individual needed to depend on others for his well-being and maintain the whole at the possible expense of the parts; no man was an island. The universal compulsory military obligation did not produce this whole-over-the-part sentiment but, rather, provided a graphic demonstration of the nature of that attitude. Popularization of the hoplite phalanx was the mid-seventh-century B.C.E. Greek contribution to warfare and raised interdependence to unprecedented heights. The circular shield introduced by the Greeks—*hoplite* translates as "shield-bearer"—covered only the left side of the body and the area to the left of the body. Each soldier needed to press to his right to stand behind his neighbor's shield. To drop one's shield in battle was tantamount to treason as you exposed another to danger and threatened the formation's integrity. Files of eight men or more stood as

Warrior Greeks. The Greeks rapidly deployed the Hoplite phalanx, in which each soldier's shield partially protected his neighbor, to gain control of much of the then known world.

close as possible to each other—less than three feet apart—with shields nearly touching to form what from the air would have looked like a perfect square or rectangle. Perfectly formed hoplite phalanxes always won set piece engagements, a fact that reified at least symbolically the Greek reverence of form. The hoplite military objective was to deform one's foes, to break their formation, to convert the whole into individual parts. Carrying a thrusting spear and wearing leather greaves and bronze helmets, hoplites attempted to march through their enemies and, once they destroyed the form of alignment, to grind them into the ground.

Archers, javelineers, and peltasts figured little in these open-field military battles, which were quite different from those portrayed in the Homeric myths. There the hero personified the Greek people and provided them with a common noble heritage. In the hoplite phalanx, pedigree was not reflected by individual heroism but rather by anonymity, by individual sacrifice in the common defense.

Religion and Philosophy

A similar transformation occurred in Greek religion. The Homeric gods—Zeus, Apollo, Ares, and the others—were an aristocratic caste, mimicking the warrior clans that had run Mycenaean and early Greek society. These Olympic gods were divine, larger than life, and perfect of form yet very humanlike. The Greeks made their mountain-dwelling gods in humankind's image, even as each city-state tailored its gods to reflect local peculiarities. By the fifth century B.C.E., however, the gods had become more distant, less human. Individual distinctions among them were sometimes obscured. Greeks often represented their gods not as beings with physical form but as metaphysical entities with an idealized invisible form, a celebration of community ideals and virtues. The gods' authority also suffered. Their distance meant that they seemed less a presence in daily life and less an explanation or reason for particular acts. Instead of attributing justice and law (and orderliness) to the will of Zeus, Greeks conceived of those qualities as products of the human community, the city-state. Laws were not divinely expressed but reflected community will. That latter stipulation was especially crucial. It granted the community the right and obligation to change the law as situations changed. And change they surely would because belief in past, present, and future as distinct, coupled with human—not divine—control, virtually guaranteed that demagogues would bend the city-state machinery to further individual ends. Laws, written and therefore known, could be cited to rein in tyrants or consciously changed to reflect new social realities.

That human-centered, developmental view of action also produced debates about the appropriateness of any activity as well as attempts to explain or rationalize a particular course. This search for causality and the effort to join specific reasons to specific acts pervaded Greek discourse. It was found in legal-social relations but also in Greek tragedy, history, and poetry. Each of these dialectical exchanges held a didactic function. Greek artists, poets, and other writers proudly signed their work, making it clear than humankind, not the gods, created the product. Formalized as a manner of investigation and explanation, the search for causality became what we call logic. As a means of understanding natural phenomenon, it was personified as the scientific method. Each was a historical process, which relied on description to establish the steps of the process. At the heart of these searches and analyses rested two critical assumptions. First, every facet of worldly activity adhered to rules that humans could understand. Explicit rules dominated things as diverse as Greek medicine and building, town and machine design. Second, form explained those rules; those rules were reducible to and derivable from forms. Indeed, the Greek veneration of form was not merely an aesthetic statement but a fundamental organizational principle, a critical concept and approach—a kind of three-dimensional holism, which, when made to confront its constituent elements cherished balance, harmony, and symmetry—provided the unifying thread.

That is not to say that Greeks agreed about the parameters of a whole, its constituent parts, or exactly what it meant to place them in balance. A healthy disagreement often revolved around these issues. Nonetheless, each of their different positions stemmed from the same considerations, considerations of wholes, parts, and the relationship among them. Form—property-dictating, three-dimensional shape—dominated Greek perception and thought. It provided the enduring cultural characteristic that marked Grecian civilization as different from other early civilizations. For example, form—three-dimensional configuration—was crucial to the sixth century B.C.E. Milesians, who posited a single material cause of things. They maintained that a single substance—water, boundless, or air—was the basis for everything but they also recognized functional differences among things. Things grew and became specially formed to fill a specific function. The Milesians pointed to the homogeneity of a seed, which yielded stems, leaves, flowers, and other apparently disparate parts. Yet none of those parts was truly materially different, they contended, but rather each fulfilled a different specialized function. Analogy also enabled the Milesians to determine the height of an Egyptian pyramid. They measured the length of its shadow at the same time of day as the height of a human shadow matched the height of its owner and assumed that the pyramid's shadow and true height were equivalent.

The shadow-pyramid determination demonstrated a sense of geometric harmonies, ratios. The Pythagoreans, a collection of sixth-, fifth-, and fourth-century-B.C.E. Greeks claiming reverence for Pythagoras of Samos, understood numerical harmonies as the "principle of all things." They postulated that the One breathed into a void and created the universe, which was marked by the separation of things. The universe, a virtually limitless distinction among things, received structure, balance, harmony from the One. Pythagoras discovered the One's principles while observing a blacksmith, whose hammer pounded out certain specific tones. While Pythagoreans talked of square and oblong numbers, they did not see their numerology as mystical, only unappreciated. The universal harmonies (the fundamental musical ratios 9:8, 4:3, 3:2, and 2:1) fixed relationships, whether manifested in observable shapes, such as the right triangle in the Pythagorean theorem, in auditory stimuli, such as musical scales, or in social affairs. In this last case, for instance, justice was equated with the number 4, the square of 2, a balanced, symmetrical, harmonious configuration. Each of these relationships had a physical representation. Indeed, Pythagoreans represented the idea of justice as a balance, as in the scales of justice.

Others in the fifth century B.C.E., the elementalists, dismissed numerical ratios as of fundamental importance and instead saw earth, air, fire, and water as the underlying principles. Yet they too returned to balance and proportion. Elementalists argued that fixed and definite proportions among these elements gave each substance its unique peculiarities. Still other Greeks rejected elementalism and numerological explanation but upheld the validity of material explanations. They only questioned the trustworthiness of the human senses and humanity's ability to discern the underlying ratios and harmonies.

Those not actively involved in finding the material cause of things also considered things holistically. The Sophists, like other fifth-century Greeks, believed in discovery through rational inquiry. Rhetoric, the art of persuasion, became their tool. The process of rhetoric would expose the argument to scrutiny. Truth would emerge as self-evident; it would change the collective mind. Protagoras, one of the earliest Sophists, put it bluntly. Humankind, he argued, "is the measure of all things." A similar premise supported the popularity of comedy, tragedy, and poetry. For these art forms to gain public backing they needed to portray experience that Greeks recognized as common, even universal. Presumption of a sense of commonality also fueled the Socratic search for rules of human ethical conduct and made that search such a threat to those in apparent violation. Socrates gladly gave his life to adhere to these laws.

Plato and Aristotle: Form and Place

Plato's fourth-century-B.C.E. attempt to achieve definitions also stemmed from a Sophist-like belief in the virtue of the collective intellect. Plato sought to determine among forms, which existed and were inviolable—the five perfect solids, for example—and their human representations, which came from the use of reason and therefore were constrained by human limitations. The methods he used were indicative. He looked to humankind—ancient Greeks—for the arguments' terms and then debated them. Plato employed a *dialogue*, a form of debate between Plato or his representative and some earlier philosopher. He named philosophers, actual persons who lived and wrote before Plato's birth, and proceeded to question and argue with them as if they were alive, still members of the present philosophical community and debates. Plato considered the issues that he grappled with human issues, timeless questions, but issues that could ultimately be resolved and applied. The dialectic, a philosophical juxtaposition that seeks to refine and articulate apparently contrarian arguments to achieve their underlying commonality, was imbedded in his dialogues. His dialogues exposed philosophical positions and showed, through their proponents' words and speech, representations of those philosophies at work. In addition to attempting to achieve truth, Plato's dialogues placed human beings in the distinctively human endeavor of rational conversation and contemplation.

The word itself and human logic were Platonic tools. The Platonic (and Greek) agenda discriminated among things while at the same time it posited relationships among things so separated. The Greeks discerned (and joined) the one from (and with) the many; the ideal from how it was represented; the universal One (who Plato said "some call god") from humankind; the state of being from that of becoming; and actual form from its representations. Plato, even when discussing the five perfect solids, reduced them to a series of commonalities—lines or levers (the right-angled isosceles and half-equilateral triangles) revolving through three-dimensional space. Equating each solid with one of the four elements—earth, air, fire, and water—and the zodiac—the heavens—Plato implicitly demonstrated the interconvertability of

Plato—Student of the Greek Philosopher Socrates. Plato's dialogues, particularly his accentuation of the One as the source of all things, provide a framework for much of Western knowledge. It is from these dialogues that we know the works of many of Plato's philosophical predecessors.

matter. Each solid was composed of lines turned in three-dimensional space. Those lines disassembled could be rotated differently on three planes to generate the other essential perfect forms. Therefore elements and, by extension, things themselves held the potential to be transformed from one to another. Plato also revealed the dependence of representation (in modern terms, property) on three-dimensional form. Things seemed as they were because of their shape, their form, their three-dimensional observable composition.

Plato found all coming from the One, which he referred to as the good, suggesting a common point of origin for all things. His most famous student, Aristotle, adopted a similar quest but from a different angle. Aristotle even erected a new school, the Lyceum, to separate himself from his master's Academy. But despite the apparent differences, the ideas imbedded in the Aristotelian program remained very much like those espoused by Plato and by Greek thinkers generally. Aristotle sought to organize the entire sum of human knowledge into fields and subfields, to put things into their natural places, and to give discipline to the search for knowledge. At the heart of this taxonomic scheme was a belief in the four terrestrial elements, but Aristotle identified each with tangible qualities. Earth was cold and dry; water, cold and wet; air, hot and wet; and fire, hot and dry. The Aristotelian elements differed from their earlier counterparts in that Aristotle postulated that they stemmed from two sets of contraries—cold/hot and wet/dry. These two contrary pairs constituted the spectrum of all possible observable phenomena and explained how the various

Aristotle—Plato's Most Famous Student. Aristotelian thought, especially its emphasis on the organization of the parts of a whole, often proved an apt counterweight to Platonic understanding.

elements transformed into one another. The contrary pairs explained, for example, how air (steam) when subjected to cold became water and how fire when cooled became air (smoke). Every substance was composed of common principles—the contrary pairs—and each substance therefore was potentially every other substance. As important, each of the four elements had a natural position. It existed in some three-dimensional earthly space. Therefore, things made up from these elements—all observable matter—must naturally assume particularistic three-dimensional place consistent with the substance's relative composition. The amount of hot/cold and wet/dry dictated the space occupied by the substance.

Form and Daily Life

Even daily life in Greece reflected preoccupation with the whole, with commonality, with form. The Greek infatuation with the human body is well known. Athletes competed without clothes and the palaestra, the place for practicing wrestling and other sports, was public. Woolen tunics revealed shoulders and legs. Dance played a prominent part in the development of the young. Instructors led youths in strenuous musical drills to teach them through rhythmic simultaneous movements the virtues of acting as one.

Homes also accentuated commonality. Greeks constructed each house from mud brick with tile roofs around a common area, a courtyard. All curtain-covered doorways—the lack of permanent barriers, doors, themselves indicated an absence of separation—opened into the courtyard where Greeks ate and even sat collectively; the multiperson couch, not the individual chair, provided the basis for home furnishings.

Form and the Military: Methods and Results—Hellenistic Greece

Philip of Macedonia's defeat of the city-states in 338 B.C.E. ended the autonomy of each state but did not diminish the Greek emphasis on form. Philip's military innovation, the companion cavalry, itself reflected a three-dimensional assessment of military possibilities. The cavalry fought on horseback in a triangular alignment. The point of the triangle charged the hoplite phalanx in order to punch a hole in the formation and attack it from the vulnerable rear. The cavalry's iron-headed spears, about six feet longer than those of the hoplites, usually enabled it to achieve its objectives. Nor did Greek ideas suffer when Philip's son, Alexander the Great, conquered much of the known world soon thereafter. Alexander used the expensive horse cavalry only for lightning-quick assaults. But he incorporated the cavalry's form when he sometimes shifted to triangular phalanxes to slice through the opposition. Because of these and other military maneuvers, Greek civilization was imposed everywhere as Alexander established colonies in conquered territory and encouraged his occupation forces and colonists to marry the local population.

The Greeks' success in transferring their civilization through domination, by inflicting it upon subjugated people, was markedly different from the ways the Sumerian, Egyptian, and Hebrew cultures had spread. Gradualism—cross-cultural influence as a by-product of trade, for example—now gave way to face-to-face cultural intersection and sometimes confrontation as the remnants of these ancient cultures were for the first time situated within territory under Greek control. Egypt, Mesopotamia, Persia, and Northwest India became Greek; people administering those places held the beliefs, conventions, and outer trappings of the Greeks as did many others living there, although the local populace generally retained most traditional customs. Coastal areas and urban centers—places of administration—became Greek quickly and relatively thoroughly. Interior populations rarely developed the same intensity of commitment to their conquerors' culture. Under the Ptolemies, the Egyptian city of Alexandria served as a base for trade with India and emerged as a main center of Greek culture. More Hebrews lived there than in Jerusalem, and Alexandrian Jews translated the Hebrew bible into Greek.

With the demise of the city-states, Alexandria-centered Greek civilization, Hellenistic civilization, looked beyond the locality as notions of civic virtue regularly yielded to cosmopolitan beliefs in the universality of humankind. Certainly the small, relatively homogeneous city-state no longer functioned as an adept model. Alexander's triumphs undercut city-state centrality, and the disintegration of his empire after his death did little to restore these political forms. Numerous different types of administration emerged. Huge kingdoms, each operating somewhat separately but affiliated with other large Greek holdings, proved most common. Unprecedented wealth was controlled by these new Greek kings. The new cosmopolitanness went far beyond geographic borders to emphasize humankind and humankind's realm. When Zeno of Citium wrote *The Republic*, he located it in Cosmopolis, a large heterogeneous area, rather than the idealized city-state. Physical representations became increasingly realistic, less idealized as freestanding statuary, raised statues, and busts emphasized three-dimensionality. Artists used suggestive outlining, movement, shading, and perspective in their attempts to represent three dimensions on a two-dimensional surface.

Private action and self-discipline, qualities possessed by each human, provided the basis for renewed collectivity. All people were to act in a similar fashion to unite them in a whole. Again, not every Greek explained the path to homogeneity the same way, but virtually all came to the question from similar precepts. For example, the Stoics (circa 300 B.C.E.) maintained that a universal law bound humans and required all to fulfill the obligations of their particular social position but never seek power and wealth outside that station. Epicureans (also circa 300 B.C.E.) felt humans should seek pleasure, which came from correct conduct and moderation in all things; pleasure stemmed from the reduction of pain, not from vainglorious hedonism or self-indulgence. Lust for wealth and power reduced contentment and therefore caused pain. It must be avoided. Cynics saw the pursuit of wealth and power as corrupt and corrupting. Only by withdrawing from worldly concerns and shunning the quest for wealth and power could humans find peace of mind.

The Greek language itself underwent a subtle shift as desire for cosmopolitan homogeneity swept the expanded Greek world. Regional dialects and variants, each originating with a city-state, had characterized the Greek of Homer and Plato; a new simplified pan-imperial Greek, called the *common tongue*, replaced and blotted out regional variations and served as potent testimony to the reconfiguration of the locus of identity. So too did creation of a huge Ptolemy-sponsored library and institute at Alexandria. Gathering much of human knowledge into one place served as a magnet for scholars from all over the Greek world interested in literary, mathematical, or scientific matters. The nature of the cosmos and humankind's place within it had long been concerns within Egyptian, Sumerian, and Hebraic culture, just as they had mesmerized Plato, Pythagoras, and numerous other philosophers in the Greek city-states. But now people came to a central location to speculate on these issues; scholars went to Alexandria, used the collections there, and shared knowledge with each other. They then returned to their native places, carrying back common understandings, and spread this communal knowledge, providing a new cosmopolitan basis as well as uniformity to scholarly efforts.

Form and the Sea

Command of the seas was as essential to Alexander's triumphs as it had been to the dominance of city-states. The strongest city-states had been on the sea. Control of the Aegean and the numerous islands and inlets meant control of trade, and the new Greek entities devoted an impressive percentage of their income to maintaining an effective navy. Greek shipbuilders set up stocks, laid the keel, added stem and stern posts and then ribs. Planks were placed together over these vertical frames and fixed to each other with thousands of closely set mortise and tenon joints, held immobile by wooden dowels. Greeks protected the ship's underwater surface against marine borers by covering a tarred fabric with a sheath of lead sheets and securing both to the ship's bottom by copper nails.

Greeks structured their merchant vessels to hold as much cargo as possible. These broad, almost flat-bottomed, boats had single movable masts, square sails, and full, round bows and quarters. They traveled at about 4 knots per hour during the April to November sailing season. To increase capacity further, cargo ships carried no means to protect themselves. Defense was the province of another type of Greek vessel, the long ship, which sought to ram and sink enemy boats. With a length to beam ratio of ten to one, the Greeks designed the long ship for speed and superior maneuverability. It could dart between obstacles and turn completely around in slightly more than its own 115-foot length. A series of windlass-tightened metal chains called *frapping* ran from stem to stern to increase hull stability. The Greeks sheathed the ram—two chisel-like blades, one below the waterline—in bronze to increase its destructive power.

Oarsmen sitting on stationary benches rowed these long ships by pulling oars against fixed vertical pegs. Arrangement of oarsmen varied over time. Following the impetus of Phoenician ships, Greeks placed two rows of up to fifteen oarsmen side-by-side on the gunwale. Sometime in the Myceanean Age, Greeks added a narrow

Trireme. These vessels with three banks of oars dominated sea warfare. The triremes' great maneuverability enabled them to ram the hulls of slower vessels and to smash and sink them.

raised deck, which ran the length of the ship, and put a second set of oarsmen there. This raised deck unbalanced the boat in high seas and the Greeks compensated by cutting oarports in the hull and repositioning the second bank below the first. Leather bags placed around the oars and oarports about 700 B.C.E. kept water from filling the hull during rough weather. A speed increase accompanied this change but paled compared to that introduced somewhat later. Beginning about 550 B.C.E., Greek shipbuilders added a third deck, an outrigger built above and extending beyond the gunwale. The outrigger maintained the center of gravity and allowed each deck to use the same length oars, about 13½ feet. This long ship, the trireme, could travel at about 10 knots at maximum effort and stay in service for about 20 years.

The trireme marked the zenith of Greek shipbuilding. The ship was swift and maneuverable, a quite effective ramming machine. Yet Greek ship design continued unabated. As early as 400 B.C.E., Greeks introduced several new models, although none became popular until the Hellenistic period. The quadrireme, quinquireme, and "sixer" each had three banks of oars but had two men pull on one, two, and three of the banks, respectively. In each case, performance of these new long ships suffered in comparison to that of the trireme. Each boat, significantly wider than the trireme to accommodate the extra oarsmen, was heavier and sat deeper in the water. A marginal increase in maximum speed did occur, but it was more than offset by a slower acceleration, a decrease in stability, and a tremendous loss in maneuverability. Yet these devices operated adequately when compared to the twelve, which had three banks of oars and four men on each oar.

None of these ships could approach the trireme as a maritime war machine. Their adoption suggests that military proficiency became less important within an imperial context as Greek generals and other petty potentates began to crave personal glory and indications of preeminence—concerns the Stoics, Epicureans, Cynics, and others warned against. In every instance, however, these new autocrats sought to express their strength in a characteristically Hellenistic way, by introducing a grander, more elegant form, a more harmonious and symmetrical design. Glory of the nation and of its leaders was reflected in the glory of its forms.

Form and the City

Similar form-based concepts undergirded town and building design. Four edifices served the entire city: the acropolis, a high, defensible place for the community to take refuge when attacked; the agora, site of discussion and, later, market activities; the gymnasium, to teach the young; and the theater. Greek authorities expected these and every other structure to demonstrate the glory of a city-state and later of its administrators. The form of each edifice needed to fit the form of the city as a whole. The building had to be designed for its specific function yet be integrated within the design of the entire city. Equally significant, each building and the entire city needed to be conceived to fit its human inhabitants and their many activities. Only the whole mattered and it depended not simply on the outward appearance of the parts but the relationship among them. To understand relationships inherent in forms required designers to know the skills of building—art and geometry—but also the skills of humankind—history, philosophy, music, medicine, and law. Each area was critical to true design, design that took into account the fact that outward form was the visible consequence of interdependence among the parts, both structural and human.

Designers employed this knowledge within the context of several design principles. They needed to identify the parts, determine the proper place of each of the parts, make sure agreement existed among the parts, see that designs reflected established principles, and implement their plans as economically and as efficiently as possible. In temple building, for example, designers maintained that these structures must be proportioned as in the human body. They demanded that the ratios of distances in temples follow a standard set of rules just as the sizes of body parts do in the body as a whole. Temple columns must be in proportion to and symmetrical with each other. The height of a column had to correlate with the intercolumn distance and the width of the column must correlate with its height. In the Parthenon, for example, the key ratio was nine to four. In actuality, however, these specifications required builders to make corner columns somewhat thicker than others. Only in that way would the human eye perceive all columns as the same width. In every case, though, column capitals must be stylistically compatible with their bases. An odd number of steps of equal width should lead to a temple entrance. Designers stipulated that doorways be a set percentage of the height of columns, using post and lintel construction with the lintel not exceeding the width of the post. Designers also considered internal space and location within a city. Temples must open to the west so that worshipers approaching the altar would face the sunrise. The temples also needed to be positioned to provide the broadest possible view of the city. Statuary was to appear as if it came out of the east. Altars had to be lower than statues so that those praying would look up to the divinities. Statues themselves would be at different heights with Zeus placed the highest. Temples also required foundations. Designers must reach bedrock and lay foundations thicker than the columns they would support.

The great numbers of relationships that successful builders needed to know as well as the abilities and skills they had to master encouraged prominent designers to record their rules so that others could learn and benefit from their experience. The physical layout of each treatise embraced organizational principles similar to those advocated for urban design; the form of the book became inseparable from its substance. Each argument was divided into constituent parts. Each question followed from the previous question. These treatises incorporated the aforementioned types of design considerations but also more, such as specifying the various decorations and decorative techniques for any particular structure. The authors even discussed topics as mundane as how to get building materials from quarries to cities. For example, for light loads designers recommended fixed-axle vehicles with slight nonrotating stubs to which linchpins held wheels, and rotating-axle vehicles, complete with center bearings, for heavier loads. Special-purpose stone slab roads from quarries were advocated for a heavy volume of traffic or to facilitate transportation of ponderous shipments. Narrow grooves cut in these roads held cart wheels in place and prevented hard-to-steer vehicles from veering off the surface. Designers devised an ingenious method to transport huge stones used for column shafts. They suggested that each of these stones be made cylindrical at the quarry and a wooden frame constructed around it. Oxen would be hitched to the frame and the column would be rolled like a drum to the building site.

Form and Agriculture

Similar precision governed Greek agriculture. The difficult Aegean climate with its hot, dry summers and rocky soil circumscribed agricultural production. Greek farmers lived in small, centrally located communities and daily walked from these common points to their individual fields. Winter wheat or barley for bread, porridge, or barley cake were staples, and farmers needed to set aside as much as one-third of a harvest as seed for the next year's crop. These subsistence farmers also grew olives and grapes. Initially, they used an iron-reinforced wooden plow, but after the seventh century B.C.E. added an iron plowshare. Again, the Greek assumption that various relationships among humans and the natural environment determined the appropriate course of action demanded a multidimensional, multifaceted approach. For example, Greeks kept sheep and goats for milk and wool and for sacrifices but cut herds of undesirables and used the meat as food in the spring. Over 50 books on the management of Greek farms were known to exist. Farmers correlated tasks to the position of the stars, which served both as a yearly farm calendar and as an astrological gauge to ensure that certain types of activities were undertaken when particular conjunctions of heavenly bodies occurred. The form of the soil as suggested by its appearance dictated technique as Greek farmers tried to achieve a harmonious balance. They "fattened" "lean" soil by plowing in animal dung and vegetation, such as beans. Farmers had to plow "clayey" soil several times, while "sandy" soils often required some bulk. "Black" soils needed no fallow period. All other soils, including those identified as "wet" and "dry," were cultivated one year and allowed to lie fallow the next.

Form and Medicine

Greek medical therapy also aspired to restore balance, harmony, form. It too proceeded from the assumption, often unspoken, that physical reality not only was a manifestation of underlying forms but also was reducible to and understood by those forms. Medical therapy also was historical, at least in the sense of disease origin; physicians diagnosed disease and then recorded symptoms to detect the malady's cause. They claimed to understand what in the past had produced those symptoms— the symptoms represented the present—and what would necessarily occur if medical intervention were not taken immediately—the future. Physicians maintained that they could often change the medical future. Medical therapy, a therapy based on the doctor's observations and notions of disease causation seen through the gauze of Greek thought, would return the body to the "normal" state, a healthy balance or form.

Several schools of Greek medicine emerged after the sixth century B.C.E. Practitioners of each school disagreed with and often dismissed those of the other schools. Disputes centered on the particulars of an instance, not the notions underlying it. Each school revolved around the same cultural precept, the veneration of form, which made Greek civilization distinctive. For example, the school that sprang up around Hippocrates of Cos in the fifth century B.C.E. believed that the body was composed of four humors, or fluids: blood, black bile, yellow bile, and phlegm. Each humor had specific properties. Blood was hot and dry and phlegm, cold and wet. Black bile was hot and wet and yellow bile, cold and dry. Health was the natural state, a consequence of a balance among humors. The human body normally maintained balance through respiration and ingestion. Disease resulted from an excess of a humor. The body ripened the humor—the cause of fever—and eliminated some of the extra humor naturally in urine, feces, vomit, or pus but not enough to regain health. Physicians examined the symptoms and prescribed certain dietetic remedies to restore humoral balance. If that failed to produce the desired effect, Hippocratic physicians recommended plant-derived drugs, diuretics and purgatives, to assist in the restoration. Cutting the body—opening pus pockets to let out the rotted humors or bloodletting to get rid of noxious blood—remained a last resort.

Each Hippocratic therapy stemmed from the same premise: Health came from a balance of the four humors. The Erasistratian school also focused on humors but in a somewhat different fashion. To these physicians, humors traveled in three kinds of tubes corresponding to our veins, arteries, and nerves, which twisted together like rope to form organs. The blood went in the veins, the phlegm in the arteries, and bile in the nerves. Disease was caused by a "plethora," when too much blood congregated in one area, placed pressure on that vein, and caused it to rupture or leak. The venous blood then infiltrated the arteries and blocked them, which impeded phlegm movement, led to stagnation, and resulted in fever. Ridding the body of the excess blood and reducing the tubular tension to normal limits would return the individual to health. Erasistratian physicians bled their patients or prescribed drugs to relax the veins, to balance the pressure within them with their ability to withstand that stress.

Two other schools ignored humoral pathologies. Followers of Herophilus recognized life regulated by four energies: nutrition, warmth, sensation, and thought. Health was a balance of these energies and was reflected in the pulse, which beat out this balance in a mathematical and musical rhythm. Physicians measured the pulse to detect disease and then tried dietetic therapies to redress the inner harmony. The Asclepian school (circa 200 B.C.E.) conceived of the body as a series of disconnected points or atoms, which attracted and repelled each other. Pores—spaces—remained between atoms. Health depended on the distance between atoms or, more simply, the size and shape of the pores. If the attracting and repelling forces did not equal their normal balance, the size of the pores would be disrupted. Too much repelling force yielded larger pores and too many body secretions. Too great attraction would constrict pores and produce fever. Mixed symptoms meant that atoms were too close together in some parts of the body and too distant in others. In each case, physicians addressed the mechanical imbalance by mechanical means: applying heat, cold, or sunshine; drinking massive quantities of water; taking baths or massages.

These four medical schools conceived of disease differently. Yet each depended upon the same fundamental assumption. Disease was a lack of symmetry, a lack of harmony, a lack of balance—anathemas to the Greeks. Only by restoring the form, only by restoring those precise mathematical ratios and harmonies, could health be regained.

Functional Machines The Greeks devised numerous machines to pursue an impressive variety of tasks. Machines designed for the relatively simple task of raising water suggest the extraordinary diversity of Greek machinery. A wide variety of machinery was necessary because each machine needed to be fitted to the appropriate activity: Greeks required different machines to secure drinking water, irrigate crops, remove floodwater from mines and bilge water from ships, fight fires, and remove standing water from cities and from dry docks. For example, Ctesibius, a third-century-B.C.E. Alexandrian known for his water clock and water organ, described a bronze force pump for use in fighting fires. A piston was fitted into a cylinder, which was filled with water. Operators then depressed the piston to urge the liquid higher. A set of valves prevented the water from falling back into the cylinder. Hero, also of Alexandria, described a tympanon, which used a treadmill and the natural current to raise water from a river. A huge, hollow wooden drum divided inside into eight compartments stood upright in the river and gathered water from it. The tympanon raised the water as it revolved only to release it into a trough through holes near the drum's center. In this way, water could be raised to roughly half the tympanon's height, as much as 15 feet. Hero recommended this machine for service in agricultural irrigation. Others wrote about a chain of "pots," which incorporated a windlass and pulleys to get water out of wells and mines. The windlass rotated an axle-like device placed over the shaft. A pulley joined the axle to an endless chain, which had leather bags (pots) attached to it. Turning the axle would simultaneously lower empty bags into the shaft and draw up full bags. Greeks also employed the Archimedean screw to lift water, often to create dry docks. Their most refined machine placed the tip of a stationary wooden cylinder in a river. Within the cylinder was a mobile screw, which could be turned by treadmill. Water would travel up the screw and spill out the top of the cylinder into buckets.

Greeks used cranes to lift materials other than liquids and presses to squeeze fluids from solid substances. Both were based on mechanical principles similar to those used in water raising. Cranes consisted of two pulleys attached to a fixed pole. A rope running through the pulleys to a windlass enabled the Greeks to lift and lower cargo. Presses incorporated the screw. Olives or grapes were placed in the press and the top

Siege Machines. Earthen walls made it difficult to overrun cities. Greek military designers created numerous weapons to scale or destroy these barriers.

was screwed ever closer to the fixed base. The juice ran from the press and was collected in a trough.

Military Machines   Military machines were as formidable in design as their peacetime counterparts. Greeks increasingly utilized machines to lay siege to a city or to defend a besieged place in the time of Alexander and after. Regions beyond the Peloponnesus lacked its rugged terrain and proximity to the sea. Only open field or siege warfare could take these places, and word spread quickly of Alexander's open field wizardry. Few wanted to tempt that juggernaut and, rather than confront his forces on the battlefield, remained ensconced behind walled strongholds. Competition for these guarded cities increased with Alexander's death. His generals fought among themselves to succeed their fallen leader and attacked one another's fortifications as they also sought to expand their realm. Although most cities fell from starvation or betrayal, devising and constructing siege apparatus was a respected occupation and a venerated way of earning a livelihood. Iron-shrouded wooden frames called *turtles* protected soldiers as they manned battering rams to break down a city's wooden gate or stone wall or dug tunnels to go underneath. Huge iron-shielded, solid-wheel towers provided mobile platforms from which attacking forces lobbed missiles and debris into a city to terrorize inhabitants and from which troops could scale unprotected sections of a wall. Bow and torsion catapults combined pulley and windlass to draw a machine into firing position. The bow catapult depended on the elasticity of the horn or wood used in the bow for power while tightly twisted skeins of hair or sinew provided the torsion device a marked increase in force. Torsion catapults employed the principle of the lever. A wooden arm, fixed at one end, lay perpendicular to and on top of the skeins. The catapultist winched down the arm and placed a stone at the free-moving end. He then released the windlass to send the missile. The machine would recoil like the kick of a mule.

Greek military machine makers quickly developed parameters for catapult design. They determined that the size of the skein established the proper size of the other torsion catapult parts, including the size and weight of the projectile. They considered the fulcrum, length of arm, and throw arc as analogous to the revolution of the heavenly orbs and learned through trial and error to predict range and distance for various missile types. Archytas of Tarentum (fl. 400 B.C.E.) and Eudoxos of Knidos (fl. 375 B.C.E.) extended the technique to use mechanical demonstrations to resolve geometric problems they could not prove mathematically. In each case, Greek machine designers, like their fellow countrymen, relied on form both as understanding and as explanation.

Form and Mechanical Principles

Issues of form provided the basis from which the Greeks understood all machinery. They identified five simple machines—windlass, pulley, screw, wedge, and lever/balance—which they called five simple powers, or talents, as the constituent parts of all machines, and maintained that "all [the talents] are related to the same natural principle." "All machinery is derived from nature," they noted, founded on "the revolution" of the heavens. The heavens "revolves steadily round earth and sea on the pivots at the end of its axis, . . . like those of a turning lathe." This harmonious, symmetrical, three-dimensional surface was a sphere, a perfect form. But Greek mechanics also recognized that the "first explanation of circles came from the balance," a lever swung in every direction around a stationary point on a two-dimensional surface. The sphere was nothing more than that lever in three-dimensional space. The screw was "really . . . but a twisted wedge . . . moved by means of a lever" in corkscrew fashion through three-dimensional space. The wedge consisted "of two levers opposite one another." The pulley "works in the same way as the lever." Form, three-dimensional form, then, explained how machines worked and how they demonstrated the same natural principle.

The Greek affection for form became working devices—the five simple machines—and gearing. Gearing transfers or translates motion, depends upon physical relationships, and takes place in three-dimensional space. Greek bevel gears stood almost perpendicular to each other and changed vertical into horizontal motion, while their parallel wheels simply engaged one another. A sense of motion as well as depth was implicit in the wheels, which engaged a toothed rack, and especially in the worm wheel. There a toothed wheel was designed to interact with screw threads, which changed angles of incidence as the device worked its way up or down a cone-shaped screw.

Summary of Form

The Greek ability to reduce mechanical operations to simple yet perfect forms and therefore to unify them ought not to surprise. Form pervaded every aspect of Greek thought and society. It provided the explanation for events and the basis for action. It made Greek civilization what it was.

For Further Reading

Boardman, John. *The Greeks Overseas.* New York: Thames and Hudson, 1980.

Carpenter, Rhys. *The Architects of the Parthenon.* Baltimore: Penguin, 1970.

Casson, Lionel. *Ships and Seamanship in the Ancient World.* Princeton, N.J.: Princeton University Press, 1971.

Castleden, Rodney. *Minoans: Life in Bronze Age Crete.* London: Routledge, 1990.

Drachmann, A. G. *Mechanical Technology of Greek and Roman Antiquity.* Copenhagen: Munksgaard, 1963.

Frost, Frank J. *Greek Society,* 4th ed. Lexington, Mass.: D. C. Heath, 1992.

Green, Peter. *From Alexander to Actium.* Berkeley: University of California Press, 1990.

Harding, A. F. *The Mycenaeans and Europe.* London: Academic Press, 1984.

Hawkes, Jacquetta. *Dawn of the Gods: Minoan and Mycenaean Origins of Greece.* New York: Random House, 1968.

Hill, Donald Routledge. *A History of Engineering in Classical and Medieval Times.* London: Croom Helm, 1984.

Hodges, Henry. *Technology in the Ancient World.* New York: Knopf, 1970.

Kagan, Donald, Rev. *Botsford and Robinson's Hellenic History,* 5th ed. New York: Macmillan, 1969.

Landels, J. G. *Engineering in the Ancient World.* Berkeley: University of California Press, 1978.

Lloyd, G. E. R. *Early Greek Science: Thales to Aristotle.* New York: W. W. Norton, 1970.

MacKendrick, Paul. *The Greek Stones Speak: The Story of Archaeology in Greek Lands.* New York: W. W. Norton, 1979.

Morrison, John S. *The Athenian Trireme: The History and Reconstruction of an Ancient Greek Warship*. New York: Cambridge University Press, 1986.

Phillips, E. D. *The Royal Hordes: Nomad Peoples of the Steppes*. London: Thames and Hudson, 1965.

Roberts, J. W. *City of Sokrates*. London, Boston: Routledge and Kegan Paul, 1984.

Taylor, William. *The Mycenaeans*, rev. ed. London: Thames and Hudson, 1983.

White, K. D. *Greek and Roman Technology*. London: Thames and Hudson, 1984.

Willits, R. F. *The Civilization of Ancient Crete*. London: B. T. Batsford, 1977.

Wycherley, R. E. *How the Greeks Built Cities*. New York: W. W. Norton, 1976.

CHAPTER 3

Roman Civilization: The Republic

In many ways, Rome emerged as the successor state to Greece, an event memorialized in the idea of a Greco-Roman civilization. To be sure, Rome did adopt many Greek constructs. But Rome never entirely embraced the substance of Greece. Many Romans even viewed the introduction of Greek concepts into Rome as cause for alarm, signifying decadence and decline. Romans took things Greek but they often interpreted and explained them in ways fundamentally different from those of the Greeks. Sometimes Romans modified them to fit better within the new context. Rome also borrowed elsewhere—Romans were the ultimate consumers of facets of other cultures—most explicitly from the Etruscans, a non–Indo-European-speaking people from which the city of Rome descended. Again, Romans readily accepted Etruscan institutions and structures but not necessarily the intellectual underpinnings; what made those forms appropriate, even sensible, to the Etruscans did not necessarily resonate with Romans.

Romans did not simply encounter a cultural construct and implement it. How they explained that structure struck at the very heart of the matter. Indeed, Romans did not—and needed not—understand the construct in a manner consonant with the civilization from which the form was initially derived. What was crucial was that the visible manifestation of the construct made sense to the Romans within the context of Roman ideas, Roman civilization, those fundamental principles upon which the Romans based their social arrangements, how Romans identified themselves. And from that perspective, the concept of a Greco-Roman civilization makes little sense. The intellectual structures of the Roman Republic and Empire were sufficiently different from those of Greece as to constitute a virtually alien civilization. At Rome's very root was a profound fear of individualism, compounded by a static sense of time; tradition played an important part in this cultural formulation as did the ability to shun established forms and traditions whenever society as a viable construct seemed threatened. Perpetuation of society, not proportion, balance, symmetry, or form, was crucial and that led Romans to make a series of modifications to maintain the whole. The Romans' conception was corporate. The whole—society—sometimes existed at the expense and to the detriment of its parts—members, institutions, and other forms. Romans would absorb or adopt many aspects of other cultures if that adoption or absorption would enable them to achieve the core desire of preserving the whole.

How Romans in the Republic approached architecture and art reflects these different assumptions. Romans expressly preserved architectural structures and statues they encountered on their conquests. But although they refused to modify the physical form or shape, Romans nevertheless adapted these works rather than adopted them. The exterior of a facility or structure was crucial to the Greeks; they had attempted to establish building façades that would appear to observers in specific, stylized ways. Romans instead concentrated on the interior of a facility or structure and the activity within the building's shell. Romans demanded exact representations of actual things. Appearance must be true, not idealized. A lighted interior unifying the entire edifice also became a characteristic Roman theme. Each piece of Roman art needed to express the virtuousness and corporateness of Roman civilization. Every modification of an established structure and every new work of art must testify to Roman virtue. Even the act of creation itself had to reflect Roman corporality. For example, although the Greeks celebrated their artists, architects, and sculptors, Roman artists rarely signed their work. Romans maintained that Roman art was not the product of the actual artist but of the eternal Rome. Roman civilization had made the artifact and that artifact embodied the values and premises of that society.

Roman Origins: Etruria

Rome as a place likely began as one of nearly 20 quarrelsome city-states of Etruria sometime before the seventh century B.C.E. Etrurian customs closely resembled those of Sumer and Egypt and the Etruscans likely originated in Asia Minor. But this culture also reflected some Indo-European practices. The Etruscan people in what is now Italy had well and circle graves like Indo-Europeans and citadel or acropolis-like structures. They were often buried in terra-cotta sarcophaguses, flanked by numerous bronze and gold artifacts. Etruscans also held a profound, Sumer-like fatalism and a belief in the inevitability of divine will. Life spans of individuals and civilizations were preordained. Civilizations would die or be absorbed according to divine plan. Etruscans even hammered a nail into the temple wall to mark each year in their civilization's passing. Belief in the divinity of laws pervaded Etruscan society. It was humankind's duty to follow precise rules of conduct. The natural world showed the will of the gods. Humanity was responsible for finding signs of that will in nature and in the heavens and interpreting them correctly. Peculiar and uncommon occurrences, such as sports of nature, thunder and lightning, and the flight of birds, provided critical clues. The liver was the seat of life and divination of an animal's liver seemed to hold particularly important insights.

Etruscan cities took on a characteristic grid pattern. Minor paved or cobbled roads about 17 feet wide intersected major thoroughfares nearly three times as broad. Specialized activities were relegated to specific locations within the city. Religious and common commercial activities dominated the central area, while metalworking took place near the city's rough-cut stone walls. Etruscans also used stone to line wells, to build storm sewers to catch runoff and take it out of the city, and to form bases for housing and other buildings. They liberally employed arches and lintels in their single-story houses, which were built from wood and sometimes covered by terra-cotta or mud brick. A slanted atrium covered by shingles or tile provided the architectural focus. House interiors reflected the Etrurian passion for ostentation. They mingled bronze mirrors with eclectic bronze and terra-cotta sculpture. Etruscans seemed to have little movement, perspective, unity, or specific themes in their art and decorative arts, which emphasized the personal and particular rather than the universal. Wood-framed chairs and four-legged tables served for informal occasions but at banquets Etruscan men and women reclined on low bed-like structures with footstools. Both men and women wore loosely fitted wool or flax tunics. They favored open baskets and boxes attached to walls instead of closed cupboards or chests as they proudly displayed their possessions rather than hid them.

Etruscan power rested in part on its raw materials. Good soil and adequate rainfall produced excellent farmland and an abundance of timber—oak, elm, beech, pine, maple, and boxwood. Nearby land bore copious amounts of copper, lead, silver, and iron ore, which was smelted on site. Commerce increased the value of these materials and Etruscans instituted several conventions to facilitate trade. They established among themselves a set of weights and measures and used a decimal-based numerical system to show relative value in commercial transactions. They also coined money, which was good throughout the realm and featured mythical creatures—griffins, chimeras, or gorgons—on one side. The Etruscans further encouraged trade among the city-states by building stone highways to connect them. These roadways, often rock cut, always had drainage ditches by the side to help keep the roadbed dry.

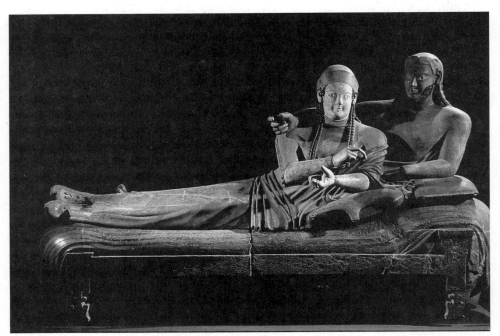

Etruscan Sarcophagus. This terra-cotta casket depicts a husband and wife. Wealthy Etruscans often took their meals reclining on a couch-like frame, such as the one pictured here.

Etruscans' religious and social arrangements revolved around the family. They believed in as many as 40 groups or families of gods (generally in threes) or fates—lesser gods—and recognized regular interaction, perhaps even a quasigovernmental organization, among them. The gods' human servants—priests—came from noble lineage and wore high conical hats and other ostentatious garb. Familial connections also provided social status in Etruscan society. Fathers passed the family name to children. Families were buried together in family plots but Etruscans excluded slaves from the tombs of the families they had served. A system of clientage joined the most consequential Etruscan families with the lesser ones in each city-state. The great Etruscan families protected and interceded for client families and sometimes provided financial assistance. These prominent men and women annually selected from among themselves several magistrates to represent their interests. These officials controlled the day-to-day operations of each city and met yearly as a council of twelve to discuss issues of mutual concern. They chose a chairman but military authority—the king and his generals—rested outside these social arrangements and took precedence.

The Etruscans dominated central Italy from the seventh century B.C.E. As the significant regional power, Etruria traded and came into conflict with the Greeks and Assyrians. The Romans chafed under the Etruscan kings and by the late sixth century B.C.E. proved powerful enough to break away. Romans dated their independence and the Republic from 509 B.C.E., but many years passed before Rome freed itself from Etruscan influence. Nor was Etruria the only hostile military power in the area. Latins and Italians, of Indo-European origin like the Romans, surrounded the early Republic in central and southern Italy, and Greece controlled the coast of southern Italy and Sicily.

Roman Ethos

Romans prided themselves on two particular tenets: their uniqueness as a people and their ability to preserve their indigenous traditions. They proposed that Romans living, dead, and as yet unborn were essentially the same. In our terms, they assumed that these people possessed a similar frame of reference, saw each situation in a similar way, and would respond to that situation in a similar manner. That not only suggests an unbending consistency and continuity among the past, present, and future, but also that modernist concepts of progressive time had little meaning to the Romans. Fundamental change, including development or regress, was in Rome inconceivable. Things were a particular way and would always remain so.

Ironically, the Roman inability to conceive of change freed them to undertake regularly what we would consider significant, even drastic, changes. Because fundamental change was virtually impossible, actions taken by duly elected Roman bodies could not constitute tradition- or stability-threatening change; by definition, these activities were merely restatements of the same basic, fundamental principles held by Romans throughout eternity. The Republic's successes seemed to contemporaries further to support the idea of Roman unity. Each instance served as a potent confirmation of the virtue of Rome as a republic and as an explication of the Roman will; it reaffirmed the idea of eternal Roman commonality and rectitude.

Early Republic to 265 B.C.E.

Stability was crucial to the early Romans and they worked to create an institutional framework that would perpetuate features that seemed to mark Romans as unique. Administration, both civic and religious, the family, and the military each in their own way served to buttress Rome. Each became a bulwark against change and a pillar of the early Republic.

Administration

Roman experience under Etruscan kings led these newly independent people to guard against tyranny and to seek solace in a republic. At the same time, however, they adopted a good portion of Etruscan administration, the administration to which they had become accustomed. The republic accentuated representative government and upper-class control.

Civic Administration

But the notion of a timeless unity among Romans also served to make a republic possible. Romans did not think of government as governing so much as administering. Officials merely implemented the eternal Roman will; they did not institute new initiatives or move the Republic in new directions. In that context, administration was a somewhat onerous responsibility, and an unpaid one at that. To ensure its successful pursuit, Romans challenged those whose ancestors had administered—those from the most prestigious families, who were generally of means (especially in the early Republic) and who therefore could afford the luxury of administration—to serve as had their forefathers. Administering the commonality was a duty, not a privilege, and not looked upon as particularly attractive. Administrators lacked authority to do more than carry out the law, and office-holding prevented them from pursuing other tasks. To ease this civic, republican burden, Romans regularly rotated public offices, held frequent elections, and stipulated through term limitations that no individual should bear an unfair share of the administrative onus.

Those long-prominent families that produced office-eligible noblemen were called Patricians. In the early Republic, a patrician-dominated family or clan assembly annually elected two patricians as chief magistrates—consuls—with executive power. Consuls executed the laws—they administered—but did not make them. Ideas of administering rather than governing even extended to the Assembly. Romans conceived of their Assembly as announcing laws rather than legislating in any modern sense. Romans considered laws as representing the collective Roman will. No single body possessed the authority to make laws, therefore, but the Republican Assembly as the representative body of the Roman people could announce eternal Roman truths. Absence of a written constitution during the Republic's earliest years supported this idea of time-honored constancy. It was a collective experience known to all who shared the Roman heritage.

Roman citizens overwhelmingly agreed to this administrative arrangement. Yet that did not stop them from endeavoring to sharpen administrative structures and practices, to change things to check the possibility of individual self-interest, without acknowledging that change occurred at all. Almost from the start, the Roman fear of a tyrant, of an ill-designing individual or megalomaniac seizing power, encouraged and permitted Romans to seat retired consuls—those individuals who had by virtue of their office already proven that they represented the eternal will of the Roman people—in a Senate to oversee the actions of the then current consuls. The Senate had no official or constitutional power, but in practice Senate approval was required before consuls could act.

In modern terms, creation of the Senate would smack of usurpation of power. Romans expressed no such sentiments. Patricians also introduced several other administrative modifications, each of which diffused authority and thus made it increasingly difficult for a single individual to control government. Assistants to the consuls—quaestors—became independent of their former bosses, including standing for separate Assembly elections, and late in the fifth century B.C.E. gained responsibility for supervising the public treasury and military finances. Two other magistrates—praetors—were detached from the consulship and charged with administering the law. One praetor dealt with cases involving Roman citizens, while the other handled legal issues concerning foreigners. At the beginning of each year, praetors announced the types of cases they would hear, a procedure that defined and circumscribed the scope of Roman law.

Each of the aforementioned adjustments lessened the responsibilities of consuls. Administrative modification also came from other quarters. Plebeians, the vast majority of Roman citizens who did not come from noble families, repeatedly sought to influence administrative forms. The dominant Patricians ultimately bent little by little to these initiatives until they had relinquished completely their special administrative claim. The Patricians' action and the willingness of the Plebeians to sustain the issue peacefully over a matter of centuries reflects three pervasive sentiments: the Roman terror of one-person or clique rule, the idea that proper Roman administration was a responsibility without significant power, and the desire to keep the body politic intact even as it meant redefining the nature of the affiliation. The last was the case even though Rome was a brutish place, rough, competitive, violent. An assembly of Plebeian families elected tribunes to represent the group and pressed Patricians to recognize these officials. By the middle of the fifth century, tribunes had formalized their obligation to inspect rulings about Plebeians made by the Patrician-dominated Assembly or Senate. Patricians formally acknowledged the tribunes' obligation after the Plebeians refused to fight in defense of Rome without such an acknowledgment. Plebeians saw this acknowledgment less as a modification than as a formalization of what they claimed was an eternal edict. Similarly, the successful Plebeian initiative in 451–450 B.C.E. for Rome to issue a written code of law—the Twelve Tables—seemed a formality, one which protected against ill-designing persons. A written (even if incomplete) law code versus a remembered law lessened the possibility for tampering or forgetting; it increased the difficulty for a clique to violate the Roman will. The right of Plebeians to hold the Republic's highest offices—the quaestorship and finally the consulship—was codified in 421 and 367 B.C.E., respectively. Prohibitions against intermarriage between the social orders had been removed somewhat earlier and personal enslavement had been eliminated as a payment for debt.

Religious Administration

Roman religious institutions mimicked civic ones. Representative priestly bodies—colleges—administered religious law. To serve on these bodies was an administrative burden and men of learning, political experience, and wealth, men with the leisure and finances to devote their efforts to the state, assumed these duties. Their exact knowledge of religious tradition, divine law, and precise ceremonial and ritual procedure constituted their credentials.

Romans had two main priestly colleges. Both added members and increased in size over the centuries. The College of the Augurs interpreted natural and atmospheric signs to learn the will of the gods before an important civic decision. A college member stood blindfolded as a civil official, perhaps a consul, reported on the skies and surrounding terrain. "Thunder and lightning, the flight and cries of birds, the feeding of the sacred chickens, and the behavior of certain animals and snakes" were potent omens, each of which could affect the timing of some critical determination.

The College of the Pontiffs presided over all other religious events. College members were repositories of the rituals, prayers, chants, and litanies employed in public worship. They directed the building, dedication, and consecration of temples, oversaw burial of the dead, and fixed festival dates. The latter activity had civil significance because courts were closed on festival days. But it was as keeper of religiously ordained tradition and custom that the College of the Pontiffs had its greatest influence on civil society. Criminal law was based on the principle that an offense against the community was an offense against the gods; the college adjudicated what was offensive to the gods and used its collective knowledge of religious tradition and divine law and, later, the partially complete Twelve Tables as precedents. In that sense, law during the early Republic never seemed to evolve. Every subsequent college pronouncement was identified merely as an expression of previously articulated precedent, a precedent of eternal Rome. Nor did the college's responsibilities end at Rome's borders. Because Romans conceived of severing and fomenting alliances as sacred acts, the pontiffs supervised declarations of war and establishment of treaties and alliances.

The King of Sacrifices and the Supreme Pontiff, the latter an elective office, sat consul-like over the priestly colleges. Their duties included supervision of the vestal virgins—Vesta was the Roman goddess of the hearth—and other priests and priestesses identified as attending particular religious entities. Each Roman deity commanded some specific activity or set of activities and Romans believed that prayer and sacrifice of foodstuffs would curry their favor. Identification of individual gods with precise spheres of life persisted even as Romans added gods to their pantheon, redefined the spheres of established gods, and identified other peoples' gods with the gods of Rome. In none of these instances, however, did Romans acknowledge that a fundamental change took place. They remained convinced of the essential consistency of their religious pursuits.

The Family

In a civilization bound by the idea that each Roman was tied to every other Roman, living, dead, and as yet unborn, it was not surprising that the family constituted the basis of socioeconomic organization. It also took on the basic form of identification both for individuals and for the state itself; Rome used the family as a metaphor for the relationship among Romans. Even education was family-based. Mothers and older female children trained their younger brothers and sisters until about age 7. Girls remained at home to study housewifery while boys went with their fathers to learn an occupation and how to be a citizen. Boys received togas at age 15, a sign of adulthood, left their fathers, and studied with a family friend. At 17, they entered the military, first as infantrymen. Their ascension to junior officers provided leadership training and completed their formal education.

The state reflected familial arrangements. The centrality of tribal assemblies was the most obvious measure of familial importance but a complex web of patron-client relationships governed most day-to-day activities in Rome. These relationships were critical to individual survival because as late as the third century B.C.E., Rome proper was a rather brutish modest city. The city had been sacked by the Gauls and was without a wall until 378 B.C.E. In the Rome of the early Republic, winding, unpaved streets skirted unimposing temples. Rectangular, mud-brick houses with stone foundations and wooden braced walls opened to central courts. Every eighth day was market day and the market area bustled with activity. A citadel high above the city housed the sacred flame, which was tended by six vestal virgins.

Agriculture

The city of Rome was the site of religion, trade, and government but the overwhelming preponderance of Romans were tied to the land. Agriculture remained the primary means to gain wealth in the early Republic. An extremely large estate of 150 acres used soil-maintenance techniques consistent with the idea of an eternal Rome. Such an estate would have over a dozen slaves, including the foreman and his wife, laborers, plowmen, a donkey driver, a shepherd, and a swineherder. The estate would use three teams of oxen and three donkeys for plowing and transportation. Six plows and plowshares (Romans plowed at right angles because their scratch plows made shallow furrows), three yokes with rawhide ropes and harness for six oxen, three wagons, presses, a harrow, rakes, shovels, and similar implements would constitute basic equipment. These large Roman estates could afford to crop two years in succession and then allow the field to lie fallow for a year. A flock of sheep provided manure for the crops and olive trees. The vast majority of Roman farmers, however, were subsistence farmers and did not have the luxury of fallowing their acreage, nor could they apply manure like their wealthier compatriots. Intensive cultivation of grapes, olives, livestock, millet, and barley provided them with enough food and meat for themselves and their families and little else.

The Military

Military service, like civic administration, was a social obligation. Roman citizenship carried with it the duty to serve in the military. In the early Republic, Patricians exclusively shouldered the administrative burden by acting as generals and other high-ranking officers. In fact, military administration was considered a necessary prerequisite for civic administration. The form of Roman military organization further reflected the hierarchical nature of the Republic's family-based society. Romans had learned the Greek-styled phalanx—the military technology of their day—from the Etruscans but modified it to make family status and then wealth the organizing principle: Each citizen's place in the phalanx depended upon what military equipment he could afford. First-class citizens had to supply their own spears, helmets, greaves, cuirasses, and metal hoplite shields. The second class bore no cuirasses and held cheaper, curved, metal-reinforced Italian shields. The third class had only Italian shields and helmets, the fourth class carried shorter spears and Italian shields, and the fifth class used only slings and javelins. The first class constituted the heart of the force. In hoplite fashion, it marched forward to crush the opposition. The other classes guarded its flanks or served to soften up an enemy's main force.

The phalanx worked exceptionally well on set piece engagements conducted on flat ground. But the topography around Rome and throughout the Italian peninsula was much too hilly and rugged for set piece warfare to remain a successful military strategy, and the Romans quickly adopted a much more flexible arrangement. The legion, a group of about 4,300 men, became the basic unit. The legion's advantage was that it could be divided into any number of smaller, closely coordinated units

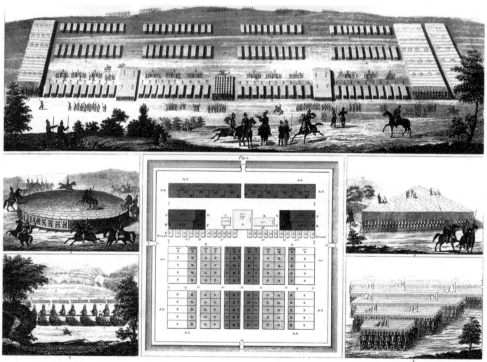

Roman Military. Romans precisely arranged and organized their forces. Their legions provided the flexibility necessary to fight in the hilly areas surrounding Rome.

that could be deployed in countless formations and situations. It could counter whatever terrain and force the army faced. This multifaceted arrangement accentuated mobility and command. It required a much larger officer corps and Plebeians began to hold places in that enlarged body. The tight, sudden movements made by this mobile body required a rigorous discipline, and Romans prided themselves on possessing that discipline, thinking it preferable to face one's enemy in battle than to face a Roman commander after failing to follow an order.

Desire to increase military flexibility led the Romans to replace the heavy circular hoplite shield, excellent for warding off powerful direct advances, with the more supple Italian shield, which provided a variety of defensive possibilities. Romans also modified their javelins, which, with the demise of the phalanx and replacement of the hoplite shield, now had new defensive responsibilities. A heavy version of the javelin was used as a pike to help protect against frontal assaults in exposed areas.

No similar change occurred in naval warfare. Never the most important part of the military arsenal, Roman ships resembled oar-driven floating platforms. Each ship possessed a grappling hook and plank with a large spike to secure enemy vessels for boarding. Oarsmen, generally poorer citizens, did double duty, rowing the boat and then boarding the secured ship to fight in hand-to-hand combat.

Conquest, Citizenship and Assimilation

Early Roman military campaigns secured the Italian peninsula and preserved Roman freedom from the Etruscans. Rome received assistance from the Latins and Italians in central and southern Italy but an alliance with these Indo-European peoples long persisted in name only. Rome conquered its former allies in 338 B.C.E. Somewhat before that time, in the late fifth century B.C.E., the Carthaginians, Phoenicians from the city of Carthage in Northern Africa, had gained disputed control of Sicily with the Sicilian Greeks. Control of that important island made conflict between Rome and Carthage inevitable.

But it was what Romans did after their military adventures that was so striking. They did not reduce their former foes to slavery. Instead, they invariably entered into some form of alliance with their defeated Etruscan, Italian, or Latin foes. These alliances always proved remarkably favorable to the conquered party. To a large degree, the terms of the alliances were based on the conquered parties' law, which the Romans codified as part of their law for foreigners; laws of the conquered became institutionalized as Roman laws, albeit only applied to those who were not Roman citizens. In general terms, the alliances usually permitted the already established social structure and arrangements of the conquered party to remain in place. The administration that led the former foe to defeat continued in power but Rome forbade it to engage in an independent foreign policy and required the conquered province during an emergency to furnish the Roman army with a relatively small number of soldiers. The beaten province retained its own customs and traditions and did not pay Roman taxes. Rome also retained the right to settle disputes among alliance partners. It occasionally permitted the conquered people to marry Roman citizens and own property in Rome. In a few scattered instances, a handful of vanquished foes gained citizenship in Rome.

Even these practices pall, however, compared to the Roman decision in 338 B.C.E. to make citizens of the Latin League citizens of Rome. The grant of citizenship was absolute. Those granted citizenship became part of eternal Rome, the Romans of the past, present, and future, indistinguishable from those born citizens of Rome. In our terms, it was not simply a matter of who could vote but rather of ethnicity or race. (Similarly, adopted children were the equivalent of natural children in Rome.) Such a fundamental redefinition of persons, particularly former foes, demonstrates just how pervasive and deep-rooted was the idea of an eternal, unchanging Rome. It could accommodate even an extension of Roman citizenship because change was inconceivable. Since change was unimaginable, no threat to the body politic—to the Roman family—was perceived from the acceptance of outsiders as Romans.

Cementing Alliances: Roman Outposts

Conquering a place or agreeing to a pact with a foreign potentate only initiated the process of bringing the land within the Roman sphere of influence. Romans demanded organic affiliation, a fact they accomplished in two primary ways. They created Roman outposts in those territories and then established roads to link these territories to Rome proper.

Cities

When Rome conquered a territory it made its former foe cede a small parcel of land, generally on a hilltop or coast. Retired Roman soldiers received this land as a reward for their valued service, and they immediately began the ritual of laying out a new town much as the Etruscans had. They dug a pit and burned an offering, consulted an oracle, and then marked out the perimeter of the city wall. A cow and bull yoked together pulled a bronze plowshare where the walls were to be built. Romans deposited the soil from the furrow inward, presumably as a symbolic moat to mark the spiritual boundaries of this Roman outpost city. The plow was lifted over the areas reserved for the three gates, dedicated to the Etruscan/Roman gods Jupiter, Juno, and Minerva, and the streets and temples were set according to the cardinal points.

These new urban places had functions beyond honoring military men. They were outposts, strategic places from which to warn Rome of any violation of an alliance, and extensions of Roman civilization. Roman towns and cities placed in the midst of non-Romans spread Roman civilization to former enemies and, by example, taught them the inherent virtues of Roman life.

Roads

Roman outposts in Italy were joined physically to the city of Rome. As early as the end of the fourth century B.C.E., a web of roads crisscrossed the peninsula, cementing alliances as well as the Republic's new boundaries. These great stone and ceramic roads, similar in style and technology to the earlier Etruscan roads, were built under the direction of Rome and tied each entity to Rome proper. They fostered communications between Rome and the provinces, speeded the conduct of business, and facilitated transport of heavy materials, such as columns. Roman armies used them to protect and defend the Republic and to respond to any imminent military threat.

Later Republic to 27 B.C.E.

Rome's triumph over the Italians and Latins soon placed it face to face with the Carthaginians. Their functional control of Sicily, which extended from the boot of Italy out into the Mediterranean Sea, provided a natural check to Roman ambitions in the region as well as a threat to Rome itself. A series of long, bloody battles, known as the Punic Wars, ensued and lasted for nearly 120 years from the middle of the third century B.C.E. These conflicts caused Rome great pain but removal of the Carthaginian menace freed Rome to seek new territory, and it quickly moved east and west. In the east, Rome captured much of the empire that had been Alexander's. Macedonia and the Greek city-states became Roman provinces. Asia Minor became a Roman protectorate. Rome forbade Egypt and Syria to have independent foreign policies. In the west, the eternal city made incursions into what is now Germany and France.

Romans reaped unprecedented wealth from these military campaigns. Plunder and tribute sparked an opulent building boom and people throughout the expanded Republic emigrated to Rome proper. But pillaging was a sporadic activity, only as dependable as the latest military conquest. Unfortunately, the Republic functioned as if massive amounts of tribute were normal and institutionalized that very idea within its various social and administrative mechanisms. When, as was sometimes the case, no or little plunder came to Rome, the populace complained vigorously. The absence of this largess, which many Romans considered the natural state of affairs, produced dissatisfaction, even rebellion and civil war.

Romans brought more than wealth to their city from the conquered provinces. They also carried a series of new religions and ways of doing things. Ways and things Greek especially captivated many Romans, who celebrated the Greeks as the height of civilization and actively copied aspects of their culture. But some Romans identified Greek civilization as an insidious force, undercutting the status quo and traditional Roman values. Romans explicitly blamed Greek ideas and ways for unleashing those forces that the Romans had traditionally feared. They claimed that the Greeks, not the Romans, were culpable for the social dislocations that marked the later Republic years.

Positing blame on the Greeks rather than recognizing that their own addiction to foreign-generated revenues had weakened the social fabric and undercut the idea of civic virtue was characteristically Roman. Indeed, little else was conceivable because Romans by definition were eternal, inherently joined, and virtuous. Only outsiders could sow seeds of dissatisfaction. The belief in the fundamental sameness of the past, present, and future promised, moreover, that, once the cause of a problem was identified, slight modification could restore tranquillity. That Romans really abandoned the character of their republic while claiming to make only minor reorganizations ought not to surprise. Romans had many times recrafted the nature of their union all the while claiming constancy. In this particular case, they opted to back a single representative to repel these foreign influences, a series of dictators and generals. To first-century-B.C.E. Romans, single representative rule was no less republican than the rule of the many and the reasoning was clear. The idea of an eternal Roman people suggested an eternal Roman mind or position. In that case, one person could administer to reflect that position at least as well as a group of representatives. This vaunted Roman flexibility enabled Romans to cleave to the fundamentally same set of beliefs for centuries but find solace in totally antagonistic expressions of that set of beliefs.

The Military and Agriculture: Social Ramifications

The Punic and subsequent wars meant that small farmers—the backbone of the military—would be away for long periods from their farms. Hannibal's invasion in the late third century B.C.E. brought the war home. It destroyed Roman crops and farm buildings and reduced the land to rubble, which devastated the small farming class. No longer able to support themselves, small farmers moved to cities, leaving their farms as partial payment of their debts. Veterans often refused to return to the now barren land after completing military service. They either accepted land in a different province as part of a colony or they abandoned farming and embraced urban life. Wealthy Romans gobbled up small farms and consolidated them into large-scale, capital-intensive *latifundia*. Using slaves from conquered lands lessened labor costs and further hindered the ability of free small farmers to compete. These slave plantations specialized in high-priced crops—animals, olives, and grapes. They would later introduce newer, even more exotic crops, such as cherries and apricots, wild game, and marine delicacies. The final defeat of the Carthaginians made small farms even less tenable. Abundant Sicilian wheat came to Rome as tribute. This crop had been the staple of small Roman farmers and had provided much of their modest income beyond subsistence. With a serious decline in the market price of wheat and with the latifundia well situated to dominate the production of exotic crops, small farmers found themselves in an economic vise. The situation was exacerbated after about 100 B.C.E. The various revolts took a further toll on the land and on the agricultural infrastructure, while the military sometimes confiscated the crops of small farmers for its needs. Many remaining small farmers, especially in central and southern Italy, could not withstand these onslaughts. They left their farms to become *coloni*, free but propertyless men who worked on a large landowner's estate for a portion of the crop.

The Military and Volunteer "Clients": Political Ramifications

As late as 120 B.C.E., Romans embraced the idea of the citizen soldier. The typical Roman soldier was a small farmer, the virtuous yeoman upon whom the Republic had been built. Armed with breastplate, helmet, greaves, and sometimes a mail shirt, Roman soldiers carried a curved, oval body shield made of fine-grain hardwood, and a short, doubled-edged sword. Behind the forces came baggage trains carrying supplies and siege weapons, and camp followers—merchants, slave traders, and prostitutes—who made their livelihood from the army.

These soldier/citizens paid for their arms, armor, and food. Such de facto property qualifications restricted military service to a certain class—those able to afford the requisite equipment—that had done moderately well in the Republic; they had a clear stake in the system and its preservation and acted as a buffer against those who might undermine republican traditions. But the years of fighting on Roman soil, coupled with the great demand for soldiers to fight overseas, reduced the supply of small farmers. Generals lengthened tours of duty but that was not enough to end the manpower shortage. Soon, volunteers were accepted without property, especially the urban poor, induced to enlist by promises of regular pay, booty, and land grants.

These volunteers became "clients" of their generals, a bond cemented by the longer duty tours. They took an oath to serve their commander—not the state—until released. Generals soon recognized that these "client armies" possessed political as well as military advantages and used these personal forces to intimidate the Assembly and Senate, which were without their own forces. Generals took an active interest in their men and provided their armies with weapons and clothing. Provision of weapons and clothing from a central supplier standardized Roman military equipment in a way not possible when each soldier brought his own sword and shield. But the desire to stamp something as distinctly Roman also led to a Roman military practice of heightened uniformity. For example, Roman camps developed a characteristic defensive formation. Two deep ditches surrounded each campsite behind which stood a rampart with timber-framed towers located at specific intervals. Even warships began to be standardized. In fact, they now resembled siege machines. Complete with towers and artillery pieces, these ponderous Roman vessels abandoned ramming, seeking instead to pummel enemies through the air prior to boarding.

The Military and the Infrastructure: Civic Ramifications

Road Building

Armies needed to be at the ready but they did not always fight. Much of the time was spent between campaigns, an especially dangerous condition with the introduction of urban rabble into the forces. Well before that time, however, Rome had a healthy tradition of using its armies to build roads. The massive, superb Roman highways, which served civilian as well as military ends, assumed a standard form. The 40-foot-wide road was bordered by a wall or green space. Beyond that barrier, which drew off and collected water from the roadbed, armies built a sidewalk for pedestrians. The road itself consisted of four layers. The *statumen*, a 10-inch-thick layer of hand-laid rock slabs, was placed directly into the level, compacted soil. Romans then positioned the *rudus*—up to 20 inches of grouted cobbles—on the statumen. They used round stones two to four inches in diameter as cobbles and a thin lime mortar or bitumen as grouting, which helped seal out moisture. The nearly 20-inch-deep *nucleus* of gravel concrete was laid on this foundation and was topped itself by the *pavimentum*. The pavimentum was composed of up to 40 inches of square stone slabs, generally of volcanic origin, which the Romans covered with pozzolana, a powdery silicate that, when moistened, reacts with crushed lime at ordinary temperatures to form cement.

Roman highways usually withstood a century of service, but extremely heavily trafficked roads might be repaired every 30 years. The military also built some local roads, although provincial authorities fought to retain control over provincial road building to reward local contractors. Few of these roads had the four layers of highways. Some country roads were simply leveled, rolled, or drained. Wooden or stone rollers flattened the terrain and a graveled surface served as pavement. Large stones acted as curbstones to keep water from running over the road. Cobble roads, laid in sand, were generally restricted to cities. Chipped-rock roads required the armies to reach subsoil and roll the chips to compact them.

Generals and other officials in charge of road building often named their creations in honor of themselves and placed monuments at roadsides to commemorate their achievements. Although all roads led to Rome or at least to other roads that went to Rome, it remained for Caesar and the Empire to take direct, firm control of road building, financing, and regulation. Before that time, military and provincial officials exercised broad discretionary powers.

Civilians and the Infrastructure

The ability to award contracts enabled provincial officials to wield influence, create new alliances, and raise funds. They found the power to grant contracts for tax collection especially critical because Rome expected them to pay tribute for their offices; by granting tax-collecting contracts, they could raise money immediately to pay their obligations to Rome. Roman nobles also saw contracts as a means to make money. Customs that prohibited them from undertaking certain occupations could be circumvented by awarding a contract and benefiting from the contract. This might be done directly, as in the case of a tax-collecting contract, or indirectly by bribery. Individuals had to bid for the right to collect taxes in a certain district. The highest bidder won the contract, paid the appropriate official the specified sum, and attempted to collect more from the populace than he had paid the official. The extra was profit. For a public works or building project, the reverse was true. The individual offering the lowest bid won the contract. He profited only when he built the building or performed the service for less than the amount of the contract.

Two things were required to bid on contracts: money and the willingness to take risks. A group of landowning citizens wealthy enough to have formed the horse cavalry in the early Republic (hence the name Equestrians) combined both requirements. Often working collectively to share the financial risk, Equestrians invested in contracts to build roads, temples, and other public buildings, to supply armies with food, to collect taxes, to lease and work state-owned mines, and to build ships for the Roman navy. Equestrians did not limit speculative ventures to public activities. They engaged in commerce, especially the highly lucrative wine and pottery trade, and shipping, always problematical because of the weather and hostile forces. Money-lending was their most profitable activity. They charged usurious rates to politicians desperately in need of funds and provincial officials seriously short on their tribute and therefore in danger of losing their throne. Equestrians often invested their profits in land and lived out their lives as gentlemen.

Public Works: Water Delivery and Removal

Rome prided itself in its public works, monuments to the Roman people and their Republic. Construction of water delivery and removal systems were typical of Equestrian-won public works contracts. Aqueducts carrying water from the countryside to urban areas comprised the heart of the Roman delivery system. The first aqueduct to Rome had been planned in 312 B.C.E. Less than one mile long, this aqueduct was little more than an underground pipe. Fifty years later the Romans completed a second aqueduct but it too went primarily underground. Tactical concerns argued for underground placement: Enemies could not locate the supply to disrupt it and force Rome into submission. Not until about 145 B.C.E., coinciding with the final defeat of the Carthaginians and the relative freedom from invasion that that defeat implied, did Rome complete its first above-ground aqueduct. Two additional above-ground structures were built during the following century.

The Roman infatuation with water is illustrative. Wells, streams, and the Tiber could have provided water enough for survival. Nor did Romans choose aqueducts for simple health concerns. Commentators marveled at the clarity and purity of aqueduct water—an indication to the ancients of a salubrious substance—but Romans used it ostentatiously, for fountains, baths, gardens, and other water displays. Copious amounts of pristine water constituted a signal of splendor to the Romans, a grandiose if somewhat garish gesture demonstrating the success of the Eternal City, and the Romans spared little expense in building and maintaining their system. Water commissioners let contracts both for building and maintenance. Equestrians receiving these contracts guaranteed the city that a specified number of slaves would always be engaged in the work.

The gravity-powered aqueducts themselves were primarily open channels, covered by raised, arch-like stone roofs. Troughs were generally U-shaped stone or concrete and because these channels carried the water, Romans could not leave room for thermal expansion. Frequent repair became a necessity. Romans tried to lay out channels

Roman Bridge and Aqueduct. Transporting aqueducts over rivers required extensive use of arches to span the waters. Sinking the pillars was never easy, and by blocking part of the river, the supports altered water flow.

at an incline of three-quarters of a foot for every hundred feet. But some water sources rested more than 30 miles from Rome and, combined with the city's seven hills, conspired to make meandering routes the rule, not the exception. After the first two aqueducts, Rome used pipes only when it lacked another option, such as when crossing a large valley. In those particular instances, Romans ran earthenware vessels, some seven inches in diameter, down the wall of a basin, across its floor and up the opposite side, taking care to place the intake pipe higher than the outgo. To decrease chances of a pipe bursting, they sometimes divided the water into several pipes across a particularly deep hollow.

Romans erected arcades—a series of semicircular stone arch spans—to provide the support for aqueducts across most valleys and similarly structured bridges to overcome rivers. In both cases, aqueduct troughs rested directly on the structures. Bridges provided additional construction problems. A bridge is essentially a dam with holes in it. The reduced surface area produces an increase in the velocity of the water, which quickly wears away and undermines the bridge base. Romans recognized this problem and took care to place bridge supports on bedrock and to lay rubble against the base to provide additional protection from water erosion. Cofferdams enabled Romans to situate bridge supports properly. Romans constructed cofferdams by driving wooden piles into the river to make a relatively watertight rectangle around the location of the planned bridge base and then used a force pump to remove the remaining water. After mucking out the spot, they laid the base and rubble and removed the cofferdam.

When aqueduct water reached the city, Romans placed it in huge settling tanks, where gravity helped clarify the liquid. The term *settling tank* was a complete misnomer; the entire water delivery and removal system was based on gravity flow and continual motion of water. From the tanks, water went to an elevated reservoir for aeration. Customers drew water from the reservoir by spigot. The most prestigious Romans received the clear water from the top spigots, while water from the bottom spigots was used for public purposes.

Some large buildings used force pumps to lift water to secondary reservoirs some 20 feet in the air to improve flow within that facility. All customers, even those without pumping equipment, relied on lead pipe to carry water from central repositories. Strips of lead held together by lead solder brought water to individual homes and public baths, gardens, and fountains where ostentatious, always-open bronze taps sent the water into view. Sewers, arch-covered stone channels placed in streambeds, ran the length of the city and carried excess water and wastes, including the runoff from public urinals, into the Tiber.

Architecture

The gaudy Roman aqueduct system, quite expensive to construct and vulnerable to enemy assault, indicated a certain celebratory confidence on the part of Rome in the wake of its triumphs over Carthage and the Greek East. Rome carried on the celebration publicly, not privately, and although individuals often built or supported various projects and named them after themselves, the celebration was of the Republic. It was the glory of Rome and the Roman people that they celebrated, not that of its leaders. When embarking upon this celebratory path, Romans quite naturally turned to the civilization that had been the acknowledged cultural leader—Greece—and attempted to

The Colosseum. This large stadium evoked Greek architectural styles and the accentuation of the arch. It was the site of numerous entertainments, including gladiator battles.

recreate its physical presence and splendor. Victorious Roman generals not only took the wealth of the East to finance the development and reconstruction of Rome, but also captured Greek craftsmen and appropriated famous Greek paintings and sculptures. Greek artists, painters, and builders taught Romans Greek methods and techniques, including the use of marble and stone and the virtues of column architecture.

Romans absorbed this knowledge and felt compelled to add their own uniquely Roman perspectives, elements, and predilections to Greek styles. The result was not quite right—too bold, too loud, not quite as genteel. Roman realism found its way into portraits and landscapes, undercutting the Greek idealization of form. Roman architecture was blatantly celebratory, not cerebral, hedonistic, and chauvinistic. Romans' use of concrete and brick, coupled with a fondness for arches and vaults, permitted construction of more massive structures, but these buildings often appeared ponderous, not ethereal. Although Romans appreciated symmetry as did the Greeks, their symmetry was based on the central axis and emphasized combinations of different architectural units. The Romans combined columns with vaults and arches, frequently constructing columns from brick and facing them with stucco.

Literature and Philosophy

Architecture was hardly the only thing that Romans identified as worthy of taking from the Greeks. In the third century B.C.E., Rome transferred entire Greek libraries to the Eternal City. An affection for Greek literature and knowledge of the Greek language became signs of refinement among the better classes, and Greek slaves tutored Roman children. By the end of the second century B.C.E., children of the wealthiest Romans went to Athens to study. Around 100 B.C.E., however, Romans began to replace the tutorial system with collective education. Rather than marking a deemphasis on things Greek, this change signaled a growing appreciation of things Roman. In these new private schools, children to about age 12 studied mathematics and learned to write and read Greek and Latin. Those boys whose education continued beyond age 12 read Greek and Latin literature. The new Latin literature celebrated Rome and also reflected the ambivalence of Romans toward Greeks. The villains in Roman literature were almost always Greek.

Exposure to certain Greek philosophies gave Romans reason to view Greeks suspiciously. Only Greek Stoicism did not cause great concern as it seemed consonant with traditional Roman notions of morality and destiny. Stoicism accentuated magnanimity, generosity, and public service. It considered duty a divinely created task undertaken by a divinely chosen group—the wise—within the context of a divinely created order. Stoic-like notions, especially that of a natural law, even resonated in Roman law. As early as 200 B.C.E., Romans took the Twelve Tables—their written law—and began to merge it with the praetors' various expansions of the law's scope to form a judicial formulary, a series of templates based upon natural law. Romans standardized lawsuit forms, rules of evidence, procedures, damage awards, wills, and contracts.

Skepticism and especially Epicureanism as then practiced seemed far outside Roman tradition and therefore potent threats. When first introduced from Greece, both skepticism and Epicureanism accentuated the absence of dogma and rejected the idea of a divinely or otherwise inspired set of moral guidelines. The blatancy of the Epicurean platform as initially presented in Rome—a lack of divine punishments and the primacy of pleasure as life's goal—offended the Roman sense of duty. The Senate banned that philosophy in 173 B.C.E. Yet even Epicureanism could be made palatable for Roman sensibilities. The Roman philosopher Lucretius's interpretation of Epicureanism about 100 B.C.E. presented the doctrine as had Epicurus himself, as completely rejecting hedonism. Lucretius based his Epicureanism on a particulate universe and postulated that upon death the soul returned to its particulate nature and rejoined the universe's other particles. To Lucretius, the particles of the universe composed a sort of collectivity—not unlike the Greek notion of the One or the Roman idea of an eternal Rome—a view that made each individual a part of a greater community. This confident sense of belonging deemphasized the need to sate the appetites of the flesh before facing an unknown eternity—it made hedonism unnecessary—and focused attention on life's simple, quiet pleasures, of a life of gentility in a villa-like setting.

Religion

Traditional Greek religion did not trouble Romans. They quickly identified their gods with those of the Greeks and adopted Greek myths as their own. The Greek idea of unity in the one, manifested most clearly in the works of Plato, gained currency after about 100 B.C.E., at about the same time that Roman mercantile practices, law, and coinage provided a sense of universality and syncretism across the western world. It was the cults, coming to Rome from formerly Greek provinces, that, with Epicurean philosophy and skepticism, led Romans to accuse the Greeks of immorality, selfishness, and gluttony. The worship of Bacchus was common among Greeks in southern Italy and tales of their drunken orgiastic revelry as well as their secret rituals and rites signaled to Romans a rejection of Roman standards of conduct. The Senate banned Bacchanian worship in 186 B.C.E. and prohibited by threat of death any private religious gathering not approved by the praetor. The worship of Cybele with its attendant ecstatic dancing, self-mutilation, and public castration, was similarly outlawed. Proselytizing Jews were banned from Rome proper in 139 B.C.E., not because of their moral beliefs but rather because of their refusal to participate in Roman ritual and society. Worship of Isis, now identified with Aphrodite, was prohibited in 58 B.C.E.

End of the Republic to 44 B.C.E.

By the time of Julius Caesar, in the second third of the first century B.C.E., less than half the people in Rome were descended from old stock ethnic Romans, the Republic's founders. Rome had assumed the mantle from Alexandria as the world's polyglot city. Rome's growth had been spectacular. Plundered riches flowed into Rome, which experienced repeated building booms, each grander and more sensational than the last. Upper-class Romans ruled much of the world. The richest Romans could look forward to lives of private baths, personal libraries, vintage wines, and exotic delicacies, all provided by extensive staffs of domestic slaves. The poorest Romans lived in stark contrast. Massive immigration from the countryside and conquered provinces led to overcrowded slums and flimsy, multistoried tenements. Those on the top floors lacked water and sanitation facilities and worried about fire, while those beneath them lived with the constant threat of a building collapse. The poor worked at semiskilled jobs for subsistence wages. Poor women took in laundry, spun and wove, butchered animals, sold fish and nails, and worked as waitresses and prostitutes.

A complex set of relationships joined rich and poor. Clients sometimes received gifts of food and money from their patrons after an important military victory. Public festivals were often a time for bonuses. Selling votes at the polls became a widespread practice and patrons able to buy sufficient numbers of votes had considerable political clout. Political clubs in support of particular candidates (collegia) became weapons by which to harass and intimidate enemies. Poor Romans sometimes organized collegia by occupation. Other clubs sought to protect an area from crime, to fight neighborhood fires, or to ensure a proper burial for deceased members. Rich individuals and the state were obligated to provide mass entertainments during religious festivals and civic celebrations, and these public spectacles reflected the grandeur of Rome. Plays were popular, but gladiatorial combat, which had been an Etruscan funeral practice, and chariot races marked by high-speed and often fatal crashes were particular favorites. Circuses featuring exotic animals, predator versus predator fights to the death, and wild beast hunts also had supporters. Caesar even created an artificial lake to stage naval battles for the entertainment of the masses.

Domestic slaves in Rome lived better than many of the free poor. Often educated and well trained, domestic slaves of wealthy masters sometimes owned slaves of their own. They often earned money and could buy their freedom as well as the freedom of loved ones. Manumitted slaves retained special obligations to their former masters but their children became full citizens of the Republic. Slaves working in mines or on latifundia, however, did not share in the good life, engaging instead in backbreaking labor under unbearable conditions.

The number of Romans living outside the city of Rome in Roman colonies increased markedly during the first century B.C.E. A policy of dispatching Rome's urban poor to colonies in the territories changed the nature of colonization. Many of these new places specialized in manufacturing products for export. Roman bronze and ceramics were well known. Wool spinning and weaving centers employed slaves and artisans as carders, combers, dyers, felters, fullers, and weavers. Relatively few except colonists in these territories were Roman citizens or would become so. The local nobility might gain Roman citizenship and would continue to administer, but Romans no longer offered sweeping provincewide grants of citizenship, although they continually adjusted and broadened their definition of who was a citizen.

The extraordinary amount of wealth flowing into Rome seemed the norm, not the exception. The Roman upper classes came to behave as if that wealth would continue

Servants Wait on a Lady. Wealth abounded in the later Republic. The wealthiest Romans distinguished themselves by employing servants, purchasing slaves, and engaging in an extravagant lifestyle.

indefinitely. They established traditions—for example, they stopped serving in the military—based on that expectation and identified the Republic's continual expansion with their own enhanced opportunity. The lowest classes, which needed the extra grain allotments to survive, also came to depend on this "regular" source of wealth. The sudden dearth of plunder-derived revenues, such as that after 62 B.C.E., then, caused a critical situation among both the wealthiest and the poorest Romans. The poor, whose very existence depended on additional revenue from outside, searched for individuals who promised to rectify their plight. Wealthy Romans, competing among themselves to maintain their living standard, engaged in recurring civil war as dictators and demagogues seized power. But even during these times of peril, Romans continued to act as if they were perpetuating the old republican order. Elections for administrative posts continued even as dictators and demagogues held virtually absolute authority. One-man rule in the Republic reached its zenith under Julius Caesar, who in an unprecedented move had his face stamped on Roman coins. His soldiers, who had tasted luxury and who were the basis of his claim to political power as well as the means to achieve it, were amply rewarded with land and bonuses. The free poor of Rome reaped copious supplies of grain and entertainment for their support.

Caesar did several things more effectively than his predecessors. First, he created a military fiercely loyal to himself and, by extension, to eternal Rome. He then adapted the military model to civilian politics, especially in the provinces, to cement his political base. Caesar lowered provincial taxes and extended citizenship to a much greater number of provincials than had his predecessors. He also stopped his lieutenants and competitors from exploiting provincial wealth without his approval. In these ways, he tied the provinces to himself personally and to Rome only through him. His organizational genius rationalized and integrated the various provinces under his personal banner. But identifying the Roman people and state in terms of its leader meant that Rome was a republic in name only. The virtual deification of its leader transformed Rome into an empire.

For Further Reading

Ashby, Thomas. *The Aqueducts of Ancient Rome*. Ed. I. A. Richmond. Washington: McGrath Publishing Company, 1973.

Boren, Henry C. *Roman Society*, 2d ed. Lexington, Mass.: D. C. Heath and Company, 1992.

Champlin, Edward. *Final Judgments: Duty and Emotion in Roman Wills*. Berkeley: University of California Press, 1991.

Cowell, F. R. *Cicero and the Roman Republic*. Middlesex, England: Penguin, 1973.

De Coulanges, Fustel. *The Ancient City*. 1864; Garden City, N.Y.: Doubleday, 1955.

Dixon, Suzanne. *The Roman Family*. Baltimore: Johns Hopkins University Press, 1992.

Fussell, G. E. *The Classical Tradition in Western European Farming*. Rutherford, N.J.: Fairleigh Dickinson University Press, 1972.

Hackett, John. *Warfare in the Ancient World*. New York: Facts on File, 1989.

Heichelheim, Fritz M., Cedric A. Yeo, and Allen M. Ward. *A History of the Roman People*, 2d ed. Englewood Cliffs, N.J.: Prentice-Hall, 1984.

Jones, A. H. M., ed. *A History of Rome through the Fifth Century*. New York: Harper & Row, 1968.

MacKendrick, Paul. *The Mute Stone Speaks*. New York: St. Martin's Press, 1960.

Macnamara, Ellen. *Everyday Life of the Etruscans*. London: B. T. Batsford, 1973.

Moore, Ralph Westwood. *The Roman Commonwealth*. Greenwich, Conn.: Fawcett, 1942.

Oleson, John Peter. *Greek and Roman Mechanical Water-Lifting Devices: The History of a Technology*. Toronto: University of Toronto Press, 1984.

Rouge, Jean. *Ships and Fleets of the Ancient Mediterranean*. Middletown, Conn.: Wesleyan University Press, 1981.

Stambaugh, John. *The Ancient Roman City*. Baltimore: Johns Hopkins University Press, 1988.

White, Hayden V. *The Greco-Roman Tradition*. New York: Harper & Row, 1973.

CHAPTER 4

Roman Civilization: The Imperial System and Its Dissolution

The seeds of the high Empire were sown in the very late Republic, although that premise certainly seems contrary to the rhetoric of the late first century B.C.E. and early first century A.D. Led by Augustus, Romans harkened back to a time before Julius Caesar, before the cataclysms of the early and middle first century B.C.E., and advocated reestablishment of the Republic. It was a rhetoric of restoration, of tradition, of the old way. Augustus maintained that Rome had lost its moral moorings and needed to recapture the celebrated Roman virtues. He emphasized family, religion, and community as the mechanisms for Rome to regain its specialness.

On the most obvious level, Augustus and most of the emperors of the early Empire were men of their word. They focused on family, religion, and community, as had their republican ancestors. Reinvigoration of republican institutions also included a new and unseemly emphasis on grandeur and glory but superficially the old ways seemed restored. A closer examination suggests something quite different had taken place, something akin to what Julius Caesar and his immediate predecessors had begun by fiat, something fundamentally at odds with the way the Republic had been established and had conducted business. Family had framed the Republic and the Roman social system. The structure of society was hereditary and tribal; individuals received the status of their birth—Patrician, Plebeian, Equestrian—and that status persisted throughout their lifetime. The crux was not citizenship but social group within the citizenry. It proved extremely difficult to move between classes. The group into which you were born could receive new rights, obligations, and duties—the boundaries could be modified—but you remained defined by your class. The Roman Empire persisted in this hereditarian orientation but it incorporated considerable social flexibility if not direct social mobility. The Empire was marked by a loosening of the notion that you were what your forebears were. The Roman Empire was not a rigid society of family, which the Republic always had been, but a society of statuses outside of family, a society of roles. What a Roman *did* in the early Empire mattered much more and the group into which a Roman was born mattered much less.

This new society was one of distinctions and distinctiveness outside of family groupings. Indeed, the idea of role itself suggests distinctions, differences among the newly perceived categories. In the Empire, training often provided the basis for distinctiveness, as in the case of the emergence of lawyers as a distinct subpopulation in

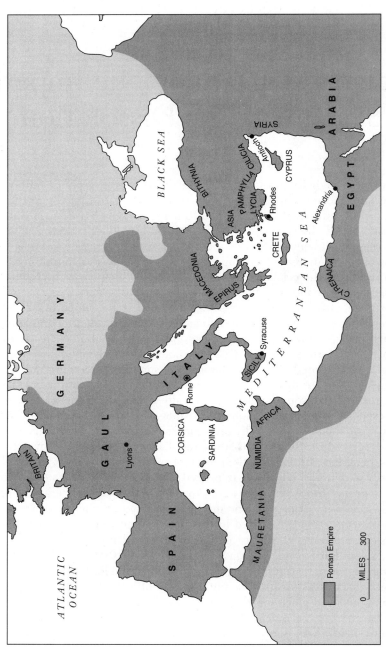

Roman Empire (A.D. 117)

the first century A.D. A desire to systematize operations and activities rested at the heart of this society of roles; there were procedures for everything and adherence to these procedures would maximize results. Emphasis on procedural rules indicated an unprecedented reliance on order, rank, authority, and grade, which was the genesis of an important social hierarchy outside familial arrangements. One person, the emperor, sat at the apex of the organizational pyramid and functioned as the arbiter for eternal Rome. The Empire was systematized and centralized in his hands.

This vision of a role-based society itself perpetuated notions of staticness, which Romans easily confused with tradition and stability. The centrality of order-establishing rules, perhaps divinely ordained, implied existence of eternal, immutable categories, the stuff from which universal rules were necessarily deduced. Categories were fixed and rigid, but individuals could move between them. This new Rome had begun to crystallize in the first century B.C.E., especially under Julius Caesar. His successors' accomplishments stemmed less from their uniqueness than from their ability to present their program as maintaining continuity with traditional Roman assumptions. Belief in an eternal, unchanging, virtuous Roman Republic continued as the basis for commonality. That the Republic no longer existed—if it ever had—and that the manner of identity had subtly changed was abhorrent, plainly impossible, to Romans. The genius of Augustus and the following emperors was that their countrymen believed they had reestablished the Republic on traditional precepts.

After the second century A.D., several major groups new within the Empire refused assimilation into eternal Rome. These new groups, especially the Christians and the Germanic Barbarians, held ideas different from those of the Romans (and each other, at least for awhile), ideas antithetical to a republic. Christians refused to participate in Roman ritual and sought a personal relationship with and salvation from the deity. Barbarians emphasized the individual—an explanation for why the Barbarians became Christians so rapidly—rather than the collective. These two groups proved an insidious combination. The Christian penchant for martyrdom and the Barbarian attacks on the Empire undermined established mechanisms of authority and encouraged others by their example to shun Rome. Emperors and their allies soon abandoned all pretensions to commonality and republicanism and relied on an iron hand to hold the Empire together. The military might and power of these entrenched figures ultimately collapsed in the face of this individualistic onslaught. Rome fell with the end of Roman ideas. That which followed it was conceived from very different notions. Rome was no longer either a society of roles or of families. It was a society of individuals.

Early Empire to ca. A.D. 190

Rome moved swiftly if not always smoothly from its Republic phase into the early empire. Augustus, the first emperor, had much to do with the transition. His program harkened backward, not forward, and promised to reinstitute what had seemed the essence of the Republic; the Empire capitalized on the myth of a virtuous Republic to create the new social and political order.

The Genius of Augustus

Augustus first secured his authority by appearing to resurrect Republican government. The assemblies and the Senate, legitimate sources of authority in the Republic, rubber-stamped his maneuvers. Augustus generally took only titles and positions that others had held during the Republic but kept these offices for unprecedented lengths of time and assumed many at once. If Augustus chose to gain a new position, secure a new power, or take a power for which he did not hold the appropriate office, his wealth, political clout, and armies virtually forced the Senate or other constitutionally empowered entity to provide him the right. For example, Augustus was granted the titles "Imperator," "princeps," "consul," "proconsul," "tribune," "Pater Patriae," "censor," and "pontifex maximus" at various times during his reign. The Senate and assemblies gave him the right to rule the imperial provinces, initially

Augustus. Augustus's genius was to evoke the themes of family, continuity and an eternal Rome, which had been the backbone of the Republic. Yet he was also savvy enough to consolidate his power in Rome and his control over the military. Augustus was revered as a god in many of the eastern provinces.

Spain, Syria, Gaul, and the fabulously wealthy Egypt, without benefit of a legislature and to appoint his deputies to administer that realm. Augustus received from established Republican institutions the power to hear judicial appeals throughout the Empire, to make Equestrians and Plebeians Patricians, and to appoint a prefect for the city of Rome. The Senate also gave Augustus the sole right to coin gold and silver in the Empire.

Augustus attempted to return the family as the core of Roman life. To that end, he encouraged marriage and child rearing and discouraged divorce and adultery. His laws prohibited long engagements and divorce and required all widows below 50 and widowers below 60 to marry within three years. Violators were fined or punished by exclusion from public games or ineligibility for public office. The public careers of married men with fewer than three children progressed less rapidly than those with three or more. Augustus set adultery as a criminal offense punishable by fines and loss of property. A man legally could kill his wife's lover. The head of a family could kill adulterous men and women within that family.

These rules may not have had a marked effect on Roman behavior but they symbolized a desire to return to more virtuous days. Augustus's revival of religious ritual was of the same character. He repaired Rome's temples and dedicated new ones to Mars and other gods. Augustus particularly venerated Apollo, the Romanized Greek god of purity, morality, and order, and built several triumphal arch-dominated temples in his honor. He also divided the eternal city into 14 sections and at each major intersection erected shrines to honor the traditional guardians of the crossroads and household. Those who tended these shrines quickly included among the spirits to whom they would sacrifice the Genius of Augustus. Similar in form to the more traditional sacrifices to the head of a family, which honored both the head and the family, sacrifices to Augustus's genius simultaneously venerated his visionary accomplishments and eternal Rome. Linkage between the emperor and the city transcended the mortal world and established him at the apex; his genius had restored Rome. The ruler-worshipping eastern provinces extended this cult of personality to Augustus himself, not just his genius. Augustus deflected this admiration by establishing a connection with Rome; he refused adoration except in conjunction with worship of the traditional goddess Roma, the spirit of good fortune for the eternal city.

Augustus established ancestral custom as the Empire's ruling principle and thus identified the Empire as the glorification of Roman traditions and virtues. Within that commonality-establishing and -perpetuating framework, he created and maintained social stability by recognizing the functional distinctiveness of the Roman population, creating an environment in which that distinctiveness could reach full flower, and then ensuring that none of these areas of authority clashed. The upper classes, including those in the provinces, gained the appearance of ruling and even held senatorial posts. He established a minimum age for manumission to prevent a glut of recently freed slaves from disrupting the political process and therefore threatening other citizens. Under Augustus, freedmen in Rome formed seven geographically distinct units to serve as ad hoc police and fire-fighting forces. Military-like ranks organized each cohort—individuals were paid for days of actual service in support of the city—and a single police commissioner coordinated effort citywide. A water commissioner with a staff of at least 240 slaves ensured that Roman aqueducts were in good repair. Augustus sealed the loyalty of the poor through forcefully pursuing the established policy of "bread and circuses." He regularized the distribution of grain, sometimes making up shortages from his personal granary, while increasing the number of spectacles to entertain citizens.

Augustus also revamped the military and created a paid standing army. Rather than demobilize troops after decisive battles or allow generals to maintain their own armies, Augustus kept a standing army of 250,000 under his control to deal with emergencies. He reduced the size of the imperial army overall, placed his friends in control of the various divisions, and, through them, centralized all authority in himself—legionnaires swore oaths of loyalty to the emperor, not to commanders. He also regularized tours of duty at 20 years, established a rank-dependent wage scale, and recruited a significant percentage of military men from the provinces, which further united the provinces with Rome proper. Retired military men received substantial land grants and bonuses. The army and its retirees, who established provincial colonies and towns, gained central government control of the provinces. Like county seats in more modern times, these colonies and towns soon dominated the economy and culture of the areas surrounding them.

Augustus's extensive road-building campaign outside of Italy further cemented the provinces to Rome. By about 20 B.C.E., Romans had created a central road board. The board met regularly in Rome to plot the routes of all major roads, direct their construction, see to their maintenance, and establish means to finance them. This centralized board systematized all imperial road-related activities. To facilitate transportation on these roads, which also carried the newly created imperial postal service, planners needed to include regular locations to change horses—Rome required locals to provide hay—and hostels and inns about 22 miles apart for deliverymen and travelers to spend the night. The board protected the roads by setting maximum weight and speed laws. Regularly placed stones—milestones—marked the road as property of the Empire.

Romans debated how to finance roads. Should conquered persons pay? Should those along the roadway contribute toward its building and upkeep? Should there be tolls? Concern about financing went far beyond roads, of course. The Empire required substantial sums of money simply to conduct its daily activities, especially in the wake of Augustus's creation of an embryonic imperial bureaucracy. Augustus tackled the question of revenue collection in much the same way he approached other "public" issues: by systematizing and centralizing the task. The new, paid imperial tax collectors conducted a census of property throughout the provinces, which enabled them to classify holdings within the Empire by province and activity. They used these categories to set a specific taxation rate for each unit and regularly repeated the census to establish local tax obligations.

High Empire to 193

The genius of Augustus heralded the Pax Romana, two centuries of a Roman-enforced state of relative peace. Rome spent less in support of the army. War devastated few farms and plundering opportunities likewise dropped dramatically.

Trade replaced funds lost from the decrease in pillaging. The Empire's single administration and coinage, coupled with its safe sea and land routes, encouraged both an agricultural and a craft boom. Military salaries, equipment, troop ships, warships, and bases remained the single largest class of expenditures, but income derived from increased trade easily compensated. Money poured into new and old hands at unprecedented rates, especially in the provinces. There as in Rome itself the wealthy responded to the traditional Roman sense of duty, combined it with the new notion of grandeur and magnificence as important signs of a grand, magnificent empire, and undertook a public works building campaign unparalleled in Roman annals. In the first two centuries after Christ, Romans not only rebuilt Rome but provincial leaders, often with Roman citizenship, tried to recreate Rome in the provinces. Every town and city wanted basilicas, temples, theaters, arenas, forums, market areas, harbors, public baths, and aqueducts. That remained true even in Britain, which the Romans solidly controlled after A.D. 80. With abundant streams and an extremely high water table, Britain needed no aqueducts. Yet a sense of empire demanded that they be built. This Romanization of the provinces was not simply a ruse to achieve political alliance but rather a shrewd policy to connect those provinces organically with Rome. Provinces were to become Roman in almost every sense of the word.

Colonization: The Western Provinces

The western provinces, especially Britain, required pacification as well as civilization. The tribal Celts, the group from whom Rome wrested Britain, knew little of Rome except its military might. Romans applied the principles that they had used for centuries to overcome this drawback. They established colonies to demonstrate Roman virtues and offered inducements for Celtic and other leaders to enter cities and towns, adopt Roman ways, teach these ways to their children, and thereby encourage supporters to follow. Indeed, the town was the instrument of civilization. It was not unusual for Romanization to take several decades. Romanization was a gradual process and, as historian I. A. Richmond has noted, Romans evinced "a readiness to work within existing arrangements provided these could be assimilated into Roman form."[1] For example, Romans permitted Druid priests and priestesses to hold Druid rituals (except human sacrifice) but required them to perform their service in Latin. Language and ritual eventually became coterminous, a source of pride among Druids in their Roman identity and in the Roman Empire.

Acculturation

Romans developed a rigid yet clear set of procedures, rights, and obligations to govern colonization. Imperial emphasis on rules and hierarchy during the first and second centuries A.D. no doubt contributed to the formulation. Retired army men secured an imperial charter, which freed them from taxes for a certain period and permitted them to make laws. Charter recipients were not excused from imperial

---

[1] I. A. Richmond, *Roman Britain* (New York: Penguin, 1955): 79.

systemization and centralization. They had to promise to conduct commerce according to Roman law, which gave businessmen the same terms and conditions throughout the Empire, and to acknowledge the inferiority of their laws to Roman laws when conflicts arose. They also received authority to establish an administrative system. Rome provided the model. Colonial senates elected magistrates, praetors, water commissioners, and the like.

The Empire even centralized town design. Surveyors in imperial service laid out the town site, usually a rectangle bisected by two main roads through the center. A grid of side streets completed the checkerboard pattern. Surveyors marked out space for the public buildings in the town center. Each public facility had a communal function. The forum's shops and stalls housed the market. Large assemblies met in the basilica's aisles. A hypocaust, an underground, stone channeled floor and wall heating system, warmed the public bath. The public games and spectacles took place in the palaestra. Imperial surveyors also designed the town's water carriage and evacuation system but aqueducts, like the public buildings themselves, depended on the beneficence of the emperor or some other public benefactor. These major projects usually gained support quickly. Since colonies served as models of the Roman way for the indigenous population, Romans emphasized the swift completion of projects that demonstrated imperial grandeur and Roman virtue to the entire province.

People filling these planned communities, like those in the Empire's other urban places, tended to assume characteristic living arrangements. A person's role—what he or she did in the community—predicted where he or she lived in the town. Traders and drovers resided near city gates. Engravers, jewelers, and goldsmiths lived and worked near the center. The noxious industries were found outside the walls, away from heavy population concentrations. The nexus between role and city location even extended beyond life. Romans buried the dead with occupation and shop address on gravestones, indicating the deceased's firm position within the Roman community. In life, the union of occupation and location spawned an extensive system of occupation-related associations. Every trade, from sailors to coppersmiths, formed an association and selected a governmental official as its patron. These associations were not unions in any sense. They did not strike, regulate who could practice the craft around which they were arranged, or attempt to set wages, improve working conditions, or shorten work hours. Their raison d'être was to raise money to fund some imperial or civic improvement and to have their association—and by extension, their occupation—identified with that improvement. They pursued honor for their social role—their kind—rather than economic advantage. These occupational organizations themselves replicated the social system of which they were so much a part. Noble titles, offices, and awards hierarchically distinguished membership. In the Empire, "people at all levels knew their place," notes historian Ramsay MacMullen. Place—social role—"was so clear, the sense of high and low so present to the consciousness, and its degrees made known so conspicuously in manners, dress, accent, cult, style, and material possessions"[2] that it seemed as if individuals did not exist outside their social role-defining group.

---

[2]Ramsay MacMullen, *Roman Social Relations 50 B.C. to A.D. 284* (New Haven: Yale University Press, 1974): 118.

Urban Life

The vast majority of Romans lived in conditions that could charitably be considered modest. Rome itself provided a striking contrast between spectacular public areas and squalor. Narrow streets and tall houses held a closely packed population. Open-channel sewers carried refuse from public, not private, latrines, while chamber pots were sometimes emptied from upper story windows. The city's seven hills prohibited construction of a checkerboard-like street pattern and Romans attempted to prevent gridlock by banning heavy traffic from the serpentine streets during daytime. As a consequence, a significant portion of the Roman work force worked at night and generated considerable noise.

Few provincial cities proved as crowded. But even there only the wealthiest 2 percent lived in relative comfort in two-story houses with roomy garden courts, cellars, and storerooms. Amenities, such as iron-grated wood stoves, domed ovens, and shelves, were extraordinary, not ordinary. So too were couches and chairs, as compared to benches. Slaves accounted for as much as 40 percent of the population in Italy and perhaps more throughout the Empire but they for the most part were better situated than the free poor. The wealthiest Romans owned most of the slaves—one well-to-do Roman had 4,116 slaves although fewer than 50 was more typical—and many worked within the household, eating food similar to that of their masters. The poor, on the other hand, ate porridge and bread. Only minute quantities of vegetables, fish, and cheese broke the monotony and provided essential nutrients. The homes of launderers, tanners, glassblowers, and metalworkers also doubled as workshops: One-room rectangular buildings opened to the street—horizontal folding wooden shutters provided a sales platform by day and closed at night—and the family lived behind. These timber-framed edifices usually rested on stone foundations to prevent the timbers from getting wet and rotting. Clay, daub, or stone filled spaces between timbers.

Work

Trade required something to be traded and the Romans proved adept at several distinctive crafts. As important, they took great pride in organizing the production and dissemination of goods. Merchant shipping and ship-owning groups built masonry harbors, constructed lighthouses, and established camel caravans to regularize river, sea, and land trade. Moneylenders lent money and bankers stored it. The military preserved the peace and kept trade routes open during the Pax Romana. These imperial armies received standardized equipment from standardized imperial production facilities: uniform helmets, made by riveting together two iron pieces under a protective ridge; standardized heavy armor (an enhanced neck guard and more substantial cheek pieces); and leather breeches and boots.

Romans also routinized and formalized training—preparing to accept a particular social role—for specific occupations. The length of training differed according to the task, but individuals seeking mastery of the same task were to be trained for approximately the same length of time. An articulated set of rules—not individual contracts—defined relationships between trainees and trainers. Training often included a graded path by which, over the years, pupils incrementally became teachers. Formal training was not the sole means of creating uniformity. Roman authors published handbooks and technical manuals of all types to standardize practices throughout the

Empire. These works relied heavily on Greek authors for material but incorporated Roman sentimentalities.

Certain productions, such as metal goods and ceramics, moved west and north from Latium and Etruria, closer to abundant supplies of raw materials. Other trades were found sprinkled throughout the Empire and served local markets. Carpenters and the basic iron tools of the trade—rule, adze, hammer, set-square, level, bow drill, mortise chisel, saw, ax, plane, and trowel—were virtually the same everywhere in the Empire. So too were ironsmiths, goldsmiths, and silversmiths, who made such different items as pots, rings, and bracelets. Some trades developed a regional dominance. Pompeii's weavers, fullers, and dyers captured much of the Italian woolen tunic and toga market, in part because area farmers raised sheep nearby. Pompeiian fullers dipped woven fabric into tubs filled with water and soda (sodium carbonate) and applied pressure to the still wet cloth with their feet to remove natural oils and dirt. The clean material was dried on a frame and bleached by placing the frame over a pot of burning sulfur. Workers then raised the nap and used shears to trim the cloth. Dyers dipped the cloth in a heated metal vat filled with the appropriate dye. A shellfish-derived purple was immensely popular.

The blown-glass industry emerged early in the Empire and superseded the cast and molded glassmaking of Etruria, Greece, Egypt, and Syria. Cast or molded glass had been a precious commodity because its manufacture required a substantial financial investment. Inexpensive raw materials—sand, lime, and potash—could be found almost anywhere but cast or molded glass required beehive-shaped furnaces, with heating pits, ovens, and cooling chambers. Glass blowing removed those constraints. Romans could make clear, smooth glass relatively cheaply simply by melting the ingredients in a pot, cooling and then reheating the mixture, and finally using a blowpipe to turn out the finished item. Mastery of this new process required considerable skill but learning how to blow was the sole restriction and in the first century A.D. artisans adept in the technique established shops throughout the Empire.

Roman Glass. Earlier civilizations had potted glass, but Rome pioneered in glass-blowing techniques. Pinching and reaming tools applied to the blown glass when still warm yielded decorative ridges and depressions.

Glassmakers tooled glass when warm to make ribs and ridges and also drew it to apply as threads and beads. They engraved or painted it when cool. Impurities placed in the pot—tin salts for opaqueness and copper, iron, and manganese for colors—produced a distinctive product. Glass found extensive use as a substitute for precious stones in earrings, rings, and hairpins, and as an adornment for walls and even floors and vessels. The wealthy also adapted it in new ways. Glass tables became common and windowpanes, made by rotating blown glass quickly on a potter's wheel to flatten it uniformly, began to appear in residences in the first century A.D.

Rural Life and Living

Rural life in the Empire, far from an individualistic enterprise, accentuated the common cause. In that sense, it paralleled its urban counterpart. The High Roman Empire had two radically different types of rural social organization. Latifundia, or villas, were owned by people of great wealth, operated for profit, and worked by slaves or hired hands. Villages, on the other hand, were composed predominantly of subsistence farmers. An occasional absentee landlord might own some land there or some property might be held in common between two or more farmers, but subsistence farming was the predominant agricultural pattern. Rural residents were not isolated, however. Traveling traders and tradesmen, entertainers, and the begging poor regularly invaded the community. On large, single-owner farms, managers neatly divided farm activities to increase efficiency and, in the process, created a hierarchical social organization marked by discrete social roles. Villagers similarly made distinctions among themselves. Certainly they recognized personal difference; for example, brutally strong individuals were much admired. But they also made distinctions among tasks. Shepherding was looked upon almost universally as the most distasteful activity. The reason for abhorring shepherding proves illustrative: Shepherds had little opportunity for assistance from other villagers and little social interaction. Even though they remained a vital part of agricultural enterprise, they functioned as individuals, not as part of the whole. Villagers jointly participated in numerous joint endeavors. Often they held village-wide religious festivals. They sometimes bought equipment or a facility, like a central storage barn, collectively. As a unit, they often petitioned a rich individual to build a needed village facility. Candidates for village office contributed a specific sum to the village treasury as part of their campaign and, when elected, showed their sense of honor and gratitude to their fellow villagers by erecting some necessary structure.

On single-owner estates and in villages comprised of subsistence farmers, agricultural practice remained similar. Hypocaust-heated granaries, human- or animal-powered rotary grist mills, barns, and ox-drawn plows with iron coulters to cut the ground in front of shares constituted basic equipment. Romans used light, two-wheeled mule carriages and heavy, four-wheeled vehicles pulled by oxen to haul material around farms. For-profit enterprises used the same vehicles and the vaunted Roman roads to take barley, sheep, goats, pigs, chickens, geese, olives, and grapes to market.

Monstrous Monuments

Almost every emperor after Augustus tried to outshine his predecessors. Building monstrosities—structures larger than life simply to demonstrate the ability to do so—became the common means to assert an emperor's—and the Empire's—magnificence. New roads were built in the provinces—one was 1,600 miles long—and completely serviceable old roads straightened. Romans tunneled through rock, placed elevated roads over marshland, and constructed arcades and bridges of unprecedented proportions. One Roman bridge traveled some 158 feet above the water line and incorporated arches over 90 feet in diameter. But erecting more and more gargantuan buildings, including imperial palaces, was the most frequent way to celebrate imperial Rome. Greek architects provided the style but Roman builders substituted their own sense of appropriate relationships and proportions. Much of what we know about Roman architecture as well as its Greek influences comes from Vitruvius, a prominent architect during the first century A.D. In a highly articulated technical manual, *The Ten Books of Architecture*, Vitruvius outlined Greek and Roman building (and machine) principles. His distinction between "the thing signified, and that which gives it significance" directly addressed the issue of larger-than-life structures. A civilization's "greatness," wrote Vitruvius, ought to be shown in the "distinguished authority of its public buildings."

Imperial Rome expressed a fondness for marble and circularity, especially circular temples, and took care to lay out these facilities as if on graph paper. An imaginative combination of forms and shapes characterized imperial architecture. The Pantheon, for instance, combined columns in the front with a huge domed cylinder in the center. Circular, square, and rectangular designs marked the interior. Light for the building came from a hole in the dome. Roman architects reduced stress on the walls by constructing the dome out of pumice-based rather than sand-based concrete, which lessened its weight. Thinning walls nearer the top reduced load on the lower parts of walls, while recessing them approximated structural ribs, which increased support capabilities.

Knowledge

Vitruvius's division of knowledge into its constituent parts assumed that such a categorization was possible and that this knowledge could serve as a template for the training necessary to assume a specific social role. These formularies were popular in the technical arts. Romans in other spheres of life also believed knowledge could be broken down, compartmentalized, and learned, but they created different training mechanisms. Each presumed that the requisite knowledge could be codified and ordered, and transmitted to a considerable degree through the written word. Proliferation of municipal libraries in the first century A.D. was a potent reflection of these sentiments. Emperors and others had slaves copy manuscripts, which municipalities housed in central repositories and permitted interested citizens to read. Romans particularly favored works that specifically ordered knowledge and reduced it to a series of concrete categories. For example, the leading Roman rhetoricians claimed rhetoric was composed of three distinct classes—advisory, demonstrative, and forensic—and that instruction in each class could be broken into five parts: "the discovery and development of material, arrangement of material, verbal expression or style, memorization of speeches, and hypocrisis, or manner of delivery." They stressed graded, repetitive exercises for students to master each part. Aristotle, a Greek dead for nearly five hundred years, gained currency in large part because his philosophy of

Interior of the Pantheon. The Pantheon symbolized the massiveness of Roman architecture. Rain falling through the hole in the dome was said to evaporate before reaching the floor. The building stands as a combination of several styles and forms, a celebration of vastness and power.

nature, his natural history, and his physics each provided a hierarchical categorization of what was known and knowable. Roman writers followed that Aristotelian lead and systematically codified natural phenomena in encyclopedia-like tomes, which acted as tombs. Ptolemy, an imperial subject of Greek heritage, reduced the motion of the heavens to an orderly series of discrete and unchanging circles and epicycles. That these cycles and epicycles—categories or at least boundaries—conformed to the heavens—they could be drawn from the data gathered from painstaking observations of the sky over an extended period—itself confirmed their virtue. Galen, a Greek physician often in imperial service, expressed similar ideas in medicine. In a number of important works, Galen reduced medicine to identification of body constituents and description of their particular functions. This unbending mechanical formula posited disease as deviation from particular function and the palliative as the mechanical means—diet, bloodletting, exercise, purging, or the like—to restore health.

Creation of law schools in the first century A.D. suggested the depths of the commitment to categorization. Romans considered law a discrete endeavor with its own category-based knowledge and believed that knowledge could be mastered by those trained in it. Law was perhaps the archetypical discipline. It presumed that rational principles were inherent in nature and that rational people were capable of discerning these uniform norms. In practice, this rationalist legal system produced the Laws of Rome and the Laws of Other Nations, the latter a precise articulation of foreign custom conjoined with Roman precedent. That Romans looked with pride on this highly organized, hierarchically systematized code as a most significant contribution of their culture to the world ought not to surprise. Its establishment embodied those notions central to imperial Rome.

Religion

The expanse of the Roman Empire exposed it to a vast number of religions. Romans approached most religions as they approached secular laws of other lands—by trying to incorporate them within an established Roman framework. They identified the new deities with traditional Roman gods whenever possible, and therefore provided means for the Empire to absorb practitioners of these religions. Many of the Empire's new initiates gravitated to the cult of the emperor, worship of the leader as divine and identification of the Empire's fate and fortune with that of its leader. This religious practice had grown substantially since celebration of Augustus's genius. His successors worked actively to encourage it.

Pagans

Religion had assumed a new centrality within Roman life. It now had a discrete existence, its own unique social role, and Romans organized religious or spiritual life just as the Empire centralized and systematized daily life. Numerous new religious groups—cults—appeared, while others were reinvigorated. Romans celebrated Mars, Jupiter Dolichenus, Mercury, Hercules, Baal, Tanit, and the Magna Mater. Other groups, such as the cults of Isis and Cybele, that had been banned during the Republic now secured a measure of state sanction. Religious groups might be most profitably equated with occupation-based organizations in cities. Each identified itself as distinct, its organization mimicking the society from which it emerged, yet each possessed a similar purpose. Each cult gave its members a collective identity, arranged them in a hierarchical fashion based on their level of training in the religion, provided a graded step-by-step process to an afterlife of some sort, and maintained that it would help its members achieve that afterlife more efficiently because they followed its tenets and rules; spiritual life, like secular life, followed natural law.

That religious life became somewhat separate from secular life did not necessarily require Romans to act contrary to imperial-era assumptions. Just the opposite was the case. Religions whose activities meshed with those stressed within the Empire provided a natural link between the secular and spiritual worlds. Most cults had certain similarities. They were tolerant of each other and celebrated rites with splendor, pomp, and ritual, their members often engaging in ecstatic displays. Cybelians, for example, often completed dances of ecstasy with self-mutilation or castration. Rituals remained secret, revealed only to members. Converts underwent initiation rites whereby they attempted to unite with the deity "after first purifying themselves through baptism, . . . fasting, having their heads shaved, or drinking from a sacred vessel. Communion was achieved by donning the god's robe, eating a sacred meal, or visiting the god's sanctuary."[3] The Cult of Isis, now portrayed as the savior of humankind, became increasingly popular and received imperial sanction. Cultists needed to follow a specific set of moral guidelines while on earth to avoid retribution in the afterlife. The Cult of Mithras proved even more popular. Mithras was born out of rock, cared for in his human form by shepherds, and became the god of light and truth, who aided the Power of the Good in a never-ending struggle with the Power of Evil. This heroic figure, whose birthday was celebrated on December 25, had the task of rescuing humankind from domination by the evil power. Mithras's life provided the template—the rules—for people to free themselves from the evil power, and cultists attempted to pattern their lives after that of Mithras. Exhibiting high standards of morality, including bravery and camaraderie, was the critical factor. Those Mithras judged successful were granted eternal life.

Mithras's rescue of humanity included his capture of the sacred bull, which, when slain, revealed plants and animals to nourish humanity's body and soul. Initiates recreated the bull slaying. A trained, professional Mithraic priesthood led the physically demanding, often painful ritual, which simulated the Mithraic legend's seven distinct stages. Initiates had to walk in Mithras's footsteps; parables of how to live a moral life, demonstrations of the initiates' valor and fraternity, and an injunction to do good works in their earthly existence were all part of the Mithraic service. Its culmination was a priest-administered baptism in bull blood in a subterranean cave—a sign of death—to purify initiates, followed by a sacramental meal of bread and wine to mark their anticipated resurrection and eternal fellowship.

Hebrews

These groups generally equated, whether formally or otherwise, good imperial citizenship with successful pursuit of an afterlife. Activities leading to spiritual success were not inimical to those for achieving temporal success within the Empire. At the onset of the Empire, the Romans permitted only one major religious group—the Hebrews—to act openly in ways contradictory to imperial control. The Hebrews' religious practices, abhorrence of idolatry, and refusal to worship earthly rulers, especially those claiming an almost divine status, violated imperial precepts. When dealing with foreign nations, imperial Rome tolerated local customs. They built on that sentiment with the Hebrews. The long Hebraic traditions impressed them as did the religion's high moral code and essentially nonsubversive character, and Romans granted Hebrews throughout the Empire the right to act as a single group. This grouping evoked a collegium: It had its own internal government, owned property, had an exclusive membership, and taxed its members to support the Jerusalem-centered religion. The scope was different, of course, as was the basis for aggregation—religion. Hebrews also gained exemption from military service and from the cult of the emperor. In Judea, the Hebrew homeland that became a Roman province,

[3]Marvin Perry, Myrna Chase, James R. Jacob, Margaret C. Jacob and Theodore H. Von Lave, *Western Civilization*, 3rd ed. (Boston: Houghton Mifflin Company, 1989): 137–38.

Romans were so aware of the Hebraic proscription against idolatry and emperor worship that Roman soldiers stationed there did not carry busts of the emperor or wear the standard military medallions bearing the emperor's likeness. Imperial coins used in Judea substituted birds or other nature scenes for the then common portrait of the emperor's head.

Hebraic Judeans in the first century B.C.E. and in the following century and a half occasionally chafed under the comparably modest Roman strictures. Major rebellions occurred in A.D. 66–70 and in A.D. 132–135. In both cases, an apparent imperial slight sparked the outbreak and the subsequent peace restored the status quo. But the Hebrews were hardly unified among themselves or beyond secular questions. Internal social-religious political disputes often led factions into alliances with Roman governors to secure religiously sanctioned temporal power. Nor did Hebrews all interpret Mosaic law identically. Disagreements over doctrinal matters were common as were charges of heresy and blasphemy. The situation within Judea remained fluid as several different groups, each with its own understanding of Hebraic tradition, competed for authority.

Christians

It was from within this framework that Christianity emerged. Jesus was a Hebraic reformer in Judea and his disciples were Hebrews. The disciples remained Hebrews after the crucifixion and persisted in their attempt to reform the Hebrew religion. Their earliest audiences and newest initiates were Hebrews. Their designation as Hebrews protected their religious practices from the Romans; they received the same exceptional treatment that other Hebrews received. Not until the Nero-precipitated rebellion of A.D. 66 when the Hebraic religion temporarily lost its special status in the Empire did Christians in great numbers claim their separation from the Hebrews. Christianity abandoned its standing as a sect of Judaism and became a religion.

Many aspects of first- and second-century A.D. Christianity resembled contemporary cults. It was rationalist, providing its followers a set of laws by which to secure their spiritual life. It was to serve the entire Empire, even all of humanity. The central Christian tenet as espoused by St. Paul was that Jesus as the messiah came to earth and then gave up his earthly existence to make it possible for humankind to receive eternal salvation and to show humanity how to achieve it. The emphasis on an afterlife, a heroic figure descending from the heavens, a specific liturgy designed to lead to salvation and including baptism and a sacramental meal, resurrection after death (overcoming death), and a refined moral code—all were similar to pagan cults. From the Hebrews, Christians took a profound belief in monotheism, but they also took an equally profound intolerance of the beliefs of others. Tradition-admiring Romans granted the Hebrews an exception and tolerated their intolerance. Christians received no such dispensation. Refusal of Christians to participate in the Roman life—to respect the imperial and other cults—or join the military, coupled with their worship of a crucified criminal, suggested to many Romans that Christians constituted a subversive element within the Empire, likely to rebel and threaten imperial stability. This fear led Romans before the end of the first century to make Christianity a crime punishable by death.

To be fair, Christianity by the later first century had begun to erect a state within a state. As Christ had redeemed humankind from original sin, Christianity was universal, which made it seem like an alternative to Rome itself, and those who believed in the message constituted a community—a church—on earth. Members of the community had responsibilities to one another, and works of charity directed toward its poorest members were common. Its members spread the word, finding the cultists in Asia Minor and Greece most receptive. Not until after about 100 A.D. did the religion make inroads in the west. There, as in the east, Christianity was initially an urban phenomenon. In major cities, Christians established churches, complete with local hierarchies of clergy—servants, elders, and overseers—to guide them, formulate their policies, and regulate their activities. Under the direction of these congregations, missionaries went out and established churches in small surrounding towns and villages, which reported to and took their lead from their urban counterparts. In that way, Christianity achieved regional integration. Overseers—bishops—of Christian churches in major cities regularly communicated with each other, especially on matters of doctrine. Church leaders understood hierarchy; they looked to those most closely connected in time to Christ and his disciples—apostolic churches—for doctrinal guidance. The result was a degree of religious systematization unmatched in the classical world, a systematization that existed wherever Christianity existed. The Christian service of common worship included a ritual meal patterned after the Last Supper. It focused not on understanding the nature of divinity but on establishing a pattern of activity that led to heaven—the Paul-translated message of Jesus, not the nature of Jesus. That would soon change.

Declining Empire to A.D. 350

From the end of the second century A.D., the Romans repositioned vast armies to defend the Empire's northern border from threats and periodic attacks from Germanic peoples. Defending exposed areas stretched the imperial purse and bureaucracy.

Barbarians: The Roman Perspective

The Germans, identified by the Romans somewhat earlier (they had repulsed Augustus's repeated attempts to expand the Empire past the Danube) posed a potent threat to Rome and not just because of their military capabilities. These people were *barbarians*, a term that came from the Greek and meant "foreign" or "strange," especially in speech. And it was the very foreignness that made these people truly menacing. Certainly they looked foreign to second-century-A.D. Romans, who marveled at the great size of these men and women with long, red or blond hair and fierce blue eyes. Romans noted the Barbarians' lack of battle armor, even helmets or breastplates, and wondered about their colorful shields, short, narrow-headed thrusting spears, and disdain for swords. Romans also complained about their lack of cleanliness, asserting that Barbarians dressed their hair with rancid butter and drank beer, not civilized wine. Their thick wool or animal-pelt cloaks and trousers seemed a sure sign of barbarism. Their actions in war appeared puzzling to Romans. Barbarians seemed to live to fight, never working for something they could acquire through plunder, and to not fear death. Romans maintained that the Germans attacked "in the shape of a wedge" and considered retreat prudent so long as it was followed by an attack. Barbarians carried off their dead even in the midst of heated battles. But "to abandon one's shield is the basest of crimes," a forfeiture of all rights. "Many, indeed, after making a cowardly escape from battle put an end to their infamy by hanging themselves."

Romans expressed shock at the Barbarians' habits and customs, some of which seemed uncouth and others of which seemed unfathomable, striking at the very core of Roman existence. The Barbarians did not even share a common language. Indeed, it would be more appropriate to say that Barbarians came together for only one purpose—to fight. Speakers of many tongues, some not Germanic in origin, joined to form an army. The first acts of this polyglot army were to meet—assembling its var-

Barbarians Reach Rome. These Germanic peoples seemed to the Romans the very antithesis of everything Roman. They appeared to hold none of the Roman traditions or even to value hard work. Their fierce, unkempt appearance revolted cultured Romans.

ious members sometimes took days—and to decide on a leader. The decision was democratic, not republican: Each individual army member, not chosen representatives, expressed his point of view. The individual deemed the most valorous by a majority of the army became the leader. Each man then pledged his allegiance—to do otherwise branded the perpetrator a coward—and each provided the leader a gift of his own choosing. The popularly elected leader led by example—he must outshine in bravery all his men or be disgraced—and received virtual life and death authority over the army during time of war. When a war concluded, he lost power. No Barbarian state existed in peacetime.

Barbarian Society: The Individual

The individual constituted the basis of Barbarian society. Possessions, which included a Barbarian's wife and children, were individually owned. A male child became an adult and hence no longer property but an individual when he received his spear and shield. Trade was by barter between two individual Barbarians. A person secured money to purchase glass, bronze, pottery, or weaponry from the outside world by selling his cattle to individuals outside his Barbarian group. Barbarians did not live in cities or even in villages. They resided in individual timber dwellings some distance apart. Nor did they own land per se. Instead, Barbarians merely worked it. Several Barbarians, generally speaking a common language and perhaps related as an extended family, divided land into smaller units or strips and annually apportioned strips to the males working the plots. The land was not divided equally but each individual received only that grain grown on the strips designated as his. The same individual did not necessarily gain the same strips year after year or even the same number of strips nor did the group necessarily work the same land in successive years. They sometimes wandered from place to place, pasturing animals and growing only grains, which required a minimum of cultivation. The Barbarians knew slavery but as a fixed payment of goods rather than of services; a slave owed his master a portion of his property, not labor.

Romans of the second century A.D. and earlier recognized the Barbarians as a superstitious people and found their disinterest in theological or philosophical debates striking. Barbarians established no mechanisms to channel such debates because none was needed; in peacetime, religion was a personal matter. No priests or religious government existed parallel to the state because there was no state, only individuals. Barbarians worshipped the sun, the moon, and fire but erected no temples to these divinities; Barbarians refused to imprison gods within walls or to reduce them to human scale by giving them human features or attributes. Woods and groves served as holy places. Individuals interpreted their own auspices to predict the wisdom of a potential personal act.

Barbarian society revolved around the individual. Romans remarked on Barbarian hedonism when not at war. They hunted, gorged themselves on beer and food, played dice, and slept a lot. Theft of property was admired when those victimized lived outside the group. Barbarian social customs also recognized the sanctity of the individual and his property. Punishments were crime-specific and almost always involved property. A debt was satisfied when an aggrieved party agreed to the terms offered by the offending party. Murder as well as any other crime could be paid for in cows and sheep. Children had responsibility for pursuing their fathers' unresolved feuds. In those instances where two parties disagreed on the commission of a crime, each of them was subjected to an ordeal, a test involving physical courage or mystical powers, to decide between these rival claimants. Even the pursuit of war incorporated an individualistic component. Men fought with their friends and kin and brought their human property—their wives—to battle. Barbarians had no camp followers. Wives fed their men and bound their wounds but also stood near the battlefield and offered verbal encouragement. If their champions suffered a setback, women were to provide a compelling inducement to fight harder by thrusting out their chests to indicate the imminent loss of property—themselves—to the opposition.

Barbarian Legacy

Roman commentators thus described Barbarians and, although their characterization of these Germanic peoples might not exactly reflect reality, it does suggest that individualism played a prominent part in Barbarian life. Romans noted the difference between Barbarian individualism and the collectivism of eternal Rome and were appalled yet fascinated by it. Intercourse between Barbarians and Romans accelerated after about A.D. 200. Skirmishes between these two peoples became common, and many Barbarians crossed Roman borders to settle in the Empire. Possibility of service in the Roman army attracted them, and the army, desperate for soldiers because of the stepped-up Barbarian attacks and the wanton unwillingness of Romans to join the military, welcomed them. The upshot was that Barbarians fighting under the Roman banner fought other Barbarians, who had amalgamated into tribes, generally kin- and/or language-based groups. Barbarians gained a further inducement to join the Roman army when in 212 Rome granted citizenship to any freeborn male within the Empire. Barbarian customs, beliefs, and practices—individualism—would now stand legally alongside Roman collectivism.

That desperate move marked a radical change in Roman history. Romans had guarded and cherished citizenship because it defined the eternal Rome. It had provided the bond—the moral code, religious ethic, and social structure—by which persons defined as Romans acted. Those fundamental notions of the nature of Roman social organization now were traded for the expediency of an army. In truth, Romans had begun to abandon the basis of their commonality somewhat earlier. The citizenship decision simply reflected the lack of commitment to ideas previously held.

Early Roman "Kingdom":
Third to Early Fourth Century

In 193, the governor of the Roman province of Syria and the generals of the Roman armies in Britain and in the Danube each declared himself emperor and rushed to Rome to solidify his claim. These declarations symbolized the decline of republican institutions, especially the Senate, which no longer participated in selecting the emperor. They also indicated the growing importance of the provinces in the Empire, perhaps eclipsing Rome and all Italy.

Septimius through Diocletian

When the numerous battles and the attendant destruction ceased, the Danube commander Septimius emerged as victor and assumed the imperial throne for almost 20 years. In the process, he remade the Empire, substituting military might for consensual governance. Septimius actively destroyed those bulwarks long cherished by Romans in his personal quest to cement his power. He pronounced himself divine and identified himself as Mithras and his wife as Cybele. Septimius claimed the right to rule by a heavenly decree, not from consent of an earthly republic. He destroyed the prestige and power of the Senate, had many of its members who opposed him put to death, and abolished the senatorial court. Septimius spent lavishly on the provinces and relatively little on Rome. He more than doubled the salary of the army, the majority of which now came from outside Italy, to ensure its loyalty to him, and encouraged army men to establish politically active social clubs to press his agenda. Septimius divided Roman law into two distinct segments: law for the upper class and law for the lower class. Definitions of crimes and the type and severity of punishments differed for each class as Septimius retained power by dividing his potential opponents.

Septimius's immediate successors continued his policy of placating the army and further drained the public treasury. This policy did not ensure stability. Between 235 and 285, Rome had about 50 emperors. Each confronted the Barbarians and other menaces and relied on the army to stay on the throne. The Goths, a Barbarians tribe, attacked Thrace and the Persians attacked Mesopotamia and Syria. The Barbarian Saxons and Jutes crossed into Britain and Gaul and the Franks moved into Gaul and Spain. The Goths mounted a huge invasion in 268 that required over 500 ships. Pestilential epidemics left millions dead. Local mints coined—and often debased—their own moneys. Pirates roamed the seas and brigands ravaged the land. Emperors doubled the size of the army, replaced the unwieldy legion system with smaller, more flexible units to defend against unpredictable Barbarian attacks, and established heavily armored horse cavalries to strike at Barbarian strongholds. They further secured the throne by eliminating likely rivals. Imperial edicts prohibited members of the Senate from high military command and declared them ineligible to govern any province with an army, actions first initiated by Augustus.

Agricultural Decline

These cataclysms seriously debilitated agriculture, which had provided the surplus necessary for military adventures and urban life. The military now chose the emperor and emperors seized whatever resources they deemed necessary to maintain army support. Ideas of commonality and consensually derived republican institutions were virtually abandoned as society fractured. The emperor-directed state actively entered the breech. To guarantee an adequate bread supply for the army, the state seized control of the bread-making trade. It set the price for wheat and bread sales and then put all collegia engaged in transporting and processing food under government control.

Government regulation of private enterprise for survival of the emperor had become de rigueur.

Imperial Pomp and Fiat

These trends reached full flower under the reign of Diocletian in the two decades after 284. He virtually abandoned Rome as the capital to move closer to the frontier, divided the Empire into four separate areas, and established an emperor-like official for each. Each of these regional emperors had his own court, bodyguards, and the right to strike coins in his image. And each was divine. Imperial pomp reached new heights as emperors no longer claimed republican or even earthly origins but rather divine provenance. Everything they touched was holy. Their portraits had halos or auras emanating from their heads, a sign of divinity. Diocletian further diffused authority and eliminated potential rivals by doubling the number of imperial provinces and by dividing Italy into 16 separate provincial areas. He completely separated civil and military authority; officials governing were different from those commanding the military. Emperors were the exception. Diocletian divided the military into two distinct stations—border guards and mobile army—and paid and fed the mobile army better. He instituted an extensive military draft, taking beggars, tramps, and sons of Barbarians settled within the Empire's borders. This was a far cry from the citizen army of the Republic and Diocletian even drafted prisoners of war, giving them the choice of service in the Roman military or death.

Diocletian. Diocletian ironically held together the Empire by separating it into four parts. Only his military power prevented a complete and permanent breakup. The Rome that persisted depended on force; the consensus that had defined the Republic and early Empire was long dead.

Imperial Building: Price Fixing and Taxation

Despite an extensive labor and money shortage, Diocletian revived imperial building. His edict of maximum prices, announced in 302, extended the policy of government regulation begun by his predecessors as he attempted to keep costs down. Arguing that citizen-gouging profiteers ran rampant in the Empire, he put a ceiling on prices for over one thousand goods and services, including clothing, ink, and wages, and instituted the death penalty for violators. Diocletian created two new taxes to help pay for his extraordinary construction initiatives and military expenditures: a tax payable in kind on production and a head tax that differed according to the individual's station. He reinforced the municipal senators' responsibility to collect taxes in their cities and surrounding environs and compelled them personally to make up the amount they did not collect. Municipal officials found themselves squeezed by that practice and sometimes they used physical force to recover delinquent taxes. That tactic often resulted in contempt for municipal officialdom and complaints that governments in "cities are set up by the state in order . . . to extort and oppress."

The economic situation of the third and early fourth centuries was quite a bit more complex than most contemporaries recognized. An agriculture devastated by war and epidemics could not provide the bounty necessary to satisfy the tax collector and the army and support small, self-sufficient farmers and their families. The already impossible situation was exacerbated by the fact that large landowners, those most able to pay taxes, were best able to resist paying them. To guarantee adequate grain supplies, military and civil commanders often contracted with large landowners for a set percentage of their crops. Large landowners received a premium price for their commodities as well as military support for tax evasion. This left municipal officials—usually descendants of the original provincial aristocracy—to get their tax quotas from smaller farmers, who could not pay. Sometimes these small farmers joined the army. Often they simply abandoned their land. Still other times they went to large landowners and secured loans of grain at usurious rates. When these loans came due, the small landowners traded their land for the debt. They became landless tenants on latifundia or villas, receiving protection from tax collectors, military recruiters, criminals, invasions, civil wars, and the other dislocations of life in the third and early fourth centuries. They worked the land they always worked and paid the large landowners a specified percentage of the yield as rent. Large landowners were free to loan the grain at high interest, to hoard it until prices rose even farther, or to sell it on the increasingly important black market.

Imperial Bureaucracy

Municipal officials fled responsibilities as swiftly as did small farmers. Entering the imperial bureaucracy—now marked by a uniform consisting of a small round helmet, a cloak with shoulder pin, and a heavy inlaid belt—exempted the individual from taxes, tax collecting, municipal service, and the draft. So too did investing the family fortune in a villa or latifundia. But these officials had done more than raise taxes in cities and their agricultural hinterlands. They had also administered cities and had devoted a considerable portion of their fortunes to maintaining the urban infrastructure and other municipal services. They abandoned these tasks when they abandoned cities.

Without these services, municipal economies declined. Large-scale pottery, glass, metalware, and cloth manufacturing collapsed. Governmental price fixing, coupled with military salary-driven inflation, rendered production unprofitable. Artisans involved in these trades frequently found work at latifundia and villas where a portion of their production went for rent. Others found positions in the new state-run armories and clothmaking establishments, which made armor, weapons, and uniforms for the military. City merchants went out of business without manufacturing or an agricultural surplus to sustain them—the state, not private enterprise, distributed the products of state armories—and urban populations tumbled. Municipal famines became commonplace and a barter economy emerged. Only governmental and religious institutions and their support structures remained fixtures in cities. Provincial capitals and cities of particular military value suffered less than other municipalities but even in these places population dropped considerably.

On every level, third- and fourth-century Romans abrogated the social contract that had sustained the Republic and the high Empire. The sense of commonality, the agreement to suffer for some common benefit, first by family and then by social role, had exploded as the Empire's raison d'être no longer seemed viable. In that way, Rome had become somewhat barbaric. Individual-based Romans paralleled the individual-based Barbarians.

Religion

Great similarities existed between what large numbers of pagans and Christians believed. Both groups contemplated the ultimate nature of their gods and both saw their deities as spiritual, incorporeal. Both, moreover, recognized the possibility of a mystical union with god, the establishment of a personal or at least a one-to-one relationship. The details of these understandings separated Christian and pagan as did the Christian insistence that only their deity was valid.

Pagans

By the end of the second century, most pagans had accepted the idea of a heavenly, incorporeal afterlife in which the earthly individual merged with a single spirit. This ethereal god barely concerned himself with terrestrial matters, preferring to leave those to lesser beings or daimons. Daimons could be good or bad. They intervened in earthly affairs and performed earthly miracles and it was daimons that pagans asked for intervention and blessings.

The abrupt separation between god and daimons enabled pagans to engage in a form of mutual toleration of others and even respect their alternate beliefs. Any number of interacting daimons might exist and the Romans identified gods of different lands with one another and wove the various provincial myths together to form a single pan-Roman story. The Roman state gods (daimons) assumed an exalted place in this syncretic pantheon. Nonetheless, Romans understood that god was different from these daimons. He existed insubstantially, without body, removed from the baseness of material life.

Roman pagans could believe in many things simultaneously. For example, they could believe in the cult of Mithras, the cult of Cybele, *and* the cult of Isis as well as worship the Unconquered Sun, (a particularly popular third-century cult), defining each as a daimon and seeing no conflict among them. But Romans could also recognize one of these cult figures as god, as the supreme being, and the others as daimons. In either case, the basic assumption was the same. A single deity divorced from day-to-day life existed, while lesser entities interacted in the world.

Pagans often sought to understand the nature of their deity and they sometimes reached to the Greek past for inspiration. Curiously they adopted Greek verbiage—shape, form, and order—to discuss a divinity they denied had a corporeal nature. This curious combination of rationality tinged with mysticism gained currency after the second century. Historians have termed this metaphysically derived rationalism neo-Platonism. The third-century Egyptian Plotinus offered an enduring explanation for the One, the Good. To Plotinus, everything came from this single, impersonal, immaterial, eternal force. Reality spread from the One in concentric spheres, rather like the layers of an onion. The outer layer, matter, was the basest level of reality. Matter depended on Nature, which depended on the World-Soul, which depended on the World-Mind, which ultimately depended on the One. Each individual contained within himself or herself all reality levels. By focusing the mind, each person could achieve the level of the World-Mind. Achievement of that level resulted in a union with the One. Plotinus's explanation emphasized the individual, not a community. The individual entered the union and did not rely on others. The process was internal. The individual focused her or his thinking inward. Union was personal, not a public event.

Christians

In the third century, pagans increasingly confronted Christians. Christian intolerance of pagan beliefs bred a retaliatory hatred of Christians. Pagans accused Christians of cannibalism, especially of eating babies as part of their sacraments, and described them as peculiar, unwilling to join with their neighbors. The pagan indictment of Christianity went far beyond slurs. Pagans called Christians enemies of the state and haters of mankind and blamed them for all Rome's ills. The Christian rejection of polytheism was the central defining question and had profound sociopolitical implications. To deny Roman deities was to deny Rome itself. Invalidation of Roman gods constituted a personal repudiation of the state and its emperor. These treasonous sentiments did not go unpunished. Early third-century persecutions of Christians sought to wipe out that treachery, but not until Diocletian was a sustained crusade conducted against the treason. Diocletian destroyed many Christian churches at the end of the third century, burned Christian sacred books, and prohibited worship of the religion under penalty of death.

Christianity had become popular enough to withstand the imperial onslaught. In a number of ways, third-century Christianity mimicked its pagan competitors. The view of salvation stressed the individual. Salvation—revelation and conversion—had become a personal private act of faith. Acceptance of Jesus cut an individual off from past and peers to join with god. Christianity also included iconography similar to that of pagan religions: worship of individuals after their earthly demise; statuary; the naturalistic imagery of serpents and lightning; portraits of holy individuals surrounded by halos or auras; angels and other supernatural daimon-like beings; a monarch enthroned on high; and battles between forces of good and evil. Christianity offered converts miracles, especially healing through laying on of hands and driving out evil, the same powers pagans sought from their daimons. These personal benefits included exorcism. Exorcism became a particular Christian practice—it confirmed (proved) both god's power and the ever-present danger of evil—and provided a practical demonstration of the superiority of supporting one powerful god instead of several lesser entities.

Ironically, the Christian penchant to martyrdom gave their faith a measure of validity and credibility. The apparent inner peace of Christians as they gave their life for their religion demonstrated a profound sense of belief in doctrine that could easily be equated with truth. Christian steadfastness, both in its absolute intolerance of other beliefs and its absolute certainty in the validity of its own beliefs, appeared attractive to a people who previously had cherished duty, commitment, and obligation. Christianity initially appealed to the downtrodden as its message of hope encouraged individuals to look not to earthly wants and concerns but to the more promising afterlife. Christianity, of course, was never entirely otherworldly. Saint Matthew's admonition to "render unto Caesar what was Caesar's" acknowledged continuity between the earth and heaven. So too did the late third-century view offered by some Christians that Greece and Rome were earthly manifestations of Christ's rule in the world. It was Christ in some other guise who established the premises of classical civilization. His minions then applied the divine schoolmaster's teachings and were bringing to a successful resolution on earth the fight between good and evil; Christ's principles, which were embedded in Rome, acted to defeat Satan's earthly legions—barbarism, hedonism, and paganism.

Constantine and Christianity

Constantine, Diocletian's successor, certainly believed this and became Christianity's most powerful friend. In 311, he ended a decade of Christian persecution with an edict of religious toleration. Christians could reopen their churches if they did not disrupt public order. Constantine's own conversion to Christianity in 312 proved a major landmark in pagan–Christian relations as his imperial pronouncements solidified the church's position. In 313, he declared that each local church constituted an individual in law, able to own property, to sue, and to be sued. Two years later, Constantine firmly established the Bishop of Rome (Pope) as head of the church. The Pope endeavored to determine Christian doctrine for the entire church and enforce discipline among local churches. Constantine granted legal standing to the Pope's decisions and to his court, in effect giving the Pope in matters Christian the authority of the imperial state. Constantine also allowed the church to claim the property of martyred Christians, exempted church lands from taxation, granted regular food allotments to churches, built large basilicas, and excused clerics from various municipal activities they might find offensive or burdensome.

Constantine's conversion to Christianity was less than absolute as he also worshipped the Unconquered Sun, Hercules, Jupiter, and Mars into the 320s. In that sense, his personal turmoil reflected that of the church. Numerous Christian thinkers offered their interpretations of the nature of god and the nature of humanity and the relationship of Jesus to salvation. Several sects gained large numbers of adherents. The most popular incorporated a sense of dualism, a radical separation between different physical states, between opposites. The Gnostic heresies, for example, considered humans composed of a divine mortal soul trapped in an evil mortal body. Christ brought knowledge of that dualism to earth and acceptance of Christ's truth would free the soul from its mortal body and thus make it immortal; true believers would never experience death. Manichaeism, another Christian offshoot, postulated two states: light and dark. Light was pure, orderly, peaceful, intelligent, and clear. Its opposite, dark, had invaded the light sometime in the past. The visible world was the product. Jesus told Adam how to separate light and dark but agents of darkness created Eve to seduce him. Cain and Abel further scattered the light. Jesus then used the moon and the sun to distill the dark out of the souls of dead men, which returned the deceased to a state of heavenly perfection. Manichaens believed that the earthly world would end with Jesus' second coming. A huge conflagration would herald restoration of the kingdom of light.

The Constantine-empowered church dealt with these matters. Constantine intervened in one particular religious question, one that struck at Christianity's very foundation. What clearly separated contemporary pagan and Christian thought was the Christian insistence on only one god. This monotheism differed considerably from the views of the pagan world, which generally believed in a supreme ethereal god but also welcomed lesser divinities or daimons in the pantheon. Christ's nature was central. Was he the same as god? What was the relation of the "father and son"? Was Christ part human and part divine? What were the proportions? Were those proportions eternal? Several positions were offered on these questions. Arius, an Alexandrian priest, maintained that the father and son were sequential in time and therefore not of the same substance. The father must have preceded the son, a view which offended the Bishop of Alexandria who believed that the persons of the trinity were one in chronology, substance, and power. Arius was excommunicated from the church but found considerable support for his position among Christian clerics in Asia Minor. Constantine, proclaiming "one ruler, one world, one creed," interceded by calling a council of bishops from across the empire to gather at imperial expense at Nicaea in 325 to consider Arianism. Over 300 bishops attended and under Constantine's firm hand formulated the Nicene Creed. The creed confirmed the Bishop of Alexandria's view of the trinity, set the date of Easter, and formulated additional rules for church discipline and uniformity. Constantine celebrated his success by announcing himself "Equal of the Apostles," banning pagan sacrifices, and abandoning the decadent and hard-to-defend Rome to establish a glittering Constantinople in Asia Minor as the new eternal city. Arius and his supporters continued their preaching—some later emperors would be Arians (ironically, Constantine himself would be baptized by an Arian a week before his death)—and found remarkable success among the Barbarian tribes in the west, especially the Vandals, Burgundians, Ostrogoths, and Visigoths.

Final Roman "Kingdom":
Fourth to Late Fifth Century

By the fourth century, the Roman west had been completely barbarized. The communitarian ideas that had provided the basis of Roman civilization had fallen under the individualist onslaught. What remained in the west was for imperial power to collapse. Those benefiting from the imperial system clung to authority as if their very existence depended on its continuation. To a large extent, it did. Imperial forces proved no match for the Barbarians, who maintained pressure on the Empire's northern frontier. After 376, various Barbarian tribes took up residence within the Empire where they remained unassimilated. Before the end of that century, Vandals, Goths, and Franks had each established significant bases inside imperial boundaries and would create autonomous kingdoms there early in the next century. The Romans abandoned Britain to protect the city of Rome, which the Visigoths sacked in 410. The Vandals sacked Rome some 45 years later. Burgundians and Ostrogoths also set up kingdoms in what had been Roman territory. The Barbarian general Odoacer ended the succession of Roman emperors in 476 when he proclaimed himself Patrician and regent of the emperor of the west.

During this period, the eastern branch of the Roman Empire became in effect a separate empire. It too surrendered Roman tradition and custom and adopted instead many of the trappings of Greece, Mesopotamia, and Egypt. It succeeded but was not a continuation of the Roman Empire.

Reform and Stability: Striving for Grandeur

Constantine's imperial reforms were as profound as his religious reforms. He welcomed, even actively recruited, Germans for the army and accelerated their ascendancy into the officer class. He converted the Roman Senate into a municipal council; the venerable Senate had authority only over municipal matters in a city no longer the pride of the Empire. Constantine also removed distinctions between the Equestrian and other upper classes, which narrowed the options of the traditional aristocracy while broadening those of the wealthy. In 314, he followed Diocletian's lead and made collegia and guilds hereditary, which forced the sons of tradesmen to continue fulfilling the same economic obligations to the Empire as had their fathers. This move to stabilize—even increase—imperial revenues was matched by a 322 edict in which Constantine bound small farmers to the soil to ensure a sufficient food supply for the army. These farmers were not free but rather were *coloni*, serflike individuals tied to large landowners who held policing and judicial power over them. Constantine also created a proliferation of titles to designate a new exalted class and instituted different levels of punishments for various offenses. The background of the offender dictated the punishment.

By creating Constantinople, Constantine tried in one way to recreate Rome. Situated on easily fortified land and possessing an excellent harbor, Constantinople was to recapture Roman glory. Constantine embarked on an impressive building campaign for this new pristine capital city and devoted proportionately less money to other Roman cities. In this action, he set a precedent for his successors. Public building in cities other than Constantinople virtually ceased.

Imperial Courts and Opulent Estates: Trappings and Tools

Later emperors followed Constantine's lead in other ways. The imperial court increasingly relied on pomp and ceremony as if to regain the outward pretensions of the materialistic past. Cities lost their right to self-government, while the state compelled ever greater numbers of children to practice the same trade as had their fathers. Local nobility, as well as its massive financial obligations, also became hereditary. An army of government agents enforced these dictates. Infertile or difficult-to-till northern farmland was abandoned as bureaucratized, militarized Rome regimented its citizens' lives. Frequent attacks by Barbarians and Huns led the remaining Roman aristocracy to barricade itself behind the walls of its fortified country estates. Depopulation of cities and flight from small farms quickened as the state instituted draconian measures to fight the invaders. Wood and grain were requisitioned; citizens were forced to repair and maintain roads and bridges; and trade beyond the locality virtually ceased. Great estates became the center of power and population. These estates remained private, not public, institutions; individual contracts between owner and supplicant or simply the whim of the owner governed them. Private estates were neither republican nor democratic and the relationship was hardly consensual.

A certain opulence characterized these estates. Landowners demonstrated they were people of means, that the relationship between themselves and each of their supplicants was and ought to be unequal. An ostentatious use of glass was one way to

A Great Estate. Formation of great estates signaled the death of the Roman Empire. Individuals possessing obscene amounts of wealth found it expedient to abandon Rome and to rely on their own devices for protection in the countryside. The result was that Roman cities possessed increasingly fewer resources to deal with increasingly more poverty.

set themselves apart from the coloni and artisans. Estate owners appreciated slightly octagonal glass mirrors backed by sheet lead and an assortment of glass lamps. Even watermills, a substantial capital investment, were sometimes found on these estates. People and animals had long turned a stone on top of a fixed stone to grind grain into meal for bread and beer. In the fourth century, estate owners replaced the people, horses, mules, and oxen usually used for this arduous task with a water-turned wheel. The earliest and simplest mill consisted of a wheel lying horizontally in water and connected to a vertical shaft. The shaft went upward through the anchored lower millstone and was fixed to the mobile upper millstone by a crossbar placed in a depression worn in the stone. Romans ground grain between these two stones. In the late first century, an undershot waterwheel appeared. It rested vertically in the water and provided considerably more grinding power than the horizontal mill. The river's current ran beneath the wheel and turned its flutes. Gearing translated the vertical motion of the wheel into horizontal grinding power. By the end of the third century, Romans had begun to use an overshot waterwheel, which combined the vertical flow of a river with the downward pull of gravity to offer the most power available in the classical world. Romans dug a wheel pit and a race from the river. The race waters came to the pit and landed on and ran over the uppermost flutes, providing extensive vertical power, which gears translated to horizontal motion.

Art

Later western Roman art also attempted to make up in stone or with glass mosaics what the Empire had lost. Statuary celebrated the exalted but did not follow classical canons. Massive rather than graceful, the figures were impressionistic and immobile. Statuary became vigorously abstract, an expression of the whim of the individual sculptor. It lacked a sense of perspective or relief, the basis of the classical three-dimensional approach. Paintings and mosaics were flat, reflecting two dimensions, and figures faced the spectator. Artists attempted to convey one and only one emotion in their frozen figures, the singular essence of their study.

Reality

These artistic and technical pretensions could not overcome the harsh reality of late fourth- and fifth-century Rome. In 378, the Visigoths and some Ostrogoths routed the Roman army and, as part of the terms of peace, became a province within the Roman Empire. This province was Roman in name only. Goths ruled the province according to their individualistic traditions. Four years later Rome gave the Visigoths in the Balkans a sort of federated status. That state retained its own leaders and military but promised to fight in support of Rome. That promise was meaningless. It was the Visigoths, not the Romans, who decided whether and when they would come to Rome's aid. Curiously, Roman law demanded that these Visigoth leaders be designated kings and that their state within the Empire become a neatly defined kingdom if the populace was to be "Roman" and continue to be commanded by their chosen leaders; in effect, Roman law welcomed the Empire's conquerors into the imperial bureaucracy, provided them exalted status, and offered them considerable power within the Empire. Other Barbarian tribes quickly adopted the model of the Visigoths. Each received a minimum of one-third of the property of the Romans—arable land, cattle, slaves and coloni—which, according to Roman law, constituted the normal cost of quartering troops. Each tribe generally segregated itself from the Romans, in some cases even forbidding intermarriage. At the same time, the Roman army found itself even more heavily dependent on its Barbarian members. Many Romans found that the decline of central authority had made it rather simple to refuse or avoid military service. Busy defending themselves from the Barbarian hoards, the army and the western emperor were unable to enforce imperial edicts or dictates.

In the fifth century, tribal animosities began to dominate imperial politics. Germans assumed the highest military commands and high imperial offices because of the prestige that the Empire implied. Romans chafed as Barbarians captured Roman property and then carved up the Empire. And these "Roman" troops were loyal to their commanders and tribes, not some abstract idea of Roman commonality. As a consequence, "Roman" troops often attacked and fought each other, a situation that further mocked the idea of an empire. The Eastern empire, worried about the Huns and Persians, was unable to intervene. Although many in the empire long harbored a desire to reunite east and west, the possibility never materialized. Eternal Rome was dead.

Religion: Christianity Ascendant

During the fourth century, the number of people identifying themselves as Christians skyrocketed from 5 million to 30 million. Intellectuals joined in significant numbers. Their conversion was generally accompanied by testimonials and confessions and in many cases announcements that they had forsaken the material to adopt an ascetic life. Some even went alone far from civilization to contemplate their faith, to avoid sin by living simply in concert with Christ's teachings, and to achieve a mystical union with god. There they fasted, wore rough, irritating clothes, and otherwise subjected themselves to deprivations, a rejection of Roman life, and a commitment to Christ. Ironically, other individuals of a similar bent soon followed them. They acted alone together, setting up small rural communities that eschewed Roman civilization and incorporated prayer and work. These otherworldly communities became monasteries and their inhabitants monks.

Both civil and religious authorities feared these ad hoc entities. Emperors worried that this life free from responsibilities to the Empire would encourage others to renounce their now hereditary civil obligations. Officials were also concerned that monks would become public nuisances, while the church fretted about doctrinal and organizational unity. Heretical views or charismatic leadership might bloom in the desert. St. Basil tried to remove these menaces in 360 by formulating monastic rules. Basil's code stressed group study and work. It kept the monks occupied and forced them to interact with one another, moves that would ensure doctrinal harmony. The church acted again in 451 to rein in these dangerous bodies. It required bishops to approve of the establishment of monasteries in their diocese and prohibited monks from leaving these compounds unless they received the bishop's express permission.

Within the Roman world, Christians began to dominate imperial affairs. Using force, brutality, and remarkable zealotry, they accused nonbelievers and heretical Christians of doing the devil's work and set about to gain converts, using coercion when necessary. After about 380, non-Christians were regularly attacked. Pagan temples were confiscated and converted into schools, meeting halls, and churches. Sometimes Christians used the temples as quarries, taking the stone to build new Christian structures. Christianity became the official imperial religion before the century's end. A decree in 407 commanded that "if any images stand even now in the temples and shrines . . . , they shall be torn from their foundations." Temple buildings "situated in cities or towns shall be vindicated to public use. Altars shall be destroyed in all places." The sack of Rome in 410 by the Visigoths did not diminish the onslaught. Some pagans pointed to the sack as demonstration of the weakness of the Christian god. No less a personage than St. Augustine disagreed. A Manichaen in his youth, Augustine suggested that the sack proved that evil was about in the earthly world and called on all Christians to do god's bidding by purging it from their midst. The City of Man was not pure like the City of God. To Augustine, pagans and nonbelievers were evil incarnate. "That all superstition of pagans and heathens should be annihilated is what God wants, God commands, God proclaims," maintained Augustine.

That was not to say that the church had resolved its internal divisions. Questions of Christ's nature continued to divide Christians. Christian clerics adhering to the Nicene Creed now were ruled by Arian-practicing Barbarians. The Vandals proved particularly fanatical. They banished over 5,000 traditional Christian clerics to the desert for their "heretical" views and punished their bishops with forced labor. Other Barbarian tribes were more tolerant but even within the traditional church disagreements raged. The bishops of Rome, Constantinople, Antioch, Alexandria, and Jerusalem persisted in their individual quests for church primacy. The church itself, like the Empire, divided into eastern and western branches. The bishop of Rome retained control of the church in the west even as the western empire collapsed, while the bishop of Constantinople, backed by the still strong eastern emperor, dominated the eastern church.

Christianity as explained in the third century and after was antithetical to Romanism. Romans had always considered themselves a unique, divinely blessed people with an extraordinary ability to preserve their indigenous traditions. Romans living, dead, and as yet unborn were essentially the same and that provided the essence of Eternal Rome. As historian J. M. Wallace-Hadrill has noted, Eternal Rome was a "mould [that] was fixed." Romans were "to fill it, from generation to generation." But individualistic Christianity was of a different character, accentuating each person, not the Eternal Rome. It posited, "in place of Eternal Rome, the eternal soul of each person, and woman, the salvation of which was the proper business of life and compared with which the fate of empires was merely irrelevant."[4] Rome fell because the assumptions upon which it was built no longer seemed germane.

For Further Reading

Balsdon, J. P. V. D. *Romans and Aliens.* Chapel Hill: University of North Carolina Press, 1979.
———. *Rome: The Story of an Empire.* New York: McGraw-Hill, 1970.
Brown, Peter. *The World of Late Antiquity, A.D. 150–750.* London: Thames, 1971.

[4]J. M. Wallace-Hadrill, *The Barbarian West* (New York: Harper Torchbooks, 1962): 20.

Carcopino, Jerome. *Daily Life in Ancient Rome*. New Haven, Conn.: Yale University Press, 1940.

Heather, Peter J. *Goths and Romans, 332–489* New York: Oxford University Press, 1991.

Heichelheim, Fritz M., Cedric A. Yeo and Allen M. Ward. *A History of the Roman People*, 2d ed. Englewood Cliffs, N. J.: Prentice-Hall, 1984.

Johnson, Stephen. *Late Roman Fortifications*. London: B. T. Batsford, 1983.

Jones, A. H. M. *Constantine and the Conversion of Europe*. New York: Collier, 1962.

Jones, Tom B. *The Silver-Plated Age*. Lawrence, Kan.: Coronado Press, 1962.

Liversidge, Joan. *Everyday Life in the Roman Empire*. New York: G. P. Putnam's Sons, 1976.

Lloyd, G. E. R. *Greek Science After Aristotle*. New York: W. W. Norton, 1973.

MacMullen, Ramsay. *Christianizing the Roman Empire*. New Haven, Conn.: Yale University Press, 1984.

———. *Roman Social Relations 50 B.C. to A.D. 284*. New Haven, Conn.: Yale University Press, 1974.

Momigliano, Arnaldo. *On Pagans, Jews, and Christians*. Middletown, Conn.: Wesleyan University Press, 1987.

Reynolds, Terry S. *Stronger Than a Hundred Men: A History of the Vertical Water Wheel*. Baltimore: Johns Hopkins University Press, 1983.

Richmond, I. A. *Roman Britain*. New York: Penguin, 1955.

Robinson, James M., ed. *The Nag Hammadi Library*. San Francisco: Harper & Row, 1977.

Sigerist, Henry E. *The Great Doctors*. 1933; New York: Dover, 1971.

Smallwood, E. Mary. *The Jews under Roman Rule*. Leiden: E. J. Brill, 1976.

Starr, Chester G. *The Roman Empire, 27 B.C.E.–A.D. 476*. New York: Oxford University Press, 1982.

Wallace-Hadrill, J. M. *The Barbarian West: The Early Middle Ages A.D. 400–1000*. New York: Harper Torchbooks, 1962.

Wheeler, Mortimer. *Roman Art and Architecture*. London: Thames and Hudson, 1964.

Wolfram, Herwig. *History of the Goths*. Trans. Thomas J. Dunlap. Berkeley: University of California Press, 1988.

Identification of the intellectual, social, and physical remnants of Greece and

Rome as touchstones for western civilization highlighted the fall of the Roman Empire as a critical event in history. The civilization that immediately followed Rome and that occupied the same lands in western Europe, the Germanic or Barbarian realms, neither adopted nor adapted many sig-

European Civilization: The Middle Ages

nificant Roman or Greek institutions. In fact, the Barbarians often appeared to disdain what the Romans had accomplished. For example, they regularly cannibalized the glorious Roman roads and used the stone to build other, much less precise structures. Tra-

ditionally, the failure of the Germans to accept what seem to be the manifest treasures of the two landmark civilizations has been explained by rejecting the Germans as barbarians, as persons so foreign, unlettered, and distasteful as to signify a fundamental break with the past.

Our present definition of the word *barbarian* reflects that analysis. Apparent rejection of the intellectual, social, and physical structures of Rome and Greece also marked the Barbarians as different from two other civilizations that flourished in the period 500–850: Byzantine and Islamic. Both seem to have behaved much more rationally and conventionally; both acknowledged a debt to and contributions from Greece and Rome.

But that abrupt dismissal by the Barbarians of the ideas and frameworks of Greece and Rome is troubling in another way. It is disturbing because the Barbarians and their western European descendants, Romanesque and Gothic Europeans (the names are taken from architectural styles that dominated Europe from 850 to 1150 and from 1100–1350, respectively) apparently were great innovators in their own right. They pioneered a myriad of exciting new ventures and engaged in a tremendous amount of experimentation.

These Europeans organized societies in unfamiliar ways and created many new institutions, several of which seem the forerunners of those of the

113

present day. And it is this relationship to the present that truly appears unsettling. Does contemporary civilization owe a considerable debt to persons long considered barbarians?

Fortunately, that last question need not be broached directly because the assumptions upon which it rests are false. Medieval Europeans, Europeans from the fall of Rome to about 1350, did not reject Greece and Rome out of hand. Instead, they repeatedly looked back to Rome for guidance.

The German adoption of Christianity helped foster and ultimately constrain that gaze. The Christian church provided the Barbarians and their successors the initial and most compelling reason to look to Rome: It was the site from which Christianity sprang and which provided them a sense of continuity with the past. Yet the church was not static during that nearly millennium-long period. On the contrary, it redefined itself several times, making its use as a cultural referent and the sense of continuity it supposedly brought mere illusion.

The repeated redefinition of the church did not make it unique but was symptomatic of a far broader cultural phenomenon. What at any given time medieval Europeans selected from Rome and how they interpreted it did not stem from an intellectual commonality or familiarity with Greece and Rome—perpetuation of similar Greek or Roman beliefs—but rather from ideas indigenous to Barbarian, Romanesque, and Gothic cultures. True, Greece and Rome served as repositories and templates but differentially, only within the context of what Barbarian, Romanesque, and Gothic Europeans sought.

Those Barbarian, Romanesque, and Gothic Europeans who examined the past did so on their own terms and through their own perspectives. The result was twofold. Each of the three medieval western European cultures chose to focus on different aspects of Greece and Rome and each placed the Greek and Roman material within an entirely new context. In that sense, the three medieval European civilizations not only lacked continuity with Greece and Rome but also were not directly continuous with each other. That each occupied similar geographic space and followed one another sequentially mattered less than the fact that each held a separate series of understandings and assumptions that permeated the culture. Considerable distinctiveness marked Barbarian, Romanesque, and Gothic civilizations as each employed its own unique set of intellectual constructs.

CHAPTER 5

Germanic Successors: Structural Transfer

Rome fell and in the west several successors emerged from the void. The significance of the emergence of these new Barbarian kingdoms has long been in question. Recent historical scholarship has rebelled against an earlier generation, which termed the period immediately after Rome's fall the Dark Ages, to stress an essential continuity between Rome and what came after. These men and women see the Barbarians gradually becoming Romanized. It was that civilizing influence, often in conjunction with Barbarian ingenuity and sometimes aided by Islamic and Byzantine civilizations, that these scholars see as producing the later or high Middle Ages. These historians correctly reject the earlier categorization of 500–950 as a time marked by ignorance, stupidity, and irrationality. But the influence of Rome in this period may be overstated. At best, Roman contributions were apparently superficial. Although the Barbarians surely learned some things from the Romans—writing, legal codes, and Christianity come to mind—close examination indicates that few uniquely Roman intellectual, social, or physical structures transferred to the successor kingdoms in any meaningful way. Those that did transfer did so in name only; they were conceived of or used differently.

This lack of deterministic transfer ought not to surprise. The civilizations of the west after the fall of Rome differed from Rome itself for the exact same reasons that Rome fell. The assumptions that had forged the Eternal Rome no longer seemed valid or even desirable. A pervasive individualism, thinking in terms of single units or monads, had made it impossible to sustain Rome. That notion had formed the basis of Barbarian civilization and of Christianity as presented after the second century A.D. It was that same idea that fueled formation of the western successor realms, which were more nearly kingdoms in which the king owned the government as if it were property. The intellectual, social, and physical structures of Barbarian civilization and post-imperial Christianity had transferred, not those of Eternal Rome.

Barbarians: Successors to Rome

By 500, the Ostrogoths controlled Italy, the Vandals occupied North Africa, and the Anglo-Saxons and the Visigoths dominated England and Spain, respectively. What

CHRONOLOGY	
500	Barbarians establish kingdoms in what had been the western Roman Empire
527	Justinian of Constantinople launches Reconquest of the West
560	Italian peninsula freed of Constantinople's forces
570	Birth of Muhammad, prophet of Islam
622	Rise of Islam
700–900	Height of Islamic interest in Greek and Roman learning
Circa 700	Rise of the Carolingian dynasty
732	Franks drive Islamic people from what is now France and begin to unify much of Western Europe
800	Pope crowns Charlemagne Roman Emperor
825	Viking invasions of what had been the Carolingian empire gather steam
840	Carolingian empire near destruction

would become France was divided between the Franks in the north and the Burgundians in the south. Relatively small Barbarian armies had taken these territories.

Military Organization and Weaponry

Barbarians considered an army of about 25,000 large. Barbarian armies were neither tactically adept nor well equipped nor mobile. They persisted in using wedge-like formations to break through their enemy's lines and continued to bring all their property, including women, children, and livestock, to battle. A certain portion of the Barbarian war effort went to defending these personal possessions. They lacked effective siege machinery to attack walled cities or villas and generally employed modest armaments. Barbarian weaponry included battle-axes, long two-edged swords, and barbed spears, and only chiefs wore iron skullcaps and occasionally chain mail armor. Barbarians took great pride in their shields. Made of wood and leather, each of these dramatically convex, almost shell-like shields protected the individual employing it, not the adjoining infantryman. The shield protected only its bearer.

Barbarians overcame these military handicaps in several ways. Their reputation as fierce foes worked to their advantage as numerous towns and villas surrendered rather than bear anticipated devastation. Barbarians excelled at encouraging treason, persuading formerly loyal subjects to open gates impregnable to German weaponry. Sometimes Barbarians captured a place simply by cutting off its water and food. Roman armies took time to respond; often they responded too late.

Social Organization

Barbarian social and military organization were inseparable—their greatest weapon was their social organization. Barbarian society remained one of personal bonds, personal loyalty. Every free man eighteen years of age and older owed his chief or king

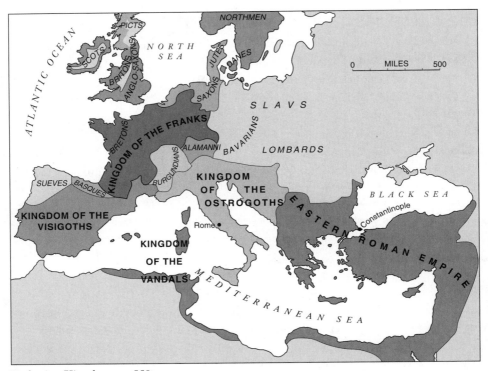

Barbarian Kingdoms c. 550

military service. The king's retinue, those he most closely trusted, were individuals who owed the king their personal loyalty. They fought with him and drank with him. As important, they advised him. Each retinue member had his own family and friends, each of whom in turn was beholden to that member. Personal bonds of honor, admiration, and friendship tied army and society together and called for commitments and efforts far greater than those given involuntarily or for less noble aims.

Law and Justice

Acquaintance with Romans and Roman customs did not sever or even lessen these personal obligations. They remained the crux of Barbarianism even after Barbarians migrated into Roman territory and formed the new Barbarian kingdoms. Emphasis on the self with its attendant rights and responsibilities framed the Barbarian law codes, written by the new kings to ensure peace and order. These codes, mere compilations of traditional Barbarian custom, were directed at Romans, not at Barbarians, who presumably already knew them. As people living within foreign kingdoms, Romans needed to know Barbarian regulations. But since Barbarians conceived of law as personal, not territorial, they did not demand or even expect Romans to practice Barbarian law; it governed Barbarians—and Romans living in Barbarian kingdoms were to adhere to Roman law.

Barbarian law codes were all similar. Since personal obligation served as the basis of Barbarian social organization, each code focused on the individual. In the centuries before tribal amalgamation (and sometimes after it) the blood feud emerged as the means to protect the individual. Relatives and even friends of an aggrieved individual had personal obligations to take up that individual's cause and to set the matter right. Often lines blurred between offender and victim and the respective supporters battled without end. Customs reflected in the codes sought to end that sort of senseless destruction by formalizing personal obligations without resort to violence. As had always been the case, whatever harmed the individual—whether physical being, property, or reputation—remained actionable. Violations were violations against the person and included such things as theft of an ox, insults, lies and curses, carrying off young females, hitting a person with an object, and even murder. To avoid blood feuds, Barbarian custom had substituted remuneration for physical violence. Custom demanded specific compensation for each offense. But all persons in Barbarian society were not equal; some had more property or more status than others. These persons had a higher value, or what Barbarians called a *wergeld*. The more valuable the person, the higher the wergeld, or price, to right a wrong to that person's physical being, reputation, or property, which included his women and children. Wergelds were not fixed at birth. Thus, an advantageous marriage or success at war could increase an individual's wergeld.

Barbarian justice required compensation for injury, not penalties for criminal activity. Once custom-specified compensation was extracted, the debt was usually squared and both individuals resumed their place in society. Difficulties emerged only when grievances were not clear cut. The accused would maintain his innocence, while his accuser demanded satisfaction. Barbarians used oath and ordeal to adjudicate these disputes. Both had arisen in an earlier era when Barbarians still believed in the godlike status of natural phenomena. Yet these forms persisted after this animistic people converted to Christianity. Christian Barbarians depended on the Christian god to reveal the truth. Trial by ordeal or oath was not a trial in our sense of the word. No evidence was presented proving a claim right or wrong. An exhibition or series of exhibitions, in our view unrelated to the matter at hand, occurred. In trial by oath, the accused and his defenders—as many as 20 hand-picked neighbors, relatives, and friends—each swore a sacred vow. The number of persons swearing depended on the status of the accused. Those with greater standing needed fewer oath takers than their less prominent counterparts. Any stuttering or hesitating during an oath constituted a conclusive sign of guilt because god would not allow liars to utter sacred words. Trial by ordeal tended to be of two types. The accused might be bound and placed in deep water blessed by a priest. If this holy water rejected him and he floated, it would signal guilt. Sinking would mean the blessed water accepted him, thus demonstrating innocence. The other common type of trial by ordeal also employed water. The accused would be asked to stick his hand in boiling water (or sometimes oil). If the burn was clean three days later—not infected—innocence was presumed because god would never hurt an innocent man.

Individuals assumed personal obligation for acts of their women, children, and slaves. Sometimes perpetrators lacked the resources to pay compensation commensurate with their offense. Kin and sometimes even neighbors were obligated to make up the difference. Failure to compensate a victim consigned the guilty individual to servitude, or worse, to life outside Barbarian society. Some Barbarian kingdoms allowed a person to renounce his kinship to a particularly wayward relative to free him of responsibility for the undisciplined person, but he also had to renounce inheritance possibilities. This uncoupling process was carried to an extreme in a few cases with slaves. Particularly indolent and irresponsible slaves were manumitted by their masters as a means of repudiating the debts these rascals incurred. Such a move isolated the former slave outside the social circle. Individuals without kin in Barbarian society were almost powerless. Kinship proved a guarantor of personal responsibility. No respectable Barbarian would marry someone without kin or do business with such a person.

Rural Life

Living arrangements also reflected the society's pervasive individualism. Most Barbarians earned their livelihoods as independent, self-sufficient farmers. Ironically, when the Barbarians entered the Roman Empire or overtook it, they rarely had to fight Romans for land. By the fourth century and certainly thereafter, Barbarians found extensive land for the taking. Small Roman landholders, unable to pay the heavy duties placed upon them by ever more desperate emperors, had abandoned their land to become coloni in villas. Barbarians claimed and settled this land in privately held lots. These lots generally congregated around a small hamlet in which a church and possibly a mill were situated. Barbarians patronized these two institutions but the pattern of their activities was decidedly not communal. Each Barbarian had his own house, shed for storing grain, barn or stable-like structure, courtyard for growing grapes for sacramental wine, and kitchen garden for beans, lentils, and peas. This was often fenced off and made private from his arable land, which he sometimes fenced off from that of his neighbors. Natural boundaries—ditches, banks, ridges, or hedgerows—were most convenient for separating parcels, but Barbarians sometimes erected wooden structures and occasionally locked enclosures to fortify the distinction.

Each Barbarian usually plowed his own land. Although a heavy, wheeled, moldboard plow capable of breaking and tilling the dense northern soil was known, its drafting required as many as six oxen, far more than most self-sufficient farmers possessed, so it found little use. The common Barbarian swing plow prepared the land adequately for wheat as well as some rye and barley. Each small farmer raised some combination of oxen, cattle, sheep, goats, pigs, geese, doves, chickens, and bees. The bees' honey became mead, a potent alcoholic beverage, and their wax made an apt oil substitute. Barbarians kept horses only infrequently and ate these powerful but expensive animals when their productive years had ended. The predominant agricultural use for these beasts was to tread on grain to thresh it, to separate the heads from the stalks. In warm months, farm animals roamed the pasture beyond individually owned and individually cultivated fields, while in winter they were penned and their manure collected to fertilize their owners' lands. The forest lay beyond the pasture belt and supplied firewood and building materials.

The very wealthiest Barbarians lived in a different fashion. They owned one or more villa-like farms, working them with slaves or coloni and sometimes entrusting their operation to stewards. Villa houses, barns, granaries, mills, pigsties, gardens, orchards, meadows, and rivers dotted the landscape of these individually owned farms, which produced far more commodities than were needed for subsistence.

Urban Life: The Center of Christianity

During the early Middle Ages, urban life continued its precipitous decline as Barbarians most decidedly shunned cities. Cities retained their governmental functions and kings occasionally used them as strongholds but, other than for formal state events, royalty hardly visited there. Rare was a city with more than a few thousand inhabitants. The Romans' grand structures for a glorious empire—public baths, fountains, aqueducts, and other public works—quickly fell into disrepair. Their multistory stone tenements also fell apart. Barbarians erected instead small wooden dwellings, sometimes on stone foundations to protect the lower levels from water damage. They chinked spaces between boards with masonry or rubble to keep out drafts. Cities persisted as focal points of what little trade remained and some Barbarians did follow some of the Romans' favored Mediterranean routes, but their haphazard coinage suggests just how little trade mattered.

Religion remained a vital urban function. As bishoprics, cities housed church government. Nearby Christians trooped to these places for baptisms and other sacred ceremonies. Cities were also sites of a huge new religious industry. Churches began to display holy relics and relics of holy men. Choices of which relics to exhibit proved illuminating. Bishops tended to display relics relevant to a particular person who had lived in or passed through the area or had some other connection—often only emotional—to it. In effect, these displays established cult-like situations, elevating a particular personality as a patron of the city. Christians from far away visited these places to ask for the patron's intercession. Their donations to the church and the money spent while at these shrines enabled bishops to rebuild religious structures, often Roman basilicas. As the only persisting source of authority in cities, bishops gradually assumed administrative duties and increasingly received petitioners at basilica churches, symbolically joining the religious and governmental functions.

Architecture and Art: Colorful Assymetry

Petitioners and visitors to shrines found land travel difficult. Barbarians had not only not repaired the Roman roads but often cannibalized them to build religious structures. The Church of Stephen the Protomartyr, for example, apparently received some stone from Roman roads. This basilica-like structure, built on the spot that would later support the incomparable Notre Dame of Paris, was an impressive Barbarian urban church. This sixth-century structure was dedicated to the Patron of Paris and resembled a Roman temple but was more stodgy and less refined than its predecessor. Foundations of this 160-by-72-foot church were nearly six feet thick and composed of neatly dressed rectangular stone, common in Roman construction. The masonry walls above this foundation, however, reflected Barbarian, not Roman, techniques. The masonry grew more irregular the higher it went until it seemed no longer to be laid in layers. Barbarians did not cut but rather hammered stone. The resulting blocks proved too uneven to stack in anything approximating rows; each stone possessed its own unique shape.

Designs on the outer walls, which included a bell tower nearly 60 feet in height, were far more extraordinary than building techniques. Emphasis on color evinced Barbarian, not Roman, tastes. Colorful tile, brick, glass, stucco, and stone were embedded in otherwise plain, ponderous, irregular outer walls in arrays designed to reflect light: triangles, hexagons, six-petaled roses, spirals, and swastikas. A polished copper alloy dome covered the roof. This chaotic external mass of colorful splendor was matched by an equally sensational interior, the main hall of which was divided into three parts. Marble pillars separated the central nave from the aisles, which ran on either side of it. These pillars were apparently taken from pagan temples. Barbarians merged several different styles of white and black pillars and capitals to form the divisions. A distinctive mosaic graced each floor in these three areas. Only fragments of one now exist. According to Allen Temko, that mosaic took the "exquisite purity" of white, "curled [it] like surf against the black shores of great revolving patterns," and had it disappear in the mass "only to reappear in the turbulent centers of the mosaic as a foil for deep reds and burning yellows; white against black, then black against red, and red against white, with wild yellows floating between, tracing ingenious crosses of Christ the length of the nave."[1] Perforated stone slab windows were similarly colorful. Barbarians placed red, green, or white crystals in each perforation to suggest a bejeweled appearance. Purple frescoes of religious figures dominated the ceiling, which led to the gold-encrusted marble altar where relics of St. Stephen rested.

Principles reflected in the decoration and design of the Church of Stephen the Protomartyr were typical of Barbarian art and architecture. Barbarians lacked the Greek and Roman appreciation for harmony and proportion. Rather than view something as composed of several parts, they tended to consider each aspect separate. Designs were superimposed upon one another, layered but independent. Symmetry demanded two or more similar (if not identical) items to balance. The Barbarian conception of each item as unique made considerations of symmetry irrelevant. Styles of two railings joining together need not match just as the church of St. Stephen's pillars varied in style and color.

Nor did Barbarians revere purity of form. Although designs may have been exceedingly intricate, they generally were slightly—or more than slightly—askew. This was not simply a matter of technique. The exquisite craftsmanship of Barbarian goldsmiths testified to their ability to produce pure forms as did Barbarian iron technology, which was on a par with that of Rome. What they lacked was a compelling cultural reason to devote time, energy, and finances to achieve that sort of perfection. Barbarians threw few pots on a potter's wheel, choosing instead to hand-build them. Pots with small differences resulted. Barbarian coinage demonstrated a similar lack of uniformity and precision. Again, the question was not whether the Barbarians lacked the knowledge to make pure forms. They lived among Romans, took over Roman places, and viewed Roman artifacts. They even used Roman materials, dismantling symmetrical, visually stunning facilities and edifices to construct their own characteristic structures. Leaders of the early Barbarian successor kingdoms considered

---

[1]Allen Temko, *Notre-Dame of Paris. The Biography of a Cathedral* (New York: Viking Press, 1955): 39.

The Plow. This simple plow and the related swing plow were the predominant means for Barbarians to prepare farm land. Although the heavy, wheeled moldboard plow was known to them, few owned the eight oxen necessary to pull the ponderous tool through the dense northern soil.

themselves part of the Roman Empire, often took Roman names, and looked to Constantinople as the imperial capital. Unawareness or lack of access cannot account for their action.

Barbarians also took no pleasure in subtlety. They juxtaposed vivid colors as if each existed in its own space at its own time, as if each were separate and therefore would not—and could not—clash with adjoining colors or seem garish. Barbarians also appeared fascinated with abstract or geometrical design, and lines, often straight but sometimes curved, usually played an important part. Their art, architecture, and decoration exhibited very few circular elements.

Representations of holy or heavenly figures, however, especially in frescoes or mosaics, demonstrated a marked exception to the preceding statement. Roundness abounded in these portraits. Halos were extremely common and Barbarians usually portrayed religious men and women as having overly round heads. Exaggerated, large, rounded eyes peered out of the soft, nearly circular skulls of these larger-

Early Christian Art. This mosaic floor from a fifth-century Christian church demonstrates the Barbarians' disregard for the Greco-Roman virtues of balance, proportion, and harmony. Each panel is treated as if it were a separate picture; representations of animals and plants coexist with geometric designs, and the Barbarians refused any attempt to balance them. Although circular forms virtually disappeared from Barbarian secular life, they remained vital in early Christian art. Halos and other circular representations abound.

than-life, almost divine figures drawn to larger-than-life dimensions. Barbarian art, like religion, clearly made a distinction between the earthly world and heaven.

Religion: Christianity

Many Barbarians had become Christians almost as soon as they confronted the Roman Empire in the third, fourth, and fifth centuries. Christianity's emphasis on a personal bond between god and the individual through Christ appealed to Barbarians, who had structured their society according to similar sorts of bonds between individuals. The nature of Barbarian society itself encouraged conversion. If a king or chief converted, the personal bond between the ruler and his subordinates would dictate that they all convert to Christianity.

Controversy: Arianism

Arianism won over early Barbarian converts. The Franks proved the only major exception by converting directly to traditional Christianity. The Arianism of most Barbarian groups put them at odds with the church, which continued to uphold the Council of Nicaea. Despite agreement on the Nicene Creed, tensions persisted among the apostolic churches. Debating the importance of the apostle who formed each became one measure by which these bishoprics asserted their priority within church affairs. Rome claimed to be founded by Peter, traditionally known as Prince of the Apostles, and demanded preeminence. The apostolic churches in the east disagreed. Yet each contended that this split was of little consequence compared to the heresy of Arianism and they repeatedly called for action against their heretical occupiers. Just who was going to undertake that action and compel the Arians to submit to the Nicene Creed remained in question. Could an imperial entity emerge and create (or restore) hegemony? What was left of the Roman aristocracy also saw restoration of imperial rule as critical. Imperial rule justified their ownership of land and other property, which they had been forced to yield in some measure to the Barbarians.

Tension: Constantinople

Both the church and the remnants of the Roman aristocracy gained an advocate in Justin, emperor of the eastern Roman empire. Based in Constantinople, Justin had superb geographic advantages. Constantinople stood at the convergence of water and land routes joining Asia and Europe. It overlooked the Danube, the Black Sea, Asia Minor, and the Aegean Sea and as such was the single most important trading place in the world. Justin tried to capitalize on these advantages. He made peace with the Bishop of Rome and in 523 announced a law to exclude pagans, Jews, and heretics from public employment. This law, aimed at bolstering the spirits of his western supporters, was followed up by Justin's nephew, Justinian, four years later. Justinian launched a "Reconquest" of the west and attempted to create a grand Christian (not Arian) commonwealth. To a large degree, Justinian's crusade was successful. He freed North Africa, the former breadbasket of the empire, from the Vandals and restored the "rightful" heirs to their estates. The church received property otherwise unclaimed and immediately began to cleanse itself of North Africa's Arian hierarchy. A series of other conquests led Justinian's force to Italy where the Ostrogoths resisted for 20 years before falling. Yet the Justinian restoration was short-lived. By the 560s, a Barbarian group, the Lombards, had recaptured Italy and Rome.

Justinian had initiated this western reconquest by first reorganizing his empire. He had increased imperial control over administration, defense, finance, and commerce. He passionately systematized the bureaucracy, rooted out pagans and religious heretics, and sponsored religious conclaves. Among his most enduring acts was the codification of Roman law. Justinian's commission divided Roman law into four parts: (1) laws still in effect; (2) classical law as it had been modified over the centuries; (3) earlier opinions; and (4) new legislation, which now came from the emperor. He also expected to be treated as if he were a deity. Justinian loved pomp and took pleasure in requiring others to prostrate or debase themselves in front of him.

Division: Eastern and Western Christendom

Whatever Justinian's personal or psychological motives, his program exposed what had become a radical, irreconcilable split between the eastern and western churches. Cut off from the east and anchored in Rome, the western church had developed in the Augustinian tradition. It brooked no compromise between what Augustine called the kingdom of god and the kingdom of man. To the western church, the important lesson of Jesus' incarnation and resurrection was that heaven and earth were always distinct. Heaven was pure, pristine, and perfect. Earth was always inferior, even base, a place filled with temptation. Getting to heaven was a matter of faith and god's law, not the product of human ingenuity. Man should spend neither time nor effort in attempting to reconcile the temporal with the eternal world; the earthly world simply was not that important except as a way to enter heaven.

Through its actions, the eastern church rejected the Augustinian synthesis. In eastern Christianity, the kingdom of god on earth was a symbol of the kingdom of god in heaven. Continuity between heaven and earth existed, and, though it was to be god's kingdom on earth, eastern Christians tended to act as if it were man's kingdom in heaven. A blend of Hellenic philosophy and Christianity made heaven less a matter of faith and more a matter of rationality. A logic to heaven existed and a neo-Platonic Christianity looked to Greece and the Near East. Logic could be successfully applied to questions of Christian theology.

The Augustinian explanation held a certain resonance within Barbarian culture. Barbarian individualism made superfluous exactly those elements of Greek and Roman civilization that post-Augustinian western Christianity found extraneous. Greco-Roman literature and the humanities generally were temporal, not germane to the question of personal salvation. God was not a logical construction but a matter of faith. Even reading and writing were important only so long as they assisted the individual's heavenly quest. The few chronicles of the Barbarian kingdoms—the history of the Franks by Gregory of Tours and the later histories of the Lombards by Paul the Deacon and of the Anglo-Saxons by the Venerable Bede—were histories of the respective group's conversion to Christianity and/or the history of the church under the auspices of various kings; they were explicitly ecclesiastical, not literary or humanistic. Excessive concern about form and design, except in the production of works to praise god or to inspire others to learn the lessons of Christ, was more than irrelevant. It bordered on sinful.

Medicine

Approach to disease within Christian Barbarian culture manifested a profound emphasis on faith. Although the individual proved the locus of disease, illness came from possession, corruption, or co-option by an evil, otherworldly agent. This agent or the effects of this agent needed to be released to remove the pernicious influence and to restore health. Bloodletting was a common medical technique but its efficacy, like that of other "medical"—usually botanical—therapies, depended upon prayer, upon an individual's relationship to the deity. Medicinal plants were gathered to prayer on the first of each month. Opening a vein made it possible for an evil agent—worms, elf shot, and venom were often pinpointed as the cause of disease—to leave a body, but only faith and Christ's charity would see that it did. In that sense, healing was very much akin to Christianized trial by ordeal or oath. God intervened to protect—in this case restore—the individual. A Christian Barbarian "prescription" read:

> A drink for a fiend-sick man, when a devil possesses the man, or affects him from
> within with disease, to be drunk out of a church bell:
> Take githrife, yarrow, betony and also other worts; work up the drink with clear
> ale, sing seven masses over the worts, add garlic and holy water, and dip the drink into

every drink that he shall hereafter drink; and then let him drink it out of a church bell, and let the mass priest sing over him after he has drunk it: Domine sancte pater omnipotens, &c.

This sort of Christian medicine mimicked pagan Barbarian practice centuries old. In that animistic universe where plants, animals, and other natural phenomena had powers beyond those of humankind, magic squares or the number of letters in a name had taken on medicinal significance. An incantation to relieve an abscess from the right eye called on the victim to touch it with the fingers of the left hand, spit, and repeat three times:

The mule brings into the world no young, nor does the stone produce wool; so may this disease come to no head, or if it comes to a head, may it wither away.

Relics and shrines played a large part in Christian healing. Mortals had no medicine against Satan's hordes, and saints gained reputations for healing certain ills. St. Appolonia cured toothaches. St. Anthony healed the mute; St. Magnus, the blind; and St. Andreas, the halt. Pieces of the true cross might halt an epidemic. Gregory of Tours even considered it blasphemous to consult an earthly physician rather than pray at the shrine of St. Martin.

Muslims: The Emergence of Islam

At about the same time that tensions with the eastern empire receded, a threat emerged to challenge the west. By 650, Islam, a new religion and culture, had swept what had been the Persian empire and parts of the Roman empire. Islam had achieved unprecedented power and, over the next several centuries, became a persistent and repeated antagonist of both the west and the east. The relationship between Islam and the west, however, was far more complicated than one of simple enemies. An extensive and continual exposure to each other's culture took place during those hundreds of years. Islamic culture adeptly selected and used aspects of western culture almost from the beginning. On the other hand, the west determinedly ignored any possible contribution made by Islam. Its interests lay elsewhere.

Muhammad and the Tenets of Islam

The Islamic peoples rejected Augustinianism, so influential among the Barbarians, out of hand. At first glance, the abrupt dismissal of Augustinian sentiment in Islamic thought seems surprising because the prophet Muhammad, who introduced Islam in the early seventh century, offered a vision, like that of the ancient Hebrews and Christians, that stressed an uncompromising monotheism. It had great respect for Moses, Christ, and others as prophets but rejected any thought of Christ's divinity as inconsistent with monotheism. Muhammad recognized himself as god's supreme prophet but he repeatedly disavowed attempts to portray him as a god. Born in

Mecca in 570, Muhammad claimed that the archangel Gabriel told him to preach god's word and reform the polytheistic Arabs. Muhammad actively pursued his mission and demanded that the faithful submit to god's will, which is a rough translation of the word *Islam*.

Muhammad's declaration that individuals must submit to god's will on earth indicated that earthly life in Islam mattered much more and in a fundamentally different manner than it had for Augustine. No dichotomy existed between a city of god and a city of man, and Islam made no separation between religious law and civil law. All law came from god through his prophet Muhammad; earthly existence was entirely consistent with religious life, not antagonistic to it. Following god's will on earth—submitting to god's rules and doing god's bidding—gained one entrance to heaven. The nature of Islamic law further accentuated the differences with Augustinian Christianity. It dictated that the members of civil society acknowledge their mutual dependence in the quest to do god's will and that social arrangements reflect a sense of fairness.

Islamic Culture: Heaven and Earth

Individualism had no place in early Islamic thought. The Islamic social vision more closely evoked the Egyptian concept of maàt. Lack of separation between civil and religious society meant that rules for action in the earthly world became the measure for entering heaven. Because these rules came from god through Muhammad, subsequent leaders, or *caliphs* (which translates as successors to the prophet), had no doctrinal or legislative power; they could only enforce Muhammad-announced law. In addition, because Islam placed such great emphasis on serving god through social responsibility, then the means to achieve eternal life for oneself was through action that furthered the interests and activities of others.

The early Islamic idea of heaven was reminiscent of Egyptian thought but also suggestive of Sumerian influences. The Islamic afterlife very much took earthly existence as its template. Heaven stood as an idealized earth, a sort of Garden of Eden in which pleasure and comfort reigned. An enhanced earthlike reward greeted those Muslims who had performed admirably in their earthly incarnation.

These basic assumptions about the nature of existence and the possibility of afterlife ensured that the Muslims would be receptive to the collectivism of the Rome of the third century and earlier. It also made Hellenic and Hellenistic Greece familiar and worth embracing, especially neo-Platonic and Aristotelian elements. Muslims certainly had the opportunity to consider the ideas of these several cultures. As the Muslims moved on Egypt, they captured the Alexandrian library as well as other Greek material. Their initiatives against the eastern Roman empire seized from that entity some of its Greek and Roman writing, although the Muslim siege of the city of Constantinople ultimately failed in 717. Frequent warfare among the Muslims, the eastern empire, and the Barbarians produced awareness of the central tenets of each of these places as well as an interchange of ideas. For example, eighth-century Muslim religious buildings looked very much like their eastern empire counterparts. Classical styles—Hellenic Greek architecture—found a substantial niche in the Islamic-dominated world. Islamic culture reached the zenith of its infatuation with Greece and Rome between the eighth and tenth centuries. Muslim scholars translated

Muhammad's Ascent to Heaven. The early Islamic view of heaven was an idealized form of earthly life marked by opulence and pleasure. Entrance to heaven depended on doing Allah's bidding on earth.

Greek and Roman writings of all types into Arabic, which remained the Islamic language even as that culture accepted and integrated multitudes of diverse peoples, and studied these documents as important sources of information. They acted as if these documents emanated from a Muslim-like consciousness and so apparently took great pride in commenting on the text or even amending it to reflect better the author's sense of the problem or situation. But the subject of these documents also mattered. It was because these documents dealt with earthly existence, not some separate heavenly state, that they proved a potent attraction. Islamic culture refused to separate heaven from earth.

Saints and Popes: Western Monasticism

The intellectual cleavage between eastern and western Christianity had profound implications. Eastern Christianity would form the basis of and be incorporated into

Byzantine civilization. The west would grow in a different direction. Although many Barbarians remained Arians, their assumption of power had not hampered the western church. They permitted it the sanctity of continuing to operate under Roman law as it had since the time of Constantine. That persisting designation gave the western church a certain legitimacy of authority as well as the right to own and keep property. The amount of property in church possession greatly increased as the Empire fell, and the rate at which the church gained land perhaps even accelerated after Rome's collapse. The Augustinian injunction against too much wealth as a barrier to heaven contributed to the stepped-up giving as did the church's active solicitation of lands. Members of the former Roman aristocracy were among the heaviest givers. Surely they had the most to give. Unable to sustain their country villas, they deeded them to the church as monasteries. By the seventh century, monasteries were Europe's largest landholders and monks the most active and successful group engaged in land clearing.

This monastic boom reflected the further disintegration of established Roman-based institutions and social units as well as the increasing desire to abandon the temporal world to establish a personal relationship with the savior. The Rule of St. Benedict, promulgated about 540, attempted to organize monastic life to help individuals achieve their goal. Benedict recognized unregulated, disorderly monks as hampering individual and church ambitions and he established a new monastery governed by rules designed to further these ends. Benedict's monastery had a communal workshop to do "the work of God." Monks would establish there a library not of the works of classical antiquity as a whole but rather those works of classical antiquity related to Christ and the Christian church. But this workshop was communal only in the sense that monks sat in the same room. For the most part, each monk in the workshop read, studied, and reflected in silence as he pursued his individual task. Benedict also budgeted a certain daily period for manual labor. Invoking the concept that idle hands were the devil's workshop, he demanded that monks keep their hands busy when not engaged in "the Work of God." Yet Benedict recognized a second, equally compelling reason to have monks engage in manual labor. The ability to provide food and equipment for the monastery—to make it economically self-sufficient— would free it from outside influences; it could be truly separate from earthly society. Benedict reinforced that provision by stipulating that no one could leave the monastery without the express permission of the abbot, the monastery's head. Benedict permitted the monks to elect their own abbot but demanded that the abbot be consecrated by the bishop to ensure that he acted in accordance with church doctrine and remained independent of the monks.

Benedict's Rules became the model for western monasticism. In the seventh century monasteries added schools to teach novices reading and writing in preparation for their duties. But Benedict was hardly alone in formulating church procedures in harmony with Augustinian doctrine. In the wake of the collapse of the Justinian Reconquest, Rome as the only apostolic church in the west gained unprecedented power. Selected in 590, Pope Gregory I took advantage of the opportunity to reorganize the church, to merge weak bishoprics, with rich ones, to establish new bishoprics and to extend papal power. Gregory's reforms lasted some three centuries. He also called for the church to increase missionary work—the Arian Lombards controlled Italy—and to seek to bring the lessons of Christ to ever more people. In this

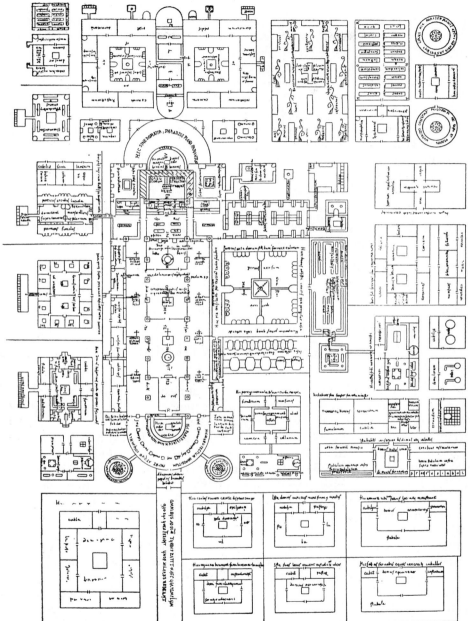

Plan for St. Gall, c. 820. Monasteries were self-sufficient islands in Barbarian Europe and took on a characteristic form. Much attention was given to providing for the monks' earthly necessities so that they were able to focus on spiritual concerns.

latter regard, Gregory urged missionaries to introduce Jesus' message of salvation, even at the expense of having to adopt some pagan or heathen forms. Such was the case with statues and other images. Gregory understood the injunction against worshiping images but just as clearly realized their utility in converting souls. He chided one cleric for destroying Christian-themed images because they permitted those "ignorant of letters . . . [to] read by looking at the walls what they cannot read in books." The proper course, he maintained, was to have "preserved the images and prohibited the people from adoration of them."

Gregory was also straightforward in his assessment of the duties of priests. He called them "rulers of the soul" and argued that they must be living guides to their parishioners. In fact, Gregory called for them to function for the soul in much the same way that Barbarian kings or chiefs functioned for civil society. Personal bonds of admiration and loyalty were to bind parishioners to their pastors and pastors to their bishops. A ruler of the soul

> should always be a leader in action, that by his living he may point out the way of life of those who are put under him, and that the flock, which follows the voice and manners of the shepherd, may learn how to walk rather through example than through words.

Carolingian Franks: Consolidation, Decline, and Rebirth of the West

At the end of the seventh century, the Catholic Franks gained new vigor under Pepin of Heristal, who seized power from the previous family of Frankish leaders to establish what historians call the Carolingian dynasty. Pepin's son and grandson, Charles the Hammer and Pepin the Short, gradually expanded the Frankish realm by stopping and then beating back the Islamic incursion into what is now France from Spain and North Africa in 732 and by making significant inroads toward conquering other Barbarian tribes. The latter Pepin's defense of the Bishop of Rome against the Arian Lombards had led the Pope to reward Pepin by officially joining in him religious and civil authority and anointing him King of the Franks. Pepin's son, Charlemagne (Charles the Great), destroyed the Lombard kingdom and declared himself sovereign over that territory, dominated most of what would become Germany, conquered and Christianized the Anglo-Saxons in modern Britain and seized much of Spain. Then, on Christmas Day 800, Pope Leo acknowledged Charlemagne's ascendancy as well as the church's dependence on the monarch by declaring the Barbarian chief Roman Emperor. The Pope's act codified a situation that had existed earlier. The devoutly Christian Charlemagne attempted to rule his earthly province to reflect glory on god and god's church. A rigorous cleansing of church doctrine, practice, and procedures resulted. Charlemagne demanded a clergy learned in church matters and capable of reading and understanding documents of the holy fathers. This rebirth of interest in material from Greek and Roman antiquity, commonly known as the Carolingian

Charlemagne. By far, the most commanding figure in eighth- and ninth-century Europe, Charlemagne gained the Pope's gratitude and the title Emperor of the Romans by freeing the Vatican from the influence of other Barbarian tribes.

Renaissance, persisted after Charlemagne's death as his descendants continued the program for nearly another half-century.

Consolidation: Military Conquest

The Carolingians' effective use of a horse cavalry helped the Franks gain control of much of western Europe. Many Carolingian horsemen rode on flat saddles with their feet fixed in leather straps descending from the saddle. These primitive stirrups appeared in Europe by the beginning of the eighth century and enabled men not expert in horsemanship to maneuver on their steeds effectively. On these relatively stable platforms, even horsemen with modest skills possessed the ability to thrust or swing a weapon. A hardwood, metal-headed lance to thrust under an infantryman's shield or armor emerged as the standard cavalry weapon, although swords and battle-axes also had their place.

The Carolingian cavalry never replaced or even supplanted the infantry. Horses were expensive to maintain and horse soldiers costly to equip. As significant, horses proved useful for only certain types of combat and environmental conditions. For these reasons, the vast majority of Carolingian forces traveled and fought on foot. The lance emerged as a common infantry weapon about 800; at about that time, the Carolingians mandated that all infantry soldiers possess a minimum of rounded, concave wooden shields reinforced with metal strips. Lances and shields were the least expensive armor and weaponry. Helmets, first leather and then segmented metal, cost on average three times as much as shields and lances together. A cuirass, a heavy leather jacket that reached to the hips and had metal scales sown on it, cost nearly twice as much as a helmet. During Charlemagne's reign, horsemen were expected to own a full complement of weapons and armor.

Consolidation: Social Organization and the Carolingian Dynasty

The Carolingian passionate embrace of the Barbarian tradition of vassalage provides a compelling explanation for that royal family's rise and subsequent domination. They capitalized on the ideas that a kingdom constituted private property and that individuals could enter into lifelong contracts with reciprocal obligations. Vassalage worked this way: Kings willed kingdoms to their sons upon death. (The Carolingians and others split the kingdom equally among the sons and then allowed each to pursue his destiny.) Sons gained power and cemented alliances by lending parts of their land to powerful individuals during a sacred ritual in return for obedience and homage, which included financial and military support. These land grants, called *benefices*, often reached thousands of acres and were temporary, ending with the demise of either party; land reverted to the sovereign upon a vassal's death or to a sovereign's sons upon his death. Carolingians increased the family's influence and might by increasing the amount of land in the kingdom and the number of vassals in their service. They confiscated church land to support additional vassals, which enabled the Carolingians to conquer new territory and use it to create even more benefices. Charlemagne added an oath of fealty to the mix. This created a bond between Charlemagne and each Frank through his vassals. In return for an oath of loyalty and military and judicial obligations, each free Frank could live and work on a benefice—land enough to support the free man's family—then in possession of one of Charlemagne's vassals.

These vassal-controlled enclaves also provided for their residents' defense. Barbarians used neither towers nor walls for defense—therefore they did not need or employ Roman siege weaponry or any other types of catapults—but relied instead on inaccessibility of location. High places, isolated buttes, earthen ramparts, and stacked stones and wood sufficed.

Decline: Drawing Inward

The Carolingians, especially Charlemagne, had sought to organize and standardize interactions among the empire's many residents. These efforts failed, almost without exception. True, military equipment and weaponry became more uniform, but attempts to establish a uniform coinage or system of weights and measures proved impossible. Civilization continued to draw within itself—trade outside the empire was deemed treasonous—and to divide itself into small units. The city of Rome, with a population of less than 20,000 under Charlemagne, was by far the largest place in the West. Small farms, villas, and monasteries became the predominant form of social organization. Each had considerable autonomy, even if they were benefices and even as Charlemagne's census takers regularly reported on and exacted a percentage of the products there. Within the context of small, agriculturally based enclaves, considerable variation reigned.

Rural Life: Manors and Monasteries

Rural life on great estates, whether benefices, monasteries, or privately held land, began as it had in Roman times, with the manor house. But manor houses built during Roman rule or even as late as the seventh century rarely continued in use. Carolingians usually did not rebuild manor houses on the same site. In contrast to the placement of churches in cities, manor houses and their surrounding outbuildings were relocated from time to time. Manor houses built under the Carolingians were simpler than early efforts. These stone-based houses had wooden uppers, cellars, and porticoes. A hedge with a stone gate often surrounded them and separated them from the outbuildings, which were often also enclosed. Hedges, low walls, or embankments and especially fences woven of hazel separated these areas. Outbuildings included furniture repositories, kitchens, bakeries, winepresses, cow sheds, stables, sheepfolds, pigsties, and haylofts. Courtyards and fishponds also were common. Houses of poorer persons were situated farther distant on these unwalled estates. The vast majority of people lived in cob-walled or timber-framed, wooden lath–latticed, mud-daubed huts as little as six feet wide and six feet in length with thatched roofs—sometimes buttressed—reaching to the ground. Often they lived there with their animals. The Carolingian poor furnished these single-room, sometimes hearthless dwellings with beds and meal tables with cloth-covered benches. Unlike the Romans, these men and women ate from plates, not bowls, and drank from goblets, and sat rather than reclined while eating. Soup—boiled meat with bread—proved the meal of choice as Carolingians gravitated to heavy fatty foods, such as bacon, smoked meat, sausage, butter, bread, milk, and cheese. A pot belly signified health and physical soundness, even divine favor, and Carolingians aspired to that station. Rude noises frequently accompanied the fat-laden diet.

Possessions and daily activities were markedly different among those living in the manor houses and in the huts. Occupants of a manor house lived in relative luxury. They slept on feather mattresses with down pillows and sheets. Wooden chests decorated tapestry-draped boudoirs. Throne-like chairs were reserved for the head of the house and his lady. Pitchers and pottery adorned with squares and triangles graced the premises, which were lit by candelabras or lamps fueled by fish, whale, poppy, or olive oil. Individuals bathed weekly in their own private bath tanks rather than in collective or public baths. The poor lived much more modestly, a condition reflected in their clothing. Tunics covered hooded linen shirts. Legs were wrapped with cloth torn in narrow strips, while heavy shoes protected feet.

It was on these people that the activities that constituted daily life descended. Two main groups of people distinguished by their relative status and freedom provided labor. Coloni did certain tasks on a regular basis and were deemed to have entered into a contract as free and equal parties. The second group, serf-like persons, owed a master labor for a specified period per week. The master decided what the person would do. The pattern of deference established by this unspoken contract indicated a subservient relationship between those in charge of the estate and those "hired" as "general laborers."

These rural units were agriculture-based, and a rigid, gender-based separation developed. Women did domestic chores. They baked bread, maintained the hearth, gathered wood, fed chickens, and tended kitchen gardens. Women ground the family's grain on saddle or hand querns. They also sewed garments, combed and spun wool, wove linen, and dyed cloth. Women in monasteries lived in separate enclosures, generally surrounded by hedges and gated. While women were responsible for household operations, men had primary responsibility for agriculture. No single pattern of agricultural practice dominated as crop rotations ranged from annual to triennial. A common Northern European rotation had workers pruning vines and sending animals to pasture in early spring, collecting forage and plowing in mid-spring, and sowing seeds and harrowing them to protect them from birds in late spring. They then harvested the hay and grain and collected and pressed grapes in early fall, threshed the grain and placed wine in barrels in November, and slaughtered pigs in December. Plowing, which permitted release of essential plant nutrients, was the primary means to increase field fertility. A few Carolingians probably used moldboard plows, sometimes with metal-capped plowshares, to turn the dense soil. These plows required a considerable capital investment since iron was expensive and several draft animals were needed to drag the ponderous implement through the heavy soil and thick turf. A simple plow would neither encounter the soil resistance nor create as deep a furrow as the moldboard plow, but, aided by a spade-wielding farmer, would turn the soil almost as well and at much reduced cost. This latter form of plowing seems to have been the norm for individuals living as coloni or serfs. Extensive evidence exists that Carolingians plowed their lands individually. They rarely pooled labor or equipment; few outside a villa manager or abbot would have had the resources necessary to make that kind of massive commitment. In addition to the land he worked for the estate, each individual living on a villa or monastery received a plot of ground to work himself to support his family. His success or failure was a matter of individual initiative. So too was the selection of the means to achieve it. Selecting annual crop rotations or a three-field system with spring and fall grain remained an individual's prerogative.

The virtual absence of trade required men and women living on estates to produce everything they needed to live. But Carolingians often went further than mere self-sufficiency. They required estates to manufacture goods and offer services in support of the king or the army. For both of these reasons, estates were the sites of a great many small-scale manufactures. A wide diversity of artisans practiced their trades.

They produced farm implements, barrels, fishing tackle, hunting weapons, parchment, and leather. They also built buildings and churches, taking care to make drawings and often build scale models prior to construction. On some of the largest monasteries, artisans did little more than ply their trades. They lived together, separate from the agricultural workers, and labored in large rooms, not distinguished by task. Parchment makers, carpenters, shoemakers, saddlers, harness makers, polishers, furbishers, turners, joiners, shieldmakers, painters, enamelers, sculptors, and cabinetmakers worked side-by-side.

Smelting, pelting, fulling, lead working, and goldsmithing required plenty of fresh air and generally occurred outdoors. Of these outdoor activities, blacksmithing held a special place. Blacksmiths seemed sorcerers, capable of transforming one material into another. Their hammers produced church bells as well as swords and plowshares. Emphasis on mysticism and magic, traditional pagan custom, extended to Charlemagne, a most reverent king. He wore a crystal talisman around his neck. Others in his retinue wore belt buckles emblazed with geometric designs to ward off evil and associated certain herbs with good luck. The church condoned most of these common magical practices because they aimed to combat a wicked earthly existence—certainly in line with the Augustinian program. The church thus attempted to Christianize magic and mysticism rather than rid them from Carolingian life. In this new view, churches became sacred enclosures with devils swarming outside. Church bells demarcated church time and holy days. The pagan practice of singing became a church staple as monks and others sang Gregorian or plainchant to open the individual mind to the contemplation of god. The blessed virgin was identified with the rose, dove, house, and lily and as a queen, spouse, and friend of the faithful. Some days became holier than others. The church designated a full forty days, in addition to the weekly Sabbath, as holy and mandated the performance of special rituals on those special days. Numerology also assumed prominence. Palm Sunday mass began at the third hour of the day as marked by the monastery water clock. The service started with three choirs singing and three crosses being raised. Three censors led the procession and were followed by seven crosses, seven deacons, seven subdeacons, seven acolytes, seven exorcists, seven readers, seven porters, and then monks in seven-by-seven formation. These monks bore the seven gifts of the holy ghost. A similar mysticism pervaded church marital doctrine. The church forbade sex between husband and wife, according to historian Pierre Riche, during "forty days before Christmas, forty days before Easter and eight days after Pentecost; the eve of great feasts, Sundays, Wednesdays, and Fridays; during the wife's pregnancy and until thirty days after she has given birth if it was a boy and forty days if it was a girl; during the menstrual period; five days before taking communion."[2]

Rebirth: The Carolingian Renaissance

St. Augustine was especially meaningful to Charlemagne, who had the saint's writings read to him during meals. Charlemagne apparently took quite seriously Augustine's

[2]Pierre Riche, *Daily Life in the World of Charlemagne*. Trans. Jo Ann McNamara (Philadelphia: University of Pennsylvania Press, 1978): 51, 240–41.

injunction that the earthly world was base and inferior to the city of god but could prepare souls for salvation after death. As important, Charlemagne believed it was a king's god-given duty to shape earthly existence to that end. He recognized the king as responsible to the bishops, who received the keys to heaven from god, but Charlemagne also realized that misunderstandings of and additions to ecclesiastical law, which was inspired by the Holy Spirit and dictated by church fathers, had corrupted that law. Through his advisors, Charlemagne knew firsthand of significant differences among Roman, English, and Gallic church law and practice. Many of his vassals had been trained in the tradition of the Venerable Bede, who, in the course of his work of Christianizing the English heathen, regularly cited passages of the Bible and church fathers out of context. To Bede and many others in the eighth and ninth centuries, the words themselves seemed holy and magical; it was their connection to church fathers and ultimately to god that made these words potent, not their interpretation or meaning. That understanding permitted Bede to roundly ignore the issue of trying to determine exactly what church fathers had meant and to routinely use their words for purposes other than those the church fathers intended.

Purification of Church Texts

Realization of the divinity of the material led Charlemagne to embark upon a multi-pronged program to reestablish the church liturgy, preaching, and calendar to reflect Christ's goal, the possibility of human salvation. Charlemagne's central initiative capitalized on an already flourishing monastic movement—400 monasteries had been formed by A.D. 750 as individuals fled earthly existence for individual solitude—to create numerous new monasteries devoted to determining the accurate textual interpretation of church books from their earliest Greco-Roman sources. In these isolated religious units, churchmen trained in doctrine could pore over manuscripts and interpretations of manuscripts to develop the "true" teachings of Christ and his church.

This plan was not nearly as sterile as it sounded. Churchmen needed to prepare themselves to evaluate and understand the classical biblical texts. Learning Greek and Latin were two obvious skills required for these tasks but setting movable feast days necessitated a return to classical astronomical texts. Designing these monasteries with workshops, bloodletting rooms, and hypocausts required churchmen to translate and explore Greco-Roman mechanical, technical, and medical texts. The actual construction of these edifices also led Carolingians back to the Romans. Vitruvius emerged as a favorite.

Few forms of Greco-Roman learning seemed inappropriate for this heaven-oriented task. Yet it would be a complete mistake to assume that the Carolingians accepted Greco-Roman learning whole or that they accepted it in the way that the Greeks or Romans conceived of it. Nothing could have been further from the truth. Assumptions and explanations were Carolingian and Christian, not Greek or Roman. The situation was most clear in Christian architecture, which, despite knowledge of Vitruvius, depended upon religious and magical elements. Even churches themselves were generally shaped like crucifixes. Walled monasteries, the archetypical effort to separate the individual from society and from the debased earthly world, provide an even more dramatic example. The Carolingians established a master plan to structure these monasteries, and sacred numbers—3, 4, 7, 10, 12, and 40—constituted the basic units for what was a modular design. The number 3 symbolized the trinity, a most sacred number. The number 4 represented the four horsemen of the apocalypse or the four humours (which represented the natural world), while 7 represented either the number of days it took god to create the universe, the seven virtues, or the seven sacraments. The number 10 stood for the ten commandments or for "perfection, in an even fuller sense because it is composed of the number seven, which embraces all created things, and the number three which stands for the holy trinity." The number of tribes of Israel and the number of apostles made 12 holy, and 40 represented either the number of days of the Noahic Flood or the years Moses spent in the desert. To St. Augustine, sacred numerology reflected god's greatness and helped each individual learn the lessons of and road to salvation. "In many passages of sacred scripture," Augustine maintained that "numbers have a meaning for the conscientious interpreter. Not without reason has it been said to praise god: Thou hast ordered all things in measure, number and weight." In a world such as this, Vitruvian ratios and relationships sometimes had no or even a pagan meaning. Rather than further building, Vitruvius's writings could seem to hamper or to be antithetical to Christian construction.

It bears noting that Greek and Roman manuscripts, both of the church fathers and their secular counterparts, existed in abundant supply for Charlemagne's churchmen. Libraries and monasteries had long preserved this heretofore little used material. That few if any had read it over the course of centuries was a matter of choice, not availability. Much of this material, especially the secular writings, seemed out-of-step with Barbarian culture, not germane or central. Only when a specific set of questions were asked did this material become relevant and then in a context totally at odds with its Greek and Roman origins. Put another way, interest in the Greco-Roman liberal arts was not the end but the means. Carolingians had no use for pagan-inspired classical humanism except as a way to achieve Christian wisdom. Indeed, some Latin and Greek writers were rejected as pernicious influences, dangers to the faith.

Salvation through Religious Education

The Carolingian religious program did not end with purification of the church and its law. Utility of the earthly world lay in its preparation for the next and Charlemagne took as his duty converting heathens. He recognized that this could best be accomplished by having a trained clergy live among heathens and, like Gregory the Great, St. Benedict, and the Venerable Bede before him, Charlemagne demanded that these clergymen become adept at presenting their case. Emphasis on oration, rhetoric, and elocution led to an increased interest in pagan masters of these skills—men such as Cicero and Seneca—as did the other thrust of the Carolingian program. To enable more individuals to find the road to salvation, Charlemagne mandated creation of episcopal and monastery schools to forge a religiously educated laymenry. He decreed "that schools be established where children can learn to read; that psalms, notation, chant, computation and grammar should be taught in every monastery and bishopric and that these institutions should obtain carefully copied [religious] books." Meditation over religious literature would no doubt unlock the secrets of heaven.

Creating a religiously educated population necessitated production of numerous copies of the crucial documents, those same documents that had been the focus of the purification campaign. Monasteries generally undertook that task. Over 8,000 manuscripts produced during the end of the eighth and beginning of the ninth centuries exist today. Copyists spent up to three months reproducing a normal-sized manuscript. Copying the complete works of Cicero required the parchment made from an entire flock of sheep. Parchment leaves resting on virtually any flat surface, horns of ink, quills, and erasing knives littered the inside of every scriptorium. Copyists, correctors, rubicators, painters, illuminators, and binders worked silently side-by-side. The copying process began with parchment making. Agricultural workers skinned calves or sheep, soaked the skins in lime for several days, stretched and

Carolingian Renaissance. Charlemagne demonstrated his devotion to the church by working to cleanse its litany. A spate of schools and other institutions of learning emerged to help in the effort. Ornate decorations on church manuscripts emphasized the teachings of church fathers.

scraped both sides of the skins, and then cut them into folios, taking care to tinge them purple. After the copyist, rubicator, and corrector plied their trades, important manuscripts went to painters and illuminators and then to binders, who might use cover plates of gold embedded with gems.

Christianity and Daily Life

Charlemagne also attempted to bring church principles into everyday life. To Charlemagne and his English-trained religious advisors, Christ's visitation and resurrection had fundamentally changed the world. Bede himself buttressed this notion when he introduced into the west the idea of marking time from the year of Christ's birth. This concept had been first proposed by a Greek and its expression by Bede was not to diminish the essential timelessness that characterized the early Middle Ages. Much as it always had been, time continued to be marked in the year of an emperor's reign. But under Bede's modification, the emperor of importance was not earthly but heavenly. It was the reign of god that now was chronicled. In that spirit, Charlemagne accepted his responsibility as god's servant and set about governing his earthly kingdom according to Christian practice. The church established each soul as distinct and each person as having opportunity for eternal redemption. Individuals shaped their lives and, when they approached death, worried about how to square accounts with god. The power and social position of each individual established a value for that individual's soul. This sort of Christian wergeld became the basis of what one paid the church to secure salvation. Although the church stressed prayer, solitude, and silence—contemplation—guilt, penance, and similar feelings of remorse were not necessary. The individual needed to acknowledge his sins—the number of times he violated god's rules—and then to pay the penalty appropriate to the number and severity of his transgressions. Fear of the power of eternal damnation demanded that the wergeld be paid, often in the form of land for a monastery. Charlemagne translated the divine concept of a Christian wergeld into earthly justice. He prohibited money lent at interest as a violation of god's property—god owned time. To accept money for time was to expropriate god's property. He also issued legislation prohibiting murder, divorce, and polygamy, and set just prices for the staples of grain and bread. These empirewide dictates were followed more in theory than in practice. They nonetheless reflect the Carolingian commitment to create a city of man that reflected the city of god.

Christianity and Slavery

The Carolingian acceleration of slave emancipations reflected similar themes. Barbarians generally had emancipated slaves in impressive numbers. These manumissions were not punitive; they did not seek to repudiate slave debt. But most emancipations stipulated that the former slave gained "freedom with obedience." Such a freed person owed his or her former master continued but now specified service; bond between master and slave remained firmly in place. The Carolingian and general Barbarian trend to this sort of conditional emancipation did not stem from church opposition to slavery. Augustinian Christianity viewed slavery as entirely consistent with a debased earthly existence. In fact, churchmen maintained that slavery resulted from original sin. It was "not nature, not god, who made slaves. It was man." Slavery was, according to Isidore of Seville in the sixth century, "a chastisement inflicted on humanity by the sin of the first (hu)man(s)." As early as the fourth century, the church had mandated that anyone leading a slave "to despise his master, to remove himself from slavery, to not serve with good will and respect," would be cursed and excommunicated.

What struck churchmen as more problematic was the ownership of Christians. Charlemagne himself forbade the sale of Christian slaves to pagans, Muslims, or Jews. But what about Christian slaves being owned by other Christians? If all Christians were equal in the sight of god, might it not be wrong for one Christian to own another? "Freedom with obedience" solved that dilemma, establishing a relationship not unlike Barbarian vassalage. Another resolution, again in line with Augustinian Christianity, was to will slaves to the church as part of a Christian wergeld. The church itself could accept Christian slaves. Humanity, after all, was owned by god; humankind were all slaves of god. The result was that the church became easily the largest owner of Christian slaves in Carolingian Europe.

Charlemagne's Successors: Fragmentation and Disintegration of the West

In Frankish fashion, Charlemagne's property—his kingdom—became the property of his sons upon his death in 814. His sons, grandsons, and great-grandsons, especially Louis the Pious, Charles the Bald, Louis the Stammerer, and Charles the Fat, attempted to maintain the Carolingian program and kingdom, which under Charlemagne was equivalent in area to the Roman Empire. They had little success sustaining either beyond the next few decades. Two major factors contributed to the demise. First and perhaps most important, those individuals to whom Charlemagne and his descendants entrusted their personal property—the kingdom composed of estates— did not always abide by the terms of their agreements. Vassals increasingly refused to return the benefices to the throne upon the death of a king or even to pay taxes or fulfill imperial military obligations. The later Carolingians proved unwilling or unable to stop this disintegration. The usurpers, each of whom had been a trusted Carolingian ally, now emerged as lords within the confines of their ill-gotten estates. They established themselves as a hereditary—not rotating—aristocracy. All authority within the estates came from them and they acquired certain specific obligations to manorial residents. Similarly, residents owed their new lords labor in return for their rights. As historian Georges Duby noted, this process was nothing less than the "fragmentation of authority into a host of autonomous cells. In each of these, a master held as his private right, the power to command and to punish. He exploited this power as part of his hereditary patrimony."[3]

Although well under way by 840, the Viking invasions and plundering of the next several decades further fueled the collapse. The pagan Norsemen sailed from Scandinavia on long ships and attacked estates and churches on their way. These mobile

[3]Duby is quoted in Paul Veyne, ed., *A History of Private Life: From Pagan Rome to Byzantium* (Cambridge, MA: Harvard University Press, 1987): 429.

marauders had reputations for cruelty and sought wealth, not occupation. They sacked monasteries as well, took their gold and silver, and often set them ablaze. Many clergymen maintained that the Viking assaults were the direct consequence of sin on the part of those attacked; it was divine retribution for unchristian living. The Carolingians did not respond as one to the Viking attacks, which they did not interpret as a threat to their collective selves. The Carolingian kings recognized their duty to Christianize heathens and maintain power, but not to protect individuals or even collections of individuals. They possessed little notion of themselves as a people, of having some kind of hereditary, emotional, biological, or cultural link binding together the geographic area they once controlled. They only protected their possessions and abided by contracts. But since the usurpers had violated terms of contracts, they could not anticipate help from the Carolingians. Carolingians and Barbarians generally would rather pursue personal vendettas than unite against a common foe.

As a consequence, each estate, church, or monastery was left to its own devices. In practical terms, each was to fend off invaders as best it could, and several built ditch and rampart fortifications and even castle-like structures. But with the responsibility of each estate to defend itself, little reason appeared to exist for estates still allied with the Carolingians to continue to defer to a family that offered them almost nothing.

The further disintegration of Carolingian society created new classes of persons. The foremost was the woodsmen. These men, formerly prominent in the Carolingian system, now shunned formal living arrangements to live in the wild. Late ninth-century men and women claimed that brigands populated the forests, waiting to attack unsuspecting individuals and beggars gathered at the boundaries of every estate. Individuation reigned supreme.

For Further Reading

Bloch, Marc. *Slavery and Serfdom in the Middle Ages.* Trans. William R. Beer. Berkeley: University of California Press, 1975.

Boussard, Jacques. *The Civilization of Charlemagne.* Trans. Frances Partridge. New York: McGraw-Hill, 1976.

Chapelot, Jean, and Robert Fossier. *The Village and the House in the Middle Ages.* Trans. Henry Cleere. London: B. T. Batsford, 1985.

Contamine, Philippe. *War in the Middle Ages.* Trans. Michael Jones. Oxford: Basil Blackwell, 1984.

DeVries, Kelly. *Medieval Military Technology.* Petersborough, Canada: Broadview Press, 1992.

Drew, Katherine Fisher. *Laws of the Salian Franks.* Philadelphia: University of Pennsylvania Press, 1991.

———. *The Burgundian Code.* Philadelphia: University of Pennsylvania Press, 1972.

———. *The Lombard Laws.* Philadelphia: University of Pennsylvania Press, 1973.

Fichtenau, Heinrich. *The Carolingian Empire: The Age of Charlemagne.* Trans. Peter Munz. New York: Harper Torchbooks, 1964.

Geanakopos, Deno J. *Medieval Western Civilization and the Byzantine and Islamic Worlds.* Lexington, Mass: D. C. Heath and Co., 1979.

Goffart, Walter. *The Narrators of Barbarian History (A.D. 550-800).* (Princeton: Princeton University Press, 1988.

Latouche, Robert. *The Birth of the Western Economy.* New York: Harper Torchbooks, 1961.

Riche, Pierre. *Daily Life in the World of Charlemagne.* Trans. Jo Ann McNamara. Philadelphia: University of Pennsylvania Press, 1978.

————. *Education and Culture in the Barbarian West, Sixth through Eighth Centuries.* Trans. John J. Contreni. Columbia, S.C.: University of South Carolina Press, 1976.

Robinson, Victor. *The Story of Medicine.* New York: Tudor, 1931.

Todd, Malcolm. *Everyday Life of the Barbarians.* New York: G. P. Putnam's Sons, 1972.

Wallace-Hadrill, J. M. *The Barbarian West.* New York: Harper and Brothers, 1962.

Wemple, Suzanne Fonay. *Women in Frankish Society: Marriage and the Cloister, 500 to 900.* Philadelphia: University of Pennsylvania Press, 1981.

Wolfram, Herwig. *History of the Goths.* Trans. Thomas J. Dunlap. Berkeley: University of California Press, 1988.

CHAPTER 6

Romanesque Search for Identity: From Individual to Group, 850-1150

As death approached on September 11, 910, William, Duke of Aquitaine, ceded some possessions to the church. He had conventional reasons for doing so. God, William argued, made men rich so that they could use "well their temporal possessions . . . to merit eternal rewards." To that end, William's impending demise made it "absolutely necessary" to "provide for my own safety" in the afterlife by now giving "some portion for the good of my soul." He expected to enter heaven, to "receive the reward of the righteous," not because he had led a life of virtue or because he had seen the errors of his ways and was now ready to assume a virtuous posture. In fact, he admitted that even at this late date and even with his immortal soul in the balance, "I myself am not able to despise" material possessions and to embrace Christ's poor. He would go to heaven simply by funding creation of a house for those "righteous and who despise the world" and having the monastic brothers "diligently direct to God prayers and exhortations . . . for me." William would buy his eternal salvation.

William followed in the tradition of a Christian wergeld. Each individual could be absolved of his or her church-stipulated sins simply by paying the church the requisite amount. But William's tacit admission that he should have been able to shun the material world suggested the slightest glimmer of what we call conscience, a belief that forces and values set by human beings other than himself were what William ought to be measured against. That William failed to measure up to this standard was perhaps regrettable, but the real significance is that he felt a twinge of guilt or perhaps sadness for not being able to achieve that standard. William had undergone the most rudimentary internal self-policing according to the standards of the Christian community. He did not need external sanction to judge him in error. William looked inside himself, recognized his shortcomings, and expressed the smallest whisper of remorse for them.

A similar sense of internalizing and accepting as the norm the commonly defined criteria of others beyond the individual also pervaded secular affairs. The Truce and Peace of God movements in the late tenth and eleventh centuries reflected not the power of some earthly prince or even the authority of an ecclesiastical potentate but a community-based expression of what constituted appropriate behavior within community-defined space. Churches served as seeds around which small groups of parishioners crystallized and declared surrounding areas off limits to any violent activity. Stressing "friendship" and "concord," these men and women swore common oaths to uphold the peace within community-defined regions. Each community acted as if its members were a single individual, maintaining that a threat to one was a threat to all, and established penalties for anyone violating the peace. Violators were expelled from the community and excommunicated from the church, and their fiefs passed to heirs. If heirs aided notorious kin in any way, they forfeited their land; the terms of the truce and peace made commitment to the whole greater than kinship ties. These groups made the nature of this union clear. Its authority to punish disturbers of the peace came not from "counts, centenaries, or officials" but from "the whole people in common."

An epidemic of attacks from marauding knights on peasants, women, and churchmen was said to have been the genesis for the truce and peace movements. But the important thing about the truce and peace movements was not whether Europe suffered an increase in knightly mayhem but that knightly mayhem and other types of disruptive activity had become socially unacceptable. Attacks on the defenseless and on holy days now violated social norms and were not to be tolerated. Reliance on the community to establish these norms and to act on them indicated that its members comprehended their essential unity; they understood that when it came to social affairs they constituted a group.

Personal identification of individuals as group members was a radical reconception. To be sure, individuals had acted collectively earlier. But the nature of earlier unions was different. Individual might, whether physical prowess or the power of one person over another, had forged union, while fear of eternal damnation had provided the unifying religious principle. Certainly Christianity and the church remained influential in this new world as the connection between heaven and earth persisted as a fundamental focus. But now individuals relinquished their autonomy and prerogatives not to more powerful persons but to others like themselves, to abide by rules set by the group.

Shift from individual to group, then, marked an important phase in western civilization. A collective conscience, the internalization of group norms, most often expressed in social regulations and moral codes, was a manifestation of that sentiment. As many of these men and women searched the fund of human experience for guidance, it was not surprising that they discovered the Roman Republic, which they immediately viewed with admiration and affection. They attempted to learn from that civilization and to adopt only those features consistent with Christianity, hoping to make their world Rome-like, or Romanesque. As it had in the Roman Republic, the metaphor of the family often expressed the new attitude toward relationships. It suggested strong familial bonds, tenacious and emotional bonds, not simply products of power. This critical shift did not occur neatly. Europeans confronted such questions as what constituted legitimate groups (or more simply what made a group a group), what was a community, and what were the limits of the bonds between community members. Similarly, they faced issues of leadership: Who leads and according to what grounds? Few asked these leadership or group questions directly. Yet the interpretation of these issues played a crucial role in designing the new society of the tenth, eleventh, and early twelfth centuries. These men and women replaced what had come to be seen as outdated institutional and social structures with others more in line with their new notions.

Land Ownership

Attacks in the ninth and tenth centuries by Muslims from North Africa, Spain, and southern Gaul and by the Magyars from the East further hastened the Carolingian empire's disintegration. Land formerly held as Carolingian benefices fell into private hands. Even some church and monastery lands left church control. Low-ranking members of what had been the Carolingian bureaucracy sometimes defended monasteries and churches but seized their lands as benefices to support the necessary military forces. Freehold land, where individual families farmed without outside assistance, became more common, as did lands leased by freemen for specified periods, but the vast majority of land remained in the hands of large landholders. Carolingian dukes, marquises, and counts, titles for officials who had administered large areas in the empire, and their descendants best withstood the fragmentation and seized much of the Carolingian land as their own. They used these huge parcels to secure vassals, who usually continued the chain of tenure to create vassals of their own. But fiefs need not have been land. A lord could grant a

End of the Carolingian Empire. A series of invasions collapsed the empire and ended the Carolingian Renaissance within one-half century of Charlemagne's death. Marauding bands attacked with impunity, and no nobles rushed to the defense of their fellow nobles.

right, a power, an office, or a specific payment on a regular basis as a benefice. By the tenth century, these and land fiefs were essentially hereditary. Custom dictated that the lord make his vassal the heir of his former vassal and grant him the same benefice.

Although these arrangements suggest stability in land ownership and use, an incredible amount of experimentation and new initiatives marked the centuries after the fall of the Carolingians. Lords abandoned cultivated land in the face of invasions or because it was too distant to defend or work. They took infertile and exhausted land out of production because it had become unprofitable. Other lands were not farmed for lack of labor to work them to best advantage; emergence of other means of income challenged agricultural work. Conversely, an impressive amount of land not cultivated by the Carolingians was farmed during succeeding centuries. Lords claimed croplands by cutting forests and by turning back the sea in what is now The Netherlands. Abandoned land, its fertility somewhat regained during the extensive layoff, went back into production. Draining swamplands yielded new agricultural vistas.

Land changed hands frequently. Numerous men and women opted to do as William of Aquitaine had done and pay for their salvation by donating manors to the church. Serfs sometimes purchased land, while others just seized it and set themselves up as mini-noblemen. After a generation, others recognized the seizure as legal. Secular officials occasionally confiscated church lands when a bishop failed to uphold the bishopric's feudal obligations; more rarely, clerics renounced title to lands as a way of shunning worldly concerns. But warfare among the nobility was perhaps the foremost mechanism for the turnover of land. Internecine battles, generally local, were rampant. Vassals quickly switched allegiance once a conflict ended, but each battle merely precipitated the next conflagration. An almost constant state of war and changing alliances among large landholders and their vassals was the status quo.

Lords and Vassals

Lords both provided and received protection from the lord-vassal relationship in Carolingian Europe and after. In return for benefices, vassals had specific obligations to their lieges. They could do their lords no bodily harm, and could not betray their plans, treat them unfairly, ruin their property, or make it more difficult for them to achieve their objectives. Vassals also actively had to advance their lords' causes, providing them advice and financial assistance. Tradition obligated vassals and the knights of vassals to provide military service to their lords at their own expense for 40 days per year when called. Failure to abide by these rules meant forfeiture of the fief. Custom also dictated that vassals continue to fight for their lords beyond 40 days only to defend their lords' estates and if lords paid the necessary expenses. For their part, lords came to the aid of their vassals when under attack, bringing their other vassals and knights to assist the compromised individual. Terms of the relationship directed that lords protect their vassals in courts of law, act fairly toward them, and give them advice. Lords also needed to safeguard the rights of their deceased vassals' minor heirs—lords could propose marriage partners but the family needed to agree—and to turn their fathers' fiefs over to them when they reached age 20.

The Romanesque Family

The stark and abject strictures of these arrangements suggest how dependent noble-men and women and would-be noblemen and noblewomen thought they were on each other. Economics certainly played a part, but protection rested at the relation-ship's heart. Not able to survive alone, individuals sought alliance and union with others. Vassals scampered to find lieges and rushed to become lieges, frequently using a portion of their benefice to secure their own vassals. Each individual's pro-tection was bound up with each other individual's protection. Wealth was not wealth per se, nor was generosity merely generosity. Being generous with wealth was simply an attempt to extend the boundaries of one's union, to buy alliances, to become con-nected with others, to further the protective net. Romanesque Europeans defined protection as had their forerunners—in terms of property and life—but added the new factor of blood. The hereditary nature of fiefs made social structure permanent, which had important implications. Each conglomeration—each group—of relation-ships in the feudal order constituted a family of sorts. Mandatory passage of benefices through lineage joined groups for eternity, even as the precise terms of agreement within each group were unique.

These communities, loosely knit with their members possessing considerable autonomy except in time of war, were the guts of society. No all-encompassing central authority existed. A number of decentralized, family-like political, social, and eco-nomic institutions, no power holding them together, dominated the territories they claimed. The typical deathbed scene of a Romanesque "family" head reinforced this idea of family, while at the same time demonstrating that the Romanesque notion of family extended well beyond kinship ties. Family heads died in their manorial homes in a public, familial ritual. Heirs, grieving women, and blood kin gathered at the bed-side, but so too did vassals and servants. The dying man left precise instructions about his death, willfully distributed his property, and recognized those who had assisted him in his patriarchal duties—blood relatives and others. Similarly, family names, such as Smith or Jones, did not mark Romanesque families. What made one a family member was not a name or blood relationship, but rather identification by the family head. That identification often employed the metaphor of the body—that is, one was part of the *whole* body, not a separate item or function, like the heart. This identification was sufficient for the entire family to act as if there were an organic affiliation.

Families and Kings

These familial groups sometimes recognized that their physical well-being required them to rely on others outside the family, especially when hostile armies—the Mus-lims, for example—provided an immediate threat. Family heads then recognized that their families comprised a family of families and appointed or elected from their number a first among equals to lead the fight against the threat. This "king" oper-ated to safeguard the whole in this community of equals, to ensure that individual feudal families would persist. The king sat at the pleasure of his equals—at least in theory—and the office of king was not hereditary; the king served at the pleasure of the family heads.

Late tenth-century France, where six feudal overlords controlled virtually the entire territory, demonstrated this principle. The last direct descendant of Charlemagne had died in 987. These six dukes felt "the lack of a leader" almost immediately and quickly assembled to select among themselves their next king. Adalbero, archbishop of Rheims, explained to the dukes why Hugh Capet, duke of the Franks, should be their next king. Capet was, he said, "a defender . . . of your private interests. His largeheartedness will make him a father to you all. Who has ever fled to him for protection," the bishop asked, "without receiving it? Who that has been deserted by his friends has he ever failed to restore his rights?" In short, Capet would aid each family's interests while doing nothing to disturb the status quo.

The dukes picked Capet, but the practice of kingship never proved as neat as the theory. Kings often tried to benefit from their position as first among equals or to pass their mantles to their heirs. Capet was no exception. But kings usually were unable to dominate. Unlike those of their Carolingian predecessors, their reigns as king were not dependent on benefices granted to vassals. Those had become hereditary rights. And though the type of kingship that arose in the Romanesque period reflected the existence of parallel, seemingly eternal communities, that same notion of parallel communities also produced a rationale for selection of a first among equals; the king helped keep order among these eternal communities. Quite simply, lack of any clear set of rules to determine a social hierarchy among these families led family leaders and their vassals to take matters into their own hands. They plotted against each other, established alliances, seized lands, forced concessions, built fortifications, and attempted to persuade individuals to break vassalage vows. Only victory on the battlefield existed to adjudicate among them. Establishing a king as titular head to unite the rival families served as a fragile stability-maintaining mechanism.

The Manorial Family

Stability also figured prominently within manorial society. Manors housed the nobility and its knights as well as several other groups of people. Serfs were part of manorial property; they were inherited with the land. Freeholders owned their own property, often within the confines of a manor, and paid manorial owners for services, such as protection, unavailable to unaffiliated individuals. Cottagers, transients with no ties to land, moved from manor to manor, helping out as necessary. They received the right to use small dwellings and to plant gardens as well as retain a share of harvests as their pay. Almost no slaves lived on manors as slavery virtually disappeared from Romanesque Europe.

Although part of the property, serfs had their own hereditary rights. They could work the same parcels of manorial land as had their progenitors so long as they labored for manor owners for a set period each week. Manorial owners recognized that hereditary entitlement made serfs part of the manorial family, and owners of more than one manor often developed rules to protect the collective family from those outside it. These regulations aimed to keep property and peace within the multi-manored family by establishing rules for inheritance and for proving one's innocence. They also penalized those in the family guilty of heinous crimes against their fellows. These laws differed from communal family to communal family. Rules for the several manors of "the family of St. Peter of Worms," collected by Burchard, bishop of Worms in 1024, typified these "familial" regulations. They made a clear distinction between St. Peter's members and those not of the family, whom they called "foreigners." On their most simple level, St. Peter's regulations detailed inheritance of widows, minor heirs, and sons and daughters, and reflected a profound commitment to keep land within the biological family. Stipulations by which serfs could sell their right to work manorial land sounded the same theme but for the communal family. Rules clarified the rights of heirs and restricted potential purchasers to St. Peter's members. Daughters could marry outside the manor with no penalty only when they married into another St. Peter's manor. Fines for injustices to others at St. Peter's were very stiff, while family members alone possessed the right to trial by oath. Foreigners suffered trial by ordeal. St. Peter's backed penalties for murderers, which included branding the felons and requiring them to pay and make peace with the relatives of their victims. In addition, the murdered parties' biological kin were obligated to accept without question the terms of St. Peter's–determined penalties, under threat of disinheritance: loss of land and membership in the family of St. Peter.

Rules of inheritance or for the public good were not the only manorial regulations to suggest familial relationships. The contract between a manor's lord and serfs reflected that between parent and child. Serfs had the responsibility to do "chores" around the manor for which they received an "allowance"—the right to do certain things. Serfs tended the lord's fields, dug ditches, collected firewood, built fences, repaired roads and bridges, and sewed clothes. In return, they received the right to use the lord's mill, oven, winepress, farmland, pasturage, forest, and artisans. Serfs lived in lord-owned huts, prayed in lord-built churches, used lord-owned tools and equipment, and were defended by lord-obligated troops and in lord-owned fortifications.

Manorial Life

Day-to-day operations of manors differed as markedly as the actual terms of each manorial families' agreement. A small manor might support a dozen families, while a substantial facility could house more than 50. Serfs generally lived in village-like groups. Each had a garden rich in legumes, tended by the woman of the home. She cared for chickens and goats and helped during harvests. Serfs often resided with their animals in single-room huts with high roofs, open to permit smoke from central fireplaces to exit. On smaller manors, virtually all tools were wooden. Only larger estates could support blacksmiths. In general, lords managed forests carefully. Trees were cut at shoulder height every seven years, ensuring a continual supply of precious wood; leaves sometimes went for cattle beds. Pigs roamed manorial forests and peasants slaughtered them in December. Serfs had exclusive right to pigs, but lords had a monopoly on forest game; only lords and their friends could hunt. Farmland and pasturage were often interchangeable. Cattle and sheep grazed on fallow land as their manure replenished worn-out soil.

Farming Practices

Farming practices are even more difficult to summarize, but several trends bear note. More than before, peasants worked collectively. They pooled their rights to draft animals and equipment—technically, the lord owned the animals and equipment but the

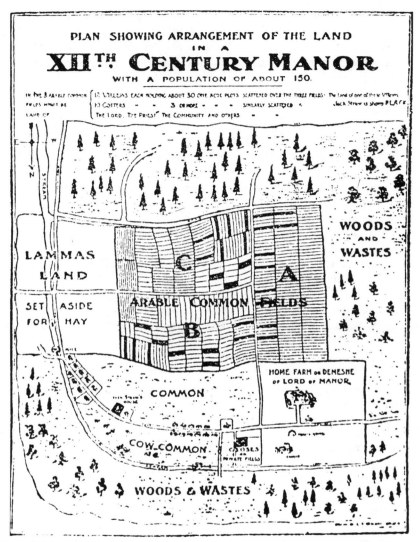

The Manor. Although a lord owned virtually everything on a manor, the most telling feature of that social organization was the great common areas. Pastures, arable lands, and forests were used communally.

serfs had hereditary rights to their exclusive personal use and housed and stored them—and sometimes labor. Each serf's farmland entitlement was divided into strips and distributed across the manor, which ensured that no individual received all the prime or barren land. That configuration encouraged collective farming since tools and animals had to be moved from place to place. Terms of manorial contracts specified that serfs work the lord's land for specified periods each week. These agreements also dictated whether serfs needed to bring work tools and animals or whether the lord would supply tools and animals for his demesne.

Use of heavy iron plows with moldboards and wheels almost always required collective action. Though hardly common in Europe, these plows temporarily increased the fertility of worn-out land by plowing deeper than simple plows and turning more soil, which released formerly inaccessible soil nutrients. Peasants also used these sturdy, substantial plows to break new land, to cut through thick, heavily rooted soil in recently cleared forests. Ironically, the type of dense soil found in these virgin forest lands and in much of northern Europe caused wheeled plows problems. The wheels regulated plowshare and moldboard depth and enabled the devices to plow at precise levels. The thick black soil clung to the wheels, increased their diameter—as if a child rolled a snowball—and raised the share and moldboard continually, which negated the wheels' purpose. Peasants could correct this problem only by stopping regularly to clean plow wheels.

Horse versus Ox   The massive drag produced by the depth in the soil of heavy plowshares was much too great for a single pair of oxen. Serfs pooled draft animals; teams of from five to eight oxen, far beyond a typical peasant's means, pulled each plow. Substituting horses for oxen multiplied costs. A horse was worth as much as twenty oxen. Effective plow horse use was a relatively recent occurrence. The padded horse collar did for the horse what the throat and girth harness had done for the ox some thousands of years earlier. It enabled horses to pull at full strength without choking; placed on the horse's shoulders, the padded collar, which was invented about A.D. 800, freed the windpipe and permitted easy breathing. Teams needed not be entirely oxen or horses. Peasants occasionally mixed the two animals in a single team.

Mixed teams of horses and oxen neutralized whatever advantage the horse might have provided. Horses and oxen pulled about the same weight but oxen pulled at a slow steady rate, while horses jerked more. Not until the twelfth century were whippletrees, which harnessed animals by chain to a bar and then collectively to a plow, used to smooth out the rough motion and permit increased flexibility and traction. Even then horse-oxen teams proved wasteful. Horses worked one and a half times as fast as oxen. In mixed-team plowing, the oxen's speed was the limiting factor. Yet the high cost of plow horses made mixed teams more common than horse teams. Only on large manors where fields were quite considerable or far from serfs' homes did the horses' swiftness provide a significant edge. That advantage generally did not offset the increased expense of horse feeding. Horses required oats in addition to grass and hay. Oxen flourished just by grazing and could be eaten when their productive years ended. But even if a manor resolved all other differences, peasants would not have derived great speed benefits from horse teams. Wheeled plows needed frequent wheel cleaning and those cleanings were based on the distance plowed, not the speed.

Horse speed paid dividends only in long-distance agricultural haulage. Perishable goods could reach farther overland markets. Blacksmiths nailed iron shoes to horses' soft, tender hooves to protect them from damage and wear, especially on rocky or damp terrain. Transformation from ox to horse haulage occurred quickly. Horse hauling was rare until about 1050. Within a few generations more than half the goods to distant places went by horse carts.

Two- versus Three-Field Agriculture   Intensification of agriculture on established fields and on newly cleared land increased food production. Yields per unit cultivated also increased. In Carolingian Europe, agricultural yields had netted less than twice the amount necessary to reserve for next year's planting. By the end of the tenth century, the ratio was at least three to one, perhaps higher. Additional production went to feed more and more people. Western Europe experienced massive population growth from the late ninth century to the fourteenth and those people, many of whom settled in urban areas, became a ready market. One other agricultural initiative also boosted production. A much greater number of manors adopted some aspects of the three-field agricultural system.

In two-field agriculture, peasants fallowed half the land each year. A crop of wheat was grown yearly on the nonfallow half. Three-field agriculture divided a parcel into three equal portions. The first third sat fallow the first year, while on the second serfs planted spring grains, such as oats. They grew winter wheat on the third portion. The next year field one had wheat, field two was fallow, and field three grew spring grain, while the following year field one produced spring grain, field two yielded wheat, and field three was fallow. Serfs then repeated the process indefinitely.

Three-field agriculture provided some manifest advantages. Serfs cultivated fully two-thirds of the available land yearly, an increase of one-third over the previous method. The system's two yearly harvests decreased likelihood of a single catastrophic harvest. Both had to fail before peasants experienced famine. Manors did not universally adopt the three-field system, however. Certain European climates proved unsuitable. Italy, for example, lacked the year-round rainfall required for two distinct crops, while Scandinavia's growing season was much too short for spring and winter crops. As important, productive manors rarely switched systems, apparently satisfied with then current methods. Only on recently cleared land and on land with worn-out soil did the three-field system make considerable incursions in planting practice. In the case of worn land, desperation probably led manors to try new techniques.

Awareness that surplus agricultural goods yielded profits sparked a second land reclamation wave as lords further extended agricultural operations. Population increase provided the people necessary to work these lands. Hereditary rights traditionally went to the firstborn. Subsequent male children frequently received no birthright. Tapping virgin lands offered these disenfranchised serfs a means to establish their families. They did so collectively. Groups of serfs seeking to improve their condition entered into a communal contract with a lord to develop some untouched area. They generally received the traditional rights of serfs, including hereditary rights, but, rather than work for their lord, they often pledged to pay him a specified percentage of their goods. Lords in what are now The Netherlands, northern France, and England pursued this policy aggressively, but Italian lords also participated as they encouraged serfs to break land that even the Romans had found forbidding. That these new production sites were sometimes located far away from established manors granted serfs a measure of independence. Their communal contracts occasionally permitted them to establish their own courts so as to not "suffer from the injustice of foreign judges," as was the case of the petitioners to Frederick, bishop of Hamburg, in 1106. Creation of separate courts, like payment in goods rather than services, stemmed from the distance of these new areas from their paternal manors.

Castles

Distance also worked to the serfs' disadvantage by placing them far from manorial protection. Massive motte and bailey castles provided refuge for a manor's population from the early tenth century. Early mottes were nothing more than huge earthen mounds topped by tall structures. Mounds might be 300 feet in diameter and 60 feet high, but few early mottes had diameters of more than 60 feet. Their slope depended on the nearby earth; clay mottes were much steeper than their sand counterparts. Wooden platforms, often on stilts and covered with protective bark, provided a view of the countryside, a stage from which to launch projectiles, and a spot to garrison troops. Picket fence-like palisades were common around edges of mottes.

Ditches, the largest of which was roughly 40 feet deep and 70 feet wide, surrounded most mottes and provided additional protection. These ditches connected mottes with enclosed, often kidney-shaped baileys (land islands). A series of earthen steps led out of the ditches or, if they held water, rope or wooden bridges traversed the span. Tenth- and eleventh-century baileys generally had large earthen enclosures at their centers, places for manorial families to gather when manors were under assault. Sometimes buildings were found inside enclosures on palisade-encircled baileys: kitchens, storehouses, barracks, and other structures necessary to sustain a populace under attack. Not until the late eleventh century did stone structures, called *keeps*, begin to replace these earth and wood bailey complexes. Early English keeps were huge rectangular edifices, up to 90 feet square. These four-story-tall buildings had buttressed walls up to 14 feet thick. Massive towers overlooked and guarded walls. Iron portcullises slid down to bar doors. Gatehouses were literally narrow rooms that could be defended from above by arrows, boiling water, and other means through small holes in the floor called *machicolations* and through holes in the walls

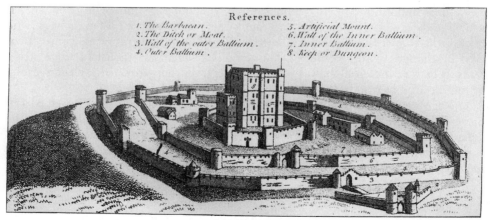

The Castle. This late eleventh-century castle represented cutting-edge technology. It replaced the motte-bailey castles of earlier generations with stone structures able to provide refuge to large numbers of persons and to withstand sieges for long periods.

called *meurtrieres;* they stood as the castles' last line of defense when the portcullises failed to keep out intruders.

Motte and bailey castles did more than protect manors. William the Conqueror used these devices to dominate much of England. In the two decades after 1066, William's forces built at least 500 of these primitive castles, locating each at a strategically important site. Although quite small—ditches provided earth for mottes—they nonetheless provided William's forces defensible positions from which to ward off attacks and stamp out insurrections.

Warfare

The great defensive-structure building boom paralleled introduction of mounted shock combat. Horsemen carried kite-shaped shields in their left hands and metal-tipped lances in their right. Early horsemen sat on rigid, flat leather saddles, but by the late eleventh century, saddles with high pommels to protect the lower stomach and groin and cantles to help horsemen absorb blows and stay on their horses became common. These horsemen were of little use against fortified structures. Their utility dwindled further with the crossbow's introduction in the eleventh century. These bows were too powerful to be drawn without mechanical aid. Composed of several wooden pieces to provide the requisite strength, the crossbows' great range compensated for their relatively slow rate of fire. Longbow-wielding archers could fire three or more arrows for every crossbow-fired arrow. But crossbow arrows traveled more than twice as far, up to 400 yards. Although crossbows were inadequate for open-field battles, they served well in defense of fortified places.

Attacking forces were not without their devices. Wheel-mounted, timber-housed, iron plate-covered, iron-headed rams proved particularly effective at battering rectangular corners of keeps or walls. Aggressors also sapped corners, by tunnelling underground and jabbing these vulnerable points with iron spears, which undermined foundations. Scaling ladders and wheeled siege towers with battlement-connecting bridges breached walls. Projectile-throwing machines, powered by thongs, twisted ropes, or counterpoised weights, demolished stone structures. The late eleventh-century counterpoise trebuchet provided a siege weapon of increased power and accuracy.

Open warfare became a casualty of castles. Infantrymen had shields shaped like those of horsemen, the bottoms of which when placed in the ground formed living defensive fortifications. These human shields were powerless to withstand a mounted assault. The infantry benefited from few other innovations. Carolingian-styled helmets protected heads, while chain mail preserved chests and legs.

Towns

Europeans established a new social form, the walled town, at about the time that they conceived of motte and bailey castles. Like manors, no single model served for all towns. But despite tremendous differences in the explanations for town formation, town creations had a common thread. This new social form, the town, had much in common with another new form, the castle. Europeans predicated both castles and towns upon notions of coherence and unity of a particular population and a desire to separate that population from outsiders. The castle or town group was seen as (and acted as if) mutually dependent and the keep, motte and bailey complex, or town wall provided a graphic demonstration of that idea. These visible barriers were nothing less than physical manifestations of the idea of the unity of the ensconced populace and its separation from those outside. Each wall marked the boundaries of the family of people living within it. Each town was differentiated, however, by the terms establishing the composition of the respective families. In other words, they differed over what made the group in fact a group.

Agricultural Towns

Towns first emerged in the tenth century in what would become southern and central Italy and in much of what would become France and Belgium. In Italy, lords frequently initiated towns. Serfs, especially those lacking hereditary claims to land, were induced by the promise of their own land in a distant place to leave manors and to settle on uninhabited spots on the lords' land. Each group of landless people starting a town agreed to a precise set of lord-offered terms. And each of these landless collectives pursued the same course. They selected a high point around which to locate their habitations, built stone or wooden houses, and erected walls to protect their domiciles. A fortified structure stood at town center. The land both in and around these new agriculturally based towns usually needed to be cleared.

The case was somewhat different in France. Town formation often was a consequence of the "dissipation of authority" as much count- or monastery-controlled land, especially in those areas where threat of foreign invasion was high, was abandoned or left undeveloped. Enterprising peasants and lesser noblemen claimed this land for themselves and then sought to enter a vassalage arrangement to protect their claims. The peasants established their hereditary right to the land by seizure. They next brokered an agreement with a liege to maintain their ersatz titles.

Freeholders apparently also formed towns. To ensure their protection, they actively relinquished their autonomy to become part of a "family." The collective interest of these previously widely scattered freeholders exceeded the desirability of private ownership because in Romanesque Europe not to be part of something was to invite catastrophe, even to risk survival. In return for their holdings, renunciation of further ambitions, and relatively modest homage, freeholders received as their fief their town and small parcels around it; they exchanged land and independence for a measure of security. They then acknowledged themselves as a family and announced a communal charter, which specified their obligations and responsibilities to each other. These communal towns grew in number from the mid-tenth century. Historians credit Huy in what is now Belgium as agreeing to the first communal charter.

Commercial Towns

Early Italian, Belgian, and French towns had agricultural foundations and drew their populations from nearby areas. In Germany in the tenth century and France a century later, towns attracted people from outside the region but grew around established population centers. Vassals had long sought to increase their wealth. To that end, they often contracted with widely traveled merchants to transport their wares away from population centers and start a market. These walled locales were trading posts from their beginnings. Merchants stayed at each of these places for about three to six weeks before they packed up their goods and moved on. The decision to place these markets outside traditional jurisdictional areas, such as cities or monasteries, enabled lords to negotiate very attractive terms that would interest these merchants in returning year after year. Lords quickly realized that securing merchants permanently rather than temporarily would enhance their town's prospects. At about the same time, the highly prized merchants recognized their own value. They understood that together they comprised a group that offered lords something they strongly desired. Merchants made that group identification a reality by forming themselves into a guild or brotherhood, thus enabling them to solicit better terms from the nobility.

Permanent retention of internationally well-connected merchants remained no simple task, especially once they conceived of themselves collectively. Lesser nobles, fearing for their ability to compete for merchants, sometimes realized that they, too, had common interests and pooled their prospects to help lure—buy—merchants. Feudal overlords also offered potent inducements to encourage merchants to settle at sites the overlords chose. These rewards generally were of two types: money and grants of sovereignty in the Romanesque sense of the phrase. Romanesque sovereignty, awarded in the form of a municipal charter, permitted the guild to act like a vassal to its lord. The guild, whose "manor" was the town, elected its own officers to run the town, levied taxes, waged war, issued regulations, and held its own courts. In return, it paid its liege a percentage of its commercial transactions or tolls.

Local nobility sometimes also offered merchants the privilege of sovereignty but rarely did they welcome monarchical support in town formation. Although in a few instances the king's intercession furthered the nobility's interests, he more commonly planted towns and awarded them charters to beat down challenges from the nobility and to maintain his first-among-equals position in the feudal family. German monarchs, for example, engaged in a deliberate policy of situating towns upriver from established ports to siphon off whatever trade existed and around monasteries and manors as an active source of competition.

Nor did many commercial towns remain simply the province of merchants. Artisans began to appear in these places, apparently leaving manors to ply their trades. No doubt the non-inheriting sons of manorial artisans saw in towns opportunity they lacked on manors. Entrance of artisans into the commercial town family was gradual and proceeded as if each craft was distinctive, as if each craft constituted its own group. First metalworkers came to towns, followed by those engaged in textiles and then leather. Only after these crafts were grounded in towns did other artisan groups arrive in measurable numbers.

Concentration of people in central places, whether towns or manors, fostered ready markets for merchant and artisan goods. The recurring military threat encouraged people to work together for their defense. This notion of commonality extended far beyond defense, of course. It tied town inhabitants together as members of a Romanesque family, which encompassed more than blood kin.

Commerce

Towns sprung up throughout Europe because they made sense to Romanesque Europeans. Conditions certainly made town formation possible. An agricultural surplus, at least in many localities, provided the food necessary to support an extensive non-food-producing population. An increase in the number of people living, coupled with establishment of the hereditary rights of the firstborn, produced a surplus of human beings on manors. Emergence of the possibility of commerce enabled Europeans to explore its potential. A clandestine trade between the Muslims and the west had grown in the ninth century, but the trade revival of the tenth century, modest by any other standards, overwhelmed it. The Magyars and the Muslims blocked major land routes, but Genoa and Pisa, commercial towns situated on the Italian peninsula, developed trade within the Mediterranean. They and other Italian towns cleared that sea of the Muslim fleet in the eleventh century and provided the impetus for a commercial revolution that lasted more than two centuries. The First Crusade at the end of the eleventh century brought Constantinople within the trade net and transformed Venice into an even more bustling commercial center.

Foodstuffs and cloth drove early Romanesque commerce. Italian towns benefited from two events: the destruction of traditional overland trade routes between western Europe and the Middle East and the Muslim desire to open Egypt to trade. Tenth-century Magyar invasions and Slavic incursions had disrupted trade through the Baltic and Russia. Italian towns capitalized on their geography to capture what remained of this small but lucrative activity. The opening of Egypt in the 960s and 970s flooded the region with cotton and grain. Italian merchants established connections there and in Europe. The area in what is now Belgium, especially the towns of Flanders, Bruges, and Ghent, utilized its North Sea location to dominate wool and wood trade. Merchants purchased English wool and contracted with others in these Belgian towns to turn the raw material into finished products. They then sold the fine woolen cloth to Germany for wood, to Scandinavia for fur, and to England for more wool.

Navigation

European trade easily surpassed that of the Roman Empire as large oared galleys hauled the cargo of the tenth and early eleventh centuries. Carrying more than 300 men, these ships had two oarsmen per bench and could be brought under sail when weather permitted. Introduction of doubled-masted, lateen-sailed round ships in the eleventh century reflected sea trade growth. These ships' triangular sails enabled them to sail closer to the wind than their square-sailed counterparts, and they held twice the cargo of galleys below the main deck. Round ships dominated the Mediterranean by 1200. Improved navigational techniques meant the loss of fewer ships and allowed goods to arrive more nearly at planned times. Astrolabes determined latitude by the earth's position in relation to the fixed stars. Sand clocks, similar to modern egg timers, and logs tied at specific intervals on continuous lines gave Romanesque sailors their nautical speed.

Trade Routes c. 1050

Watermills

The people of the Belgian towns led European manufacturing and were among the first group to use water power in manufacture. Artisans in Flanders and the other towns employed watermills to raise triphammers to simulate the constant foot kneading associated with fulling cloth at home. These falling hammers condensed fibers and thickened—fulled—fabrics. Waterwheel-powered triphammers entered other types of manufacturing before 1150, but their extensive use occurred after that date. Even during the Romanesque period, however, tanning mills broke oak bark into little pieces for tanning, and hemp mills slashed stalks to expose the valuable inner material. Nor did Romanesque manufacturers restrict their watermill use to triphammer-dependent tasks. Agricultural products needed milling, and towns and manors milled mustard and poppy seeds as well as dyes and pigments. But for all manufacturing use of watermills, manors were the site of their real popularity. Watermills (and animal mills) replaced manually powered stone rollers and grindstones to mill grains.

The explosion of watermill construction and use confirmed again the importance of the idea of collectivity, of unity. Each site, whether manor or town, required its

Water-Powered Gristmill. Waterwheels powered an extraordinary number of devices after the mid-tenth century. These simple machines converted the flow of a river or stream into mechanical effort.

own mill. The attractiveness of watermills was new. Historians have found little evidence from the sixth through the early tenth centuries to show that watermills existed in Europe to any significant extent. Barbarian law codes rarely mentioned them, a gross oversight—if mills really existed in meaningful numbers—for a people consumed by the idea of individual property and of listing virtually every contingency in their codes. Only occasionally did watermills appear in monastery records and almost never in the records of manors or urban places. Archeologists rarely have uncovered watermills. Barbarian individualism rendered watermills generally impractical. Watermills worked on volume; they were group, not individual, sized. Watermills flourished only with the idea of group.

By the mid-tenth century, mills began to appear throughout Europe—in France, Germany, Britain, Italy, and the Balkans. Tidal mills (those anchored in bodies of water and powered by tidal ebb and flow), undershot mills, bridge mills (where the bridge and mill shared supports and were in essence a single structure), and floating mills, which could be moved so as not to obstruct river traffic or water flow (rapid water flow near bridges quickly undermined supports and led to bridge collapses) received frequent and repeated mention both in towns and on manors. The

Domesday Book, compiled between 1080 and 1086, noted 5,624 watermills at 3,000 locations in England alone, an estimated one for every 50 persons. The Toulouse region of France had at least 60 mills in 1100, while Picardy had more than 40 some twenty years earlier. These mills required a steep investment and were often pointed to with pride, as a group product and manifestation of a collective identity.

Wheels and Circles

Community interest in mills and increased mill usage simply could be the consequence of population growth and the extensive clustering of people. But a possible symbolic basis for the Romanesque adoption of the wheel ought not to be dismissed out of hand. Symbolism played a crucial role in Romanesque thought and the actual shape of the mill wheel is intriguing. Like castles and walled towns, its shape permitted no division or intercession; the wheel was indivisible, a totality, complete unto itself. Nor was the waterwheel the only circular object reborn during the Romanesque era. Coins, which had been triangular, octagonal, and other straight-line-dependent shapes, again became circular, and potters returned to wheels to throw pots. The fascination with the unity of circularity also extended to an interest in millennialism. Millennialism both before and after A.D. 1000 was predicated on the earthly world coming full cycle, being completed.

The Romanesque Church

The Romanesque world's search for identity led it directly to the church. Christianity alone operated beyond the immediate area; it remained the one institution capable of organizing the vast majority of the west. The church bound humans together as well as heaven and earth. But the Romanesque church did not resemble a theocracy. It emerged instead as a subject of concern and attracted those outside church governance as well as the clergy. Some examined church institutions, found them flawed and demanded revision. Others aimed at expanding church influence, seeking to bring it to bear on more souls. Still others sought to brighten the church and its edifices to prepare for Christ's second coming. In every case, however, the goal remained the same. Romanesque men and women placed the church at the center of Romanesque affairs.

Cluny and Monastic Reform

The gift of William, Duke of Aquitaine, in 910 created a monastery at Cluny, a small town in what is now France. This monastery was different from previous monasteries. No workshops existed at Cluny. For the first time, monks were not supposed to engage in manual labor. Cluny required monastic brothers to separate themselves from the earthly world and do only one thing, pray. Nor was their abbot appointed by an earthly potentate from outside the house. In direct repudiation of prior practice, the brothers elected their own abbot. The abbot was the first among equals.

Rather than sit in an office and take his meals alone, the abbot ate with the other monks and slept in the communal dormitory.

The Cluniac reforms proved so successful that they inspired nearly 2,000 similarly structured abbeys over the next two centuries. Barbarian Europe's monasteries had each been independent, free to adopt their own practices within the Benedictine tradition. Cluniac monasteries thought of themselves as a founding house–affiliated family. This familial affiliation translated into an organizational scheme. Each house elected its own prior to head the abbey and all looked to the abbot at Cluny as their leader. He stood at the head of the greater Cluny monastic family, a heavenly community bound together in Christ.

A minuscule twinge of conscience had led William to fund the Cluny venture. A similar twinge caused its monks, led by Berno—Cluny's first abbot—to attempt to regulate themselves, to set monastery life right. Cluny's monastic reform program aimed to rid the church of the taint of earthly influences. Monks seemed to have grown worldly and neglected their education, while religious service had lost focus and meaning. Cluny railed against the buying and selling of ecclesiastical offices—simony—and sought to diminish secular interference in church affairs. Grand, splendid processions (the grander the better to show the glory of Christ's sacrifice) marked Cluny's elaborate religious service. Certainly the monastery could afford its trappings. Rich people wishing to persuade holy men to pray for their eternal salvation—men with a conscience praying for those beginning to develop one—could do no better than support these most pious brothers. Cluny soon became by far the wealthiest and largest property-holding monastery. Ironically, its success as an ascetic institution enabled it to accumulate incredible material rewards. Within a century and a half, however, other men of conscience concluded that the incredibly wealthy and ostentatious Cluny had lost its way.

Cluny's rise and fall suggests that the church faced the same dilemmas as civil society. Its membership and its limits were basic questions. The church also considered the roles of the clergy, monasteries, and the pope and the relationship between the pope and civil society as well as between the church generally and civil society. The parallels to feudal society were obvious, a fact that may not surprise because religion played a huge part in everyday life. Saints were god's vassals and pledging oneself to them was comparable to the earthly act of commendation. Threat of excommunication became a way of influencing moral action, while excommunication itself meant unaffiliation, abandonment by the Christian family. But more practically, the church had long been a feudal bulwark. From the seventh century people left property to the church, first to pay for their sins (the Christian wergeld) and later to persuade pious men to use their influence with god on the donors' behalf. The church thus acquired a fantastic number of estates, which it sometimes worked or converted into working monasteries. Bishops and abbots controlled these estates and monasteries. In Carolingian Europe, these estates acquired the crucial military responsibility of supporting men fighting for defense of the Holy Roman Empire. Indeed, the concept of a Holy Roman Empire, headed by a secular emperor upon whom the pope depended for his protection, neatly summarized the intertwining of religious and secular affairs. Demise of the Carolingian dynasty did not free bishops and abbots of feudal obligations. They became vassals to secular lords or became lords themselves with critical military responsibilities. Church lands supplied a full 76 percent of the military forces used by Otto II, Holy Roman Emperor, in his 982 campaign.

Lack of a hereditary basis for the offices of bishop and abbot made the church a distinctive part of Romanesque feudalism. Control of property could not be passed from kin to kin. A new bishop or abbot, freed from hereditary constraints, might choose a different course or set of relationships, which could make or break lords or kings. Secular potentates took succession of bishops and abbots quite seriously as these clergymen could tip the military balance. Kings and lords worked to select and appoint these church leaders because of their feudal, not religious, positions.

Monastic Life

Cluny's organizational scheme, majestic religious service, and restriction of monks to prayer separated it from other monasteries. But many of its day-to-day activities were quite similar to those of other monasteries. Although Cluny established its own definition of monastic life, which its houses practiced throughout Europe, community standards also overlay other monastic houses. The locus of community was the difference. Prior to the end of the eleventh century, non-Cluny houses each constituted a separate community. Distinctions among each monk in a house were made only by the date of entry into monastic life, the date at which the person left the outside world and joined this heavenly community. Each monastery's monks defined together what was appropriate behavior within the Benedictine tradition and framed these collective agreements as *customaries*, books of rules, regulations, and procedures. Customaries told the monks precisely what the group had agreed upon, specifying the clothes community members should wear, the foods they should eat, and when they should pray.

Time and the Church

Customaries derived from the consent of the governed. Yet agreement to act communally in a precise fashion required means to alert or remind widely scattered monks of their agreement's particulars. Bells served to announce common meals and common prayers. Meals and prayers generally took place at particular times of the day, and monasteries relied on clocks to tell them when to ring bells. Sand clocks (larger versions of those used aboard ships), waterclocks similar to those employed by the ancient Greeks, or candle or oil clocks—a quantity of a combustible material burnt for a specified length of time—provided the necessary information.

Bells announced monastic community life and marked community time but did not drive monks. Moving from activity to activity when bells tolled was a voluntary, community-based decision. Nor did Romanesque monasteries conceive of time as a commodity they could own or manipulate. Time belonged to god and was a heavenly, not earthly, construct. To attempt to shepherd it, to benefit from it, or to make money from it by charging interest on a loan, for example, was sacrilege. Heavenly time was a manifestation of divine orderliness, of god's plan. Ordering procedures on earth had a purpose and that purpose was to demonstrate the road to salvation. Use of time by mortals for their own ends constituted the sin of theft.

Romanesque Europeans approached the concept of the earthly day seriously. Following god's plan, they divided days into two parts, daylight and night. This heavenly division was no accident, of course. The light represented god—good—and the night was identified with Satan—evil—reflecting the bifurcated nature of the struggle for man's eternal soul. Incorporation of sundials in religious architecture taught and reinforced that important lesson. Romanesque Europeans were especially fearful at night, recognizing it as a time of danger and malevolent spirits. The allegorical salvation message continued with division of daylight and night each into twelve periods, the number of apostles. But dividing the daylight and night into units of equal number, although spiritually rewarding, had practical drawbacks. Length of hours varied daily and the length of a day's daylight hours and night hours was never the same, except for two days a year. The situation was hardly insurmountable. Monasteries possessed the type of timekeeping devices perfectly adapted to their needs. Monks easily adjusted the amount of sand, water, or oil daily—the length of a daylight or night hour increased or decreased essentially linearly—to correct their clocks for daily variations. Romanesque clocks attached to bells exactly suited Romanesque desires.

Order, Symbolism, and the Christian Community

Affixing the length of hours for prayer occurred within the larger context of belief in Christ's Second Coming. Christ's Second Coming—this grander sense of time—would mark the end of earthly affairs; they would come full cycle. Earthly believers would ascend heavenward as per god's plan, while those denying god's domain would be left behind. This, like other facets of god's plan, struck Romanesque Europeans as understandable, essentially logical and orderly. Rarely if ever did they think of human activity as linear, evolutionary, or developmental. Time to these men and women did not progress or regress. Events were signs of god's plan, not cumulative milestones on the way somewhere (as we tend to think of occurrences today). Sports of nature, such as two-headed kittens, and natural phenomena, such as earthquakes, comets, floods, and eclipses, fascinated them precisely because they were abnormal. The abnormal (which indicated a common understanding of what is normal) seemed portentous, meaningful. It was not something that Romanesque Europeans sought to put back into balance, to correct or ameliorate, but rather to understand. The abnormal was a conscious sign from god that demonstrated the path to salvation. God had established order. If he chose to disorder something, to produce an abnormality, it could only be to show Christians the divine will and way to eternal life.

Romanesque Europeans recognized divine symbols in just about everything. Good things were miracles, while bad occurrences were demonstrations of god's wrath. Baptism and the Eucharist involved miraculous transformations, but earthly magicians blasphemed or worked in league with evil. The uncorruptedness of the heavens showed the perfection of heavenly order while earth seemed base. Humans were composed of matter and the soul. The soul was pure and matter corrupt. Nature itself, not just anomalies, provided salvation signs. Bestiaries, volumes describing earthly animals, focused on how animals' lives and habits reflected divine truths. It was not what the animals did that was important but what that action represented, god's plan. For example, the alleged fact that lion cubs were born sleeping only to be awakened by their mother's roar on the third day, confirmed and proved the reality of Christ's resurrection after three days. Similarly, description of the ant-lion—half ant and half lion—as constantly at war with itself over what to eat (the ant half would eat only vegetables, while the lion half wanted only flesh) proved the existence of one god; man could not serve two conflicting masters.

Other spheres of intellectual activity also fit this symbolic, allegorical assessment. Geometry and arithmetic proved god's orderly plan. The precision, grammar, and rhetoric of the divine Latin evinced an orderliness that showed god's hand and the road to salvation. Earthly tones constituted a corrupted version of the music of the heavenly orbs. Religious chanting combined four or more voices as if they were one to constitute a timeless, monophonic vocal community, a community that symbolized the monastery and ultimately all of Christendom. Human productions, such as art and literature, accentuated the message, not the medium. Heavenly figures were drawn or written much larger than life. It was common to picture a bearded Christ, not a baby, in the Madonna's arms. Divinely inspired individuals continued to fight on even after their vital organs had been destroyed. These literary heroes possessed extrahuman qualities as their creators provided them with exaggerated, allegorical attributes, not realistic ones.

In the Romanesque world, Christians explicitly considered themselves an earthly community. The designation *Christendom* reflected this new sentiment. It stood as a collective identity, complete with collective obligations and concerns. This statelike entity began to serve as a moral compass for its members—the saints seemed appropriate Christian models—and announced rules to guide interactions with others. Christendom's conscience was collective, not individual; the Christian position was the community position and guided people on how to act toward those outside the community rather than inside it. God dealt with individual Christians at Easter, the Eucharist, and death—William, Duke of Aquitaine recognized that—but the community governed relations with the broader world.

The dying institution of slavery itself served as a model of Romanesque Christianity's communal/personal dichotomy. Christendom's notion that all Christians were equal before god made Christians owning other Christians undesirable and the church had great success discouraging warring Christian factions from taking Christians as slaves at the conclusion of battles. But a more personal agenda fueled the final wave of slave manumissions during the Romanesque era. It took Christ's sacrifice as its template. Christ had suffered for all men and freed them of original sin through his blood. Slave owners imitated the savior in great numbers by freeing their Christian slaves in a Christlike endeavor.

Acknowledgment that people and communities existed beyond Christendom was important because it further defined Christendom itself. Christendom—the whole—was defined in part by what it apposed, by what it touched but was different from, by what was foreign. On its most simple level, evidence of the devil confirmed the existence of a Christian community, Christendom. Within that context, Christendom viewed Muslims, Jews, and heretics as demons whose purification was demanded for Christendom's triumph.

The Second Coming and the First Crusade

A sense of the imminence of Christ's Second Coming pervaded Romanesque Europe. From about 970 to 1100, as the millennium approached and receded, Christians

The First Crusade. Pope Urban's call to Christendom to free the Holy Land from the Muslims was greeted enthusiastically by knights errant and others seeking adventure or religious enlightenment.

recognized numerous symbols of the earthly end. Following the biblical prediction of a battle between the forces of good and evil—Armageddon—Christians prepared both to fight and to see Christ's arrival. The Muslim capture of the Holy Land and threat to Constantinople provided a focus for action. At Pope Urban II's behest, representatives of Christendom's leading forces gathered in 1095 to consider collective action. They demonized Muslims as committing unspeakable grotesquenesses and of having destroyed things Christian. Urban II best summed up Christendom's position. The infidels were "wholly alienated from God." They destroyed Christian churches or "defiled them with their uncleanness." They circumcised Christians and then spread the blood on church altars. They routinely raped and tortured their victims. Urban II pointed to a particular kind of torture as a sign of the devil incarnate. Muslims perforated the navel of a person "and dragging forth the extremity of the intestines, bind it to a stake; then by blows compel the victim to run around the stake, until the viscera gush forth." He asked Christendom to recognize its common obligation, mobilize, and begin that final battle. "Let therefore hatred depart from among you, let quarrels end, let wars cease, and let all dissensions and controversies slumber," called Urban, and Christendom responded with a crusader army.

Cathedral Mania

Christendom's crusaders engaged in what its leaders considered a Christian war, a just war, and by doing so confirmed that Christendom constituted a terrestrial community. But the Crusades were not the only attempt to root out evil in preparation for Christ's return. In what is now France and Germany, anti-Semitic literature became common in the eleventh century as did pogroms, systematic routing and slaughtering of Jews. Mass burnings of heretics, such as the burning in Orleans in 1022, also were part of the cleansing process. Christendom instituted other initiatives to prepare for Christ. An incredible wave of church and cathedral construction gave city after city grand new buildings to welcome the savior. New structures were erected on land reclaimed from the Muslims in Spain and elsewhere and in established places, even small towns and cities. Although nobles sometimes built these churches after suffering pangs of conscience, the enormity of the moment caused townsmen and women to overlook the obvious financial strain and to support construction of imposing new facilities. As time approached full circle, Romanesque Europeans reached for the beginning of time as they understood it. They found it with Christ's birth in ancient Rome. Rome ironically was identified as Christian, as the spiritual base from which Christianity rose. Resurrecting Rome symbolized time's conclusion, then, and architectural ruins provided inspiration. Roman imperial architecture, especially the basilica, became the model. Cluniacs were very active. Reformation of Christian structures paralleled their reformation of the clergy and service.

Romanesque—Rome-like—architecture marked the first all-European style since the Roman Empire's fall. Romanesque architecture accentuated grandeur and holism and thus complemented the notion of unity implicit in the term *Christendom*. Bishops were housed in the grandest structures. Bishoprics were important local administrative centers both before and after Charlemagne. Bishops sat on thronelike chairs—cathedras—and by virtue of their position spoke with authority; they spoke from these thrones, ex cathedra. Bishops assumed even further prominence in this new world of Christendom as high-ranking officials in the Christian community. That their churches, which housed cathedra and therefore supported administrative functions, would be Christendom's grandest ought not to surprise. Nor should use of holy numbers in their design and construction, as divine symbols.

Romanesque Cathedral. Roundness abounded in these ponderous religious structures. Thick pillars and walls supported ceiling vaults made of stone. The largest cathedrals could hold over 10,000 persons.

Romanesque churchmen took early Christian basilicas as their paradigm but soon abandoned these square and rectangular models to produce cathedrals in which circularity and circles—roundness—abounded. Expressions of completeness and indivisibility, circular elements in cathedrals included rounded arches, circular or octagonal keeps, groin and tunnel ceiling vaults, ambulatories, pillars, cylindrical central spaces, and domes. Thick, oversized walls and small windows marked these structures, the consequence of massive stone ceiling vaults that pressed downward. The Romans had known of these permanent, fireproof, acoustically excellent vaults but they had fallen into disuse. Tunnel vaults were single curves of stones mortared together. Groin vaults were composed of intersecting tunnel vaults and pushed weight to the corners. Both made thin walls all but impossible. They also influenced building height. The great thickness needed for walls led to accentuation of the horizontal rather than the vertical and to disproportionately short buildings. Bell towers were frequently built next to the cathedral, not atop it.

Internal decorations also differed from those of Roman basilicas. Ornate capitals topped pillars painted to simulate marble. Stones of different colors reflected geometric patterns or suggested plants. Colorful mosaics and paintings representing lives of saints or New Testament scenes highlighted interiors. Curtains, tapestries, and even carpets bore these spectacles as Romanesque Europeans rarely missed an opportunity to demonstrate the way to salvation and to acknowledge Christendom's monopoly of that pathway. An emphasis on roundness persisted. Europeans made no attempt to provide artistic perspective in their religious and other art. Two-dimensionality also dominated sculpture. Form was rigid and the work never free-standing. Relief, if it existed at all, was exceedingly shallow.

Church versus State

Christendom as announced in the Romanesque era explicitly rejected those tenets of the Augustinian program that had served Barbarian Europe. Augustinianism had renounced the city of man as hopeless, useful only because it helped individuals enter the city of God. Charlemagne's Augustinianism attempted, for example, to train clergymen in Christian matters and declamation to prepare them better to spread god's word. The anti-Augustinianism of the Romanesque period took the city of man—earthly society—as Christian and therefore part of god, perhaps even the city of god. Christendom rejected not the earthly state but incorporated heaven and earth together as a single Christian community. It embraced a Christian state as part of the heavenly plan.

The Crusades and the cathedral building craze were tangible demonstrations of that union. Need to purify the world for the Second Coming meant that the world mattered. The group identification of Christendom defined a collective conscience, manifested in a Christian morality, which provided Christian rules for life on earth. Everyone understood that god established these Christian rules. But controversy raged over who was god's representative. Who should lead, who should stand first among equals, and express god's will? This fundamental question resulted in recurring battles for control of the church and of secular society.

The Cluniac movement's attacks on simony and the laxity—even irreligiosity—of the noble-appointed clergy demanded that the church, not secular authority, guide Christendom. It confirmed a union between what had been the city of god and the city of man and demanded that the clergy—a reformed church-led clergy, to be sure—lead this Christian community. Within that context, Cluniacs and their supporters began to articulate a number of Christian moral positions. Many had to do with family. In addition to simony, they deplored the practice of clergymen taking wives and/or mistresses, maintained the necessity of a clerical blessing to constitute a valid marriage, urged lords to bear arms for Christian goals, and recognized the bishop of Rome or pope as Christendom's leader.

Feudal lords rejected this formulation. Harkening back to Charlemagne, they claimed divine inspiration and the right to select and invest bishops and priests. They also maintained it their god-given responsibility to reform the church, which required them to select churchmen. That included the pope; secular nobles had gained control of papal selection after Charlemagne. Few secular leaders were more successful and committed than Otto I of what is now Germany. Building on Henry I's defeat of the Magyars in 933, Otto assumed power in 936 and retained it until 973. He used a crack cavalry to fight dukes as well as his relatives, and ultimately set himself up as their liege lord. His strength stemmed from his ability to undercut his adversaries' institutional base. German churches overturned the traditional rights of the dukes to appoint bishops to bishoprics and abbots to monasteries and declared it Otto's divine right alone to appoint clergymen. Church-related fiefs provided Otto's power and when the pope called for his assistance in defeating a noble who claimed to be king of Italy, Otto proclaimed himself Holy Roman Emperor and used his forces to vanquish the usurper. The rapprochement between Otto and the pope did not long persist. Otto assumed that his new title empowered him to appoint bishops and abbots in Italy and to have them pledge fealty and homage to him. When the pope objected, Otto had him driven from Rome. Otto then installed a pontiff more to his liking.

Otto's successors continued his policies and the Cluniacs led the complaints about several Holy Roman Emperors' treatment of successive popes. Christian morality needed a Christian basis, not a secular one, and they labored to position clerics rather than secular liege lords to appoint church leaders. Bishop Odo of Cluny argued in the first half of the tenth century, for instance, that kings received power from god, which permitted them to act in secular affairs. That authority did not extend to church matters but undercut their ability to act in a Christian moral manner. Indeed, those very things that made them apt secular leaders—aggressiveness and ruthlessness—and gave them wealth signaled moral turpitude. Rather than act like saints, they took advantage of the weak and poor to build their strength. They succumbed to temptations, temptations unavailable to persons of lesser station, instead of casting them aside.

Establishing the pope as Christendom's leader was a consequence of this new separation of church and state. The Cluniacs were intimately involved. As a Christian monastery, they remained distinct from and without ties to civil society. But their reform initiatives strengthened the pope by exacerbating the need for a clerical leader of Christendom to demonstrate Christian morality. The situation intensified in 1059. The clergy of Rome—the cardinals—claimed sole right to pick the pope from among themselves, as the first among equals. Divine inspiration guided the decision, of course, but the pope thus selected led a church-based crusade to purify itself and to assert its preeminence over secular authority. Penalties for refusing to acknowledge the cardinal-selected pontiff or for enshrining another in his place were severe, reflective of the idea that abandonment by the Christian family was the supreme punishment. Usurpers and their allies were "expelled from the holy church of God . . .

subjected to perpetual anathema as Antichrist and the enemy and destroyer of all Christianity." Curses followed excommunication. Each stressed the individual's eternal isolation, his disenfranchisement from the Christian family. "Let his habitations be desolate," the papal decree continued, and "let his children be orphans and his wife a widow." Let "his sons beg" and "let the whole earth fight against him . . . and let the powers of all the saints in heaven confound him."

The pope, Nicholas II, also moved to limit secular authority. He called papal councils to prohibit the buying and selling of ecclesiastic offices, clerical marriages, and interference of laymen in church affairs. The cardinals were the true power behind the throne of St. Peter—a sort of first family of the family of Christendom—and they ensconced themselves in the Holy See and established a nascent papal bureaucracy. Hildebrand, archdeacon of the Roman archdiocese, provided the intellectual justification for the pope's boldness by arguing that church superiority stemmed from the basic differences between religious and temporal spheres. The church reigned supreme because it dealt with spiritual, not basely material, matters. But not all cardinals held this view. Some claimed that god granted authority to both the church and the state and therefore both had validity. The church should ignore temporal power so long as the power did not act against church interests or attempt to perform sacraments, including investing clergy. To that end, Nicholas II prohibited investiture by laymen with or without oaths of fealty.

Henry IV, Holy Roman Emperor, ignored this last stricture as did his vassals and opponents. The church did not press the issue until 1073 when Hildebrand became pope. Taking the name Gregory VII, the pope attacked Henry and the other secular leaders, claiming that the state bore the mark of Cain; the state was a human creation, originated by a murderer whose greed led him to kill his own brother, and liable to the same temptations and forces. Each human had one road to salvation, the subjection of his or her selfish will to the divine ends which the papacy pursued in the world. A pope-led Christendom would provide the morality needed to achieve a true earthly Christian community. Temporal powers were "beloved sons," family members but not the paterfamilias. Gregory then drew up his *Dictatus Papae*, which promulgated in no uncertain terms what he claimed for the throne of St. Peter and Christendom generally. God alone created the Christian church and gave the pope "universal" power, power over everything and everybody. The pope could "be judged by no man." The church "has never erred nor . . . will it ever err, through eternity" and the pope as the church's human embodiment could have his decrees "annulled by no one," while "he c[ould] annul the decrees of anyone." No religious meeting could occur or edict be announced without his approval, and the pope could break vassalage agreements and even "depose emperors." Anyone disagreeing with the pope forfeited the right to be part of Christendom.

Henry dismissed these clerical dictates and continued to appoint and invest clergymen. The investiture ceremony was largely symbolic. A lord, duke, or Holy Roman Emperor would give the incoming cleric a ring and staff, symbolizing marriage to the church and leadership of the Christian flock. Gregory objected and in 1075 opposed some of Henry's bishop appointments. Henry proclaimed Gregory "not pope, but false monk." He acknowledged his "respect for the papal office," but cautioned Gregory for mistaking "humility for fear" and daring "to make an attack upon the royal and imperial authority which we have received from God." Henry claimed himself "anointed to rule among the anointed of God" and according to scripture could "be judged by no one save God alone." He further maintained that god never called Gregory "to the rule of the church." Instead, Gregory's ascension came from secular sources. He used craftiness to gain wealth, wealth to gain favor, and favor to gain "the power of the sword," and Henry demanded that Gregory relinquish his immoral hold on the papacy.

Gregory refused to resign and declared Henry no longer king of Germany and Italy. Henry then declared the papacy vacant and scheduled a conclave to elect a new pontiff. Gregory excommunicated Henry for that act. The German nobility then rose up against Henry and he found himself in no position to beat back the challenge. Fully two-thirds of Henry's military might stemmed from ecclesiastic lands. Church-men refused to support an excommunicated individual, the penalty for which was also excommunication. Gregory prepared to select a new king, but Henry traveled to the site and, before the pope announced his choice, pleaded for absolution of his sins. The pope let Henry wait outside for three full days but determined that he would lose moral authority if he did not offer absolution to a truly contrite individual. The pope granted Henry an audience and Henry lay prostrate at his feet. The absolved Henry then was restored to the throne.

Henry's subservience to the pope was more apparent than real and did not end the secular-church debate. Henry stopped confronting the pope outright but his policies did not change. Nor did the pope feel free to excommunicate Henry a second time. A guerrilla warfare ensued in which German incursions into Italy kept papal author-ity down, while Gregory and his successors fomented rebellions in Germany. Not until 1122 was the controversy resolved. At the Concordat of Worms, Pope Calixtus II and Henry V reached a compromise. The concordat confirmed that both emperor and pope received their positions from god. Each had equal claim to the leadership of Christendom. Both also agreed to "make a true and lasting peace" with the other, his supporters, and followers. But neither now was more powerful than the other. The new dual leadership had the pope lead the heavenly quest, while the emperor guided its earthly counterpart. Investiture now became a fused ceremony. Clerics selected and ordained other clerics, giving them the ceremonial ring and staff. But all ordained clerics received from the emperor a scepter, which signified feudal obliga-tions, and the concordat required them to "perform all the [feudal] duties." Bishops and abbots needed to serve both secular and heavenly potentates, to be responsible to the Christian community.

Learning: Secular and Christian

Extension of Christendom to encompass both heaven and earth, manifested so pow-erfully in the investiture controversy, legitimated the examination of earthly occur-rences. Fascination with bestiaries and cataclysmic natural phenomena came from that union. The apparent imminence of Christ's Second Coming and the end of time focused interest on the time when he first came to earth, when Christianity began. As in art and architecture, the Roman past demanded consideration and its poetry and literature drew unprecedented attention. Cathedral schools, such as the one at

Rheims formed in the late tenth century, were run by bishop-appointed chancellors and introduced young men training for the clergy to this material. An educated clergy was the goal of these schools but concentration on grammar and rhetoric qualified what an educated clergy meant. Studying these Christian texts—even those written by Cicero and other pagans now seemed almost Christian—was didactic and demonstrated the fundamental unity that undergirded the concept of Christendom. Everywhere in grammar and rhetoric abounded symbols of god's fixed plan, his order. Salvation came through observation of things Christian and recognition of that glorious pattern; it could be reasoned. Introduction of dialectical thought around 1100 at Chartres and elsewhere initially did not undercut that meaning. Examination of the writings of church fathers and divine scripture produced instances that we would perceive as irreconcilable conflicts—as would later scholars—but these early logicians brooked no such disagreement. Both the church fathers and scriptures were absolutely true. Neither contradicted or disagreed with the other. God's plan, often presented symbolically as with bestiaries, ran through both and it remained the task of the reader to reveal it. Students even approached the new didactic dialectic through rote and declamation, just as they had Latin grammar and rhetoric.

Didactic investigation was not restricted to cathedral schools or the humanities. In the Italian cities of Pavia and Bologna, interested persons gathered to learn from Roman law. Again, as Christendom's home, Rome assumed monumental importance. Roman civil law was Christian law (although not church or canon law) and Christian order. There no formal establishment presented the subject. Masters, persons noted for their profundity and insight, attracted others wanting to learn of god's message from the study of Roman law and continued in that capacity until interest had been exhausted or better opportunities presented themselves. Unlike many at cathedral schools, these unaffiliated itinerant masters often had not taken religious vows.

Interest in Roman law did not stem from the sudden availability of new texts. It had always been known and early Barbarians had permitted Romans to practice it. But Barbarians themselves had found little use for Roman law. It reflected communal concerns, not individual ones. Concepts of wergelds and individual worth did not fit neatly in Roman codes. Only with the reemergence of a sense of a civil community was a body of civil law vital. It provided a sort of group conscience, broad parameters to inform this very public family, to oversee civil society in what was supposed to be a true Christian fashion. Earthly Christendom understood Roman law and gravitated to it for both ethereal and practical reasons.

For Further Reading

Adelson, Howard L. *Medieval Commerce*. Princeton: Van Nostrand, 1962.

Bloch, Marc. *Feudal Society*. Trans. by L. A. Manyon. London: Routledge & Kegan Paul, 1961.

Brandt, William J. *The Shape of Medieval History*. New Haven: Yale University Press, 1966.

Brooke, Christopher. *The Twelfth Century Renaissance*. New York: Harcourt Brace and World, 1969.

Cantor, Norman F. *The Meaning of the Middle Ages: A Sociological and Cultural History*. Boston: Allyn and Bacon, 1973.

DeVries, Kelly. *Medieval Military Technology*. Peterborough, Canada: Broadview Press, 1992.

Donnelly, James S. *The Decline of the Medieval Cistercian Laybrotherhood*. New York: Fordham University Press, 1949.

Duby, Georges. *The Chivalrous Society*. Trans. Cynthia Postan. Berkeley: University of California, 1980.

Duby, Georges, ed. *A History of Private Life: II-Revelations of the Medieval World*. Trans. Arthur Goldhammer. Cambridge, Mass.: Belknap Press of Harvard University, 1988.

Ennen, Edith. *The Medieval Town*. Amsterdam: North-Holland, 1979.

Fichtenau, Heinrich. *Living in the Tenth Century: Mentalities and Social Orders*. Trans. Patrick J. Geary. Chicago: University of Chicago Press, 1991.

Ganshof, F. L. *Feudalism*, 3d ed. New York: Harper Torchbooks, 1964.

Kunstler, Gustav, ed. *Romanesque Art in Europe*. New York: W. W. Norton, 1968.

Langdon, John. *Horses, Oxen and Technological Innovation: The Use of Draught Animals in English Farming from 1066 to 1500*. Cambridge: Cambridge University Press, 1986.

Le Goff, Jacob. *Time, Work, and Culture in the Middle Ages*. Trans. Arthur Goldhammer. Chicago: University of Chicago Press, 1980.

Lopez, Robert S. *The Commercial Revolution of the Middle Ages*. Englewood Cliffs, N.J.: Prentice-Hall, 1971.

Mundy, John H., and Peter Riesenberg. *The Medieval Town*. New York: Van Nostrand, 1958.

Nicholas, David. *The Medieval West, 400-1450. A Preindustrial Civilization*. Homewood, Ill: Dorsey Press, 1973.

Ovitt, George, Jr. *The Restoration of Perfection: Labor and Technology in Medieval Culture*. New Brunswick, N.J.: Rutgers, 1987.

Painter, Sidney. *The Rise of Feudal Monarchies*. Ithaca: Cornell University Press, 1951.

Phillips, William D., Jr. *Slavery from Roman Times to the Early Transatlantic Trade*. Minneapolis: University of Minnesota Press, 1985.

Pirenne, Henry. *Medieval Cities*. Princeton, N.J.: Princeton University Press, 1925.

Radding, Charles M. *The Origins of Medieval Jurisprudence*. New Haven: Yale University Press, 1988.

Rait, Robert S. *Life in the Medieval University*. Cambridge: Cambridge University Press, 1931.

Reynolds, Terry S. *Stronger Than a Hundred Men: A History of the Vertical Water Wheel*. Baltimore: Johns Hopkins University Press, 1983.

Rosenwein, Barbara H. *Rhinoceros Bound: Cluny in the Tenth Century*. Philadelphia: University of Pennsylvania Press, 1982.

Toy, Sidney. *Castles: Their Construction and History*. 1939; New York: Dover, 1985.

Trevor-Roper, Hugh. *The Rise of Christian Europe*. New York: Harcourt, Brace and World, 1965.

White, Lynn, Jr. *Medieval Religion and Technology*. Berkeley: University of California Press, 1978.

———. *Medieval Technology and Social Change*. New York: Oxford University Press, 1962.

White, T. H. *The Book of Beasts*. New York: G. P. Putnam's Sons, 1954.

Whitrow, G. J. *Time in History*. New York: Oxford University Press, 1988.

CHAPTER 7

Gothic Search for Order: The New Social Order, 1100–1360

St. Anselm, archbishop of Canterbury, set out about 1100 to prove the existence of god "by the force of reason alone." He looked at the material world and found many good things there. He then noted that comparisons between any two good things suggest that one or the other can have more goodness, that quantities of goodness may vary in things. He reasoned that goodness was a quality not dependent on context—things received a precise quantity of goodness at their formation—and that everything received its quality of goodness through another being. This being was pure goodness, "supremely good . . . neither equaled nor excelled." It "alone [was] good through itself . . . the highest of all existing beings." Humankind called this being god.

Nearly a century and a half later, St. Thomas Aquinas proved god's existence in much the same way. His senses showed him "the gradation to be found in things." One thing was hotter than another, for instance. All members of any graded category "resemble in their different ways something which is the maximum [in that graded category], as a thing is said to be hotter according as it more nearly resembles that which is hottest." In the same fashion, there exists "something which is truest, something best, something noblest, and consequently, something which is most being, for those things that are greatest in truth are greatest in being. . . . Now the maximum [in any graded category] is the cause of all [in that graded category], as fire, which is the maximum of heat, is the cause of all hot things. Therefore there must also be something which is to all beings the cause of their being, goodness, and every other perfection; and this we call God."

God and Humankind

Neither the proof offered by Anselm nor that put forth by Aquinas would satisfy modern philosophers or theologians. That is, of course, besides the point. Both seemed compelling within their time. More important, both employed techniques and relied on assumptions that Gothic men and women applied to virtually every activity in their daily lives. The difference between these saintly theologians and those of more modest social standing was area of emphasis and field of inquiry. Like their Gothic compatriots, Anselm and Aquinas both fervently believed in the existence of categories of things, real units typified by their members. Both also held a conceit new to the Gothic period, the conceit that god could be known, proved, or explained and that humankind had the power to achieve that knowledge. Humankind's hubris opened a new chapter in medieval history. If god was knowable by humans in some sense, even an elementary one, then was it not likely that less distance existed between god and humans? Was god not less awesome? And if god was knowable by humans, was not god more like humans? While few would have reflected on the god–human relationship in this explicit fashion, humankind's hubris

The Blessed Virgin. Mary's transformation from Queen of Heaven to mere mortal child in thirteenth-century art and literature reflected the narrowing of the gulf between god and humankind that characterized Gothic thought.

anthropomorphized god and diminished that all-powerful entity. In its place humankind erected a much more human god, one who loved humans and, because of that affection, was willing to die for their sins. By the thirteenth century, god was regularly portrayed as a human being, doing human-like tasks. Perhaps the most common rendering of god was as an architect of the universe, employing tools similar to those used on earth. Even the blessed virgin was changed. Frescoes, statuary, and other artistic forms had traditionally pictured the Virgin as the Queen of Heaven, a regal figure. In the thirteenth century, she too was reduced. She became a young girl, childlike, a most approachable and sympathetic creature. By virtue of its knowability and relative nonjudgmentalness, this merciful, comparatively nonjudgmental god played a less central part in human existence. In a real sense, humankind's newfound ability to approach knowledge of god made god a more distant, less immediate, less potent force in human affairs.

Making god less immediate also reflected humankind's new reliance on itself, on creating situations and mechanisms through which newly empowered humans could take an unprecedented measure of control over their affairs. It emphasized human solutions, designed by humans and implemented by humans for human needs. Governance was a primary beneficiary of this new optimism. Indeed, that men and women in the Gothic world contributed anything to Western civilization certainly would have astonished seventeenth- and eighteenth-century Europeans who viewed the era with such contempt that they dismissed its cultural style as barbaric, the style of the Germanic tribe, the Goths. And while the culture of the later medieval period in no way was reminiscent of the Goths some thousand years earlier, the moniker remains. Gothic Europe continues to be identified with a culture it hardly knew.

Reason, the Senses and Human Behavior

Humankind used reason and applied the dialectic method as then constituted, but human senses gathered the information upon which to reason. Observation therefore proved at least as important as reason. What the senses recognized was what was reasoned, and the senses determined only observable phenomena. To Gothic men and women, what was on the outside—observable—was the key to and generally consistent with what was on the inside—reality. Put more boldly and in personal terms, behavior, habits, or public action constituted a window to the soul; it was a window to what you were and how you defined yourself. In a period in which categories, including social categories, assumed a significance that affected virtually every sphere of human endeavor, behavior gained unprecedented station. Appearances were not deceiving. How you acted dictated to which group in the social hierarchy you belonged.

Behavior also claimed new importance in religious thought, and outward display proved its public measure. The new dictum of contrition, an inward state, required sinners to be truly penitent to remove their sins; it was not enough simply to pay a Christian wergeld. But contrition's inward nature forced reliance on outward activities, public behavior. Although the church believed earlier that any baptized person "fallen into sin [can] by true repentance . . . always be restored," it remained until

1215 for the church formally to detail true repentance and to stipulate the procedure to achieve that state. It mandated that each Christian confess his or her sins publicly—the private confessional is a much more recent invention—to a priest at least once a year. This acknowledgment and recounting of sinfulness as well as the protestations of remorse needed to be followed by demonstrating penitence through performing of specified church-ordered acts, acts of contrition. Only in that way could an individual "prove" himself or herself absolutely contrite. The heart's transformation was judged by the mouth's utterances and the hand's actions.

Gothic Order

Anselm's and Aquinas's proofs of god's existence depended not only upon categories but upon graded categories. Things contained or possessed different quantities of a quality and were more like that quality according to how closely they approached total purity. This focus on hierarchies was not limited to the saints but constituted a fundamental Gothic cultural form. Ordering things, constructing hierarchies, emerged as twelfth-, thirteenth-, and early fourteenth-century Europeans tried to establish lines of organization (and often authority) from the lowest form to the highest in virtually every human activity or endeavor. For example, Gothic Europeans coalesced into a number of elites differentiated by function and by outward display of social role. Distinctive intellectual, political, clerical, occupational, and bureaucratic elites crystallized during this period. These new elites were definitely not equal. Elites attempting to mark out their precise place within the social hierarchy contributed to social unrest.

Ancients and Moderns

Gothic clerics and others considered Greco-Roman writings more extensively than their Romanesque predecessors and generally with profound appreciation. The oft quoted observation of Bernard of Chartres that, "we are as dwarfs standing on the shoulders of giants" reflected that appreciation. But Bernard and others saw classical writings not as an end but as a beginning. "Thanks to their gigantic size" and "because we are carried and elevated" by these giants, we can use their works, Bernard noted in 1115; "we perceive many more things than they."

   Bernard's appreciation of Greco-Roman writings was not unconditional. Like others in the Gothic period, he emphasized those works consonant with Gothic notions. Aristotle, known simply as the Philosopher, became the single most important ancient author. His explicit classification schemes, rules for logic, and musings about the first cause of things resonated in the later Middle Ages. But Aristotle was not alone. Works of reason—dialectics, logic, grammar, law, and mathematics, for instance—and works of the senses—descriptions and taxonomies of natural and astronomical phenomena—were prized. Works of literature and the humanities—Greco-Roman tragedies, comedies, poetry, and history—were ignored. Ironically, European monasteries long had housed many relevant Greco-Roman texts. Previous generations had passed over these now crucial documents as not germane. The redis-covery of already available documents, which began in the very late eleventh century, was matched by an equally aggressive effort in the twelfth century and after to secure and translate additional appropriate material. Much of this new material had earlier fallen under Muslim control when the Muslims conquered a considerable part of what had been the Greek and Roman Near East. Muslim commentators had avidly translated the works into Arabic and added their remarks to them. Western Euro-peans translated into Latin these writings, as well as Greek manuscripts, whenever they came into their possession. As Christian Europe cleared Spain and Sicily of the Muslims, these two areas became translation centers. Aristotle's advanced logic texts reached the West just before 1100 but his *Physics* and *Metaphysics* were not available until the early thirteenth century. Euclid's *Geometry* came to Western Europe in 1126, while algebra arrived some two decades later. Ptolemy's astronomical *Almagest* was translated into Latin in Sicily before 1160, and Gerard of Cremona translated numerous works of physics, optics, biology, mechanics, and meteorology in about 1180 at Toledo.

Stairway to Heaven

These Greco-Roman works helped give final shape to the Gothic depiction of the nat-ural world. Emphasis on hierarchical arrangement of categories differentiated this view from Romanesque conceptions. For example, Romanesque Europeans embraced bestiaries because they believed that lessons for salvation abounded in the natural world. Gothic Europeans, on the other hand, held a more realistic view of nature. As the creation of a reasonable god—a god formed at least in part in humankind's own image—they expected nature to be reasonable. They set about to learn and understand that reason so as better to approach knowledge of god. Europeans in the twelfth cen-tury and later focused on nature's hierarchical character—it was as if nature was god the builder's construction, meticulously laid out from the foundation to the upper floors—and proclaimed it a ranked series leading from stones, which were the lowest things on earth because they lacked souls, to god. Angels sat beneath god in heaven but above the saints and earthly humanity. Humanity in turn resided above animals and plants. Nor were heaven and earth alike. The earth was immovable and at the uni-verse's center, the focus of god's attention. Up to nine spherical nesting heavens revolved around it. Each of these hierarchical heavens moved in pure circles and was made of quintessence, a perfect substance not found on earth. Outside these heavens rested the boundless, motionless abode of god, angels, and saints. Earthly motion was linear, not divinely circular. Four elemental substances comprised all terrestrial bod-ies—fire, earth, water, and air. Each had its own quality. Fire was hot and dry; air, hot and wet; earth, cold and dry; and water, cold and wet. The senses confirmed this rea-soning. It seemed natural for heavy things to fall and for smoke to go toward the celes-tial world.

Numerous Europeans carried the analysis of the natural hierarchy far beyond that outlined here. Dante Alighieri in his early fourteenth-century *Divine Comedy* divided earth into the populated northern hemisphere and a mountainous southern hemi-

Dante's Hell. Dante's Hell was a series of concentric circles. The more dastardly a person's sin the closer that person rested near the center for eternity. Satan, portrayed as an unspeakable monster, ruled these hierarchically organized, low depths and subjected sinners to cruelties consistent with their sins.

sphere of purgatory. Paradise rested far beyond the earth in the heavens, while hell descended from just beneath the soil to the center of the earth. Nine circles comprised Dante's hierarchical hell. Each soul resided in the circle appropriate for his or her sins. Those with the most heinous sins sat at the center of the earth and received the most terrible punishments. But Dante was not content simply to categorize hell into nine circles. He also divided some of the circles into rings and others into chasms, thereby further differentiating between sins—quantities of the quality of sin—and their respective punishments. To Dante, the palpable sins of lust, gluttony, suicide, blasphemy, simony, and schismatics were quantitatively different. Souls of individuals who had committed each of those sins received a different punishment and were confined to a different place in hell. For example, Dante's god consigned virtuous pagans and persons not baptized to hell's first circle. Original sin confined these persons to darkened hell, out of god's sight, but because they personally had done nothing wrong, no pain befell them. Contrast their fate to those souls in the fourth ring of the ninth circle, the lowest pits of hell. Three men had committed what to Dante was the ultimate sin, being a traitor to your benefactor. Judas Iscariot, the betrayer of Christ, remained imprisoned there as did Brutus and Cassius, the betrayers of Caesar and of Rome, which continued in the Gothic period to be viewed as Christendom's birthplace. Lucifer ruled this icy "realm of pain." He clamped his teeth around each of these betrayers as "blood slaver" dripped from his three mouths onto his chin. Each horrible sinner went through eternity "racked with torment keen" and often had his "spine flayed completely bare."

Order and Society

Acknowledgment of social station was a characteristic Gothic stance. Liberty seemed a product of society. Without society—the stability of social organization—and especially understanding of social position, liberty ceased to exist. This view depended upon several beliefs: humankind's ability to form society; fear that absence of society would produce a far worse situation; and recognition that society so created needed to approach expectations for it among a considerable portion of the population. We know that when society failed to approximate expectations, riots and other social disruptions occurred. Such was the case, for example, with the English nobles' refusal to support King John financially, an event that produced the Magna Carta, or with the Flemish laborers' revolt in 1255. Basic inequities among population groups were taken for granted as equality never figured in the social formulation. A late medieval principle of justness (perhaps even fairness) provided much of the social glue. Society was predicated precisely upon inequalities; inequalities were the pillars of social organization. Gothic justness was group-based, not individual-specific. It reified that individuals per se were important only insofar as each reflected a facet of society, a social group. Put another way, any individual served as a representative of the group of which he or she was a member. That conception made representative governance possible; individuals represented their group in governmental and administrative forums.

The Nobility

Each individual represented her or his group any time that group took public action, and no group was more conscious of that fact than the nobility. Its members recognized an essential tautology: Their standing dictated their public behavior and their public behavior justified their standing. In the years after 1100, the nobility labored hard to establish and create its uniqueness. Expenditure of moneys at a prodigious rate became one way to mark the distinctiveness of this elite. The nobility acted as if their social class demanded that they spend far more than their estates produced. They craved the most expensive silks, the rarest spices from the Far East—saffron was worth more by weight than gold, and ginger, nutmeg, cinnamon, and pepper were almost as dear—and the largest, most ostentatious dwellings. None of these extravagances made economic sense; they were not investments. Nor were they for defense. Rather they functioned to delineate the nobility.

The castle's form and purpose testified to this changed milieu. Earlier castles quartered troops and provided havens for inhabitants of the manors' hamlets when attacked. Twelfth- and thirteenth-century castles were residences for the nobility. Often the size of small towns, these monstrous structures had huge outer walls—

some were 32 feet tall and 10 feet thick—with defensive turrets, towers, parapets, and ramparts upon them. Nonrectangular walls, without bad sight lines or corners to attack, proved easiest to defend. A second wall was often placed inside the outer wall as was a large bailey—one measured 435 by 650 feet. Food, water, and troops could be stored inside these walls. A single extremely well-fortified drawbridge, gate, and gatehouse complex offered entry to each of these most protected castles.

The focus of each of these castle formations was the center where the nobility resided, generally in a stone keep. Rectangular keeps, some more than 30 feet square, dwarfed their circular counterparts. These several-story-high structures catered to the nobility's comforts. The lord and lady's chamber dominated the upper floor and in turn was dominated by the great bed. Interlaced strips of leather supported feather mattresses and ensured that the lord and lady rested comfortably on their wooden-framed, curtained bed, which went with them whenever they traveled. Wooden chests and wardrobes stored clothes, which sometimes were hung on pegs on the chamber's walls. A small anteroom led to the chamber and, after 1200, to a small family room with a large window and fireplace. Children's bedrooms remained nearby. Sometimes, too, the lord and lady each had his or her own sleeping chamber. Frequent baths, the conspicuous use of water for a nonessential purpose, became popular among the nobility in the thirteenth century and the most prestigious nobles began to take them indoors. Latrines also found their way indoors. Situated near bedchambers, latrines were made distinct from those rooms and usually cordoned off from the rest of the keep. Gravity carried the noxious wastes in earthen pipes from latrines to moats. Ironically, latrines sometimes threatened castle security. Enemies climbed up latrine shafts to enter bedchambers.

The more mundane acts of living and governing occurred on the keep's lower floors. An executive headed each household and ministerial department. For example, a household steward maintained the household accounts, making sure that sufficient quantities of bread and other commodities were on hand. The estate steward kept track of the manor's earnings, expenditures, and possessions. The chaplain ran the chapel and also kept the lord's seal, which required the chaplain to act as secretary and handle the lord's correspondence. The chamberlain presided over the bedchamber, the keeper of the wardrobe took care of clothing, and the usher regulated the door to the great hall, the site of ceremonies and business transactions. The butler controlled the beverage area and the cook headed the kitchen. The stable was the marshal's province.

Paralleling the formal division of authority within castles was the merger of nobility with knighthood to create a single, formalized elite. Knights, renowned for their ability to fight on horseback, had traditionally owed service to others; they were not truly free. Noble persons had been persons of property, persons of position and power within society but only so long as they controlled that property. In France at the very end of the eleventh century, persons of property and standing began to adopt the title of *knight*, an event memorialized in court documents. In the early twelfth century, nobles took *knight* as a hereditary title, an attribute of family. The title no longer stayed with the property owner but went to all his sons, even those receiving no inheritance. The sons then passed the title on to their male heirs. A similar co-opting of the term *knight* occurred throughout Western Europe a bit later. At about the same time that the French nobility called itself knights, traditionally

The Nobility. Knights and nobles merged to become a single group in the twelfth century. A code of behavior, chivalry, separated nobles from others as did their garments. Family emblems distinguished noble families as early as the thirteenth century.

defined knights began to imitate the nobility. Again first in France and then through Europe, knights restructured their houses to mimic castles. They dug moats and raised turrets—even when there was no clear military advantage. They also copied other customs of the nobility, including primogeniture. By 1200, differences between knights and noblemen had virtually disappeared. That disappearance enabled kings further to expand the nobility in the thirteenth century. Royal treasurers wanted to tap wealthy urban merchants, who lacked only status. These well-to-do men rectified that shortcoming when kings sold them patents of nobility. They now had gained the appearance of nobility, which was akin to nobility itself.

Nobility came with fixed rules of descent, status, inheritance, and even behavior. The church contributed to this precise formulation by seeking to turn the nobility into Christ's knights. The nobility was to be in Christ's service, fighting for Christ's cause, a church-defined objective. Participation in the Crusade to free the Holy Land struck many church officials as the exact sort of task Christ's knights should undertake, and numerous military religious orders emerged to fight the infidel. The Knights Templar became the most famous and later would become masters of the pope's treasury. Others in the church focused on knightly behavior during peaceful times and advocated a model ethical behavior to justify social position and military vocation. For example, Stephen of Fougeres called on knights always to defend the weak and perpetuate justice. They were brave and loyal and obediently submitted to the church. The innate superiority of these men of honor showed in their public behavior. Knights were always courteous, Christian, and ethical, men of honor even without an inheritance.

Such a precisely defined state required training, and a pattern of knightly preparation developed. The church further formalized the process of becoming a knight by converting the ceremony of dubbing to a sacrament in the twelfth century. At age 7, boys of noble birth went to the house of a great lord to learn the arts of war and manners. Actual fighting experience began about age 13 and in his late teens a youth became a squire, a servant to a knight, caring for his horse, armor, and weapons. A lad in his early twenties was then ready to become a knight. The dubbing ceremony began with an all-night vigil at a chapel. The knight-to-be was clad in special robes and dressed in special armor. A priest presided over the dubbing mass, which included numerous speeches outlining the knight's Christian duties and communion. The knight's father then touched his sword lightly to his son's shoulders as he knelt. Knights also had knelt at earlier dubbings. There, however, the father smashed the young knight about his shoulders, usually knocking him to the ground, to symbolize the roughness of earthly life.

Expansion of who could become a nobleman, coupled with primogeniture—granting the firstborn male child the entire holdings—guaranteed that a large portion of the nobility in the relatively peaceful Gothic period would be landless. The manorless nobility nonetheless had manners as a chivalric code governed their affairs, especially when in the presence of other nobility. Behaving like a knight constituted part of the training because knightly behavior identified a knight. Beginning in the late eleventh century in France, nobility followed precise rules of behavior and decorum. Failing to cleave to those rules marked the offender as ignoble, a potent sign of inner strife. Gallantry, courtesy, and honor characterized the chivalric code, but so, too, did a profound admiration of noble love. This courtly love was ethereal, emotional, spiritual, true. It was a product of mind, of conscience. Physical consummation was not the point. In that sense, love differed markedly from marriage. Marriage remained the union of families and possessions, the forging of alliances, and the transfer of property by dowry. The church insinuated itself into marriage in the twelfth century but only to sanctify that act. The church served as the guarantor that the bride and groom willfully entered into the marriage contract, that the persons pledged fidelity to one another—an important protection of property—and that they were not related. Priests commonly officiated at noble weddings in the thirteenth century and often blessed the marriage bed. Heirs further solidified property agreements.

Courtly love's ethereal nature required a fitting subject of admiration and noble-women soon accepted that role. Only women of superior virtue, refinement, devotion, and loyalty would be worth any sacrifice. Older women watched and taught younger women. Castles and smaller noble dwellings housed a ladies' chamber, off limits to men. Women engaged in acts of personal refinement there: sewing, embroidery, and prayer. The archtypical noblewoman assumed a characteristic form: creamy complexion, blond hair, long face, regular nose, and thin lips. Real women tried to approximate those outward indications of nobility and used dyes and various formulas to achieve it. They also masked their bodies. Large-breasted women bound their chests, while slender females wore bulky clothing to appear heavier. No true noble-woman or nobleman would permit even a spouse to see them naked, even during sex—public nudity was the act of a maniac. Outward appearance defined the inner person.

Noblemen labored to win the hearts of these noble females. Noblewomen demanded gentleness and mastery of the fine arts from their spiritual suitors. Lyric poetry, declamation, letters, and song showed a lady a knight's virtue and adherence to the stipulations of courtly love. These Gothic humanities, which included the legend of King Arthur and the Knights of the Round Table, constituted rules for noble behavior. Tensions between love and calling and duty and honor as well as questions of conflict of loyalties and the nature of fidelity focused concern. Instrument-carrying troubadours and trouveres sang ballads and recited poems of adventure and romance throughout southern Europe. Like the vernacular literature of the day, which these ballads and poems so closely resembled, these manuals of how knights and ladies acted were extremely detailed and precise, and reinforced courtly love behavior.

Noblewomen and noblemen welcomed these generally landless knights into their courts and provided them sustenance for extended periods. Propitious marriages remained possible but most knights errant earned their livelihoods through force of arms. The Crusades and other wars siphoned off a considerable percentage of these surplus knights. Others supported themselves through tournaments. Held by great lords, these later twelfth-century tournaments had their own formalized rules. Two groups of knights charged each other. They then chased through fields until one group captured the other. The captured group ransomed its freedom with its horses and armor. The victorious knights could dispose of their booty as they wished.

Jousting began in the twelfth century but did not figure prominently in tournaments until two centuries later. By then, blunt wooden-headed lances less likely to cause fatalities had replaced their more dangerous counterparts. The church fervently opposed tournaments but failed to end them. Tournament violence was less a problem for the church than the debauchery that accompanied the games, especially the excesses of food, sex, and drink. Like debauchery, heraldry was part of tournaments almost from their beginning. Noble families each designed symbols to mark them as distinct from non-nobles and from each other. These character- and status-testifying symbols first appeared on banners. By the thirteenth century, armor and surcoats bore them, and a nobilitywide system of rules developed to govern these heraldic emblems. Nothing was left to chance. Shields were partitioned in precise ways and certain animals situated in various positions held special meaning.

Merchants

The nobility's desire to behave in a fashion equal to its station increased the number and influence of merchants, and encouraged their coalescence as a discrete social group. Merchants purchased spices and silks from the Far East and other fine goods to sell to those persons whose social standing depended on ostentatious display. Merchants also benefited from the church's concept of a Christian knight. Tens of thousands of Crusaders required transportation to the Holy Land as well as supplies. Knights errant comprised much of these crusading forces, but so, too, did the landed nobility; even sitting kings—England's Richard the Lion-Hearted, France's Philip II, and Frederick I, Holy Roman Emperor and King of Germany and Italy—participated in the third Crusade in 1189. Merchants in towns on the Italian peninsula found themselves especially well situated to profit from the Crusades and the Far Eastern trade. Muslims blocked land routes to the East, and Western Europeans could reach Jerusalem and the Orient only by water. Merchants, their ships equipped with astrolabes and mariners' compasses to chart direction and rudders to steer that course, reaped tremendous fortunes on these transactions. But the Far East trade was only part of the Italian trade penetration. Italian merchants took Far Eastern and other goods by pack train into Europe, especially the Champagne area of France. Located on a plain in northeastern France, Champagne was easily accessible from Germany, England, Flanders, and Scandinavia. The counts of Champagne set up a series of six international fairs yearly, providing merchants the potent inducements of safe conduct and swift justice. Each fair ran for several weeks and each specialized in a particular product. Cloth, leather, and fur merchants met once a year in Champagne as did merchants offering products by weight, such as spices and gold. Merchants from throughout Europe journeyed to Champagne to exchange their wares with other merchants, who then took those products back home and sold them to locals.

The Champagne and other lesser fairs met regularly. Homogenization of goods throughout Western Europe was not the only product of these fairs. The same merchants repeatedly encountered one another and familiarity bred agreement. Merchants used the same system of weights and measures and pledged to uphold the same regulations, the basis of a particularized commercial law, distinct from other types of law. Familiarity also produced trust, a sense of interdependence, and credit because immediate payment was not always possible or even desirable. And credit fostered extensive record keeping since memories sometimes failed or could be disputed. Quills, wax tablets, parchment, seals, ribbon, and ink constituted Gothic office equipment. Contracts also formalized procedure and drew their inspiration from the assumption the transactions would occur at regular intervals in regularized quantities at regularized rates. Some traveling merchants in Germany went further. They seized upon the regularity of their arrangements over a particular trade route to refuse to trade with merchants working other routes.

Regularized rates and contracts meant regular income, a luxury few medieval men or women possessed. Some merchants employed it to generate additional income. They formed themselves into collectives to undertake high-risk, high-profit ventures. Merchants voyaging to secure raw materials or to sell finished products generally risked less of their funds—and received proportionately less profit—in these short-term partnerships than did those who just put up capital and remained at home. Italian merchants specialized in these speculative risk-sharing enterprises, which usually lasted only a few voyages. They also pooled resources, using convoys and caravans to take products overland or across the Alps. By the mid-thirteenth century, Genoan merchantmen had sailed through the Strait of Gibraltar to France, Flanders, and England. Direct water access to European markets ultimately killed the Champagne fairs. At the same time, these merchants increased the importance of smaller, local fairs as commodities previously available only through Champagne now directly penetrated the North. German merchants found their way through the North Sea to England and the Low Countries.

Other merchants used their regularized income to purchase status. Christians long had viewed trading, profiting from the labor of others, as tainted. Usury, the earning of money off of god's time, smacked of debauchery. The church had relegated both to the Jews, persons outside Christian society and restricted to living in specific urban enclaves. The social stigma persisted even as the extensive Italian trade began depending on Christian money changers in the early twelfth century. By the thirteenth century, the transformation of the merchant class from Jew to Christian was so complete that Jews could conveniently be expelled from much of Europe or persecuted without damaging commerce. Banking, installment buying, and even credit were tasks assumed by Christian merchants. Men participating in these morally objectionable occupations sometimes also had feudal obligations. Although many transformed their feudal duties into a single financial payment, maintenance of feudal commitments marked them as not totally free. Purchase of their freedom became the next logical step and an always overextended nobility generally welcomed the one-time influx of new funds. Purchase of the accouterments of nobility, including noble patents and heralds, frequently followed as did large payments to the church, a public suggestion of benevolence and piety.

The merchants' regular purchase of the same raw materials and sale of the same finished products encouraged them to invest in the activities that went in between. This merchant intrusion into manufacturing did not introduce factory production. Merchants entered instead into a series of contracts with artisans and others to carry the raw material from farm to market. Italian cotton cloth making provided a most dramatic example. Cotton cloth, like silk, long had been a luxury. Introduction of the cotton plant into new areas increased cotton's availability as did expanded trade between the Muslims and the Christian West. Italian merchants joined these factors with the desire of individuals to express their station through material possessions. They first gained from a noble the right of self-governance for some locality. They then used that right to establish a governmental unit, contacted artisans situated elsewhere, and attempted to get them to relocate. As inducements, merchants offered rent-free shops, tools, and loans without interest as well as citizenship rights. Sometimes legal protection against foreign creditors joined the mix. In return for these privileges, merchants expected artisans to sign contracts pledging to produce cotton cloth from cotton. Artisans and their assistants separated fibers from seeds by hand and with rollers, beat the bolls to separate fibers, and then carded the cotton by raking it through wooden-toothed boards. Others spun the cotton into threads, classified the threads by length, and wove them into cloth. The cloth required bleaching with wood ashes and lime and by laying it in the sun for several weeks. The garment was then washed, stretched to its original size, and dried. Artisans raised the nap and sheared it, finally pressing the cloth to consolidate the fibers.

English and continental wool merchants adopted a less communal, more businesslike approach. They signed long-term advance contracts with flock-owning monasteries for large quantities of wool. Merchants took possession of the wool and then "sold" it to artisans who would prepare it as thread and agreed to purchase the cloth after dyers had colored the material. That type of agreement provided artisans with incentives to achieve production economies at every turn. More work than ever before was done by apprentices, who labored for room and board. Apprentices divided out damaged wool and sorted the rest into grades. They washed, dried, beat, combed, and carded the fibers and then spun them into yarn on a distaff and spindle or, in the thirteenth century, a spinning wheel (which made cloth more standard by producing a more uniform thread). The stronger warp thread was sized and wound. The woof thread was wound around a bobbin and placed in a shuttle. Another group of artisans—the weavers—then blended the material together and transferred it to fullers to consolidate the fibers. The fullers stretched the thickened cloth on a tenter by means of tenter hooks and used teasels to tease the nap. A long shears shortened and evened the nap, which was brushed. Dyers then added color, which increasingly became a way to mark social distinctions. Darker colors were favored: black, greens, blues, purples, and oranges proved most popular but grays, yellows, and beiges also were used. White reflected mourning.

Artisans

Cotton and wool manufacture demonstrated the considerable specialization of function within each area of production. Status distinctions accompanied functional differences. Weavers and fullers had different statuses as did cotton and woolen workers. Demarcations extended beyond particular industries. Goldsmiths and silversmiths proved the most highly respected artisans while clothmenders and dishmenders—nothing was thrown away—were much lower on the social hierarchy. Butchers had more status than candlemakers but less than bakers. Social hierarchies also operated within trades. Three distinct statuses comprised most occupations: master, journeyman, and apprentice. These designations reflected degrees of technical proficiency as determined by other trade members. Masters had mastered their craft. These experts had made a *piece* their peers had deemed worthy of a *master*, a masterpiece, and headed a small workshop in which others learned and practiced the craft. A master goldsmith's workshop, for example, needed a quantity of the precious metal on hand, a small furnace for heating and refining it, and a full complement of the little anvils necessary to fashion wares. It also required work space for a handful or more of individuals. Journeymen were nearly as proficient at their trades as masters but lacked experience or the funding to establish their own shops. Apprentices were new to the trade. They watched the journeymen and masters and learned from their example. But the masters' and the journeymen's example was more than craft-related. Apprentices, generally adolescent boys, almost became members of their masters' families, living in their homes usually for four or more years. There they were taught social as well as craft responsibilities.

Guilds. Guilds regulated most aspects of their members' lives. Guilds specified who could be members and how they could achieve membership, guaranteed that products were made in particular ways and to certain minimum standards, and that members behaved in a manner to bring credit to their fellow guild members.

This highly articulated occupational status system was especially pronounced in towns or cities, although villages increasingly became sites of large-scale production after 1300. Often complete with walls and other fortifications, these towns or cities rarely had radii of more than one-half mile. Only a handful of places throughout Europe, most of them on the Italian peninsula, had more than 25,000 persons. Radial or grid street patterns predominated, but rapid growth and terrain-produced problems often resulted in disarray. Urban sites were generally crowded and dirty. By the twelfth century, cities and towns had identifiable quarters, places in which persons with different identities lived. In the case of artisans, their identity was their special occupation but other measures of identity included place of origin or religion—Jew or Muslim.

It was the acceptance of identity by quarter—places were by no means limited to having only four quarters—that proved particularly illuminating. Gothic artisans conceived of each craft's members in a locality as a brotherhood. Members of the same craft not only congregated together in a certain section of a town or village but these men generally socialized together, established common charitable obligations—such as providing for a member's widow and children—and engaged in common religious festivals. Masters guided these hierarchically arranged units but each member represented the entire group. Individual behavior ceased to exist per se, a fact recognized quite early by these collectives. To protect against renegade, untutored, or corrupt practitioners of a trade, these men established governments among themselves. Elected guild masters headed these guilds, which worked ceaselessly to protect their members' collective reputations. Guild members met regularly in guild halls, purchased or rented buildings demarcating social space. Each guild rigorously scrutinized each candidate for inclusion. Persons lacking good moral character were excluded. Guilds also created codes of personal and occupational ethics to regulate members and to guarantee their common reputations. Perjurers were prohibited from work for a year and a day, for example, while certain minimum acceptable production standards protected crafts from unscrupulous or unprepared workmen. A standard of roundness, for instance, governed bead makers. By their very existence, guilds restricted participation in a craft to members of the brotherhood. Others in the area practicing the trade were shunned, isolated, left without brothers. Regulation of entry and participation were very important to guild members' survival and prosperity. The medieval concept of justness, of fairness, required artisans to ask for a fair or just price for their goods, not necessarily the top price. Their demonstration of fairness in pricing reflected the brothers' inner justness. They were not greedy or selfish. In fact, guilds often required all masters to charge the same price for their goods. The pricing monopoly, coupled with the membership monopoly, ensured that guild members made a satisfactory livelihood. The concept of a just price also justified limits on the number of guild members. Few begrudged a tradesman a livelihood but many objected to an artificially high price used to support numerous shops when a handful would have sufficed. To ensure members a living wage—a just wage—guilds sometimes restricted membership to a relative few to keep prices up or, less frequently, mandated the maximum number of hours a guild brother could work (and therefore the number of pieces he could produce in a day).

These guilds governed public behavior (even economic behavior) and were ubiquitous. Paris had over 130 guilds in 1292, for example. In addition to the numerous food guilds (butchers, bakers, candlemakers, brewers), transportation guilds (teamsters), or esoteria (bookbinders), Paris had 18 guilds that cut or gathered materials, such as fire-wood or broken glass, and 5 that engaged in sculpture or building trades. Paris also was the home of 22 guilds that worked in some type of metallurgy, a similar number that produced cloth or leather, and 36 that turned cloth and leather into finished clothing or jewelry. Ten Parisian guilds built, mended, or modified household furniture, and 15 engaged in financial, banking, or clerking pursuits.

Not all these guilds produced goods. Nor were they viewed as equal. Some occupations had more status than others. But each functioned among its membership in a similar way: to regulate each individual member's behavior to bring credit on—or at least not reduce the standing of—that occupation within the community. In guilds that produced a good (not a service), the workshop stood as the fundamental site of production, the focus of both manufacture and social organization. The master-journeyman-apprentice structure dominated the shop but the wives of masters and sometimes of journeymen also worked there. On occasion, widows of masters took their husbands' place within the shop and the guild hierarchy. Much less frequently was a woman admitted to a guild in which her husband or father was not a member. Women without previous familial connections perhaps gained guild recognition only during periods of shortage. They received less pay than their male counterparts and could not hold guild office or train apprentices. A few occupations, such as lacemaker or laundress, were clearly given over to women. Rarely were these occupations organized by guilds.

Prime Movers

Also new to the Gothic European manufacturing trades was an intensified interest in and reliance on waterwheels. Human and animal power remained important, but waterwheels powered an increasing number of trades. It would only be a slight exaggeration to claim that the Gothic period was gripped by waterwheel mania as virtually every population center built these devices. Artisans often located near waterways to use these prime movers. Mooring a mill to a bridge provided access and stability as tradesmen could enter stationary mills from shore. But joining mills to bridges constricted stream flow, which undermined supports and sometimes caused structures to topple into rivers. Floating mills required no cofferdams for erection and proved a popular alternative. Two forms prevailed. A single hull mill was flanked by two small wheels or a single large wheel was surrounded by a double hull. Floating mills did not block streams but mill pilots needed to move them to permit boats and ships to pass. On numerous occasions inept pilots rammed bridges with their mills. Creation of separate watermill races had neither bridge nor floating mill drawbacks but were very expensive. Construction of dams, sluices, and watergates gave these race mills great power.

Windmills offered watermills competition beginning in the twelfth century. Popular in windy areas without nearby waterways, windmills generally were underpowered, used primarily as grain mills. Post mills, the earliest windmills, probably developed in England. Builders pivoted these little houses to rotate whenever their large crossed sails caught a breeze. The sails' horizontal axle was geared to a vertical shaft used to rotate grinding wheels. Watermills, however, found much more extensive applications. They milled mash, mustard, pigments, and dyes. Watermills produced olive and poppy oils. Introduction of camshafts and camwheels in the twelfth century enabled wheels to raise an object and to drop it repeatedly in the same spot. Ore stamping mills and triphammers for consolidating iron blooms on a hearth incorporated cams and combined them with great weights. Fulling, hemp, and oak bark mills also employed cams but linked them with knife-like projectiles to tear apart fibrous substances. Cams or use of mill-powered cranks, a late twelfth-century adaptation, produced sawmills, grinding mills for metal or stone sharpening and polishing, and water-powered wood lathes. Waterwheel-driven, crank-raised bellows permitted iron smelting to occur at higher temperature from the thirteenth century and yielded a better quality iron. Fourteenth-century Gothic Europeans used mill-turned cranks to draw iron through a series of ever narrower templates to yield wire.

Raw Materials

Wire manufacture and bellows-produced iron point to the centrality of that metal in late medieval Europe. From horseshoes to farm tools and from crossbows to building materials and reinforcements, iron was heavily used. So, too, was wood. Wood charred in a diminished oxygen supply became charcoal, the primary fuel for refining iron ore (Europeans did not use coal in any appreciable quantities until the fifteenth century). Wood heated buildings and ships, and most structures were made of it. Timber-framed houses, waterwheels and windmills, bridges, looms, casks, and wheelbarrows, a thirteenth-century invention, required tremendous numbers of trees. As early as the 1170s, the incredible demand for wood, coupled with the clearing of farmland, gave rise to fears of deforestation and eventual crippling wood shortages.

Artisan Life

Successful masters in highly prized trades had a modestly comfortable existence. They had their own several-story homes. The second floor, placed above the workshop that in most occupations also served as salesroom, was the most interesting. Connected to the shop by a steep staircase, the second floor was directly beneath the bedchambers. It usually included a hearth for light, heat, and cooking, oil lamps, and small oiled-parchment-covered windows. Dyed linen cloth covered the walls of this low-ceilinged room. Benches and an easily dismantled trestle table converted the room into a dining hall. A series of cupboards, some of which were simply for display, surrounded the hearth. Wooden chests stored pots, kettles, and other goods. A broad cloth served as a tablecloth. Two-handled bowls, knives, and spoons were dishware.

Artisans craved public approbation as much as merchants and nobles, a fact reflected in the great concern over manners. These status-seeking and status-hungry men and women attempted through their public actions to convey a sense of gentility, a sign of higher social station. At the same time, displays of gentility would mark those exhibiting the behaviors as separate from and better than the lower social orders. Formalized table manners were a product of that sensibility. Gentlefolk, artisans were warned, "eat slowly, take small bites, do not talk while eating, do not drink with their mouths full. Knives are never put in the mouth. Soup must be eaten silently, and the spoon not left in the dish. One does not belch, lean on the table, hang over his dish, or pick his nose, teeth, or nails. Food is not dipped into the salt cellar. Bread is broken, not bitten. Blowing on food to cool it is commonly practiced but frowned upon. Because the

Noblewomen. Noblewomen characteristically wore garments with deep necklines, gathered waistlines, and detachable sleeves. Such clothes denote a noble station, but they also reflect the Gothic period's desire to make distinct men's and women's apparel.

wine cup is shared, one must wipe the grease from one's lips before putting them on the cup." Women of the artisan class tried to imitate the nobility whenever possible, seeking to write, add, embroider, or play the lute. They also learned to guard their public demeanor. To appear refined, women were taught to walk calmly and straight, but not alone. Never did a cultured woman look a man in the face on the street; she always looked at the ground. Hiring a wet nurse proved a sign of elevated station but being hired as a wet nurse was not. Women in church were told to kneel courteously, pray, not to laugh or talk too much, hold themselves upright at communion, and sing boldly. Robert of Blois, a thirteenth-century commentator, also warned women to watch their countenance in church, "for one is in the public eye, which notes good and evil." Clothing was used to differentiate among social strata. Earlier differences had been of quality, not style. By the later twelfth century, however, different colors in clothing began to connote different statuses. Social demarcation, boundaries among identified parts of society, were not restricted to occupation or class. A differentiation of the sexes, extending far beyond the idea of the lady, also occurred. To a significant degree, women stopped being considered property and became persons, different from and likely inferior to men. The church's demand of consent in marriage came from the notion of women as a distinct part of the social order as did different social roles for men and women. Women of the merchant or artisan classes learned housewifery at home and raised the children. They engaged in business activities only in extraordinary situations. Distinctions between the sexes also extended to dress. Members of both sexes had worn simple wool or linen tailored gowns, with high necklines and long sleeves. Gothic men and women dressed differently from each other and their predecessors. They also dressed in layers, each distinct from that above or below it. Underwear came first to the aristocracy in the twelfth century and soon this mark of status spread to the merchant and artisan classes. Men's cotton or linen undershirts and drawers were sewn and fitted. Women's underclothes were looser fitting, like a gown. Men increasingly wore trousers, a tight-fitting combination of breeches and stockings. Long-sleeved tunics covered their upper torsos and in turn were covered in the north by a sleeveless, pocketless woolen hooded surcoat. Cotton quilted jackets came into vogue in the later twelfth century. Noblewomen wore gowns with plunging necklines, detachable sleeves, distinct waistlines, and padded bodices. Women of lesser status dressed in tunics with sleeves that laced from wrist to elbow. These tunics were covered by belted surcoats gathered at the waist. Thin-soled, soft leather shoes finished the wardrobe.

Social Order and Individual Identity

The noted French historian Jacques Le Goff maintained that each twelfth-century man had a "new consciousness of himself" and that new consciousness, that new identity "came to him only through the estate to which he belonged, the professional group of which he was a part, or the trade in which he engaged."[1] Le Goff's statement ignored women as well as other forms of identity but his point that each person's identity stemmed from his or her membership in a social group certainly reflected the Gothic passion for differentiation. Yet differentiation was tempered by a recognition that the various social groups, no matter how distinctive, achieved their distinctiveness when compared to others. In that sense, Gothic distinctiveness was based on a group's relationship to other groups, groups larger than families. These differentiable groups together constituted society, which took on new force in medieval life. Identity was in part dependent upon participation with others of different identities.

[1]Jacques LeGoff, *Time, Work, and Culture in the Middle Ages* (Chicago: University of Chicago Press, 1980): 114.

That remained true even in villages where the vast majority of Gothic men and women lived in circumstances similar to those of their parents and grandparents: as serfs on manors. Widespread adoption of the three-field agricultural system, heavy plow use—a foot-adjusted lever permitted plowmen to vary plow depth—horse hauling and plowing, and especially the almost universal pooling of labor and equipment reflected the new social emphasis, an emphasis on cooperation with those outside the biological family. Many who wrote about identity during the period likened the social unit to a human organism in which each social group corresponded to a body part. As in humans, all parts of this social human were necessary for proper functioning; a body could not live well without hands, for example. But also as in a human being, all parts of society were not equal. Some were indispensable, such as the brain or heart, while the organism could survive the removal of others. Peasants and day laborers were sometimes referred to as society's feet and craftsmen became the arms.

Social Order and Time

The notion of group identity emphasized uniformity of practice and observance among persons claiming membership in or affinity to a particular facet of society. Standard observance or practice required a means to measure standardness. Gothic men and women often sought that standard in time. Divisions of night and day into 12-hour blocks, an approach that made the length of each daylight and night hour change daily, gave way to 24 equal hours. The standardized hour enabled clerics—in principle at least—to regularize prayer. Their much more human god was the great orderer. Monks over a large area achieved a measure of grace by praying at the same time each day. Other social units and groups besides monasteries and monks gravitated to uniform time. Clocks connected to bells unified activities in urban areas. They announced regularized mealtimes, work breaks, and the closing and opening of markets and gates. They marked the time for regular assemblies and daily curfew. They helped guilds regularize their members' activities. For example, merchants in Italy as early as 1200 relied on clocks to divide the business day, establishing different times for considering dowries, contracts, and partnerships. Clocks became so important that guilds of clockmakers could be found occupying specific quarters in many larger towns in the late twelfth century.

Water clocks measured Gothic time but the shift to equal hours—first employed in these water-driven devices—made mechanical clocks practical. Gravity-powered mechanisms marked time while escapements regularized it by ensuring that units of time had equal lengths. These ponderous mechanisms worked extremely poorly—personal clocks remained a Renaissance phenomenon—but they became increasingly common by the late Middle Ages. Virtually every city came to be dominated by a public clock. Perhaps part of the Gothic fascination with mechanical clocks stemmed from the similarity between their mechanisms and then current ideas of social organization. Both society and mechanical clocks seemed composed of discrete yet related parts. Each worked properly only when each part fulfilled its special function.

Gothic men and women went one step further. They seized time from god and appropriated it for humankind. Lending money at interest was one example of earn-

Mechanical Clocks. Mechanical clocks quickly incorporated design features consistent with church and cathedral architecture. Like cathedrals and churches, clocks seemed to join the heavens and the earth. Their mechanisms depended on the idea that each unit of time was the same length.

ing money from what had earlier been god's time, but the idea of time-derived profits stands as an essential underpinning of modern capitalism. It found expression first in agreements among Italian merchants and then spread throughout Europe. The concept of earning money from time even undergirded the late medieval idea of teaching. Students paid for their teachers' time as much as their knowledge and as a consequence exacted significant penalties for those not providing the agreed-upon quantity. Ending a lecture early resulted in financial punishments as did missing a scheduled meeting period.

Social Order and Governance

The Gothic period produced two new forms of governance: the municipal corporation and the kingdom. Both established hierarchical relationships between society's disparate parts and both derived their authority to a large extent from the consent of the governed. Gothic men and women generally understood the necessity of inequalities and expected government to provide many opportunities to some and less to others. Both kingdoms and municipal corporations were forms of representative governance. Both selected individuals from specific groups to represent the views and interests of all members of that group. That all groups were not accorded the same rights to representation did not mean that representation remained a hollow shell. It merely suggested that representation need not be equal throughout the social sphere.

Municipal Corporations

Gothic town and city creation outstripped its Romanesque forebears. Lords continued to plant serfs, freemen formed communes to fight collectively against a higher power—associations under private law for limited times—and kings and other lords established commercial towns. Some cities became specialized: In central Italy, municipalities functioned as the pope's bankers. Although most municipalities continued to depend on the agricultural lands surrounding them, Gothic men and women increasingly made distinctions between rural and urban places.

A dramatic rise in population accompanied the urban boom. The relative peace and prosperity of the century after 1150 resulted in a 35-percent population increase across Europe. The population of Europe in 1250 would not be reached again until the eighteenth century. Much of this surplus population found its way from rural estates to urban areas. Establishing towns or making them bigger provided numerous occupational opportunities. New jobs, new skills, and more extensive trade drove town and city creation and enlargement.

Merchants generally led the move to separate towns and cities from the nobility and to establish town and city governments. In Italy, minor noblemen joined merchants in seeking freedom from landed, more powerful nobles. In both cases, financially strapped nobles received an immediate influx of cash in return for granting a municipal charter, which gave recipients the right of self-government. Trading rights for money demonstrated the financial stress under which lords and ladies operated as well as the increased importance of money and a money economy to the later Middle Ages. Only those persons stipulated in the charter received the privilege of self-government and the exclusive right to shape municipal administration. Purchase of a municipal charter made them truly free men. They shed all feudal obligations, including labor service, support of the manorial miller, and marriage and inheritance taxes, and generally rebuffed efforts of their former lords to institute head taxes—annual taxes on their persons—which would keep them servile. As important as bestowing "liberties and free customs" upon grantees, charters awarded recipients powers to regulate the affairs of others within the neatly circumscribed social space of the municipality. Charter holders gained the power to specify who could dwell or work within a municipality, to establish and control municipal courts, and to enforce contracts.

Although municipal government was nominally separate, merchant guilds in practice exclusively held the earliest municipal charters. Most towns and cities were established for one end, to foster commerce, so it was not unreasonable for those directly involved in that activity to receive total authority. Merchants decided among themselves what form of governance a town or city would have and which of their number would hold the appropriate offices. Provosts and councils proved popular in northern France, while consulates were more common in the south and in Italy. Yet other guilds in municipalities soon recognized that they possessed a significant stake in a town's or city's affairs. Guilds erected to regulate a specific group's activities demanded to regulate that group's interactions within the larger community and worked to wrest control from the merchants in those precise areas. Members of these other guilds sought freedom, which Gothic Europeans based on stability and just-ness, not necessarily equality. They too sought to free themselves from the feudal nobility, a sentiment fully in line with the merchant class. As part of their municipal charters, merchants often received power to establish municipalities as safe havens; those living in a place thus chartered for a year and a day were no longer bound to feudal conventions. Merchants used that right to attract desirable workmen and women to the town or city as promise of freedom served as a compelling inducement.

These artisans claimed the same right of self-government as the merchants and demanded that that group establish these artisan guilds as part of municipal govern-ment. Merchants surely had the power to incorporate these artisans. Their charters granted them the right to define municipal government. Merchants generally shared authority with these artisan guilds but occasionally physical violence broke out. In a few instances artisan guilds circumvented the merchants altogether and purchased the right of self-government directly from a prince or king. There, merchants and artisans received authority over the same area. Conflict was almost always the first response but power sharing remained the eventual outcome.

These new municipal governments always redefined guilds in terms of the munic-ipal whole. Guilds remained occupation-based, but municipal governments draped a layer of authority over all of them. For example, theft, formerly a guild violation, became the province of the municipality. Penalties for many violations now rested with the mayor or aldermen, not with guild masters. The guild had become part of and subservient to municipal government. Masters now had a responsibility to the municipality. They were expected to serve as an emergency police force when called by municipal authorities, for example. Guilds also established penalties for those interfering with the work of municipal governments. Any guild member harming a mayor or council member suffered both municipal and guild penalties, including possible forfeiture of the right to ply one's trade.

In some cases, guild regulations became a part of the municipal code. Municipal law, for instance, often specified the type of sail material and shape of sails or that wax candles have cotton wicks of certain lengths. Such laws did not indicate a collapse of guild power but rather a thorough integration within municipal government. Munic-ipalities accorded guild-derived standards the force of law.

Kingdoms

Just as municipal government eventually coordinated and oversaw the various guilds, kingdoms emerged in Gothic Europe to integrate cities, towns, and manors into a larger whole. Throughout Western Europe—except in Italy and Germany, which had to grap-ple with the legacy of the Holy Roman Emperor—royalty assumed new authority. This authority often came at the local nobility's expense. Romanesque kings had been first among equals. They owed their power to their peers. Nor were Romanesque kingships hereditary. Although kingships often remained in families, nobles approved a king's successor. Gothic kingships at first depended much less on the nobility. Indeed, the nobility would redefine itself within the terms of this Gothic kingship.

The relative prosperity of Gothic Europe, coupled with the development of a significant money economy, weakened longstanding feudal bonds. Currency rather than barter or service had become a mainstay in the twelfth century and after. Classic feudalism had been intensely personal: An individual pledged his fealty to another with personal service usually accompanying the pledge. Increasingly in the Gothic period, money supplanted service, either in a one-time buyout of feudal obligations or in lieu of recurring service. The Gothic kings recognized quite early the power of money. They purchased men at arms, and these mercenaries freed the kings from dependence on feudal arrangements.

Kings acquired funds in many ways, including sale of municipal charters. Merchants and others gladly went to the king rather than to a feudal lord. By appealing to the king as the highest power, they willfully subverted feudal relationships, those relationships that had defined them as servile. But the merchants' act also acknowledged the king as the highest authority in any part of the realm. The king was of a different and higher social station than other overlords; his authority surpassed and could overrule theirs. Monarchs even commissioned chroniclers to sound their praises and maintained that the power of physical healing accompanied their office. This new hierarchical relationship marked kings as supreme, yet ironically less distant. And it undercut personal bonds, the essence of feudalism.

Later twelfth-century kings capitalized on this sentiment to assert a franchise theory of justice. They argued that all rights originated in a grant from a superior and that these rights provided the basis for unity throughout the realm. Put more bluntly, they established themselves as the apex of the social hierarchy, the single authority for law and justice, and employed that position to systematize and universalize relationships across the kingdom, while destroying long-standing personal lord–vassal bonds. The king as the ultimate source of power stood at the center of all activities, which radiated from him. Immediate lords were bypassed and thus rendered obsolete.

Creation of kings' courts often was an early manifestation of this social organization. The courts separated vassals from their immediate lords by imposing realm-wide edicts in lieu of uniquely local customs or agreements and then protecting vassals from the lord's retribution. Circuit judges regularly went from place to place, heard cases, and carried the kingdomwide dictates to the general populace. This top-down administration often included functional specialization. Kings appointed administrative, judicial, and financial officers. These men usually served at the pleasure of the king and were paid money rather than fiefs. Kings learned that better record keeping increased their wealth and, in the Gothic world, increased wealth translated into power. To that end, they found that employing men trained to fulfill the task for which they were hired made sound economic sense. Expert administration required experts and the training of administrative, financial, and judicial bureaucrats became a lively endeavor.

The local feudal nobility found themselves in an untenable position. The basis of their power and social position had been removed. Placid acceptance was impossible. The nobles either had to battle the king or acknowledge his preeminence. They needed to establish a position in the new hierarchy.

Many lords initially fought their kings rather than submit. Almost always they encountered problems. Gothic weaponry was increasingly expensive. Horses and massive iron equipment became a necessity. Horse-driven lances easily penetrated traditional armaments. So, too, did crossbows, which the church tried to outlaw in 1139 as too ghastly for Christian warfare. Crossbows came into common use within a half-century of the church's attempted ban. Gunpowder, a mixture of sulfur, charcoal, and saltpeter in precise quantities, found military applications from the mid-thirteenth century. By about 1300, gunpowder cannons—bronze and iron vases lying on their sides and ignited by a hot iron through a breech hole—were used in siege warfare and occasionally on the open battlefield. Defensive equipment tried to keep up. Conical open-faced helmets, popular in the First Crusade, gave way to huge pot- or tin-can–like devices that covered the head, face, and neck. Infantrymen sometimes wore wide-brimmed hats covered with segmented iron plates. Shirts of mail yielded to chain mail, which itself began to be replaced by even more expensive and heavier plate armor in the later thirteenth century. Leg armor was improved as were shields, and thick leather blankets protected horses, which were bred to handle the increased weight of fully armored riders. Among their first acts, kings established armor manufactories in their realms, which, by monopolizing skilled metalworkers, placed dissatisfied lords at a further disadvantage.

Although many lords initially opposed the king, they generally made their peace with him. In return for acknowledging the king's preeminence, lords often became the king's representatives in local affairs. They quickly adopted the royal technique of depending upon their own administrative experts and also received a significant voice in the realm. In that fashion, kingdoms became true hierarchical systems in which the consent of the governed played a large part.

A rise in interest in Roman law paralleled the ascendancy of the kings. This law ultimately would be used to reaffirm royal prerogatives. Apparently struck by Roman law's logic and rationality, late eleventh-century jurists in the Italian town of Bologna began its resurrection. They claimed it announced human reason–derived universal principles of social organization and justice. As the law of the empire, it had centralized administration and reduced many seemingly chaotic events to a coherent whole. Because of the striking similarity to what they felt surrounded them in their present day, they worked to organize Roman law. In the years before 1150, these masters of jurisprudence systematically cataloged and taxonomized the ancient documents. They searched out parallel passages, physically joined them with sections that discussed those passages, and systematically commented on those areas as if they were a complete body of legislation. This process, the reconciliation of contradiction by "bringing related parts into vital connection," generally rejected the idea that these contradictions were in fact contradictions. Adherents claimed instead that a close reading of these passages would reveal their essential unity and truth; human reason would expose the underlying principle generating and joining them.

A key to the quest to rationalize Roman law was the notion that humankind could uncover the principles of jurisprudence and apply them. Roman law seemed a body of knowledge that when mastered could provide principles on which to erect governments. Contemporaries conceived of Roman law as the opposite of feudal attachments. Feudalism was individual, a de facto negotiation between two unequal parties. Roman law was impersonal, the law for all, the law of groups rather than individuals.

While both appeared predictable, based on precedent, feudal law extended only to that single relationship. Roman law was universal law. Its universality, coupled with its appearance of rationality, persuaded many litigants and petitioners to claim Roman precedents to argue their case.

The hierarchical nature of Roman law could provide the basis for contemporary social organization—for kingdoms. Jurists and lawyers argued that Roman law had come from the Roman people, who had surrendered their prerogatives to the emperor for the good of all; Roman law had assumed the superiority of the emperor. Roman law offered kings a legal, terrestrial raison d'être for the establishment of Gothic kingdoms. Lack of a secular explanation might have forced kings to rely on a Christian explanation, which almost certainly would involve church politics. Such was the case of Italy and Germany, which, because of ties to the church, never developed full Gothic kingdoms. Introduction of Roman law was a part of the secularization of civil society and ethics.

England

From the early twelfth century, the king's courts recorded their rulings as a guide for future cases. When royal judges traveled the countryside, they often attempted to use these court rulings as the basis of subsequent decisions. This substitution of a law that would be common for an entire realm (known as common law, which of course is not common but royal) was to prevail over local custom (known as customary law, the way that people had done things for centuries). Strong financial administration accompanied these legal initiatives.

Henry II (1154–1189) explicitly translated this legal principle into fact. He maintained that the king had privileges not enjoyed by any other lord, and he established his own administrative representatives—sheriffs—throughout the realm. Henry used his sheriffs to control local overlords and even had them knock down castles built without his express permission. Henry also created mechanisms to undercut feudal legal relationships. His court became the court of appeals for local court rulings. Any aggrieved party could appeal a customary decision to the king's court, which served as the court of last resort. Henry had, in effect, put into practice his claim that the king was the source from which all law in the realm originated.

His son John upped the stakes by charging feudal overlords extravagant fees for privileges they thought theirs by inheritance. A group of nobles rebelled and forced John to submit to a series of conditions before they would pay to support his armies. This 1215 document, the Magna Carta (the Great Charter), served John as much as the nobles. It established John and his lineage as king, as different from and above the other nobles, and his institutions as superior to theirs; all authority stemmed from the king. To this the nobles acceded. But the nobles compelled John to concede that he must operate according to law. He could not cavalierly institute new measures, and the agreement checked him in two ways. First, John promised not to levy taxes not provided in feudal custom without counsel of an assembly of overlords (now considered his lieutenants, which provided them a central place within the kingdom). John's capitulation to this point made it part of law, which meant he could not operate contrary to

The Magna Carta. King John's signature on the Magna Carta had two consequences: It guaranteed the English nobility certain rights and privileges and forced the nobility to acknowledge the King as the grantor of those rights and privileges.

it. Second, the nobles forced John to agree that it was illegal for any "free man [to] be taken, or imprisoned, or deprived of his land, or outlawed, or exiled or in any other way destroyed . . . except by legal judgment of his peers or by the law of the land."

Consolidation under this arrangement proceeded so quickly that by 1250 a treatise on common law in England had appeared. Consent of the former feudal leaders rested at the heart of this new form of governance. First an inner group of feudal overlords met to consider royal objectives but that small group soon gave way to much broader representation. Knights, barons, and burgesses were contacted and their advice solicited whenever the king needed money. They almost always gave their consent. The putative power of consent had given them the appearance of a stake in the system in return for their money. In the 1290s, King Edward institutionalized the process and further expanded his constituency. The British Parliament stemmed from that development.

France

French lords avoided the embarrassment and trauma suffered by the English nobility in 1066 when William conquered that island and granted large estates to his fellow Normans. The French nobility remained free to cement alliances while their active urban program and the success of the Champagne and other great fairs enabled them to afford to hire soldiers. Not until the reign of Louis VI (1108–1137) did the French monarchy begin to assert itself within France. Louis greatly expanded the number of royal charters issued and, under the pretense that the king was the vassal of St. Denis and thus, beholden to no earthly person, granted protection to all bishops not already joined through vassalage to an overlord. Both acts established direct lines of authority between the king and others previously linked only locally. His son, Louis VII, accelerated consolidation of the kingdom by using excommunication of feudal barons as cause to march against them and to confiscate their property. A theory of the king as keeper of the peace, as the single entity that decides what is just within the realm and then metes out that justice, emboldened him to pursue that course. To Louis and his descendants, the king was the realm's conscience; Louis VII thus established the principle that anyone could appeal to the king's court if he or she deemed a decision in an overlord's court unjust.

Such a grand theory did not go unchallenged and Louis VII's son, Philip II, began to create an administrative structure to implement and cement the program. He divided the realm into numerous small, royal bailiff–governed administrative units, explicitly not coinciding with traditional jurisdictional areas, to disrupt conventional patterns of authority. As important, his bailiffs demanded little from the king's subjects—much less than had their feudal overlords—a move that popularized and promoted centralized authority. But it remained for Philip's grandson, Louis IX, truly to complete a bureaucratic structure to unite France. Louis became the embodiment of France's conscience. His locally situated courts determined virtually all disputed questions with an unprecedented sense of fairness and thus created numerous precedents that they and other royal courts later applied. Persons throughout the realm felt confident that the king's courts would rule fairly—in Gothic Europe, stability and consistency were often synonymous with justice and fairness—and that no potentate would interfere with the decision. To that end, Louis formed the Parlement of Paris from among his closest advisors. The Parlement heard appeals from local administrators as well as appeals from cases decided in courts of feudal overlords. It reaffirmed the king's place at the head of the realm.

Also during Louis's 40-year-reign, the idea of the king as keeper of the peace was transformed to suggest that it was the king's peace. That slight modification held profound implications. To disrupt the peace in any fashion—and almost any activity could be considered a threat to peace—was to commit a crime against the king; it was a realm-wide violation and the authority of the realm could be brought to bear on miscreants. Louis demonstrated the breadth of his position when he announced rules to govern private wars between nobles. Parties had to give notice prior to attack. Blood kin could choose not to participate in the war and both sides had to honor that decision. A truce must be granted when an enemy requested. Neither side could slaughter peasants or burn crops. Violation of any of these provisions meant royal intervention.

The Rest of Western Europe

Louis IX integrated the feudal hierarchy into the new social system without creating a representative assembly. That proved unusual. The need of kings for money to hire soldiers and for other purposes led them to solicit the assistance of the social elites— lords, clergymen, and merchants. Lords, in particular, demanded a voice in the new system. They had been central to feudalism. The new social order was established around them, generally at their expense, and gaining the appearance of recognition and standing was perhaps as important as acquiring decision-making power. Representative assemblies provided that appearance by granting feudal lords entry into the new social system without measurably restricting prerogatives. Such was the case throughout Europe. The Kingdom of Leon created a representative assembly in the twelfth century, while the kingdoms of Castile, Aragon, Catalonia, Valencia, and Portugal did so a century later. The Netherlands and France would join the movement in the fourteenth century. Only Germany and Italy never developed a strong representative assembly–monarchy.

It bears repeating that Gothic representative government was no democracy. Those seeming to have the greatest stake in the system possessed the most power. There existed in government no modern sense of equality but rather a sense of the justice of stability and a responsibility for fairness, a fairness built upon social station. People needed to be treated fairly, not equally. Each person's obligations and rights were a function of his or her rank in society. However, persons were not identified as individuals per se but instead in reference to others, as members of a group typified by certain characteristics. That latter assessment provided the basis for representation. Any one member represented the interests and perspectives of his or her group and those with the greatest investment deserved direct representation. Under the medieval concept of fairness, other groups were implicitly represented; they needed no formal representatives.

The tidiness of its social organization ought not to suggest that Gothic Europe suffered no unrest. The situation became particularly strained after 1300 as the population began to decline. Famines in 1315 and 1317 pressured local populations and eliminated the agricultural surplus that had fueled the Eastern trade. Food prices skyrocketed and the money payments that often had replaced service or crop obligations no longer proved comparable. All hurt the nobility. Food price–driven inflation forced up manufacturing prices, which stressed the new, salaried government bureaucrats. These experts paid fixed incomes found their purchasing power significantly lessened, and they sometimes turned to bribes and other forms of corruption to restore their economic position. Complaints abounded of venal, greedy ecclesiastical and royal officials. Merchants and manufacturers also felt the strain. Beyond the medieval doctrine of fairness, no rules existed about how to treat workers in various occupations. Day laborers were especially victimized and, in the late thirteenth and throughout the fourteenth centuries, they complained and sometimes rioted. Financially strapped merchants and other masters rarely looked upon these efforts with favor.

Despite these economic hardships and despite the different and tortuous paths that medieval kingdoms took to reach the same point, these new social organizations were characteristically structured as a well-delineated hierarchy of statuses and social states ranging from serf to king. No two groups held the same social position. In urban society, for example, the poor constituted the lowest order, lower than day laborers. Apprentices were beneath journeymen, journeymen below masters; masters were under guild masters, and guild masters were inferior to merchants, who dominated municipal government. Municipal government was subservient to a lord, and a lord was lower than the king. This great chain of social being constituted a human counterpart to the Gothic depiction of the natural world. Both were stairways ascending from the lowest order to the highest.

For Further Reading

[See the end of Chapter 8]

CHAPTER 8

Gothic Search for Order II: Structuring Heaven and Earth, 1100–1360

Many late-eleventh-century Europeans judged the Cluniac experiment corrupt. The increasing ostentatiousness of the Cluniac monasteries demonstrated that the order had lost its spiritual base. Rather than separate themselves from the world to pray exclusively as had been their plan, church politics, intrigue among the nobility, and a grotesque opulence consumed Cluniac monks. The Cluniac decision to rely for their survival on property donated to the order seemed ironically at fault. Struck by the piousness of the initial enterprise, many wealthy sinners had turned their excessive bounties over to the monks. The massive human and material resources that the order then controlled had seduced the Cluniac clerics into playing a major role in church and world affairs and led to the extravagant adornment of their buildings. Forgoing manual labor to live off the sweat of the brows of others resulted not in humility and contemplation of the deity but in regalness and pretense.

Religious Innovation: The Cistercians

To Robert and 21 other monks at the Benedictine abbey in Molesme, the Cluniacs were an abomination. These rebellious monks even found that the Benedictines had gone astray. Dependence on tithes, ground rents, knights' fees, manor rents, and tolls chained Benedictine and other monks to the world of princes and nobles. Commentators also chided monks and priests for drunkenness, dicing, lending money, wenching, carrying swords, and fighting. Only by refusing these inducements and temptations could churchmen remain pure. To Robert and his followers, action was demanded and their course was clear. They needed to shun worldly affairs and to embrace the simplicity of manual labor. In 1098 at Citeaux, located on a heavily traveled Italian trade route, they formed a new order, the Cistercians. The Cistercians renounced earthly wealth and sought only to produce enough food and goods to survive in an otherwise inhospitable setting. Bare walls, plain glass windows, wooden altars, and no images, silver, or precious stones, the very opposite of Cluniac excess, underscored the Cistercian abbey church.

This hard, austere life apparently had its charms. St. Bernard, his friends, and some relatives joined the order in 1112 and established a daughter house in a particularly bleak section of Clairvaux three years later. The rules at Clairvaux and of the Cistercians were straightforward. No idleness was permitted, and no talking was allowed except during choral service. The Cistercians believed in the orderliness of silence, which forced persons to conform to it through fear; no one wanted to be the one to break the silence. Clairvaux soon spawned its own daughter houses, and by Bernard's death in 1153, the order had over 350 houses. Relations between Cistercian daughter houses and motherhouses proved markedly different from that of the Cluniacs. Each house could form one or more daughter houses and each house was a daughter house of another house, except for Citeaux. Despite their different origins, all houses hewed to the same set of rules. The abbot of each motherhouse had to visit each of that house's daughters at least once a year to ensure that each place followed the order's rules. All the order's abbots in this rigidly hierarchical administrative structure gathered at least once a year to discuss possible changes in the order's rules.

The Cistercians' separation of labor into physical and spiritual components proved striking. To free choir monks from the terrestrial world, the brothers in 1100 created a lay brotherhood, who farmed or practiced a trade to support the monastery, leaving choir monks to devote themselves entirely to prayer. Lay brothers cleared and cultivated land at remarkable rates and in England produced significant quantities of wool. In France and Germany, Cistercian lay brothers specialized in growing grapes and making wine, which was in high demand throughout Gothic Europe. A passionate embrace of water power proved the single most distinguishing Cistercian characteristic as almost every house had at least one watermill. By the mid-twelfth century, proximity to a river became a crucial factor in locating new Cistercian houses.

The Cistercian experience suggested that Gothic Europe was no less alive with religious innovation than it was with social innovation. Both religious and social inventiveness spoke to a pervasive sense of uncertainty, a sense that institutions and other social and religious structures in Gothic Europe had failed. But both also heralded a sense of possibilities. Things could be changed and what was wrong could be made better. A profound sense of renewal swept Europe but one that harkened far backward to the Gothic understanding of the Roman Empire and Greece rather than forward. It called for throwing off the immediate past in favor of a more distant past and presumed that Gothic Europeans had lost their way, that the pathway they had traveled was flawed.

Most important, Gothic men and women claimed the ability to discern that these social and religious institutions had failed, to understand why they had stumbled, and to fashion alternatives. To the Cistercians and numerous others, the outward behavior of the Cluniacs revealed inner turmoil. Observation of the Cluniac errors, when interpreted through the gauze of reason, led Gothic Europeans to contemplate new religious initiatives. Each initiative strove to overcome the failures that its proponents maintained they had observed. The Cistercians, for example, paid particular attention to deriving precise statuses among monks—lay brothers and the like—and among monasteries—daughter houses and motherhouses. Rules based upon these hierarchical statuses became the rules of the order; they gave the order a hierarchical structure.

St. Bernard and the Cistercians. Pictured here taking control at Clairvaux, St. Bernard established silence, rigor, and austerity as the rule for the monastery. Lay brothers worked the fields and performed everyday tasks to permit the monks to devote full time to their prayers.

Varieties of Religious Experience

But creating a hierarchical order and attempting to shun the material world to behave like Christ were not enough to guarantee success. In the early 1170s, for example, a wealthy Lyons merchant, Peter Waldo, turned his back on the sinful life he had led. Waldo gave all his worldly possessions to the poor and, although he lacked formal theological training, began to preach the gospel in Provence. Waldo spoke of a loving Christ and the need to emulate the savior's earthly existence to receive salvation. Twelve men quickly gravitated to Waldo and devoted themselves to spreading his message to the region's small villages and towns.

At first glance, Waldo's work seemed very much like that of Francis some 35 years later. In 1207, Francis, the dissolute son of a wealthy Italian merchant family, abandoned his possessions to the poor, dressed like a beggar, and visited villages throughout central Italy. At every stop the untrained and theologically naive Francis preached the gospel of Christ's life and called on his contemporaries to imitate the savior. He quickly attracted disciples, who became known as the "Little Brothers."

Despite the similarity of their crusades, the careers of Francis and Waldo had dramatically different outcomes. The church condemned Waldo in 1179, while it supported St. Francis of Assisi's efforts, canonizing him after his death in 1226. To be sure, a few distinctions existed between the Waldensians and the Franciscans. Waldensians wore sandals as had the apostles and denied the validity of oath taking as a measure of guilt or innocence. They also maintained that in emergencies anyone wearing sandals could consecrate the Eucharist. But their biggest sins were preaching without church blessing and criticizing the church and traditional clergy as corrupted by material wealth and therefore powerless in the next world. Franciscans avoided both pitfalls. Francis was explicitly not anticlerical, even as he complained that the church too often forgot its mission to the soul in pursuit of material advantage. Francis repeatedly sought the pope's permission and blessing to preach. He also tried to forge the Little Brothers into a permanent religious order, but when he submitted his rules for governing their activities to the pope in 1211, he was turned down. He submitted new rules in 1223. Francis had wanted the brothers to be a lay order, not permitted to hear confession. The pope instead approved three statuses of Little Brothers, including friars, who could hear confession. Francis wanted the order to be mendicant. He asked that it be prohibited from owning property to guard against seduction by the material world, forced to beg for alms to survive. The pope overruled him and empowered the order to engage in corporate ownership, which included accepting gifts. Francis wanted only itinerant brothers, circulating among the poor and preaching Christ's love. The pope urged formal theological training as a brotherhood prerequisite.

Church Power

The tales of Francis and Waldo reflected the power of the church in enforcing standardization and conformity within the earthly realm. It attempted to organize virtually everything and to place everything under its control. Headed by the pope, the emerging church bureaucracy and administrative structure proved at least as rigid and formal as the most powerful earthly kingdom. The church's centralizing structure even speeded the Cistercians' downfall, who like the Cluniacs before them, proved much too successful to remain free of papal orbit. The order's energy and austerity program had led the European pious to shower the order with such large gifts of land that, even though the Cistercians had created more than 500 Cistercian monasteries by 1200, it still leased huge amounts to peasants. The order reaped great material profits from these transactions. In England, Cistercian monks used their monasteries and other holdings to become influential wool traders. Their virtual wool monopoly angered British merchants, who chafed at their lack of control of that profitable economic sector. The Cistercian lay brothers proved no less adept as producers of meat and iron. By the later twelfth century, the Cistercians' acquisition of wealth and property made them a tantalizing prize in the unseemly world of papal politics and no pope allowed their extensive holdings to rest apart from his authority.

The Cistercian experience demonstrated that the papacy won significant authority over earthly affairs. This physical world success came at the expense of its heavenly preeminence. The heavenly and earthly worlds increasingly seemed distinct. Crystallization of a papal monarchy weakened its claim to god and salvation. The church's diminishing spiritual power encouraged establishment of other agencies, manifested in the period's extensive religious experimentation. New orders arose within the church structure. For example, the church avidly tried to harness the significant internalization of piety that persons took great care to exhibit outwardly in the twelfth century. Numerous individuals made great show of renouncing society to live life in imitation of Christ or the saints, claiming to use his story or the psalms as guides. These men often rejected the church to live as hermits. To draw them back into the fold—and to prevent them from attracting others to form splinter groups that might threaten the status quo—the church sponsored Charterhouse and the Carthusian order. Organized by St. Bruno in Savoy in 1084, the Carthusian order kept individuals who might pose a threat to the church within church confines. In effect, the order organized the act of being a hermit under church auspices as members lived alone together in a church-approved manner. The order established its monasteries as walled complexes in the wilderness. There each monk maintained a small hut in which he alone slept, worked, prayed, and studied in silence. These huts surrounded a central, common courtyard, a physical reminder that the monks together constituted a social unit. Only for meals, mass, or refectory did monks meet collectively.

Dominicans

Creation of the Dominican order provided a potent contrast, but it too emerged from the church's desire to organize nonconformity. As important, the order's origins demonstrated the new emphasis on human reason, on man's ability to approach knowledge of god. The Spanish nobleman Dominic (1170–1221) wanted to fight the pervasive heresies that he saw in his native land, and he adopted a two-pronged approach. He demanded that clerics match heretics in virtue and exceed them in knowledge. Monks needed to be expert in their knowledge of Christianity so as to refute the heretics' contentions and to expose them as shams. But knowledge without precise articulation was insufficient and Dominic's disciples gave form to their ideas. They first identified the heretical notions and then systematically refuted them. Dominicans brought orderliness and formality to preaching, and even wrote manuals about how to dispute certain common heretical arguments.

Such an impressive program could not long remain outside the papal sphere and in 1220 the pope approved a rule for the Dominican order. The rule called for the brothers to conduct themselves with obedience, poverty, and chastity, to accept no money or property, and never to be idle. Within that framework, the brothers received extensive regulatory powers. They could examine and select applicants to the brotherhood, standardize dress for novices as well as the term of novices, differentiate among themselves by apparel, and establish rules for eating and fasting. A general minister headed the brotherhood but he was selected by the provincial ministers—heads of smaller geographical units—who met at least once every three years. Each province's brothers met whenever the provincial brothers gathered.

Like the Franciscans, the highly disciplined Dominicans became closely aligned with the papacy. Both roamed through Europe, carrying information and recommendations to Rome and announcing and enacting papal policy in localities. They functioned for the church in a manner similar to local arms of the king's court in civil society and quickly received formal positions within the church bureaucracy. The Dominicans' superior knowledge of Christianity and training in formal logic led the pope to appoint them teachers of theology at cathedral schools and at the new universities, to send them to convert heathens, and to select them to head a new initiative to root out heretics, the Inquisition. The Inquisition fought heresy by presuming guilt. Defendants had to prove innocence, needed not be told the names of their accusers, and were not permitted representation. Confessions obtained through torture held the same status as voluntary admissions of guilt. Burning at the stake often seemed a suitable punishment.

The church viewed heresy as a deadly infection, which, left unchecked, could spread and contaminate the entire Christian body. That menace led the church to supplement local efforts to crack down on heretics with the papal-controlled Inquisition. As early as 1179, the church issued a mass excommunication of those in southern France blamed for "abominable heretical tenets . . . unheard of cruelties against the Christians [and] demolishing churches." As permanent symbols of papal authority in localities, the papacy directed bishops twice or more yearly to visit their areas, bind inhabitants by oath, and actively seek out heretics. The church issued formal laws to guide the search in 1229. Each bishop was to select and swear to an oath two or more individuals in each parish to uncover heretics and deliver them to papal authorities. Anyone harboring a heretic lost all property. Any sacrament-abstaining person was suspected of heresy. Recanting heretics had their houses destroyed and were forced to move from the village or town. When they settled in their new locations heretics were stigmatized by wearing clothes bearing two crosses of different colors. To ensure that bishops carried out their obligations and to finish the work of centralization and standardization, Pope Gregory IX in 1232 created another layer of bureaucracy and appointed "pontifical inquisitors," who reported directly to the pope.

Albigensians

Existence of the Albigensians helped stimulate the church to form its Inquisition. Situated in southern France, the Albigensians were exponents of the Cathari heresy, which permeated Italy and France during the twelfth and thirteenth centuries. They railed against the church's scandals and vices and demanded that it focus on only the spirit, leaving earthly matters to kings and princes. In that sense they differed little from the Franciscans or Cistercians. But unlike those two groups, which remained inside the church, the Albigensians demanded destruction of the church, total rejection of its theology, and repudiation of its teachings and erected their own religious hierarchy.

The Albigensians, like other Cathari (which meant pure), juxtaposed the forces of the god of evil, which they associated with the god of the Old Testament, darkness, and flesh—the material world—with the forces of the god of good, light, and the soul. Their theology precluded Christ having taken human form. He could not have been born of flesh, suffered on the cross, or been resurrected. Christ was instead an angel, pure spirit, sent to fight the god of evil, who had created the church and the papacy to enslave humankind. The Albigensians maintained that the church's wicked pursuit of power and wealth proved their thesis. Its sacraments were the work of the flesh. Marriage and infant baptism were especially abhorred.

The Albigensians believed in predestination, the belief that one's ultimate fate and prospects were preordained at birth. The god of good had chosen the Perfecti to lead the group. That god had predestined these people to live simply and to avoid courtly manners, dress, or habits. They rejected flesh, abstained from sexual contact, and renounced the products of animal sexual contact—eggs, cheese, milk, and meat. The Perfecti were known by how they acted; outward manifestations of their earthly behavior reflected their inner, god-preordained purity. The Imperfect held no such stringent moral code. Yet it would be incorrect to suggest that no check existed on their behavior. Albigensians believed that the god of good could reveal to humans their Perfecti status at any time in their life.

Tensions between the Albigensians and the church had long been high, but open conflict broke out in 1208 when the Albigensians murdered a papal legate. Raymond, Count of Toulouse, came to their defense as Pope Innocent III declared a crusade against these infidels, which the king of France joined. Repeated warfare and slaughter continued until 1229 when the forces of Raymond's descendants capitulated to St. Louis.

The church solidified its temporal control by urging removal of other groups of nonbelievers, such as Jews, from parts of Europe. The crime of deicide—the crucifixion of Christ—was held to have stained the Jewish people as a whole, made them bloodthirsty, and led them to spill the blood of others. Christian children seemed especially at risk, it was argued, as Jews used their blood for ritual purposes. That Jews had lent and changed money for centuries and thus benefited from god's time confirmed their depravity. The church did not call for wholesale slaughter of Jews but maintained that Jews should live in humiliation. As early as 1215, formal church policy barred Jews from public office, required them to wear distinguishing badges on their clothing, and prohibited them from public streets during Christian festivals. Jews were excluded from international trade, banned from guilds, and not permitted to own land. England expelled them in 1290 and France did the same in 1306. A wave of expulsions and massacres swept Italy during the early 1290s.

The Papal Monarchy

The church's centralization policy placed the Roman pontiff at the system's apex. Innocent III's claim that the pope was "lower than God but higher than man . . . judges all and is judged by no one" was an expression of and provided justification for papal fiat. That sentiment certainly had existed earlier. A twelfth-century pope, Alexander III, determined carte blanche that sainthood required direct papal authorization and, to that end, he created a formal procedure as well as a bureaucracy to screen candidates. The pope received a petition, which he turned over to a commission. If that commission deemed the application worth consideration, it formed a court of inquiry, complete with defendant and devil's advocate. Witnesses testified at this trial and a scribe kept a written record. That record was sent to the papal curia for comment before being judged by the pope. Popes also took action to reform church practices. Struck by the number of monks leaving monasteries to engage in the lucrative medical profession and afraid that these monks would return full of pride, arrogance, and idle habits, Pope Innocent II in 1131 banned monks from practicing medicine for money. The papacy renewed the restriction in 1139 and issued a more stringent decree in 1163, which prohibited monks from being absent from monasteries for more than two months for any reason.

Empowerment of church and papal courts proved a potent force for standardization throughout Europe and centralization in Rome. Bishops headed church courts but petitioners dissatisfied with a bishop's decision could appeal to papal court, which set the pope and his minions as the ultimate arbiter. The church assumed responsibility for behavior; it sought to regulate marriage, oaths, promises, and sex crimes. Its rules for knightly behavior called on individuals to honor church laws, defend the church against heretics, and save unfortunates. The church even tried to restrict jousting tournaments in the twelfth century to certain days of the year. Its marriage pronouncements were more detailed. Regulations included age (girls 12, boys 14), consent, and that marriage partners not be even distantly related. Consummation of the marriage awaited a priest's marriage bed blessing. The church refused to recognize Christian–heathen unions. It limited grounds for annulment to age, consent, and consanguinity and established procedural rules for divorce in the twelfth century, stipulating that a divorce remained incomplete until the groom returned the dowry.

The church recognized the seven sacraments as the sole way to achieve salvation and, since only it could deliver them, the church was the organizer of Christian life from birth to death. As the single entity spanning Europe, the church's activities and court rulings—the papal court was the only pan-European court—provided whatever commonality existed in late medieval life. Papal selection demonstrated the new earthly emphasis. Romanesque popes had been monks, separate from society and absorbed with theological matters. Twelfth- and thirteenth-century popes were lawyers, not theologians. They focused on administering the earthly church, establishing consistency in its pronouncements, and extending its influence into virtually every endeavor. Experience in papal court offered excellent training for the papacy as did stints as masters of church law—canon law—at universities. By the thirteenth century, teaching canon law became a de facto church administration prerequisite. Once in power, popes collected and harmonized papal announcements and court decisions to further consolidate the church. Gregory IX issued the most extensive compilation in 1234 but canon law codification had been ongoing for over a century.

Although the pope resided at the church's apex, he depended on the structure beneath him. To signify their importance within the system and to gain their support in various matters, church officials were provided the appearance of decision-making power through legislative conclaves meeting in Rome. Representatives of the stages of the church hierarchy attended these infrequent meetings where papal-dominated policy was proposed, analyzed, and announced. The gathering of 1215, the Fourth Lateran Council, drew nearly 1,200 clergymen and a few secular leaders. This group asserted the Roman church's preeminence over secular institutions and the Eastern church, and backed Rome's ascendancy with specific strictures. It prohibited secular leaders from taxing church properties, declared laws detrimental to the church null and void, forbade secular powers from appointing Jews to public office, and directed governments to punish known heretics. The council also defined the obligations and boundaries of the church's constituent parts. It stipulated type of raiment of each clerical status, regularizing them by rank while making ranks distinctive. Post-conclave cardinals, for example, began to wear red hats to mark their station. The council mandated certain minimal moral standards for clerics and banned them from bloodletting or performing surgery. It reaffirmed the bishops' responsibilities to uncover heretics in their dioceses, compelled them to preach regularly, and commanded them to erect and sustain parish schools. The council forbade priests to officiate at ordeals and to change the sacraments in any manner. The conclave required all Christians to confess their sins to a priest at least once a year, be contrite for their failings, do penance as an outward expression of contrition, and accept the Eucharist. It prohibited aid to or countenance of heretics. The representative body also countered the Albigensians when it mandated that married persons as well as virgins could enter heaven.

The idea of a papal monarchy produced tension between secular authorities and the church throughout Europe. Nowhere were tensions higher than in Germany and Italy. Wounds caused by the investiture controversy failed to heal, and the ambiguity of the Holy Roman Emperor remained. As important, personification of god in human terms unleashed two conflicting movements. It encouraged princely powers to identify themselves with him, an understanding that weakened the position of the church within secular administration, while simultaneously emboldening the pope to demand control over parts of earthly existence formerly deemed royalty's province. Conflicts were inevitable and appointment of bishops provided a flash point. Twelfth-century German bishopric elections always occurred with the emperor or a high emissary present. Few dared to defy the emperor, and his candidate almost always won. Beginning in the thirteenth century, the papacy declared that the pope should decide any contested bishop election and when some half-century later the papal position had triumphed, the Holy Roman Emperor's control of bishoprics ceased. German princes remembered the bishoprics' importance in sustaining the emperor's military power and many local leaders rose to confront him. At the same time, the emperor strove to regain control and to resecure his realm. He removed bishops appointed by Rome and taxed church assets to enhance his power. The papacy also recognized its bishoprics increasingly as a source of operating income. It taxed them and charged them for basic services to support the church bureaucracy in Rome. To expand revenues further, the pope often appointed the same individual to several different bishoprics. Only a single person and staff needed to be maintained and moneys saved could be drawn off to Rome. The German princes joined the church to prevent the emperor from reestablishing preeminence and, although they never overcame him, they nonetheless prohibited the emperor from consolidating his power and Germany never developed into a centralized kingdom.

The papacy also had a history of countering the emperor in Italy. The papacy understood that imperial control of Italy meant imperial domination of Rome. It hampered at every turn ambitions to subdue the peninsula. Ironically the Crusades to free and maintain the Holy Land made it easier to resist the emperor. The vast moneys pouring into Italian cities to launch crusaders had made these places even more formidable powers. Frederick Barbarosa's attempt to exert influence over the Italian cities failed in 1176 when his knights lost to Milan-sponsored infantrymen. Barbarosa ultimately recognized the Italian cities' independence but his successor, Frederick II, sought to capture these prizes a half century later.

Pope Gregory IX challenged Frederick II's initial success by calling a council of prelates in Rome. Frederick learned of the conference and attacked the vessels carrying the prelates. Most drowned or were captured. In 1245, Gregory's successor, Innocent IV, called a council in Lyons, declared Frederick's position and possessions forfeited, and proclaimed a crusade against the emperor. Frederick gave up what remained of his German ambitions and continued in Italy. The northern cities freed themselves of Frederick's grasp but southern Italy and Sicily remained firmly under his control. Frederick's death in 1250 did not resolve the situation. His heirs still controlled the southern peninsula, a state of affairs no majestic pope was willing to permit. The papacy continued to preach Crusades, tax clerics, and send cardinals to lead forces against the Germans, and it even called on foreign kings for assistance. Henry III of England and St. Louis came to the papacy's aid, finally defeating Frederick's family in 1266.

The papacy had rid itself of the German prince but never succeeded in consolidating the peninsula. It lacked the might to force compliance from the northern cities and the nobility around Rome also proved fractious. The papacy's crusade against the emperor and his descendants tarnished further Rome's claim to heavenly mastery. The several popes acted like secular kings. They taxed their constituencies to raise funds to protect their kingdoms, entered into alliances with foreign potentates, and labored to cement their earthly authority. They seemed to hold no particular moral authority beyond that of any secular leader, and less than some, such as St. Louis. Even when the cardinals chose a deeply spiritual pope, such as Celestine V, who had lived as a hermit on Mount Vesuvius, he proved unable to restore the papacy to its former glory. Celestine lasted less than a year. He became the only pope to abdicate the throne of St. Peter.

His replacement, Boniface VIII, selected in 1294, tried to establish the papacy as the first monarchy among a system of secular monarchies. He had no chance. After attempting to deny the English and French potentates revenues from church property, and after they prohibited Rome from receiving any taxes from the French and English bishoprics, Boniface relented. He then maintained that clergymen were not subject to secular law, that the church stood over the secular state. Put simply, Boniface claimed that "it is altogether necessary to salvation for every human creature to be subject to the Roman Pontiff." The Estates General, a representative assembly of French clergy, nobility, and burghers, rejected that contention and, when the king accused the pope of heresy, a force was sent to capture Boniface. Boniface died before he was brought to France and the cardinals dared not select a pope unfriendly to the French king. Clement V had been the archbishop of Bordeaux and when he received rumors of unrest in Rome, moved the holy see to Avignon, under the French king's protection. It would remain there for 73 years.

The Papal See at Avignon. The papal resettlement at Avignon forced the papacy to depend on the French king and to erect an additional bureaucracy to retain control over affairs in Rome.

Ironically, papal resettlement in Avignon encouraged institutional development mimicking secular monarchies. Located far from Rome and needing funds to supply two distant homes, the papacy sought to free itself of secular influence and to assert itself as Christian Europe's leading force. Its two-pronged approach included seeking to make itself wealthier than any other kingdom, which placed extensive pressure on its bishoprics, and further centralizing all church business within the papal court. The former would ensure independence, potentially buying a large army or becoming the leading financier of European intrigue. The papacy justified its centralization of power as the only way to remain clear of secular interference.

The Avignon popes' zeal resulted in creation of the largest Gothic European government. The papal chancery handled routine administrative work, dividing tasks among its seven functional branches. The camera apostolica broke finances into two parts—administrative and policy—and appointed a hierarchically structured staff to serve each. The judiciary established numerous new layers of legal bureaucracy. These new courts operated throughout the social spectrum: They refined the arguments heard at the highest levels, distinguishing among them through formation of new courts, and granted new options for the lowest classes seeking redress.

These new institutions of earthly governance and control undercut further the church's claim to the soul. To be sure, the church had long been abandoning other-worldliness. Even the portrait of the Crusades as a holy war, as using the sword and lance to do god's work and of granting blessings and, through penance, perhaps salvation to those engaging in it, suggested a profound earthly involvement. Transformation of the Crusades from episodic adventures as they had been at their origin to regular, expected, and formalized activities for modest terrestrial ends trivialized claims of spiritual significance. The church's new concern for the poor, demonstrated by St. Francis and others, often in the face of attacks on the church as uncaring, grounded the church within the contemporary social order.

The Church and the Soul

What religious and cosmological speculation that existed during this period was very much of this world. The church condemned Peter Abelard as a heretic in 1140 because he maintained that a person's intent was more important than the act itself. To Abelard, "to sin and to perform the sin are not the same"; sin was contempt for god, or consent to what one believed should not be consented to. Human will and understanding framed Abelard's concept and his lack of spirituality engendered criticism. With Abelard, St. Bernard maintained, "vices and virtues are discussed with no trace of moral feeling, the sacraments of the Church with no evidence of faith, the mystery of the Holy Trinity with no spirit of humility or sobriety." Soon after Bernard's polemic, however, the church incorporated Abelard's sentiments within its penance-contrition nexus. Individuals needed to be truly sorry that they had committed egregious acts before they could experience a measure of grace; they needed to understand the acts' sinfulness and to recognize their shame for having done wrong. Both acts presumed human understanding. To medieval men and women, reason fashioned the universe. God the architect (or creator or maker or builder) had erected a structure that was logical, hierarchical, orderly. God gave humans reason, which leads humankind "rationally to those truths of which, without reason, he has no knowledge." God provided humankind with the tools to understand, rather than simply behold. God was a loving deity and humankind's spirit soared hopefully because of this love. God was compassionate, no longer awesome.

The Church and Education

Humankind's reasonableness was evident in the flourishing of institutions of learning. Each body stemmed from the same fundamental assumption: that humans could use reason to deduce or uncover relationships that would bring them closer to god. God had created everything in a precise, systematic, hierarchical way. Manifestations of his plan were everywhere. Humans needed simply to observe and decipher through their reason, a god-granted attribute.

Institutions of learning incorporated the idea of expertise. Some individuals had knowledge others wanted to achieve. Expertise presumed such a thing as knowledge existed—whether observations or procedures—and could be transferred from person to person. Different statuses among those who had the knowledge—expertise—and those who sought to achieve it were the natural consequence. These formal and precise roles each operated according to specific rules.

This notion of expertise placed a premium on the past. The past became the treasury of human experience and the embodiment of human experiment. In that sense, the past was expert, a place and time in which knowledge was gained and rules exposed. The past need not be the beginning of a continuing (and developing) knowledge nor the sum total of everything required about a particular subject. It merely comprised a vast storehouse of expertise.

Not all pasts were equal, of course, and Gothic Europeans especially looked to Greco-Roman antiquity. That time produced Christ and his earthly social organization, the Roman Empire. The Greco-Roman past often provided the insights to establish the social organization of the late medieval present.

Cathedral Schools

Cathedral schools embraced this Gothic formulation earliest. Established by bishops in most major towns, cathedral schools drew teachers to them and served the surrounding area. These relatively small schools initially focused on the *quadrivium*—arithmetic, geometry, astronomy, and music—and the *trivium*—grammar, rhetoric, and logic. The quadrivium dealt in facts. Knowledge of the structure of the created world provided knowledge of the creator. Quadrivium subjects served as instruments to learn about the created world and therefore about god. The trivium constituted the expression of that knowledge. It was elegant, rational, orderly.

No cathedral school embodied this quest for human understanding more clearly than Chartres. One of its earlier masters, Berengar of Tours, argued that in reason, not authority, humankind resembled god. Bernard's early-twelfth-century injunction to examine Greco-Roman experience inspired his younger brother, Thierry, to produce a mid-twelfth-century organization of the seven liberal arts in one volume. Thierry's organization of humankind's products came directly from a presupposition of a personal god made in humankind's image. This god's goodness led him to order the universe and to give humankind reason with which to appreciate him. In that context, the search for knowledge, order, and even cause and effect became dignified service to a benign, loving god.

Universities: Bologna

Creation of the medieval university is traditionally traced to Bologna in the mid-twelfth century. Its jurists' embryonic codification and rationalization of Roman law led other interested individuals to come to the city and study with these masters. Other jurists, especially Burchard of Worms and Ivo of Chartres, pioneered study of canon law. Unlike Roman law, embodied in Justinian's *Corpus Juris* and its many commentaries, canon law was composed of numerous sources: the Bible, writings of church fathers, laws of church councils, decisions of church courts, papal pronouncements, and centuries of commentaries on all the preceding. Bologna emerged as a canon law center in 1140 when Gratian's compendium and organization of a great part of canon law made systematic study possible. Gratian had harmonized canon law by arranging the laws and principles according to categories of questions and further focusing on faith, morals, and discipline. In Gratian's hands, canon law remained otherworldly. Miracles, spirits, magic, charms, and the power of relics figured prominently, but he also recognized the ascendancy of the papal monarchy.

Later compilations and codifications considered the power of the pope and the substance of papal canons in greater detail.

The situation of both canon and Roman law in mid-twelfth-century Bologna mirrored Gothic society. Two sets of universal law competed for attention. Both were studied but since the two contained numerous contradictions, an extended opportunity crystallized for regular study and explanation of those contradictions. In every case, however, study depended on those legal experts who had mastered material now of importance to Gothic Europe. As both secular authorities and the papacy worked to erect hierarchical structures to govern all or part of Europe, the mechanisms by which this had been accomplished in the past assumed immediacy, likely to have a bearing on the present and future. The law thus attracted those seeking to govern and to understand the god-ordained order.

Centrality of codified law and emphasis on expertise helped explain why thousands from across Europe gathered in Bologna. The emperor certainly recognized the importance of expert-led legal considerations. He granted the experts a charter to act collectively in 1158, maintaining that the study of law, especially Roman law (which predated Christianity) would lead men to obey god and, because of their obedience to god, to obey the emperor, who as god's leading earthly servant received his power directly from that heavenly being. Individuals desiring to learn law contracted individually with the experts to establish a course of study. But the existence of large numbers of people from places outside the city posed a critical problem. They had no legal rights in Bologna; they remained outside the law. City residents claimed that students were rowdy—drinking, fighting, and gambling. Few Bolognese would do business with persons not accountable to local statutes and these "foreigners" responded by forming themselves into a *societates*, a collective responsible for the debts of its individual members. That ameliorated the money problem but the lack of civic rights continued to gall students, who maintained that their lack of legal status encouraged city residents to take advantage of them, overcharging for rent, food, and books. Not part of a guild or members of the civic commune, students were without legitimate means to combat these atrocities. They demanded for themselves special status and privileges and used the clergy as their model.

The city refused their entreatment so students took matters into their own hands. They constituted themselves into a *universitas*, a guildlike creation comprised only of students. Universitas members paid dues, established rules to regulate themselves, and elected officers called rectors, who handled day-to-day affairs with the advice of a council. The universitas adjudicated disputes among members, paid for damages inflicted by members as well as their release from jail, and worked to secure repayment of debts. It also sought to order the dealings of students with others. As early as 1193, the universitas established rules for interaction among students and masters. Since they paid fees for the masters' expertise, students felt they deserved to hold the upper hand. The universitas demanded that masters take an oath of obedience to universitas regulations before they became eligible to receive student fees. Student regulations included fining masters for starting a minute late or going a minute long. They required masters to announce the course's nature and precise dates that subjects would be discussed prior to the first lecture. Students fined masters glossing over difficult passages for lack of expertise. Masters needed to deposit surety before each course to ensure payment of fines. Masters delivering a lecture not attracting five students were fined as if absent from that lecture. Masters needed to receive student permission to leave Bologna and had to deposit additional surety guaranteeing their return. The universitas secretly elected four students to spy on masters to ensure their regulatory compliance. Whenever two spies reported an irregularity, the rectors—universitas officers—assumed the report accurate and fined the offending party.

Masters rebelled against the student universitas. They held their own imperial charter but, more important, masters were citizens of Bologna, part of the commune. Student attempts to regulate masters seemed to violate the commune's sanctity. The universitas' decision in 1270 to pay masters a salary rather than pay them on a course-by-course basis stood as the height of its power. It permitted students to choose who would teach and what that person was paid. From that point on, however, the universitas lost command. Bologna began paying the masters' salaries in 1300 and by 1350 had secured appointment power. City preeminence benefited both masters and students. The city established dormitories to house students living away from home and built lecture halls. It also granted students temporarily the rights of Bolognese but did not make them commune members; students gained legal standing and protection while in school. The city specified the price at which booksellers could resell student books and the rates that landlords could charge students.

By the city's ascension, Bolognese course of study rules were well fixed. Students attended three lectures weekly and church daily. Exams were given weekly. Becoming a canon law master required a four-year course of study and Roman law took a year longer. Student life also developed several conventions. Students made distinctions among themselves according to their place of origin and the number of years in school. Newer students were often taunted; treating them as if they were wild animals was considered sport.

Universities: Paris

The universitas of Bologna was the creation of people who gathered there to learn about law from experts and found themselves without legal rights, without a defined place in the social hierarchy. A status-seeking universitas was also formed in Paris, but the masters initiated it. A school under the bishop's control had long existed at Paris, specializing not in law but in a general curriculum. Students studied grammar, rhetoric, logic, arithmetic, geometry, astronomy, and music, logically precise disciplines and techniques. These arts were later joined by theological, law, philosophical, and medical curricula, each with its masters. The school's chancellor, a representative of the bishop, held authority to appoint teachers to each of the five faculties and to award degrees. As early as the 1170s, masters formed themselves into a universitas, but not until 1200 did they act collectively. Under threat of group migration, they received concessions from the city, state, and church. Gaining power to appoint a representative to plead the masters' case in papal courts enabled them to circumvent the chancellor's and the bishop's authority. The chancellor demanded oaths of obedience and fealty as well as significant payments before he licensed a master to teach. The chancellor also could withdraw a master's teaching privileges at any time and even excommunicate an offending scholar. The masters boycotted the chancellor, who refused to relent. The pope interceded in 1212 in favor of the masters, forcing

Seal of the University of Paris. Creation of universities to train persons in law, medicine, theology, philosophy, and the arts led such centers of learning to take the medieval guild as their inspiration. Masters gathered together to provide a specific training and then certified that each graduate had achieved a certain minimum proficiency.

the chancellor to license all candidates recommended by the masters; experts gained authority to designate experts.

The arts faculty led in establishing self-government. It divided itself by place of origin, selecting a proctor to lead each geographically based group, and then elected a single rector to head the faculty. In effect, the arts rector became the head of the universitas. The arts rector secured this authority because members of the theology, medicine, law, and philosophy faculties had first received arts degrees—it remained the first stage to achieving an advanced degree—and recognized the arts as the discipline binding the universitas together. Each subordinate faculty elected its own dean, who acted like the rector among his faculty but took an oath of allegiance to the rector. Deans were to a rector as princes were to a king.

Masters expected students at Paris to speak Latin. Lecturing technique incorporated the dialectic method through which each word was defined, identified, and amplified. The sentence was then tested by reference to previous arguments. For example, masters explained one Bible passage by reference to another biblical passage or a canon law judgment with respect to papal pronouncements or council decisions. Texts considered in courses seemed sacrosanct, never changing, but required continual scrutiny to reveal true meaning. In addition to church fathers, legal documents, and Aristotle, monumental texts included works of Euclid, Ptolemy, Hippocrates, Galen, and other Greco-Roman authorities. Public disputations, a sort of intellectual jousting, occurred in October and at Easter as students and masters both sharpened their dialectical skill and shared information.

Other Universities

Universities—organized faculties of masters given special privileges—spread across Europe in the thirteenth and fourteenth centuries. For example, Toulouse received a papal charter in 1229 to establish a university specializing in the seven liberal arts and in canon and civil law. Montpellier and Salerno date themselves from the twelfth century but achieved maturity only in the later thirteenth century. Medicine was their specialty. In university cities and towns, cathedral schools restricted themselves to the trivium, as a kind of stepping stone to the university. Poems, fables, and songs of university students portrayed student life as different from that pictured in courtly love literature. Students' ballads were bawdy and suggested a rough life. Sex figured prominently and priests caught in flagrante delicto emerged as a running theme as did old men taking young brides. That universities drew students from across Europe suggested that they served to create a pan-European consciousness or identity. Students congregated at central places, learned the same material, and carried it to their native lands. The consequence was a homogenized culture, at least among the elites. But the reverse could also be argued. Students gathered at universities to learn specific subjects and to study certain texts precisely because a commonality already existed. Most were clerics or the sons of nobility, two groups already imbued with a sense of extra-local identity. Universities were as much, if not more, manifestations of a pan-Europeanism (Christendom) as cause.

Paper and Papermaking

Introduction of paper into western Europe lowered the cost of writing material and facilitated distribution of monumental texts, the heart of universities. A vegetable substance manufactured by techniques acquired from the Muslims, paper became common in Spain after 1150 and quickly spread east with the reconquest. Water-powered stamping mills entered the process about a century after paper's Spanish appearance. In 1280, Bologna-produced paper was one-sixth as expensive as parchment, the animal product paper replaced. Papermaking required reducing vegetable matter to its crude fibers, generally through pounding, tearing, or stamping. Papermakers transferred the fibers to a water-filled vat and mixed them. They then dipped a mesh tray with as many as twelve wires per inch into the vat. Artisans lifted out the tray and shook it from side to side to distribute evenly the remaining fibrous material. They turned the tray upside down and deposited the wet mass on felt cloth. They repeated the process several times, making sure to separate each paper piece with felt. Papermakers used a press to consolidate the paper and to remove excess moisture. They finally hung the individual sheets to dry, sometimes rubbing them with gelatin from the hooves and hides of animals to protect the paper.

God and Nature

Study of nature required no written texts. As an observable manifestation of god, nature's explication through reason brought humankind closer to understanding the deity. Interpreting nature to understand god rather than to find the way to individual salvation suggested a new optimism about humankind's possibilities. Albertus Magnus (1206–1280), St. Thomas's teacher at Paris, trumpeted reason as enabling observers to "view" god. His contemporary, England's Robert Grosseteste (1175–1253), identified light as a material manifestation of god—god and light both emanated from the universe's center and both permeated all things, which proved them identical—and spent the remainder of his career attempting to classify light's properties and the rules for its behavior. His student, Roger Bacon (1214–1294), also accentuated light but concentrated on the eye. Bacon noted that god had chosen to make eyes with seven coverings to express the seven gifts of the spirit, and, evoking St. Anselm, the seven grades of perfection. To Bacon, the past held keys to unlocking nature's complexities and ultimately god. Rules for astrology, the effect of the position of heavenly bodies on terrestrial phenomena, and alchemy, the transmutation of one substance into another, had been known to the ancient Greeks. Recovering these lost hierarchies through reason brought humankind nearer to knowing god.

Debates of the Schoolmen

The dialectical method dominated Gothic formal thought. It constituted a pan-European approach to intellectual problem solving as Schoolmen used it as a tool to reason. But although all employed an agreed-upon method, debates raged over particulars. The true nature—the reality—of categories (or, more simply, what constituted a real classification) dominated the early years. This problem of universals, of what were real groups and what were convenient mental constructs to organize individual entities, struck at the heart of both the dialectic method and the campaign to reason to god. Did outer manifestations always signal inner realities? Were they always identical? What were the characteristics that individuals held in common and did those characteristics constitute a "true" basis of unity and identity? And most important, what was the relationship between a thing—a presence in physical reality—and the word used to designate it? Were they the same? Did one have more meaning than the other?

Abelard

The debate over universals held much in common with the debate over the nature of sin. Not surprisingly, Peter Abelard involved himself in both. As he would do with sin, Abelard made a concrete distinction between reality and the word used to signify something. The thing existed as itself; the word was different, a human construct, an approximation of the god-created thing. Things, therefore, as god's products held a greater amount of truth than the reason-derived words of god's creation, humankind.

Abelard's realism considered both the thing and the word true. To his mind, the dialectic method enabled him to distinguish among them—to determine which possessed more truth—and to establish a hierarchical relationship among them. Abelard broached a similar issue in his classic *Sic et Non* but in the context of rationalizing church teachings. Like the lawyers at Bologna, who studied and attempted to reconcile the seemingly endless contrarieties that developed over the centuries in Roman law, Abelard asserted that dialectics could reconcile the apparent contradictions among the church fathers and the Bible. He set out 150 sets of texts juxtaposing the words of church fathers and scripture. Each of these sets seemed mutually contradictory but Abelard maintained that each could be reconciled "by doubting." Through the process of doubting—looking for the thread that wove these apparently antagonistic dyads together—"we come to questioning, and by questioning we perceive the truth." This fully articulated, hierarchical list of positions identified as dualities then required explanation. Abelard's task was to show through logical argument why each set was not contradictory. His demonstration of each group's internal consistency included selection of those passages that portrayed god as a father, characterized by love, wisdom, and other human emotions and expressions. Abelard also made the three branches of the trinity less distinctive, often using those attributes given to the very human Christ as if they were of almighty god. His highlighting of these human qualities was contrasted by his downplaying or ignoring sections that pictured an awesome or a wrathful deity.

Abelard died before translation into Latin of Aristotle's advanced logic. Although Abelard lacked access to these texts, his prose, like his arguments and like Anselm before him, exhibited the same penchant for categorization, juxtaposition, and systematization that exemplified the strict canons of what later would be known as Aristotelian logic. That passion for hierarchy and order made Aristotle central; as Gothic Europeans understood Aristotle, his works confirmed a framework already in place. Others seized the initiative. Peter the Lombard, a master of the Parisian cathedral school, wrote the *Books of Sentences* about 1150, a systematic treatment of Christian doctrine. Each focused on a single question: god; the world before Christ; Christ's earthly existence and resurrection; and judgment—heaven and hell. Each consisted of paired points and counterpoints and culminated with syntheses demonstrating the fundamental consistency between what had seemed opposing positions. Paris's Stephen Langton rationalized the Bible a half-century later. He carried the passion for organization to its natural conclusion by numbering the text and organizing it from start to finish by chapter and verse.

Scholasticism

Scholasticism, usually defined as applying the logic of Greek philosophy to Christian teachings, marked the formal apex of the quest to taxonomize and help explain god, Christianity, and Christian dogma through human reason. St. Thomas Aquinas, a Dominican at Paris, disputed the contention that Aristotelianism undercut and circumvented faith and set out to demonstrate reason's utility in determining religious truths. In his classic mid-thirteenth-century *Summa Theologica*, Aquinas maintained that faith and reason never conflicted. Both came from god and therefore both supported one another. Not all things could be proven by reason, he admitted, and in

Thomas Aquinas. This rendering of Aquinas and his world provides a graphic representation of the scholastic method. It divides a whole into a series of parts, each of which has at least two contraries. The two matched contraries are then compared, and a synthesis is fashioned out of the seemingly disparate match. These syntheses are then joined to provide a greater truth.

that sense faith always was superior to reason. But faith assisted reason, argued Aquinas, because when reason and faith appeared to disagree, reasoning must be in error. That acknowledgment led to a careful examination of reason and its subsequent improvement.

That preamble set the stage for an extraordinarily detailed and orderly exposition. *Summa Theologica* was exhaustive, a tour de force. Each section adopted the same precise formality and exactness. Aquinas always set the general area of inquiry ("article") and divided that area into issues ("questions"). He began with the negatives of each issue ("objections"), taking care to articulate each negative separately and to be as complete as possible. Scripture and church fathers were juxtaposed ("on the contrary") with each negative and then Aquinas outlined his conclusions ("I answer that") to each objection. He ended each question by systematically refuting each of the negatives he had articulated earlier ("reply to objectives").

Not everyone agreed with Aquinas's presumptions. His Parisian contemporary, the Franciscan St. Bonaventure, did not reason contraries among scriptures and Greco-Roman fathers but tried to identify the hierarchical formulation of the rational god's universe. Bonaventure accentuated faith even more than had Aquinas. God created humankind in his image; humans possessed god-given reason and therefore were able to appreciate the universe's god-ordained order. Bonaventure's heavens and earth anticipated in structure Dante's hell. For example, Bonaventure claimed that god constructed part of the heavens as nine spheres of angels, which were divided into nine hierarchically arranged ranks. These ranks were in turn organized into three groups. Each group had three subgroups. Bonaventure's human was the universe's key being. Humans had affinity with the natural world because of their body but their spirit gave them a kinship with the angels. The soul most interested Bonaventure. God logically created it in the image of the trinity. Its three components—intellect, will, and memory—allowed the human spirit to look inside itself as well as at the world around it and to use its reason, which led to god.

Cathedrals: Joining Heaven and Earth

Cistercian strictures toward simplicity, lack of church adornment, and hard, laborious work were potent forms of imagery. These outward acts suggested a brotherhood rejecting earthly wealth to suffer as the savior; they identified the Cistercians with the very human Christ's tribulations. Others identified with the very human deity by dedicating to him something extremely human and valuable in human terms as a means of symbolizing camaraderie and thanks. Church buildings often became the locus of largess. Grand buildings glorified god, just as grand structures had glorified the emperor at times during Rome. An unprecedented church building boom swept Europe as bishops and other prelates demanded large, splendid facilities. In the two and one-half centuries prior to 1350, over 600 large church buildings were erected in France alone. More stone was quarried for French church structures in the two centuries before 1300 than in the entire history of ancient Egypt.

Local clergymen, especially bishops, almost always spearheaded the new, magnificent church projects. Bishoprics were generally located in Europe's largest places and these successful commercial and artisan centers could afford the grandest structures. Thirteenth-century cities and towns were tiny by present standards. Then contemporary metropolises, such as Paris, had populations less than 50,000. London remained half that size. Nor was population evenly distributed throughout Europe. The French accounted for about half of all Europeans. Present-day Italy, then split among the papal monarchy and the autonomous city-states, held the next greatest number. These two most prosperous areas experienced the greatest and most sustained church building boom.

Church building became a matter of city and class pride. Cities competed with each other to erect the grandest church buildings. Sometimes cities bankrupted themselves in the pursuit. Bishops tried to outdo one another and have their diocese house the most splendid structure. These cathedrals (bishops resided in cathedrals, which housed their thronelike cathedra) were massive, the largest similar in size to modern indoor basketball arenas. A medieval cathedral could cover an area as great as 7,700 square meters, be constructed on a foundation 10 meters deep, possess a spire over 105 meters tall, and seat well over 10,000. Some took a half century or more to complete. Wealthy merchants lovingly gave to church building funds to secure a measure of grace, to recognize god's contribution to their success, or to substitute for Crusades or pilgrimages. The truly penitent could demonstrate contrition by contributing their fortunes to church buildings while still living.

The religious building boom extended from the eleventh through the fourteenth centuries. But it remained until the mid-twelfth century for a religious building style to reflect Gothic Europe's fundamental tenets. Earlier church buildings had been low, thick-walled, ponderous structures with few windows. Rounded arches served as the predominant structural unit and murals, pilasters, and frescoes provided decoration. The new soaring, light-bathed, curtain-walled Gothic cathedrals joined heaven and earth. Their structural elements were their decoration.

Abbot Suger and St. Denis

Abbot Suger of St. Denis, the greatest of French monasteries and burial place of kings, revamped his church in the mid-twelfth century to create the first Gothic-styled religious structure. The king of France, peers, bishops, and archbishops attended the building's consecration in 1144. Suger, a political and administrative advisor to Louis VI, remembered his elation at that event when he wrote later that in his church "the admirable power of one unique and supreme reason equalizes by proper composition the disparity between things human and divine; and what seems mutually to conflict by inferiority of origin and contrariety of nature is conjoined by the single, delightful concordance or one superior, well-tempered harmony." Suger's articulated vision of god and the cosmos hardly marked him as unusual. His statement simply had laid out a series of hierarchies, announced that reason, which god granted humans, stood as means to distinguish among things, maintained that apparent conflicts were illusory and that everything conformed to the deity's perfectly harmonious ordered plan. Like his contemporaries, Suger understood order was good, order was beauty, and order was god. Anything that gave structure—unifiers of apparent opposites, such as the material and the immaterial or heaven and earth, including light, geometry, mathematics, or reason—was god, was like god, or was touched by god. But Suger went a step further. He maintained that his reconstructed building's physical presence reflected those mighty principles. Suger claimed to have built theology.

Suger used "geometrical and arithmetical rules" to harmonize the parts of St. Denis. Suger purposely charged every structural element. Each skeletal element became a facet of what could be called theological art; Suger had no need for murals or geometric designs to illustrate the divine. The entire building accomplished that goal through, in Suger's words, "concordance of parts."

St. Denis. As envisioned by Abbot Suger, this first Gothic cathedral united heaven and earth. Pointed arches reconciled the teachings of the church fathers and divine scripture. Curtain walls and huge windows permitted light to bathe the church's interior. Pointed ceiling vaults diminished lateral thrust and enabled builders to add height to the structure. A window shaped like a gigantic rose carried the setting sun's rays directly to the altar.

St. Denis's nine chapels embodied Suger's vision and typified the entire structure. Their spherical outer walls served as mere frames for paired tall windows. While architectural sight lines directed observers out and up, light poured through the seemingly porous walls into the outward-radiating chapels and then to a double ambulatory, which surrounded a choir. In that manner, "the entire sanctuary is thus pervaded by a wonderful and continuous light through the most sacred windows."

Suger conceived of the chapel-ambulatory-choir complex as a single unit, a "circuitus oratorium." To Suger and other Gothic men and women, light, like god, was invisible and, like god, caused humans to see. Paired windows flooding a single section with light suggested a physical representation of the resolution of apparent contrarieties. The union of two windows to make one wall indicated a similar sentiment. Voices emanating from the divinely inspired choir sounded like "an angelic rather than a human melody" as the assembled sang "so festively, so solemnly, so different and yet so concordantly." Celebration of mass in the revamped structure joined "material with the immaterial, the human with the divine" as "God transfers the present kingdom into the celestial one." Suger took immense pleasure in this theological building and considerable pride in its completion, placing four likenesses of himself in the church and leaving 13 stone inscriptions citing his accomplishments.

Gothic Style and Symbols

Others refined the Gothic style. The Gothic arch, a pointed arch, dominated later buildings. Structurally, it removed from the walls some of the load-bearing pressure produced by the roof. Lessening pressure—in Romanesque architecture, rounded arches had placed ceiling and roof weight directly on the edifice's thick walls—enabled builders to make windows even larger and walls thinner. Ribbed ceiling vaults distributed weight more evenly. Gothic walls were progressively more glass and less stone the higher one went. The Gothic arch itself suggested height, pointing upward. Tracery, delicate carved decorations, and colonettes, thin round shafts giving vertical sight lines, furthered the appearance of a soaring structure. The scholastic arch carried vision higher yet. A material representation of the thought embodied in such characteristic Gothic works as Abelard's *Sic et Non* or Aquinas's *Summa Theologica*, the scholastic arch collected two highly articulated Gothic arches and merged them into a single greater Gothic arch. It reconciled apparent contraries and appeared to push the structure to new elevation. Scholastic windows, mimicking scholastic arches, also became common.

Gothic architecture replaced load-bearing walls with pillars. Pillars inside the main part of the structure, the nave, bore the stone ceiling and roof. Side aisles remained outside these pillars and the large windowed curtain walls stood still farther away. In the most daring of Gothic structures, architects replaced internal pillars with buttresses located outside the edifice's walls. These flying buttresses kept lateral thrust off the walls and removed massive pillars from the nave. An even more ethereal structure resulted.

Other features contributed to the Gothic style. Cathedrals exhibited a cruciform layout. The altar rested at the head of the cross, pointing east, the direction of the rising sun and symbolic of Christ's resurrection. Rose windows, glorious huge, round stained-glass orifices suggestive of magnificent roses, graced the western as well as other facades of numerous churches and cathedrals. The setting sun shone in these rose windows, which generally had twelve escalloped "petals" around their circular centers. The rose became a symbol for the Blessed Virgin in the twelfth century and it long signified love. The number of petals may have represented the Twelve Apostles. But another possibility also presented itself. Greeks marked directions on their maps with what they termed a wind rose, a starlike design. Medieval mapmakers surrounded the known world, pictured as circular, with the twelve winds, strikingly similar to the petals of rose windows. They called their new wind-oriented maps *wind roses*. Rose windows may simply have symbolized the physical world rather than Mary.

Building decoration was less abstract but no less allegorical. Stained-glass windows were the poor's picture books and recounted Bible scenes or lives of saints. Dozens of small statues of Christ, Mary, the apostles or saints adorned each of a structure's several portals. Often religious and secular objects were joined. The incarnation of Christ at Chartres' royal portal was surrounded by worshipping angels and representations of the seven liberal arts. A man who excelled at each art was sculpted beneath the appropriate art. Portraits of Greeks—heathens—accounted for six of the seven figures. Christ's Second Coming was depicted to the left of these sculptures. There also the seven liberal arts were shown as yielding medicine, canon law, and theology. At the Sens and Notre Dame of Paris cathedrals, sculptors showed the liberal arts as holding dominion over beasts; humans reign over the animal kingdom. The liberal arts were often placed in a hierarchy. Philosophy and geometry usually vied for primacy. Builders used segments of circles or circles within circles to represent the relationship of one liberal art to the liberal arts generally or the liberal arts to the Bible or to god. Whether through inner or outer circles or outer rings around circles, miniature statues expressed ordered relationships among constituent intellectual elements.

Building Gothic Church Buildings

Constructing Gothic church buildings, especially cathedrals, required great labor, considerable skill, and much time and money. Localities recruited diggers, common workmen, lime-burners, tool-carriers, hod-bearers, and pulley-workers from the surrounding area. These men, like the more highly skilled hewers, layers, wallers, marblers, paviors, and image-makers, erected lodges at building sites for eating, naps, and tool storage but slept at their homes. Work on cathedrals began at quarries. Masons selected quarries because of rock quality and closeness to building sites. For example, stone taken from under Paris's streets went to build the city's church structures. Suitable stone often lay under rock, and teams of quarrymen, generally in units of eight and headed by a master quarryman, tunneled to reach it. Quarrymen sometimes roughhewed pieces underground or at the quarry to reduce transportation costs. Water transport on barges proved much less expensive than overland drayage. After about 1250, some cities conscripted men to work as quarrymen, paying them by the piece and placing them next to waged workers.

Stonecutters—masons—enjoyed much greater prestige than quarrymen. These men finished blocks and often cut statuary. Masons used plumb rule, mason's level, compass, and square to cut pieces precisely and to line up walls. They carved positioning marks into stone on the ground to ensure that joints measured there fit when placed in the structure. Masons scored each block with their own identifying marks. Fathers handed family marks down to their sons. Prominence of marks suggests that these craftsmen took great pride in their work; each piece constituted a work of art.

Medieval Master Masons

The masonic art achieved new status in the later twelfth century. One sure sign of this new status and power was the assertion of a tradition of masonic knowledge and craft. Masons sought to recover the secrets of "squaring the circle" and attaining perpetual motion and tried to reduce most technical questions to plane geometry, especially intersecting circles. The Greek Euclid emerged as a hero to masons, who claimed him as a founder of their artistry. As with most crafts, masonry skill depended on oral transmission and practical hands-on experience. Literacy was not necessary, although some grammar schooling at a monastery or cathedral might be advantageous. The quadrivium received short shrift there but a basic knowledge of Latin grammar and literacy would have helped masons read one or more of the numerous translations of Greek or Roman geometry books. Mathematics books appeared in the vernacular—and some master masons surely read vernacular—only after 1200.

Master masons gained responsibility for constructing large church structures and served as both designers (in conjunction with a bishop or an abbot) and contractors. They toured the continent looking at standing structures and learning new building techniques. A handful of Greco-Roman building books remained to guide them but little evidence existed of their use. *The Ten Books on Architecture* by Vitruvius would have had the most applications. With the new responsibilities of master masons came jealousy. Underlings complained that a master mason merely "gives orders and never puts his hands to work yet receives more than the others [just for saying] to others 'cut it this way.'"

Master masons shared information with each other and considered themselves an important occupational group. At least one master mason wrote of a masonic spirit that bound masons to one another and to god. Their hands and labors created god's beauty, joining heaven with earth in church edifices. Rise of the medieval master masons occurred just as skilled technicians began to replace virtuous heroes in poems and stories and as representations of the deity marked him as a great architect, the architect of the universe—heaven and earth. The respect church officials gave master masons reflected their considerable prestige. Tiled labyrinths ran the length of the central floors of most Gothic cathedral naves. Entering the church, dropping to your knees, and crawling through the labyrinth symbolized a pilgrimage to the Holy Land. At the center of the maze—at the end of the pilgrimage—rested several circular or octagonal metal or marble plaques. Instead of representations of god, the Blessed Virgin, or even the saints, portraits of the master masons who guided the cathedral's construction (and sometimes the bishop or abbot) were found there. These men were vessels through which god joined heaven and earth.

Constructing massive structures, like medieval cathedrals, required more than a sense of identity and spiritual belief, of course. Masons generally laid blocks one level at a time around buildings and mortared them together with a lime and sandstone mixture. Wax, pitch, or resin waterproofed the mortar. Workers cut scaffolding and ramps in walls to reach high places. Foundations became increasingly common.

Other Cathedral Craftworkers

Metalworking smiths and woodworking carpenters joined masons to fashion buildings. Most tools combined wood and iron; wooden-handled, iron-headed imple-

Stained Glass. Mosaic-like in construction, stained glass windows were exceedingly colorful and graced virtually every cathedral. Contemporaries took advantage of these huge glass spaces to recount biblical stories or to thank patrons for financial support of the church.

ments proved most common. Carpenters built scaffolds to reach high places, supports to bear up ceilings for masonry vaults and roofs. They sometimes constructed large Ferris wheel–sized wheels with treadmills inside as hoisting machines to help raise heavy loads to great height. Smiths participated in those endeavors and also made metal frames from which to hang stained-glass windows and thin, lead strips with grooves called *cames* to affix and hold the glass. Gothic Europeans colored glass either by painting it with a paint made from a metallic oxide, pulverized glass, and a binding agent or by adding a coloring substance—generally a metallic oxide—to the molten material in the pot. The poured glass was cut to the appropriate size with a red-hot iron. Gum arabic preserved painted material. Iron-protected wooden piles were often an essential part of foundations and metallic covering of roofs increased longevity.

Bellmaking required other skills. Medieval men cast bronze church bells. They crafted a clay and plaster of paris bell, covered it with wax to the desired thickness of the bell, and placed a layer of clay and plaster over the wax. Bronze pins sandwiched the mold together. They then heated the mold, let the wax run off, set the hollow mold in sand, and poured in molten bronze. Bellmakers destroyed the mold after the bronze had cooled.

The Gothic Arts

Church buildings, especially cathedrals, were far from sacrosanct. People ate and slept there, talked, and even brought dogs. Cathedrals served as city halls and community centers. They joined ethereal heaven with mundane earth. As with other Gothic institutions and conventions, a cathedral's outward appearance and activities provided a glimpse of what lay underneath. Precious stones decorated altars and statuary aimed toward realism. Gothic architecture emphasized totality, yet demanded that individual architectural elements be sufficiently separate and striking as to remain clearly distinct from each other. The outer significance of art showed its inward virtue. Recurrent phrases provided speech with an acoustic articulation, while rubrics, numbers, and paragraphs brought visual articulation to written words. Gothic music, articulated by the exact and systematic division of time, employed notation indicating rhythm as well as pitch. It popularized the arpeggio, the division of a chord into discrete parts played at a rate to maintain that distinctiveness yet to provide a sense of coherence. Thirds and the keys of F major and D minor, notes and keys formerly considered dissonant and unsuitable for church music, became reconciled. Thirteenth-century cathedral music incorporated polyphony, the idea of several separate voices in one piece that together constitute music.

The soul was the organizing principle of the body. Reason elucidated or clarified experience into sections, subsections, and chapters. Senses were extensions of soul-derived reason and therefore contained inherent order. The senses "delight in things duly proportioned as in something akin to them; for, the sense, too, is a kind of reason as is every cognitive power." Wholes were divided into parts, parts into distinctions, and distinctions into articulations. Gothic men and women recognized and gloried in their classification mania. The world was composed of "division into many parts as do the dialecticians; rhythmical consonances as do the grammarians; and forced harmonizations as used by the jurists." Identifiers of divisions—authorities—were never rejected. Only their interpretations could be flawed. They remained authorities even if reason did not immediately reconcile them. Gothic scholars worked to deduce what was there, to find the hierarchical categories implicit in the works of authorities.

The Fourteenth Century

The quiet confidence that had undergirded Gothic thought was shattered in the first half of the fourteenth century. A manure shortage, coupled with heavy rains and early frosts, produced agricultural shortfalls during the century's first two decades and famines from 1315 to 1317. Shortage of silver led to debased coinage and spiraling inflation. Nobles, who required luxury goods to maintain status, sought to increase their means through taxation and war. Apocalyptic predictions identified Jews and lepers as plotting against Christendom.

The Black Death

These economic setbacks paled compared to the devastation caused by the Black Death of 1347–1351. An estimated one-third of the European population died during that bubonic plague pandemic. Some places had mortality rates approaching 80 percent. Markets dried up, villages emptied, and farms were abandoned. Daily life stopped. Conventional mechanisms and institutions failed to end the chaos and deterioration, and Gothic Europeans tried numerous alternatives. Seeking divine intervention was common but Gothic men and women placed themselves at the center in a characteristic way. They flagellated themselves, dressed ostentatiously or bizarrely, or danced of death or of hell. In each of those ways, individuals showed in their public behavior outward indications of contrition, indications that god would understand and stop the retribution of the Black Death. Others in the fourteenth century recognized a force at work more powerful than the god of the Christian church and called upon that higher power to remove the scourge. Those who found this power in Satan practiced black magic or witchcraft or engaged in some sexual ritual. Yet others found the cause of the plague not in the next but in this world. They translated the rampant anti-Judaism of the period into blame for the pandemic and accused Jews of poisoning wells. Massacres followed.

Production of food and goods fell precipitously after the Black Death. During the plague, peasants had seized upon the drop in land prices to buy themselves free of some if not all customary obligations or to work at fixed wages for their lords. With the plague behind them, an increasingly desperate nobility tried to reinstitute those customs and to add additional ones. Riots resulted. The nobility treated the rioters as if they were heretics—those violently complaining attacked a hierarchically constructed, god-ordained social system. Urban workers joined the social heresy a few decades later. Again, force of arms restored the status quo.

Whether the product of new economic conditions, a consequence of the Black Death, or for some other reason, Gothic confidence had vanished after mid-century. Humankind remained at the center of concern but terms of discussion had changed. The possibility of rejecting the past, of rejecting authorities, was one manifestation of this change. As William of Ockham, an English Schoolman, bluntly stated at mid-century, "What Aristotle thought about this, I do not care."

For Further Reading (Chapters 7 and 8)

Bridbury, A. R. *Medieval English Clothmaking*. London: Heinemann, 1982.

Brooke, Christopher. *The Structure of Medieval Society*. London: Thames and Hudson, 1971.

Clagett, Marshall, Gaines Post, and Robert Reynolds, eds. *Twelfth-Century Europe and the Foundations of Modern Society*. Madison: University of Wisconsin Press, 1966.

Cobban, A. B. *The Medieval Universities: Their Development and Organization*. London: Methuen & Co., 1975.

Duby, Georges. *The Chivalrous Society*. Berkeley: University of California Press, 1980.

Fitchen, John. *Building Construction Before Mechanization*. Cambridge: MIT Press, 1986.

Gies, Joseph and Frances. *Life in a Medieval Castle*. New York: Harper & Row, 1974.

Gies, Joseph and Frances. *Life in a Medieval City*. New York: Thomas Y. Crowell, 1973.

Gimpel, Jean. *The Cathedral Builders*. New York: Grove Press, 1983.

Gimpel, Jean. *The Medieval Machine. The Industrial Revolution of the Middle Ages*. New York: Holt, Rinehart and Winston, 1976.

Haskins, Charles Homer. *The Renaissance of the 12th Century*. Cambridge: Harvard University Press, 1927.

Herlihy, David. *Opera Muliebria. Women and Work in Medieval Europe*. (Philadelphia: Temple University Press, 1990.

Holmes, Urban Tigner, Jr. *Daily Living in the Twelfth Century*. Madison: University of Wisconsin Press, 1964.

Kealey, Edward J. *Harvesting the Air*. Berkeley: University of California Press, 1987.

Mazzaoui, Maureen Fennell. *The Italian Cotton Industry in the Later Middle Ages 1100–1600*. Cambridge: Cambridge University Press, 1981.

Panofsky, Erwin. *Abbot Suger on the Abbey Church of St.-Denis and Its Art Treasures*. 2d ed. Princeton: Princeton University Press, 1979.

Panofsky, Erwin. *Gothic Architecture and Scholasticism*. New York: New American Library, 1957.

Pieper, Josef. *Scholasticism: Personalities and Problems of Medieval Philosophy*. New York: McGraw-Hill, 1960.

Radding, Charles M., and William W. Clark. *Medieval Architecture, Medieval Learning*. New Haven: Yale University Press, 1992.

Rorig, Fritz. *The Medieval Town*. Berkeley: University of California Press, 1967.

Rowling, Marjorie. *Life in Medieval Times*. New York: Charles Scribner, 1968.

Smith, Cyril Eugene. *The University of Toulouse in the Middle Ages*. Milwaukee: Marquette University Press, 1958.

Strayer, Joseph R. *On the Medieval Origins of the Modern State*. Princeton: Princeton University Press, 1970.

Talbot, C. H. *Medicine in Medieval England*. London: Oldbourne, 1967.

Von Simson, Otto. *The Gothic Cathedral*. Princeton: Princeton University Press, 1974.

The term *Renaissance* means "the rebirth of learning," a view that people living in the period 1350–1630 certainly claimed about their time. They dismissed medieval Europe as a millennium-long epoch governed by superstition and ignorance, an era of stagnation or regress. Such a view was incorrect, of course, and what contemporaries proposed instead revealed their

PART THREE

Renaissance and Beyond

agenda. They demanded a renewal of commitment to explore the earthly realm, a terrestrial, human-focused inquiry. As a source of inspiration and information, Renaissance men and women championed the Greek and Roman past, the cultural referents that have played such a large part in the idea of western civilization, and maintained that medieval Europeans lost knowledge that had been common in these two classical civilizations.

Investigation of the Greek and Roman past was undertaken differentially. Literature explicitly dealing with humankind—poems, orations, social tracts, plays, and the like—captured the Renaissance's attention in the voyage of rediscovery. These humanities enabled individuals to ask the central question of what were humankind's strengths and weaknesses as Renaissance Europeans struggled to explore and map out humankind's realm, a heady sentiment of almost limitless possibilities.

In contrast, the term *Baroque* refers to something a bit unnatural, such as a misshapen pearl. It was coined some centuries later to disparage a period of time in European history (1630–1715 here) as a perversion of the much-revered Renaissance. To be sure, Baroque Europeans maintained the Renaissance's concentration on humankind and its earthly realm and continued its veneration of Greece and Rome. But unlike the Renaissance, the Baroque sought to define humankind's boundaries, its limits, its constraints, and to arrange and design agencies to act within them.

Both Baroque and Renaissance Europe have been much praised for their emphasis on humanity, especially human reason. The stories of Leonardo da

Vinci and Isaac Newton, preeminent men of their times, are well known. Their genius is said to be a forerunner of modern thought; these men were ahead of their time and part of ours. Such a view is mistaken. These men were celebrated in their times because their ideas and actions resonated with their times; they reflected their times. And their times were not nearly as familiar to us in the modern world as we would like to believe. Da Vinci, Newton, and their contemporaries repeatedly tried to learn about and master the forces of creation, to act almost like gods on earth. To that end, they tried to become what they called magicians, seeking to employ god-given white magic to transmute things in their world. Both white and black magicians of the Renaissance and Baroque, the latter group denigrated as witches or other practitioners of the devil's art, held similar courses; they hoped to conjure up and tap into a sort of universal force and to channel it to serve their very human ends. For example, mapping the heavens to learn how the alignment of heavenly orbs at any given time would affect individuals on earth—astrology—became a most favored and most rational endeavor because of its predictive nature. Making a golem, creating a living creature from clay by replicating the actions of god in the biblical Genesis, was another overwhelmingly popular attempt at manipulation. So too was the search for a means to change the character of things, especially base metals such as copper into gold. Newton himself was captivated by that quest and he devoted at least as much effort to it as he did to his much celebrated theory of universal gravitation.

Those assumptions separate the civilizations of the Renaissance and Baroque from our times but they do not separate these two often similar cultures from each other. Only the notion of limits or boundaries served to demarcate them but that proved no small matter. Many Renaissance intellectual, social, and physical structures differed dramatically from the Baroque because of that important difference. Renaissance Europeans worked to undertake new avenues of exploration, to push further as they labored to define their intellectual, social, and physical existence. Baroque Europeans struggled dramatically with the consequences of limits and their existence took on a desperation—an inward glance—unknown in the Renaissance. They desperately sought to regularize procedures, activities, and performance, even social arrangements, simply to reduce waste and increase output in their constrained world.

Out of this constraint came two of the main features of modernity—the steam engine and the modern state. Both drew their initial inspiration from a sense of limits; both first appeared as attempts to maximize wealth and well-being. That these two seminal inventions function in other capacities stems from their adoption by later civilizations. Their genesis, their creation, occurred in and from the Baroque.

CHAPTER 9

All the World's a Stage and All the Men and Women Merely Players: Age of Humankind, 1360–1630

In early-fifteenth-century Italy and later in England, small groups of men attached themselves to the courts of the nobility and began to reenact Greek and Roman plays. Although these productions were of plays written more than a millennium earlier, fifteenth-century performers were not the first Europeans to act in a thousand years. Medieval Europeans had performed in public but only to religious themes. Guilds had dramatized the lives of saints, while their university contemporaries occasionally reenacted Bible stories. Both types of productions pointed the way to salvation as did the civic pageant, a month-long or more municipally sponsored recreation of Christ's life. The fifteenth-century Greek and Roman dramatic revival was quite different, however. It took humankind, not methods to achieve salvation, as its focus, seeking to identify traits, situations, and behaviors common to humanity. It held that humans, no matter their social situation, had fears, predicaments, wants, and needs that were far more compelling than those factors that divided humankind.

These new full-time performers learned to play numerous parts and as they continually expanded their repertoire, they exposed themselves to the full scope of human emotion. By the later fifteenth century, some actors had become playwrights and were creating fresh material and roles in the Greco-Roman style. Soon thereafter, they began to fashion original plays; they shed the confines of Greco-Roman form for more novel venues. Development of stock characters—personality types—and then improvisation, to see how these interesting characters would react in different settings and different relationships, was one new area that they explored. Often these works would include music and dance. The masque, a courtly performance in which masked actors performed a dramatized debate with song and dance in a decorative setting and then incorporated their noble patrons in the production, blurred distinctions between audience and actors. The balletto, a several hours–long costumed spectacle of themed dancing, poetry, and song with elaborate humanmade scenic sets and generally held outdoors, joined the masque as the most popular new forms.

The popularity of these and other staged forms encouraged popular acting troupes to sell their services from court to court. Touring acting companies were soon joined by other actors seeking to broaden the definition of audience. These fulltime performers put on productions in front of large masses of people; they erected temporary stages and gave public presentations. Many productions, particularly after about 1530, were of new material that proved extremely popular to a mass audience. Actors and playwrights recognized humankind as emotionally multidimensional, and so mixed tragic and comedic elements while carrying the action over time and space, as if both flowed continuously across the stage. The mania to explore humanity through the play found such broad support that it yielded over 6,000 plays in England alone in the half-century after 1580. The most famous British company, William Shakespeare's The Lord Chamberlain's Company, persisted for over two decades and employed about 20 actors. Its actors gave at least six performances weekly and each

William Shakespeare. Probably the most performed playwright in the western world, Shakespeare was instrumental in popularizing theater among the English. His Lord Chamberlain's Company had a standing repertoire of some 50 plays.

needed to master a large number of different roles; the company had a standing repertory of about 50 plays. By the later sixteenth century, special facilities to stage these productions—theaters—served the public and gave this form of spectacle a permanent home. Acting company members often pooled resources to erect these highly profitable theaters and to purchase the costumes and properties that their companies required. The Globe Theater of Shakespeare's company typified the trend. The Globe was a large, circular, roofless building, which held 3,000 spectators in pits beneath stage level and in boxes along walls. The stage, a large flat platform, visually dominated the interior. Smaller theaters were usually court property and generally fully enclosed.

The new public theater required actors to explore through themselves the many dimensions of humanity as they played onstage numerous different roles. Their mastery of the emotional gamut, their ability to express the range of human feelings, marked them as skillful, masters of their craft. But acting company members were not the only individuals to assume a multitude of public roles. Virtually all Europeans in the period 1360–1630, the age of humankind, acted repeatedly in public, assuming several public roles or personas. Humanity as an identifiable group appeared a useful construct. It was plastic and complex and its parameters demanded exploration. In any number of ways, humankind had developed as a distinct focus, not overshadowed by god or visions of heaven. The long heretofore denigrated humankind had its own realm and its extent, depth, and arenas required and deserved intense scrutiny. All the world seemed a human stage and all the men and women seemed merely players.

The Spectacle of Misrule:
Society's Necessity and Arbitrariness

Acting in public was not restricted to full-time, paid acting troupes. Others acted in public as they engaged in public action. Such was the spectacle of Misrule. Abbeys, guilds, or houses of misrule or some similar fanciful title emerged in fourteenth-century French, Italian, and German cities as men of all ages joined with others in their neighborhoods to establish these institutions. At set times during the year, men in these fraternities dressed in costume to ridicule conventional religious or civil society. They "turned the world upside down," burlesquing the Mass and celebrating fools as leaders. They often even forced the animals on which these ersatz leaders rode to walk backwards. Portraying the pope, the king, and a fool playing catch with the world represented as a globe constituted typical fare. Even the offices of these confraternities mocked social norms. Leaders of a mid-sixteenth-century house in Rouen were titled, for example, the prince of improvidence, the cardinal of bad measure, bishop flat-purse, duke kickass, and the Grand Patriarch of Syphilitics. Despite the merriment and the derision they heaped on the established order, these organizations rarely ran afoul of the church or government. Authorities tolerated if not countenanced them.

Role-playing as part of church celebrations long had been a medieval custom. The church-sponsored Feast of Asses, a dramatic reenactment of the pilgrimage of Mary and Joseph to Bethlehem for Christ's birth, had been a staple for nearly ten centuries.

To commemorate Holy Innocents' Day and the gospel's reverence toward childhood, the church had reserved December 28 for the Boy Bishop, a day in which young boys masquerading as bishops carried out all priestly chores except celebrating Mass, which remained in clerical hands. The church acknowledged the importance of society's lower orders in god's eyes by carefully choreographing an annual Feast of Fools. Held about January 1, the feast celebrated the earthly downtrodden but heavenly equal and was the occasion of great ribaldry and license. And occasionally in medieval Europe, young, single, male villagers would don costumes and mock violations of marriage customs, especially unions of aged men and young women.

Fourteenth-century and later activities were quite different from these medieval festivities. Like the contemporary theater, misrule resided beyond church control— the church began to ban misrule from using cathedrals about 1500. But unlike acting troupes, misrule's secular demonstrations incorporated a great strata of persons, from laborers to artisans to small merchants. No city or other government or patron directed these events. Nor was misrule restricted to specified days during the year. Spontaneous events grew increasingly common in the fifteenth century.

Although they adopted buffoonery and costumes as their methods, misrule houses engaged in quite serious practice. Tolerance of their pointed attacks on political and clerical misrule was instructive. It suggested that the church and government considered protest legitimate, appropriate undertakings by persons not in leadership roles. Such a view might reflect a belief in the fundamental similarity among those in the governmental and church bureaucracy and those to whom government and church agencies ministered. Rather than conceive of society as a hierarchy of fixed orders— or (to continue the acting metaphor) of parts for which individuals spent their entire lives preparing, the characteristic Gothic formulation—introduction and toleration of misrule could be construed as reflecting the absence of a legitimate basis for fixed orders; misrule was allowed because contemporaries understood that social position was arbitrary. The final function of houses of misrule supported that assumption. These houses served as extragovernmental authorities, assuming policing or peace-keeping authority whenever they deemed necessary. Their activities were not channeled into some controlled time during the year; rather, they acted to keep the peace and good order whenever sitting governments did not. Houses of misrule actively rid communities of dangerous influences; they attacked individuals likely to contaminate others or defile property and forced them to flee. Blasphemers, hoarders of grain, and those magistrates giving overly harsh or overly mild judicial sentences all were subject to misrule's rule. Misrule houses operated according to a simple principle: It was wrong for an individual to take the law into his or her own hands. Only the public could move for the good of the public in place of government. Put baldly, misrule's criticisms aimed at the social structure as well as at rules for that social structure. In that context, the farcical masks and official titles for misrule's leaders mocked the false, outward dressings of social structure and pretension. Only the public truly could make public decisions.

The Spectacle of the Danse Macabre

The danse macabre, or the Dance of Death, demonstrated humankind's essential equality by celebrating death's inevitability. Perhaps first performed in France in the wake of the Black Death but offered more consistently later in the century after the great plague had long passed, the classic dance had but three actors, all of whom appeared on stage at the same time and played the same part. The death dance portrayed a man as a living being, that same man as a recently deceased shadow of his former self, and finally that dead man as a skeleton. This play, which soon featured women in a similar sequence of roles, spoke directly to the question of the universality of humankind. Since all must die and suffer putrefaction, all humankind was in some fundamental fashion equal.

But considering the social order arbitrary while not attempting to abolish it indicated that men and women in the later fourteenth century and after regarded the stability of an ordered society as necessary and useful. They generally proved willing to abide by its inequities even as they acknowledged its lack of basis in reality. The public, or, in the greater sense, humankind, an essentially undifferentiable whole artificially divided, emerged as the dominant social construct. Authorities even took great care to destroy publicly material confiscated from individuals as threats to the social body. Cards, dice, excessive finery, and even suspect books were gathered and burned with great pomp at large public ceremonies. As never before, men and women acted in public as mass events became critical social conventions.

The Spectacle of Execution and the Idea of Treason

A mid-fourteenth-century English execution for treason had much in common with a then contemporary stage production. The traitor, convicted and sentenced to death, could expect his punishment to commence almost immediately. Town criers announced the impending execution, red flags hung on city walls announced the forthcoming event, and broadsides heralded the task ahead. On the morning of the day following his sentencing, which had occurred before an attentive audience in open court, the authorities awakened the traitor, attached him to a hurdle, which was a low wooden frame, and dragged him for all to see through town to the gallows, the site for which was selected to provide excellent sight lines for the anticipated crowd. The throng, usually several thousand strong and including royal dignitaries and judicial officials, saw the traitor mount the gallows. There he was expected to speak, to confess his treasonous act, to ask for the forgiveness of those he had plotted against, and to pray for their good health. With a priest at hand, he confessed his sins against god and professed his faith. The executioner, who had earlier directed the torture that led to the condemned man's confession, then took over. The traitor absolved the executioner for any blame in the ritual ahead and prepared to meet his maker. Sometimes mutilation would precede the execution. Hands were removed from those who raised their hands against the king, tongues forfeited by those who actively plotted against the government, and ears sliced off of those who listened to traitorous talk and failed to alert the proper authorities. The condemned man was next led up a ladder with his hands tied in front of him, a noose around his neck. The ladder was kicked out from under him and he was hanged.

Punishment did not end there. In many cases, hanging was not meant to kill the traitor or even render him insensate. The executioner quickly cut the condemned man down and dragged him—on more than one occasion the hanged man rose to his feet and had to be tripped—to a fire nearby. The traitor was first emasculated and

Punishment. Punishment for treason and a number of other crimes against society was a public affair. Criminals had the responsibility of imploring the public not to follow in their nefarious footsteps, and the public needed to 255show that it would be just and severe when its commonly derived laws were breached.

then disemboweled; his genitals were cut off, stomach slit open, entrails pulled out, and heart removed. The heart was thrust into the man's mouth—a sign of his false heartedness, the act that had led to his demise—and then the genitals, entrails, and heart were cast into the fire and burned. The rest of the criminal did not escape further punishment. He was beheaded and his body chopped into quarters. It was taken from the scene to be parboiled and the various pieces were posted in public places— on town gates or walls, on pikes near the market area, and nailed to the scaffold. Birds and other scavengers ripped at the flesh until nothing of the traitor remained.

England's treatment of traitors was not unusual. Simon Pouillet was heard uttering that Edward III, not Philippe de Valois, should be king of France in 1346 and was subsequently executed "like a side of meat in a butcher shop . . . stretched and bound on a slab of wood." Traitors in Germany had fleshy parts of their bodies torn off with red-hot iron tongs, were strapped to huge heavy wheels to have their forearms, upper arms, lower legs, and upper legs individually pulverized, had their limbs attached to four separate teams of horses set to gallop in four different directions, and were then beheaded. Their entrails and heart were removed and what remained of their body was further cut into four pieces and left as carrion.

The huge crowd's attendance was essential to the production. A century earlier, executions for any crime had been quiet affairs, performed in front of judicial authorities. Persons beyond these officials could attend but they rarely, if ever, did so. Now the situation had changed. Executions done in private or not witnessed by the public were deemed illegitimate. The public was not merely expected to oversee the event but to participate in the performance. It rated the performers—the actors—with cheers, jeers, and taunts. Each person on the gallows—priest, executioner, and judicial representative—played a special part, and all—the traitor excluded—were simply stand-ins for the public. The public carefully scrutinized each part of this public play. For example, the traitor's gallows confession, a confession reissued without the duress of torture, indicated that the authorities conducted their investigation humanely and fairly and that the penalty that was to be meted out had been justly rendered. That spoke well of the authorities, who, by the later fourteenth century, had been given the charge of uncovering truth, of determining innocence or guilt, and of presenting evidence to the public for confirmation. In that sense, the authorities simply represented the public; they accomplished the work of the public for the public with the consent of the public. A condemned man's suicide brought the authority's methods into public question. It indicated that the judges and torturers had abused their fact-finding powers. The lack of public confirmation of confession, coupled with the traitor's sacrifice of his immortal soul through suicide, suggested that interrogation procedures had been violated and generally led to an investigation of those officials in charge. The executioner dispensed the public's judgment. He needed to exhibit competence and impartiality in his role. Failure to do either would reflect badly on the public and could result in the crowd taking action against the executioner. The public also rated the traitor's performance. If he had conducted himself with quiet dignity and seemed genuinely sorry for or ashamed by his treasonous act, the crowd might show compassion and urge a quicker, less painful death. On more than one occasion, crowds were moved to tears by the forbearance of the condemned. But generally crowds jeered the criminal and urged the executioner to do his deed without mercy.

The lack of empathy for condemned traitors stemmed from how the public recognized their crime. To men and women in the age of humankind, which began about 1350, high treason was the most heinous act short of deicide. The traitor had assaulted society, the public, the sovereign power. His execution constituted a social celebration, the restoration and preservation of society that the criminal through his treasonous act had attempted to murder.

The crime of high treason was new and originated from the notion of humankind itself. Prior to the mid-fourteenth century, crimes between unequals—slaves attacking masters, wives murdering husbands, or lesser clerics bludgeoning prelates—had been deemed either riots—violations of the peace and therefore threats to property—or treasons—violations of personal relationships within the social hierarchy. In Dante's terminology, the latter series of crimes was the crime against one's benefactor. This new crime of high treason was a crime not against the social order or a person within that order but against the sovereign, society itself. The king and his affiliates—government—had come to represent and embody society; society as the sovereign power ceded its authority to an individual and his associates and tacitly committed to obeying this artificial institution's dictates.

Hanging, disembowelment, and quartering were not the only punishments for treason. Burnings, beheadings, burying alive, and drownings also were common, either individually or in combination. Drowning and beheading, widely perceived as more humane forms of execution, increased in popularity during the later sixteenth and early seventeenth centuries. Women were most often drowned or buried alive, while treasonous clerics usually were drowned. Larceny, murder, witchcraft, adultery, incest, and infanticide also were identified as crimes against society, punishable by death. But as with treason, the death penalty needed not be exacted in every instance. Simple mutilation, flogging, branding with a red-hot iron, or a combination of these penalties sometimes sufficed, especially prior to the sixteenth century. In any case, these punishments, like so many others for lesser offenses, were carried out on stage-like pillories in front of large, vocal crowds. Even without formal execution, punishment remained a public spectacle.

Each nonlethal punishment for treason was designed to mark the criminal for life and therefore to separate these heinous criminals from society. The criminal's act defamed and disgraced the person who had committed it. The act was corporeal, not of the soul, and the disgrace was permanent, irredeemable. The person must remain forever outside society. Dismemberment of criminals guaranteed that the disgraced person would never again injure society. Just as the limb that had been severed, the individual no longer belonged to the social body.

Torture

The concepts of crimes against humankind's social artifice—society—and the authorities as acting for the public also transformed the idea of torture. Torture was removed from the exclusive province of the church and introduced as a legitimate means to ascertain the truth from suspected societal villains. From at least the Inquisition, the church had considered torture appropriate to force heretics to admit their crime and perhaps even recant their heresy. Heretics menaced the Christian community, the Christian body. Their crime was against god's earthly realm; they were traitors to god. Not until the fourteenth century, however, did torture become a socially and legally acceptable method to achieve confessions from persons strongly suspected of crimes against society. The term had been introduced considerably earlier. The Romans' use of torture was documented in the Justinian Code and the term began to reappear in Western Europe shortly after the code's translation in the eleventh century. But torture as initially reapplied did not reflect its Roman antecedent. Torture in the eleventh, twelfth, and thirteenth centuries was akin to the Barbarian concept of trial by ordeal. Persons known to possess questionable character—liars, thieves, and the like—were tested by ordeal to prove the accuracy of their statements.

Torture to wrest confessions for crimes against society came into vogue in the fourteenth century and, during the next two hundred years, each European sovereignty developed its own tortures. England used the rack, a bedlike frame on which persons were stretched and limbs dislocated; the brake, where iron bands squeezed individuals already hunched over in the fetal position; and manacles, the hanging by wrists with feet unable to reach the floor. Germany adopted thumbscrews and leg screws, viselike iron plates compressing human tissue; the rack; and pine-wood slivers driven under fingernails. The Spanish attached heavy weights to a suspect's legs, lifted him by pulley, dropped him a certain distance, and broke the fall with a start before he hit the floor, a process that generally dislocated the limbs. They also jammed rags down the throat of the accused and forced water into his stomach, a method certain to distend that organ painfully and perhaps rupture it. The Spanish also bound bodies with rope and then slowly tightened the cords, which cut through the flesh. The French used the rack and water methods and developed the strap, a thick leather device tightened around the victim. It was a cross between the Spanish rope and English iron band methods.

The Spectacle of the Past as Present

In 1556 Guillaume Paradin sought to justify Misrule, an aim that led him to trace masked social protest to the classical world. He claimed that ordinary Greeks and Romans regularly disguised themselves and acted as pseudo-magistrates, pointing out the failings of others while issuing summary judgments. A half-century later Claude Noirot, a judge in Langres, maintained that public humiliation, including forcing individuals to ride backward on asses, constituted government-approved penalties in Greece and Rome. Both commentators discovered historical precedent for contemporary action, but a more important point was that they felt compelled to adopt that approach; they believed it necessary to look to the past for approval of then current practice. Their quest for legitimacy through the examination of humankind's historical acts reflected the way that men and women in the centuries after about 1360 thought of and used the past. To these persons, the past and present were contemporaneous in the sense that the past existed for the present to select from; the past as a collection of things previously undertaken served as a repository for the present. The past was not a sequence of events but rather a non-ordered set of points, of humankind's former endeavors. It became the job of the present to connect the points that it desired to frame whatever relationship it sought.

Such a view made the past relevant precisely because it was not truly past. In the danse macabre, for example, the past, present, and future were blurred; their simultaneous occurrence in the form of actors playing the same role onstage at the same time raised several critical issues. Which of the states of humankind was humankind's true state? This matter of corporeal or material substance was joined with the equally vexing question of the validity of observation: How were people able to determine which state was "true," a puzzle that even challenged the entire concept of reality? This humankind-centered view of the past stood in direct opposition to its medieval predecessor. Christ's birth marked a fundamental cleavage in medieval thought. Darkness framed the world prior to Christ as true knowledge and meaning—faith—arrived only with his birth. Post-medieval European scholars overwhelmingly rejected the medieval period (in their taxonomy generally after 410 and before 1200) as an age of darkness, an irrelevant age because of its lack of concern and appreciation for things human. Faith, an otherworldly construct that scholars joined with ignorance and superstition, not reason, an attribute of humankind, seemed to dominate. They looked instead to times earlier for usable pasts.

Reason as Separate and Almost Equal

Separation of faith and reason into distinct spheres destroyed the carefully crafted Scholastic union. Christianity and Aristotelianism, joined in Gothic Europe, now seemed incompatible. William of Ockham's dismissal of Aristotle signified that disjunction. To Ockhamists, Aristotle had nothing to offer Christianity and Christianity had little to provide toward understanding the natural world's intricacies. That latter task was not a matter of faith but of reason. Humankind needed to employ reason to define, describe, and elucidate its realm.

Rejection of the Scholastic or Thomist synthesis was not a rejection of Greek and Roman philosophy, or even of Aristotle. It simply indicated that religion depended upon faith and that classical philosophy was helpless there. Ironically, separation of faith and reason emancipated both. Neither required confirmation of the other. That proved particularly compelling for reason. Faith had dominated or guided reason for a millennium or more. Reason now gained separate and almost equal footing. Faith remained belief in god's willingness to create for humankind an eternal salvation. Reason became the god-provided ability to understand earthly existence and the natural world. Reason emerged as the tool to explore and to comprehend humankind's realm.

Humans without reason did not seem human and were not treated as such. In France and England, persons without reason—mentally ill persons in our parlance—were made to perform like circus animals or placed on display for the amusement of others. The apparent inhuman treatment drew virtually no outcries. Humans lacking reason were mere animals.

Separation of reason and faith was synonymous with separation of heaven and earth. That latter separation was symptomatic of a new cleavage between god and humankind. Just as heaven and earth had been separated so could god and man be separated. The soul remained god's province but the body—the corporeal, material, or earthly world—became humankind's dominion. Humankind ruled the world through use of reason, but reason compelled humankind to learn and understand the realm. Exponents of this humankind-centered view often reversed the traditional equation between god and humans. The noted early-fifteenth-century Italian architect Leon Battista Alberti even referred to humankind as a deity, "a mortal but happy god." Alberti brought the idea of god making humankind in god's own image to new arenas when he maintained that the divinity of both god and humankind stemmed from the ability to "combine capacity for virtuous action with rational understanding." Later in the century, Pico de la Mirandola, prince of an Italian state, argued that "God clearly and especially manifested his wisdom in the creation of man," a statement that established the existence of humankind as the tangible evidence of god's virtue and omnipotence. Humankind had the hubris to consider itself and god each as master of its own domain. Exploration of humankind's realm constituted a multidimensional enterprise. Humankind sought to consider its length, width, depth, and time. What the past had to offer humankind became a crucial facet of that investigation and ultimate mastery.

History as Technology

Medieval historical writing chronicled the world from creation to the last judgment or to the reign of a particularly noteworthy Christian potentate. In either case, the past had functioned as a backdrop to illustrate god's omnipotent but loving relationship with man and to guide Christians to salvation. History in the age of humankind had quite different purposes. It stood as a tool to separate humankind from god and earth from heaven and as a means to solve contemporary problems through the rediscovery of lost knowledge. Treating events in the past as allegorical or symbolic was replaced by a desire to locate past acts within the context of other contemporary past acts; events in the past had occurred in conjunction with others at the same time. This contexturalist history ironically incorporated a sense of timelessness within it, even as it depended on process and procedure. Lorenzo Valla's demonstration in the early fifteenth century that the Donation of Constantine, the text upon which the pope claimed authority over Christendom and the papal states, could not have been written before the ninth century A.D. became the new history's touchstone. Valla proved the document an obvious forgery by showing that several of the concepts and phrases had not occurred until some six or more centuries later. Medieval historians had ignored the question of the document's veracity. But even if they had noted the apparent contradictions, they likely would have failed to consider them contradictions at all. Such was the case with the twelfth-century French cleric Abbot Suger, who located three St. Denises in the past separated by hundreds of years but identified them each as the true St. Denis. The threefold St. Denis, a logical impossibility to the modern mind, was altogether logical to Suger. Its uniqueness demonstrated and proved god's vast power; the threefold St. Denis justified Christian faith even as its reality was a matter of faith.

Valla's efforts and the efforts of other like-minded historians both reflected and fostered distance between god and his human minions. It showed that the Roman Emperor Constantine never recognized or ceded authority to the pope or even acknowledged him as Christianity's leader; the legal basis for assuming the church's priority over humankind's earthly endeavors as well as the pope's position within the church was fabricated well after Constantine had died. Valla's belief that the medieval past—the immediate past—had been corrupt led him to a renewed examination of already available ancient writings. He also demonstrated that medieval translations of the New Testament were in stark disagreement with earlier Greek texts of the purportedly same passages. But the sense that the corruption of the past also caused documents, ideas, and knowledge to become lost or ignored revealed the importance of collecting and translating new materials. This two-pronged attack led not only to a reexamination of extant documents—church, Christian fathers, nature, and senses— but also to a search for and translation of other ancient writings. This "new" ancient material was explicitly in those areas previously considered irrelevant or heretical. Works of literature and the humanities—Greco-Roman tragedies, comedies, philosophy, poetry, and history—were elevated to prominence as humankind searched into the past to learn of and revive lost social possibilities. Valla, an ordained priest, also participated in this elevation, resurrecting a form of Greek Epicureanism to maintain that the pleasures of the senses constituted the greatest good and therefore should serve as the basis for social organization.

Greek literary and humanistic works long gathering dust in monasteries and cathedrals were now translated into Latin, and similar Roman works became popular. Western Europe also received a great quantity of new manuscripts from Byzantium. Many scholars in late-fourteenth-century Constantinople feared the rise of the Ottoman Turks and left that city, carrying with them their books. Prosperous Italy became the new home of these scholars, who earned their livelihoods teaching Greek to Europeans interested in uncovering the wisdom of past ages. Rome, Venice, and Florence emerged as centers of Greek philosophy and literature. Florence, for example, supported its first Greek scholar as early as 1390. Within a half-century, Venetians established an academy for Greek studies and Florence opened Plato's Academy for the study of Greek philosophy. Great Greco-Roman libraries were created in Italy, almost always under private auspices—the papal library remained the most notable exception—but for public utility. Patrons—individuals or whole families—supported scholars to translate manuscripts in their libraries and to make these translations public. Translators labored so assiduously that the entire Greek corpus—poets, dramatists, philosophers, orators, all of Plato, Plotinus, Herodotus, Thucydides, and new medical, mathematical, and astronomical manuscripts—had been translated by 1600.

Scholars from throughout Europe came to study these new works. They read the texts in the new Italian repositories and, in many cases, copied them and brought them to their native lands. Byzantine and Italian scholars found their knowledge prized in France, Germany, and elsewhere and left, often with manuscripts, for more lucrative positions in these countries. Greek philosophies, including Epicureanism, stoicism, and skepticism, spread across Europe in that fashion. But although these and other philosophies were merely being revived and reconsidered, men and women of the age of humankind cast them as universal truths, as essentially timeless pearls of wisdom. They quoted from these philosophical manuscripts extensively as demonstrations, as proofs of particular premises, but the quoted passages were not always used in the sense that the Greco-Roman authors had written them. For example, virtually no one sought to reinstate the religions of pagan antiquity. The quintessential validity, a validity that existed for humankind without respect to social or political situation, was what they sought, what they recognized, and what they employed. These quoted passages, elegantly written and coherently organized, served as evidence of humanness; they explained human causes and motives, set precedents, and espoused policies considered timeless, part of humanity. As an early translator wrote about his art, which he considered the uncovering of essential human truths, "Learning and training in virtue are peculiar to man; therefore our forefathers called them humanitas, the pursuit of activities proper to mankind."

The understanding–application continuum converted pursuit of understanding as well as its fruits into technology. In that sense, the humanities of the age of humankind had much more in common with later-twentieth-century social science than with contemporary humanities. Humankind was akin to a *magus*, a magician, able through use of reason to interpret knowledge and fashion the material world in any way it chose. Pico summed up that perspective neatly. God formed humankind, he wrote, as a "free and proud shaper of [its] own being, to fashion [itself] in the form [it] may prefer." Several important focal points emerged from this eternal search. A belief that the glories of Egypt lay behind Greco-Roman greatness thrust attention on identifying those truths transmitted from the Egyptians to the Greeks. In 1463, Marsilio Ficino found the key in the thrice-great Hermes, Hermes Trismegistus. Working for Cosimo de' Medici, ruler of Florence, Ficino translated from Greek to Latin the Corpus Hermeticum. These ancient documents identified the Greek Hermes with the Egyptian god Thoth and the Roman Mercury. Hermes Trismegistus unlocked the secret of the All. He had learned how to tap into the One, the unity that gives everything its outwardness. Since everything was inextricably joined, Hermetics considered outwardness in a sense an illusion. But they also believed that different things had different virtues or qualities, different outwardnesses. Outwardness permitted persons to discern among things—no matter how artificial—and outwardness enabled people to use these things in ways that were different and based on the outwardness—as actors temporarily assumed a stage role. (The idea of outwardness or quality or virtue was not at all similar to our term *property*, which suggests something fundamental, indigenous, or inherent within a body.) What remained was to find techniques to manipulate the outwardness.

Ficino and other Hermetics recognized the corpus as providing that universal information. The thrice-great Hermes was a magus, a learned human who had uncovered essential secrets of manipulation and gave them to the Egyptians, Greeks, and Romans. These secrets allowed their holders to act as lenses, to serve as gatherers and conduits. What they accumulated and conducted were influences, something akin to three-dimensional shapes. As part of the One, these influences reverberated throughout the universe. Their reverberation or shape permitted them to resonate only with some material substances and not others. Hermetic secrets were combinations of words and powers that would focus or modify reverberations. The secrets would place the reverberations in harmony with other outwardness-accompanying reverberations to create a resonance with that particular outwardness to change that outwardness. Precision was essential and talismans, words, or figures inscribed on appropriate materials and said aloud at specific times were the means by which Hermetics accessed these occult harmonies and sympathies. Their sympathetic magic granted Hermetics entrance to the One and enabled them to change the present material reality.

Alchemy had a similar intellectual construction. Its proponents sought to replicate and harness the awesome power of creation to change the outwardnesses of substances. Alchemists maintained that alchemy dated back to Moses or Hermes but had been lost and only now was rediscovered. To these men and women, god created the universe through separation—the light from the darkness, the waters beneath the firmament from the waters above the firmament, and the earth from the waters, for example. But separation was only one facet of the act of creation. At the heart of the alchemical analysis rested the assumption that god placed the same essences, qualities, or principles in all things. These universal essences were but a handful in number (sometimes they were identified as soul, body, and spirit and correlated with the trinity and humanity) and each as part of the omnipresent One was inherent in all things. A thing's outwardness was simply a manifestation of the proportion, ratio, or structure of this handful of universal essences within it. "Alchemical extraction, separation, sublimation, and conjunction" also explained the origin of volcanoes and springs, the growth of metals in veins, and fermentation. Alchemists claimed that rain was similar to condensation on glass and that thunder and lightning were equivalent to gunpowder explosions. Equating processes of nature with processes of humankind proved to alchemical adherents that humankind through mechanical manipulation of substances could act on earth as god did in heaven and transform the outwardnesses of things. All that remained was to uncover the long-lost techniques to accomplish these transformations.

Astrology was magic's scientific complement. Astrologists maintained that the heavens and the earth were inextricably tied together, in a manner not dissimilar to the Hermetic One. Within that unity, the motions and position of heavenly bodies

The Alchemist's Laboratory. The Renaissance science of alchemy took god and creation as its model. Just as the deity separated heaven and earth and the waters from the firmament, alchemists tried to separate substances into their essences, which would enable them to transform one substance into another.

caused influences to be emitted—spatial situations produced specific physical emanations—that caused sympathetic vibrations in the earthly realm. Those individuals or places in tune with the vibrations—astrologists called these harmonies between heavenly and earthly bodies "correspondences"—received them—they resonated—and were affected by the astral influences; influences from a heavenly correspondent changed the outwardnesses of its earthly counterparts. As one commentator put it, "All the virtues of earthly things depend on the stars and their images." Measurement and identification of influences and correspondences constituted the predictive nature of astrology—its science—but a few astrologists claimed that humankind could, through various procedures and processes, create its own influences. These influences would correspond with and change the position of those resonating heavenly structures, which in turn would generate another series of influences to reverberate on earth and modify sympathetic bodies there.

The alleged antiquity of the Hermetic corpus led Europeans to consider it the root text. When Ficino at the direction of the Medici translated Plato's dialogues after completion of the Hermetic corpus, he naturally assumed that the Egyptian Hermes had influenced Plato. Plato's emphasis on moving from the multiple to the One and on union with it echoed Hermetic vision as did Ficino's explorations of post-Christian Platonists, such as Plotinus whose emphasis on will and love provided the basis of union. To be sure, Ficino and others engaged in rediscovering Plato Christianized the Greek philosopher's thoughts. God became the divine intellect, with "innumerable Ideas" and patterns for all things in this divine mind because "above every multiplicity there must be a unity." Humankind's ability to approach god's mind required almost harmonic convergence—resonance—between ideas of celestial beauty—part of the deity—and the shining brightness of the human contemplation of god.

The Platonic revival resonated nicely with the renewed popularity of Pythagorean numerology, especially the dictum that the number one was the cause of all other numbers. Numerology in the form of numerical ratios framed both the pre-Socratic Greek Pythagoras's music of the soul and music of the ear. The eight tones of the audible scale—the eight regular vibrations—formed themselves into an octagonal shape, which could resonate with the Pythagorean harmony of the heavenly spheres. The twelve intervals within the scale corresponded to the signs of the Zodiac. Consonance and dissonance as proportions approaching unity or plurality tuned the music of the ear to more nearly approach the music of the soul. The soft harmony of the third interval demonstrated the wisdom of the Pythagorean approach.

Pythagorean numerology was not the only numerology current in the age of humankind nor were the Greeks the only ancients explored. During the last decades of the fifteenth century, several Italians turned to an examination of Hebrew texts. Hebrew had been virtually ignored during the Middle Ages but emphasis on the Egyptian origin of the Hermetic corpus and a belief in religious syncretism provoked interest in other early texts. Pico spearheaded the Hebrew revival and sought to translate the most ancient material. Pico naturally gravitated to those works most consonant with the Hermetic tradition, the Jewish Kabbalah. To Pico and other early Christian Kabbalists, Hermes was the Egyptian lawgiver and Moses held the same position among the ancient Hebrews. Kabbalists further believed that when Moses received the Ten Commandments god gave him a second set of information, god's names—generally believed to be ten in number. This incredibly potent information enabled its human owners to create life and matter. According to the Old Testament, god created the universe and everything in it simply by speaking (And god said, "Let there be . . ."). Moses wisely entrusted god's names and their awesome power only to the most holy Hebrews. Only on a few rare occasions had these high priests used god's names. In one particularly desperate time, they fashioned a clay sculpture of a man, wrote god's ten names on ten verticals, which represented the ten spheres of celestial harmony, and placed the material in the clay man's mouth. The clay sculpture of a man, a golem, immediately came to life and began to slaughter the Hebrew's enemies. The rabbis removed god's names from his mouth to end this avenger's existence. God's empowering names had been lost and Pico searched the early texts for their identity.

By stressing learning and saying god's names, Kabbalists recognized humans as capable of achieving virtual omnipotence, of creating as did god. But it was not enough to simply know or recite god's many names. Kabbalic operators needed to say them in the proper order or to write them in the proper form; numerology without shaping or configuration would not unlock nature's secret powers. Kabbalists understood that the keys to creation, to changing the outwardnesses of material—even life into death and vice versa—as if the operator was joined with the One, would not be carelessly or easily revealed. But they believed the requisite information was encrypted in ancient Hebrew texts. They concentrated on examining the shape and position of letters within these old documents and formed magic squares with these letters to deduce divine ratios that would reveal Kabbalist secrets.

Humankind as Master and Measure

Humans attempted to manipulate virtually every aspect of their environment and to refashion or describe that renewed environment on a human scale. Humanists, social thinkers, poets, and artists sought to make all earthly questions human-sized and therefore to facilitate human attempts to resolve them. In these senses, humankind truly emerged to master its realm and served as its measure.

Human Dignity, Versatility, and Virtuosity

Biography and shorter written portraiture emerged as primary literary forms in mid-fourteenth-century Europe and grew even more popular over the next two centuries. Although these works testified to an interest in personal experiences, opinions, and achievements, they did not signal an incipient individualism. Personal experiences, opinions, and achievements proved of interest not becaue of their uniquenesses but because of their typicality. Biography showed the range of human emotions and situations and thereby helped define what made humankind human. Chaucer's character studies, for example, outwardly separated humankind by occupation, but his genius rested in his characters showing human foibles. What united Chaucer's men and women was their humanity, their typicalness, not their exceptionalism. François Villon's mid-fifteenth-century discourses on tavern life and dens of thieves showed them as much a part of the human experience as courtly life. Homages to the simple piety of an aged pauper or to the last thoughts of a condemned criminal sought to reach the root of human experience.

A rebirth of portrait painting accompanied the biographical boom. Artists increasingly painted humans, not heavenly scenes or beings. They portrayed noble men and women as human, not as perfect Greco-Roman gods. Artists sometimes drew portraits in family quarters or placed the subject in the context of the family. Portraits of working people often pictured them at work in their shop or office with the tools of their trade featured prominently.

Artists and writers portrayed humankind as multidimensional, able to cope with and even master most situations. Humankind was malleable enough to adapt and thrive in the many social roles it was called upon to play. Humankind's capacity to perform numerous social roles stemmed from its reception of reason, which provided it dignity. Dignity separated humankind from other natural forms and liberated it from god. Human dignity enabled humankind to operate independently of god in this world, as fundamentally outside established frameworks, including the old Gothic conception of the Great Chain of Being. Definitions of humankind as god's favorite creature, as a currier of god's favor, or as recipient of god's special gift or focus would have centered on god and placed humanity in the role of supplicant or dependent. Humanity's dignity put it on a par with god in its realm. God mastered heaven and humankind mastered the earth.

Humankind's inherent dignity, coupled with its malleability, held out hope of preparing people to play a panoply of social roles. What was required was the training necessary to achieve masterful performances. Education became paramount. Study of ethics, Greek history, poetry, rhetoric, and grammar, the human disciplines, set out the confines of what humankind could achieve. This humanistic education built versatility, and versatility vigorously pursued became virtuosity. Rigorous efforts to master the broad stage of human affairs yielded actors especially adept in playing several leading roles. Virtuosity was its own reward. Virtuosos stood as models for humanity generally, their acknowledgment offered to inspire their contemporaries to equally great heights. Virtuosos—Renaissance men in modern parlance—were not considered great men or women per se—they were not explained as extraordinary or remarkable individuals—but ideally as typical men and women, what every person ought to aspire to become.

Human Government

Notions of virtuosity and versatility in the age of humankind rendered social distinctions illusionary. The outwardnesses of persons differed, of course, but the essential means of identification remained their humanity. It demanded that persons humanistically trained naturally become active participants in government and that government provide social benefits to a wide range of people. Humankind's dignity gave it liberty and its governments were obligated to furnish liberty-pursuing stability. Only through stability could liberty and its pursuit exist. But stability had its costs. It required cooperation—responsibility—from all those agreeing to its terms, which entailed a loss of individual liberty. Citizens maintained social stability to guard liberty, but not necessarily their own personal liberty; each citizen could not focus on maximizing his or her own liberty, but needed to pursue the maximization of the group's liberty. Through preserving liberty and pursuing stability, government sought to insure the greatest social good, which frequently meant the greatest good for the greatest number.

The "greatest social good" and the "greatest good for the greatest number" were relativistic concepts. They depended on definitions of liberty, of the nature of participation (was the simple act of acquiescing to government active participation, for example?), of the social good and how to measure it, of the means to measure the greatest good for the greatest number, and a wide range of similar concepts. These questions rested at the heart of humanistic and public inquiry. They were the age of humankind's fundamental questions as its men and women strove to separate earthly affairs from divine considerations and set out with confidence to restore dominion over their realm. They turned first to the Greeks, who they recognized as the earliest group to have grappled with human issues. Not surprisingly, the Italian city-states led the way. Their law centers, Bologna, Padua, and Ravenna, used and consulted classical humanistic texts to explore liberty, despotism, independence, the public good, and the like. It was in the city-states themselves, especially the northern states, where these principles were initially put into practice.

Northern Italian City-States: The Public and the Familial

In the heady atmosphere of the fourteenth and early fifteenth centuries, each northern Italy city-state pursued liberty through the stability of cooperation. Citizens accepted at least two identifications: members of the public—the city-state—and members of a biological family. In modern terms, northern Italians had neither a private life per se nor did they possess a sense of individualism. Their communalism insisted that the biological family and the family of humankind residing at the particular city-state serve to organize their affairs. From the start, these city-states recognized no civic role for the church, arguing that Christ explicitly denied his church dominion over earthly activities. City-states also possessed a clear identity, because they long had competed against and battled each other as well as the papal monarchy and the Holy Roman Empire. City-state governments of the fourteenth and early fifteenth centuries depended on a broad franchise. Citizens selected two councils to represent them. The larger council conducted affairs in public, while the smaller group met quietly. Together they appointed a magistrate to a six-month tour of duty to execute council mandates. The councils could remove the magistrate for cause.

Strong familial identification certainly figured prominently to citizens of these city-states. Deemphasis or outright neglect of primogeniture extended family unity well beyond an individual's lifetime. But family property was not split among the several sons. They kept it intact, holding it collectively generation after generation. Marriage practices also perpetuated intergenerational continuity. Northern Italian brides and grooms were typically of different generations; each union forged a span of nearly two entire generations. Grooms remained for life part of the family into which they had been born. Their mothers had provided their early education and their fathers the requisite discipline. Sons continued to live unmarried at home until well established in their professions or occupations. These mature men, often 40 years of age, married young girls, who joined the marriage family and left their birth family, quickly became pregnant, and almost as quickly became widowed. Widows, often with young children, were actively discouraged from remarrying, and urged instead to remain within the marriage family. The status accorded these women within their marriage families proved powerful inducements against second marriages. Adoption of family names, ways of demarcating familial boundaries, also demonstrated family coherence. Families, even those men and women of relatively modest means, owned property and land in common. These corporate families sometimes lived together, purchasing property around a city square and building dwellings there for brothers, sisters, aunts, uncles, cousins, and parents. The family also marked its territory to celebrate its bond. Fences, walls, and other barriers separated blood kin from others. The wealthiest families built ornate yet precise brick and stone collective fortresses to commemorate and perpetuate their collective existence. The windows, decorative ironwork, marble colonettes, and imposing entrances of the facades achieved perfect classical balance. These bastions of familydom contained up to 30 rooms and opened to an inner courtyard. Family memorabilia likewise identified the biological group as distinct from the surrounding public. Families established family altars, chapels, and tombs. They selected family saints and collected busts and paintings of their ancestors as well as present members. Family meals and family rites of passage—weddings and funerals—indicated an intimacy not suggested by banquets.

Familial reputation even provided impetus for civic action as individuals donated their efforts on behalf of their families and as families pooled their resources to glorify the family through undertaking some project that would promote the city-state's general good. A family's refusal to participate in civic affairs suggested selfishness, lack of responsibility. To set a family outside of society reduced the family and its members because their lack of participation seemed to threaten society, to place the family and its members' well-being ahead of the common good. An individual's identity came from his or her family and a family's identity came from its participation in civic affairs.

Family-based civic action joined the dual identities of family and city-state. Dwelling-attached loggias with benches along walls to facilitate conversation spatially linked the same two communities. Affixed to family houses but resting outside of them, loggias served as central gathering and meeting places for persons not related—informal gatherings were extremely popular in northern Italy—as well as convenient discussion sites for blood kin. In many ways, the city-states mirrored the family. City walls marked city space and frequent elections reaffirmed government's public basis.

Of the two identities, creation of a civic community has received the most historical attention. Modern scholars focus on what they see as the peculiarities of northern Italy, especially the absence of a strong, ensconced rural nobility, and assign those rural men and women the role of encouraging the northern Italian city-states to form representative governments. Unlike most European nobles of the fourteenth and early fifteenth centuries, the Italian nobility engaged in commerce, not agriculture, and resided in cities, not on country manors. The Italian nobility's reliance on commerce in cities is said to have created economic liquidity, at least in comparison to its rural counterparts elsewhere. This liquid wealth—money, not land—fostered social mobility by facilitating physical mobility among those persons to whom wages were paid. Payment of money rather than produce enabled persons to move, take their property with them, and sell their services to the highest bidder. Patronage extended the social leveling process. It brought many acts outside of guild control as artisans followed the demand and secured for themselves the best deal. Scholars working in households as secretaries or teachers also received monetary payments, which freed them from control of university masters.

Several factors argue against this economic/environmental explanation. Northern Italian cities certainly did not appear socially leveled. While the rich resided in palatial structures, the poor lived in much more modest circumstances. Several poor families shared a single room in a wooden structure or a family had its own room in a multifamily dwelling. Accommodations improved with wealth. Two-room domiciles had a combination kitchen and living room and a separate bedroom, while three-room houses generally meant separation of the kitchen and living room. Houses of master artisans frequently had a hall chamber, kitchen, garden, and larder. A second-floor master bedroom and underground storage facilities were signs of true luxury. The palace-like homes of wealthy fabric merchants and fur dealers contained anterooms, studios, great halls, and other areas far beyond the reach of poorer persons. A complete range of basement service and storage rooms served the household.

Wealth also distinguished household furnishings. The wealthiest citizens had several beds and mattresses, oak benches, walnut trestle tables, and jewel-encrusted iron and wood chests, in which they stored their possessions. The poor hung their meager possessions on wall pegs. Wall fireplaces with external chimneys cut across classes, as did tallow candles and oil lamps. Household security proved important to both groups. Shuttered or barred windows and locked doors protected the inhabitants and their possessions. Wealthy northern Italians frequently had servants, generally girls as young as 6 hired out by poor families as maids, and slaves, purchased from the Middle East when young and assigned the most onerous jobs. Indeed, slavery persisted among Muslims, making it possible for good Christians to purchase slaves from Muslim traders in the Mediterranean for the most despicable labors without violating the prohibition against owning a fellow Christian.

Despite gross disparities among the wealth of the citizenry, northern Italy's city-states maintained a sense of collective identity. Each city-state's identity was tempered by its persistent warfare with other geopolitical units, including other city-states. Their separate identities led city-states in the early fifteenth century to establish diplomatic bureaucracies to maintain each city-state's position vis à vis the others. Ambassadors, embassies, and intelligence reports were formalized in these bureaucracies as city-states consulted, negotiated, and formed alliances with each other. Nor was the sense of identity weakened in the second third of the fifteenth century as city-states increasingly relied on mercenaries rather than citizens to fight, although it reflected a significant shift in the application of representative government. In several city-states, citizens chose to enhance freedom-enabling stability by permitting government to be placed under the direction of a single leading family and imbuing that family with major executive and legislative powers. These leaders, often an already established aristocratic family, reflected the communal will. They were virtuosos and treasured virtuosity. Their virtue—their judgment and example—created a stable atmosphere for virtue generally to flourish. This consensual, communal despotism, whether attained through force of arms or by election, gained favor because of its stability-ensuring success. It acted as a virtuoso in fulfilling community ambitions to achieve a greater good and thereby improved public works, strengthened city defenses, streamlined tax codes, and patronized the arts and letters. It protected the city-state from foreign intrigue and controlled mercenaries, defined simply as persons outside the community. Mercenaries, who received wages, were not indebted to the community traditions and were unwilling to relinquish a pervasive selfishness.

The situation was not exactly the same in every city. In Venice, for example, a council of ten, made up of doyens of the old aristocratic families, ruled, while in Milan a single figure, Gian Galeazzo Visconti, consolidated authority. His familial dynasty was overthrown by Francesco Sforza, who declared himself Duke of Milan and established his family as head of the principality, which it ruled for over a century. In Florence, a city noted for its wealthy merchant bankers and textile manufacturers, the case was different still. Repeated electoral turnover and continual revamping of the republic's constitution with each electoral change led citizens in 1434 to sacrifice gladly the freedom of discord for the stability of a wealth-dominated oligarchy. Headed first by banker Cosimo de' Medici, who came to power on his avid support of artisans, and later by his son and grandson, the government maintained its republican appearance but the oligarchy's power virtually guaranteed that its forces won every election for 60 years.

Fifteenth-century northern Italian governmental efforts provided the backdrop for sixteenth-century speculations on the nature of government and political union. The Florentine Niccolò Machiavelli, known today as a political philosopher but also in his own time as a playwright, accentuated the means of government. His books, *The Prince* (1513) and *Discourses* (1521), explored different governmental forms, but both sought the same ends—the greatest good to the greatest number. *The Prince* started from the premise that the community to be governed lacked virtuosity. Machiavelli argued that the role of the prince was to supply it. Through his actions, the virtuoso prince uplifted the population and provided the environment that ultimately prepared the populace to assume a political role. Until that time, the prince furthered the community by maintaining its stability. To Machiavelli, a community without virtuosity when left to its own devices naturally descended into chaos, political upheaval, and war. A virtuoso prince respected persons, property, and traditions,

NICHOLAS MACHIAVEL.

Niccolò Machiavelli. In his classic *The Prince*, Machiavelli outlined how a leader needed to act in a community lacking virtue. Often forgotten is his *Discourses*, in which he discussed the opposite side of the question, leadership among virtuous individuals.

and promoted material prosperity at almost all cost. Use of violence, preemptive acts, and political suppression were essential for the prince to maintain stability, but his judicious employment of these techniques marked the prince as virtuous. The community's interest demanded maintenance of the prince, and the duty of a virtuous man was to do whatever was necessary to perpetuate his authority, which furthered community interests.

Machiavelli's *Discourses* examined the question of governance from a radically different presumption: a community of virtuous citizens. The virtuosity of the citizenry compelled Machiavelli to argue for a self-governing citizenry. Their civic virtue guaranteed stability. Communal sentiment made disagreement borne of the free exchange of ideas and repeated public debate tolerable, even desirable. Inherent within virtuosity was the critical idea that the well-being of the community as a whole took precedent over that of any of its parts or members. That alone ensured maximum freedom and stability. Leadership or governance was simply executing the public will.

The Great Geopolitical Entities of the Fourteenth and Fifteenth Centuries

The question of liberty/stability dominated European social thought, although few expressed themselves as explicitly or as completely as the northern Italians. Thomas More, a contemporary of Machiavelli and soon the Lord Chancellor of England, proved an exception. His classic treatise, *On the Ultimate Republican State, Found on the New Island of Utopia*, was a work of fiction published as social criticism and social vision. He professed that Europeans recently had discovered a heretofore unknown isle named Utopia, whose government was unlike any then in power in Europe, and More's purported examination of this "unique" situation helped define humankind's societal possibilities. More's *Utopia* stemmed from then current social theory. Like his contemporaries, he considered government a human creation, instituted by and among humankind, that could assume numerous shapes and forms. More looked first to the repository of the past for ideas to apply to his hypothetical ideal state and incorporated several from Greco-Roman antiquity. *Utopia* as published took humankind's fundamental equality as a starting point and gave government the task of preserving that equality; Utopia's government secured the greatest good by equalizing the good of each of the parts. Such a result could maximize both liberty and stability only if virtually all citizens had achieved virtuosity. (Virtuosity's centrality, of course, eliminated the desirability or even possibility of individualism or free will.) Utopia's government was an idealized form of the government proposed in Machiavelli's *Discourses*, and it demanded a citizenry in which almost all were virtuosos. All arbitrary differences—the differences that separated humanity and the differences upon which societies of the late fourteenth, fifteenth, and early sixteenth centuries were established—were erased. More explained Utopia's success by referring to the failure of then contemporary English society. Its citizens lacked virtuosity and humanity. There existed, he maintained, "a conspiracy of the rich who on pretense of managing the public only pursue their private ends." "By private fraud . . . and common law," the rich "do every day pluck and snatch away from the poor some part of their daily living." But More refused to place blame simply on the greediness of wealthy Englishmen. He maintained that virtuosos were made, not born, and therefore condemned society's lack of humanism for social problems. "If you suffer your people to be ill-educated and their manners to be corrupted from their infancy," he claimed, then they will commit "crimes to which their first education disposes them." What else "is to be concluded from this but that you first make thieves and then punish them," More contended.

Utopia's resolution was to frame for its citizens an environment in which virtuosity would be created and nourished. Children went to a government-run school for humanistic study while parents worked. Government controlled all commerce and manufacturing. Each person worked six hours daily, three before and three after lunch. Government supplied each person with his or her wants—food, clothes, and the like. Each citizen in turn would undertake progressively more detailed duties during his or her lifetime. Each family lived in its own little house, complete with flower and vegetable garden. Concentrated humanistic activities followed the evening meal. Families sang, played instruments, and danced. Children recited poetry and rhetoric under their parents' watchful guidance.

Disparities of wealth ceased to exist in Utopia. Utopians despised silver and gold and used the two metals simply as garbage vessels. Criminality was almost unknown on the island, the occasional theft the product of inadequate training. Government dealt with thieves without prisons. It sentenced them to work to develop good habits and to repay their debts, to become virtuosos. When thieves made restitution and recovered their humanity, their sentence and stigma were removed.

Monarchies, Production, and Mercantilism

Republican governments, even governments much less ambitious than that outlined in More's *Utopia*, did not exist in Europe. A single strong ruler, generally with blood relations to his or her predecessors, governed each great European geopolitical entity. These large geopolitical entities were new, built on new trade routes and new industries, such as bell and cannon founding. Production, especially producing for export and securing new wealth for the nations, dominated their economies. Nowhere was the new production economy clearer than in agriculture. Small subsistence farms could not compete as many large agricultural estates jettisoned thoughts of estate self-sufficiency in favor of a single crop or, in the case of England, animal agriculture. Commons quickly disappeared as hereditary rights were abrogated. As landlords increasingly enclosed land, the strip agriculture of the Middle Ages, which helped ensure that a large part of the peasant population would share in the best land, gave way to farmsteads that held all their land contiguously. Leasehold farming and farming for wages replaced manorial obligations on estate after estate, except in the Slavic East. Whenever leases ended, landlords were free to raise renewal prices. Wage workers lost job security and were often let go as the market dictated.

The situation was similar throughout Europe. Enclosure was most pronounced in England as many peasants were displaced from their manorial homes. Freeing Castilian Spain's peasants of manorial obligations in 1480 forced them to lease land—often having to pay before the harvest—or to work for wages. In France and Germany in the mid-sixteenth century, 90 percent of farmers leased land. Only 5 percent retained the benefits and penalties of serfdom.

The Dutch maximized production further by dispensing with the three-crop rotation, especially its wasteful fallow period, and replacing it with "convertible" husbandry. The new Dutch system balanced crops to maintain the soil for perpetual production. They grew soil-depleting cereals for two years and followed that with a year of soil-enhancing peas or beans. Every fifth year or so, they pastured their animals on the fields and worked the enriching manure into the soil.

Wages also played a central role in reorienting manufacturing. Most manufacturing took place in cities and towns. Merchants and manufacturers demanded flexibility to sell their goods to the highest bidder; some markets grew increasingly large in scope, from local to national to international. Medieval-styled guilds stymied flexibility. They restricted the number of persons plying a craft or trade in a place or limited the number of products produced by each person. Enabling all members to make an appropriate wage and permitting each the security of a livelihood no matter the economic travails prevented guilds from accepting the new production ethos. Wage labor offered manufacturers the requisite economic flexibility and freedom to respond by allowing them to set production quotas and by absolving them of formal responsibility for wage workers when markets collapsed. Although in a few instances manufacturers were able to install their wage-based systems in urban places, they found greater success in the country. Cloth manufacturing led the way. Merchant-manufacturers, savvy in the methods of double-entry bookkeeping, purchased wool from England, for example, and "put it out" to rural villages. Villagers, many of whom had been displaced from their manors, spun, dyed, and wove the cloth. These dislocated workers proved willing to work for less than urban guild members, and merchant-manufacturers paid them only for work done. The village putting-out system benefited manufacturers immediately, but it also assisted them by undercutting urban-based guilds as well as the master-apprentice relationship. To retain a significant share of the work, guilds needed to compromise with or accede to the new production ethos.

To a considerable degree, these profound economic and social changes made taking refuge in court-centered, antirepublican hereditary monarchies voluntary and popular. Often the firm establishment of these autocratic regimes came at the end of a period of unrest, even open warfare. For example, the French monarchy emerged in 1453 from the horrors of the Hundred Years' War. The English War of the Roses produced stability two years later. The marriage of Ferdinand and Isabella, representatives of two warring provincial houses, placed what would become Spain in the position to become the strongest European power. There seems little doubt that those Europeans willing to accede to a king or queen often viewed their fellow citizens as lacking virtuosity and therefore incapable of effective government participation. Yet they also recognized that the state's success—and the success of its members—dictated collective action. Keeping the good public order—stability—was a major governmental responsibility but only when coupled with maximization of the public good.

In the new production Europe, a society's accumulation of wealth seemed one measure of its social effectiveness. This mercantilist vision meant that states increased their total wealth only by bringing additional wealth into the community.

Exporting goods and receiving money proved a peaceful means to accrue community wealth—the opposite would dissipate wealth. But mercantilism pitted those in the community against those outside it. Seizing wealth from others outside the community increased the community's common wealth. Using force to plunder other lands required both coordination and military might. Enabling a community to withstand an assault from without was at least as crucial to the preservation of the public good. It necessitated either the achievement of military superiority or the formation of alliances with lesser nations. Alignment of nations proved a delicate activity and balance—stability—was the key. Less-powerful nations joined together to ward off a stronger foe but rarely did powerful nations come together to dominate large areas. Weaker states entered into alliances only when their position seemed desperate. It remained preferable to act without allies whenever possible, to maintain sovereignty at all but the most precious cost.

The public good, gauged in part by a nation's accumulation and retention of wealth, justified establishment of a strong hereditary monarchy. But that same human measure, the public good, also dictated and circumscribed the leader's duties, activities, and responsibilities. It required kings and queens to act in precise ways as they played leadership roles. Maintenance of power depended on the consent of the governed, not in a simple electoral fashion but through their active social participation. Kings and queens were not creations of a handful of nobles—the nobility and the representative agencies of the nobility dramatically lost power—but were absolute, representing and relying on far broader segments of populations even as those populations were excluded from regular deliberations. Absolute monarchies thrived as their virtuosos embodied their communities' ambitions.

A handful of officers directly dependent on the monarch alone carried out the monarch's policies. These local arms of royal policy facilitated the regal program and were the instruments through which it reached most of the population. They could offer advice to the monarch but he or she had no obligation to listen. The fate of these functionaries, whether Spanish corregidors or English justices of the peace, rested in the monarch's hands; they had no security nor tenure of office, serving only so long as they effectively delivered royal prerogatives and therefore pleased their patrons. Functionaries managed the royal estates, collected custom duties and sales taxes, leased monopolies to merchants and others, kept the peace, and sold government bonds. Churches were not immune from taxation. Separation of humankind and god had converted church property from heavenly to public property and functionaries not only collected taxes there but often served as prelates. Monarchs demanded the right to appoint clergy.

In extraordinary times, royal officers often collected taxes on the personal properties of the monarch's subjects. Direct taxation of private property generally came only with the explicit consent of the governed; a representative body would permit the monarch to assume that power. During these crises, the public seems to have understood that their private property became "public." Stability was threatened and nations as wholes authorized their leaders to maintain the status quo, to protect the communal existence. In these instances, the community determined what was public and what was private and those definitions were not absolute. They shifted depending upon what dangers communities thought they faced.

Much of the funds raised through direct taxation went to purchase mercenaries to defend the country. Monarchs had their permanent mercenary armies of Scottish archers, Swiss pikers, and French infantrymen—a necessary requirement of monarchy was to perpetuate and defend the country, but additional soldiers required additional funds. German, English, Italian, Polish, and Greek mercenaries sold their services to the highest bidders. Generally not as well trained or disciplined as a monarch's regular mercenaries, these men nonetheless often made the difference in defense.

Balance: Italian Style

Emergence of the great European geopolitical entities jeopardized the Italian city-states. Not until the later fifteenth century did the potential threat become clear. For much of the fourteenth and early fifteenth centuries, the greatest European menace to the city-states was the most powerful city-state, Venice. It threatened to overwhelm and capture its less-powerful compatriots. The other city-states—Florence, Milan, the papacy, and Naples—responded as the great geopolitical entities would do soon after. They forged an alliance strong enough to beat back Venice but not so powerful as to crush it. As one commentator noted, the aim of each city-state was "to preserve its own territory and to defend its own interest by carefully making sure that no one of them grew strong enough to enslave the others." This defensive strategy made each nuance crucial and "each [city-state] gave the most careful attention to even minor political events or changes."

For nearly 50 years, this balancing act enabled the city-states to maintain their integrity. But in 1494, Charles VIII of France invaded Florence and Naples at the behest of Milan, which feared a Florence–Naples plot, and destroyed the city-state balance. To protect their own interests, the other city-states solicited aid from Spain and the Holy Roman Empire, which caused the French to retreat north. For another 60 years these great geopolitical entities and city-states continued the delicate balance between conquering and being conquered with no side willing to risk either. Rise of the Ottoman Turks provided a potent counterweight to these European powers. The lack of a final resolution served the European and Italian powers as it provided its own stability, if only by continuing the balancing act.

Life in European Monarchies

The citizenry's virtuosity differentiated the great European geopolitical entities from the Italian city-states. Each required a different form of governance. In the later fourteenth and early fifteenth centuries, northern Italians clung to the idea of representative government. The European states ceded or delegated their sovereign powers to individuals to serve as artificial leaders of each state. That same sentiment suggests that social life outside of northern Italy was at best a pale reflection of that within it. Certainly peasant and tenant farm life proved very modest. Long houses from 15 to 20 feet wide and 40 to 90 feet long sheltered both humans and livestock as well as rats and mice. Generally built of wood on stone foundations to prevent rot, peasant homes usually lasted only about a generation. Their center entrances opened to halls, which served to separate humans and farm animals. The family area averaged less than about 350 square feet for a family of six and was dominated by a central hearth. A hole in the wooden-framed, thatch-covered roof permitted smoke to escape from the hearth. On tenant and other farms bound up in the new production agriculture, the number of animals necessary to sustain each farm required tenants to build separate facilities to house livestock. Only in those circumstances were animals removed from the homestead. These more prosperous farmers had clay-roofed brick or stone houses, complete with room divisions, bedrooms, and larders.

Cities built during the fourteenth century and later in the great European monarchies also lacked the grandeur of their northern Italian counterparts. But these walled cities were more impressive than their medieval predecessors. Their 40-foot-wide thoroughfares were more than double the width of those of medieval cities, perhaps a sign of the new emphasis on production for export. Houses opened directly onto the street. In several French cities, facades on homes of successful artisans ranged from 16 to 23 feet, and houses were 23 to 33 feet deep. These wooden houses with thatched, tiled, or slate roofs generally were two stories high but frequently incorpo-

Fifteenth-Century London. Overlooking the Thames, London in the fifteenth century was a typical, prosperous Northern European city. Its citizens engaged in an impressive variety of social and cultural activities, playing numerous social roles. Its guilds created a surplus of products, which London merchants traded on the export market.

rated attics and basements. Walled fireplaces, which were vented through chimneys, heated bedrooms and kitchens. Shutters covered the oiled parchment windows in winter and wood paneling kept out the north wind. Packed-earth floors were most common but the more successful urbanites increasingly preferred wood.

Social life, especially urban social living, required participants to relinquish a measure of liberty for the blessings of stability. Achievement of stability included following a number of human-derived rules to regulate behavior. Rules were of two types. Those offered without government supervision aimed to help persons develop their virtuosity. Those enforced by the power of government were protective, not of the individual per se but rather of society. These rules strove to defend society from the possible deleterious effects of individuals not yet virtuous.

The first type of rule usually was to be taught, often in the form of a treatise. These "how-to" books taught individuals, for example, how to behave in society without making social gaffes, how to rear children, and how to prevent illness. People in the age of humankind might also pass rules by word of mouth. The virtues of cleanliness formed one such set of rules. Wives and mothers learned to comb for lice in daylight. People were taught to place their tub in the warmest part of the house—near the fireplace—and to cover the vat tightly with fabric to trap steam. They were also told how to prepare an herbal bath, taught the responsibilities of a host to prepare a guest's bath, and admonished to bathe frequently.

These informal social rules even extended to issues of style. Persons of some means commonly coordinated the colors and designs of canopies, bedspreads, curtains, and wall hangings. As important, they routinely switched to different fabrics and patterns whenever fashion changed. They apparently felt it socially necessary for the decoration of their homes to reflect their station and for them to appear in tune with the latest fashion. Fashion likewise demarcated social role. Peasants dressed much as burghers had earlier: tunic, fur-lined coat, and a hat. For the rich, clothing was a work of art. Women ignored their waists but bared shoulders and provided a hint of breast. Men bared arms. Women and men alike dressed up when appearing in public, especially at ceremonial events such as weddings. Silk, decorated with silver or gold, was common for finer dresses for women, and furs were marks of distinction. Families retained their own symbols and heralds. Noblemen—princes and dukes—often provided uniforms, complete with insignias, to their staff. Businessmen also adopted that custom. The House of Fugger expected its employees to don Fugger-provided uniforms for special occasions.

Dress and style were essential to the performance of social roles. Appearance—outwardness—differentiated persons in society. So, too, did other simple public measures, such as manners. Persons filling prominent social roles were expected to act accordingly, to act as a person should for that part in the social play. For example, royalty began to demand chamber clocks in the later fourteenth century. These poorly conceived devices kept miserable time and had little but symbolic purpose: They showed that kings and queens held time for society. Humankind owned time on earth and royalty preserved and coordinated it for the social whole. Books of manners, each geared to a particular social role, became commonplace and even extended to the regal court. Baldassare Castiglione's *Book of the Courtier*, based upon discussions at the Court of Urbino in 1506, provided the script for persons cast in those supporting roles. But it would be a mistake to take this role-playing lightly. These outwardnesses reflected definite social commitments; they defined and demanded certain activities on the part of the actors and actresses. Failure to provide those activities was cause for severe social sanction, as in the case of misrule. Introduction of extensive, regularized pomp and circumstance, which helped identify what the perks and habits of a leader ought to be, merged style and substance. The roles that these people filled were permanent, but performers were interchangeable. These men and women merely played recurring parts (as would others after them) and were to be replaced whenever they deviated unsuccessfully from the script. A certain amount of improvisation or ad libbing was tolerated but significant alteration brought rebuke or worse.

The situation was most clear in urban areas. There society formed itself into regiments, or clubs. Each cofraternity, each of these social families, had its own symbols or heralds. Each had its own rules. For example, guilds regulated trades, conditions of apprenticeships, and wages of journeymen. Guilds also indirectly controlled marriage and family life for their members. Men generally waited until they became masters to get married and then usually married younger women. The nature of apprenticeship encouraged marriage. Among the masters' duties was provision of a familylike setting for apprentices. In that sense, wives were helpmates; they married into the guild. As a consequence, guilds seemed associations of families rather than of workers. Guild masters often followed set tracks in guilds. Their guild responsibilities dictated that they hold their first guild office about 6 years after joining and achieve their highest office 8 years later.

But it would be incorrect to assume that identity was limited to guilds. Cities and towns were awash with cofraternities and brotherhoods, which cut across guild and socioeconomic lines. Some associations segregated membership by age. Others organized citywide festivals. Still others focused on residential areas, almost all of which had populations socioeconomically and occupationally mixed. These wards provided the basis for organizing the night, wall, and gate watches, taxation, and the militia. Each ward controlled its area and provided a specified number of individuals to serve the city. These people might supervise when work began, when gates opened, when gates closed, when persons were paid, and when there was a curfew. Often churches recognized these forms of identity. Cofraternities had private chapels, separated from one another by wood or iron grills, and their own furniture and crypt.

Playing social roles was not restricted to those within contemporary social norms. Licensed and badged prostitutes, walking the streets, housed in public brothels, or cruising public bathhouses or young men's associations, followed a precise, socially defined standard of behavior. In that sense, they were no different from any other group of people pursuing a specific activity in the later fourteenth, fifteenth, and early sixteenth centuries. Urban areas enacted ordinances and regulations to control people and merchandise and to protect public health and safety. Individuals were expected to adhere to those commonly considered behaviors. Multiple identities, multiple social roles, required each fourteenth-, fifteenth-, and sixteenth-century man and woman to don one of several costumes when in public.

Society forced humans to adopt disguise. Men and women chose to live in society. Society rested upon consensus, upon group understandings. Costume, public dress, and public manners were among the most important understandings. If humans differed little at birth, then the common good prohibited any public displays of arrogance. Actions outside the norm, outside the socially defined norm, threatened society. What each person felt inside was far less important than how she or he acted outside. Individuals' outwardnesses might not have been real, but they were established to serve the common good.

For Further Reading

[See the conclusion of Chapter 11]

CHAPTER 10

Religion in the Age of Humankind

The Scholastic synthesis joining heaven and earth placed the church at the apex of both the earthly and heavenly worlds. William of Ockham's curt dismissal of human reason as an aid to understanding god or the immortality of the soul struck at the very core of the Thomist formulation. God could not be proved but had to be believed. Radical separation between humankind's reasoning faculties and faith in a supreme deity willing to grant some humans salvation was not restricted to the Ockhamists. Others argued similar precepts and then labored to use the distinction between human reason and god's existence to reconfigure or reformulate religion. Many of these religious modifications proved immensely popular. But at their heart rested a simple premise: The Christian church as then constituted did not suit the age of humankind. Church agencies built on a Scholastic foundation could not open heaven's gates and guarantee eternal salvation.

From that simple issue emerged a wide range of questions and options. What was the role of the church in salvation? Was there a role? If such a role existed, what church reforms were demanded? Could the church be reformed or would it have to be disbanded and some other edifice erected in its place? If so, who should erect that edifice and what should it look like? What were the appropriate measurements of church effectiveness? What exactly were the failings of the church? Who would perform the analysis of church failings and of the efficacy of possible solutions? Could salvation occur outside the church? Was the church universal? What was the relationship of states to Christendom? Was there a Christendom? What roles were the pope, cardinals, bishops, monks, and even parish priests to play? How should they act? Each question became a critical point of contention as Europeans in the age of humankind struggled to put their Gothic church in line with their new notions.

The Church in the Age of Humanity: The Great Schism

A new understanding of the relationship between humankind and god could not help but seem to exacerbate the status quo. On its most basic level, it converted situations and conditions long tolerated or even ignored into "problems" that now demanded immediate attention. But it also worked in a paradoxical way. It encouraged persons

270

in authority to question the way things had been done and to attempt to do things somewhat differently, to "expose" situations or conditions long unknown or unconsidered by a larger audience as well as to "cause problems."

In all those senses, the age of humankind proved a period of great turmoil within the church, perhaps the most unsettled time in its history. As early as the late fourteenth century, Europeans began to react heatedly to church initiatives. The great expansion of the papal bureaucracy during the Avignon captivity was among their first targets. Men and women complained about the church's involvement in their daily affairs and claimed that the bloated entity only craved money and influence. Kings and other nobility disapproved of attempts by the pope and his bishops to secure a central place in the governance of their countries. Nobles disliked the church's practice of collecting money, whether through simony, indulgences, or some other means, and sending it to Rome. Church ownership of property, which could be taxed only at great peril, lessened royal coffers. Critics especially objected to the pope's contention that from his distant office he deserved to control European affairs. This last criticism smacked of localism but that disguised its true meaning. A great number of men and women in the fourteenth century and after absolutely rejected any attempt of the church to assert preeminence (and in many cases any authority at all) in terrestrial matters. If the church retained a domain, that domain was heaven.

The church did little to encourage that sentiment. Popes residing at Avignon became more and more monarchical and, once freed, developed their own military machine. Nor did the local examples of the church help improve its divine image. The clergy shed its exclusive use of heavenly Latin as the church language in favor of the vernacular and even regional dialects. Nepotism seemed the surest way to enter the clergy, and multiple bishoprics appeared the rule rather than the exception.

Perhaps more important, a Great Schism split the church and exposed the humanity of its highest officials. The schism began when Pope Gregory XI died as he prepared to return to Avignon from Rome in 1378. A Roman mob demanded an Italian pope and the fearful cardinals elected an Italian bishop—Urban VI. Urban demanded that his staff reform its practices and the again fearful cardinals, many now in Avignon, claimed that the first election had taken place under duress and selected another pope, Clement VII.

Two popes now headed the church and each repeatedly excommunicated and cursed the other. Each pontiff erected his own resource-draining bureaucracy and both attempted to cement their claims in the manner of modern-day political bosses; each offered secular authorities various inducements to align themselves with him. Each pope also established his own college of cardinals, indebted to him.

This very public battle appalled those outside the high church bureaucracy. The University of Paris faculty called a general church council to decide between the rivals and maintained that such an action was possible because the general good of the church constituted a higher authority than the pope. This view was markedly different from that of medieval Europe. There the pope sat atop the church pyramid where he "judges all and is judged by no one." In the terms of the age of humankind, however, Paris's move recognized the church through its members as sovereign. These men and women willingly had placed their sovereignty in the pope's hands. It remained their right to reclaim their sovereignty whenever he proved incapable of exercising it for their collective good.

Paris's call failed to sway either Urban's or Clement's supporters. The church continued on two more or less parallel lines even after these two men died in 1393 and 1394, respectively. The conflicting colleges of cardinals elected new rival popes, who each continued to treat the other as an anathema. Not until 1409 did the cardinals on both sides agree to a joint meeting. This gathering in Pisa of 500 prelates, including many not in either college, deposed both sitting popes as "schismatics and notorious heretics" and elected a new pope. The newest pontiff was immediately denounced by his predecessors whose alliances with temporal authorities enabled them to remain ensconced and in control of their bureaucratic empires. The new pope moved quickly to consolidate his position by disenfranchising the special meeting and, in the tradition of medieval pontiffs, by maintaining his superiority to any and all parts of the church.

The new pope's initiative infuriated those who had gathered at Pisa and they worked to force a second meeting to resolve the now triple schism. The Roman-based pontiff ultimately recognized his position as untenable and called such a meeting in 1414, claiming that his call demonstrated the pope's superiority over any council and the primacy in the church of Rome and the Roman clerical line. He then abdicated, hoping perhaps to be the new gathering's legitimate selection.

The gathering met at Constance in 1414 and after three years of discussions agreed upon yet a new pontiff as the foundation for the true line of papal succession. The Pisa-elected pope was forced to abdicate but the Avignon pope refused to resign. Only at his death in 1423 was the schism fully sealed.

The Constance meeting also established periodic councils as the mechanism to supervise church reform. Placing councils above the holy see did not sit well with the new pope and he mobilized his forces to undercut the effort. In this action the pope reflected sentiments found among monarchs in civil societies. They rejected attempts to formalize control over them but proved willing to accede to the dictates of their sovereign constituencies whenever the situation demanded. Such proved the case with popes, who recognized the inevitability and real (if never publicly acknowledged) primacy of councils during the succeeding centuries.

Heresy Against the Church as Treason

The Great Schism could not help but suggest that the Christian church, especially the papacy, had little claim to earthly predominance. At about the same time that the Great Schism began to develop, the church experienced a potent challenge to its heavenly predominance. John Wycliffe, an Oxford University philosopher, involved himself with a parliamentary bill that asserted that clerical abuses—simony, the selling of indulgences, the moral turpitude of the clergy, and the like—negated the church's spiritual authority in England and, therefore, that the state needed not offer the church financial support. Wycliffe had become embroiled in this cause because of his theology of terrestrial righteousness. Only those clergymen righteous on earth could claim the right to heavenly sovereignty, which included the right to confiscate a portion of a state's earthly goods for their support. As important, Wycliffe contended that only civil authorities, not ecclesiastical bodies, could decide on the church's worthiness.

The English crown backed Wycliffe when he was called before the archbishop of London in 1377 to explain his philosophy. His supporters angrily defended their man and a general riot ensued. Wycliffe returned to his writing and expanded his doctrine. He first questioned how and even whether ecclesiastic censure could affect a person's civil situation and then stated before Parliament that that body should defy the pope's monetary demands. Wycliffe continued to enjoy the support of the crown and his university even as he was called before the church again to explain his views. This time the mob, the common people of London, intervened violently in his behalf and the proceedings ended without Wycliffe's censure.

Wycliffe did not moderate his views but extended them. He maintained that the power of the church to provide asylum was far from absolute and that civil authorities could invade churches with impunity to bring fugitives to justice. Wycliffe turned his attention to the Great Schism and argued that it showed that the church failed to achieve even the patina of righteousness. Failure to act righteously disqualified the church from intervening in earthly matters but its insistence that it held a critical role was to Wycliffe an abomination. He branded the then contemporary popes (and all popes since the Donation of Constantine) Antichrists. The immoral Christian clergy and its princely, tyrannical popes constituted nothing less than the "friends of hell."

John Wycliffe. Wycliffe initiated the first English translation of the Bible, an act that signaled his rejection of the papacy. For this and other similar acts, the Catholic church declared him a heretic and some 30 years after his death had him disinterred, quartered, and burned at the stake.

Rather than look to the impure church for religious sustenance, he called upon Englishmen to find god through the true authority of the Holy Scriptures. Wycliffe assisted his countrymen by creating "poor priests" to go through England and to spread Wycliffe's message. These poor priests were not ordained; they simply followed Wycliffe's pronouncements and their existence undercut the need for a separate priestly caste. He also translated the Bible into English so that any literate person could experience the Word himself or herself and began religious instruction in English.

Wycliffe's program gained him a substantial following among England's common people. He also continued his philosophical assault against the church within the university. In 1380–81, he labeled the sacrament of the Eucharist, especially transubstantiation, "blasphemous folly," a "deceit" that "despoils the people and leads them to commit idolatry." Wycliffe did not object to the idea of wine and bread being converted into Christ's body and blood. Christ countenanced such a transformation at the Last Supper. Wycliffe rejected the breaking of the bread into pieces as breaking apart Christ and dismissed the idea of ingesting parts of the deity as clearly not creditable. He instead proposed that the body and blood were essentially there but not actually there; they came primarily in spirit, not substance.

This last set of beliefs forced the university to condemn Wycliffe. He appealed to the king, a procedure that Wycliffe maintained followed from his religious precepts, rather than to the pope, the traditional ultimate authority on religious matters. The king refused to intercede and commanded Wycliffe to stop uttering antichurch doctrines, a decision that appeared wise when in 1381 persons claiming to follow the Wycliffian program encouraged the great Peasants' Revolt. Wycliffe withdrew from public life and died a few years later.

A sect of poor Christians called Lollards continued to practice Wycliffian Christianity into the early sixteenth century. The state refused to condone their beliefs and even passed the "Statute on Burning the Heretic" in 1401 to dissuade them from openly advocating their religious views. But Englishmen were not the only Wycliffian disciples. John Hus, native of Bohemia, fashioned Wycliffe's thoughts into his own. Hus maintained that the Bible was the only true source of authority, that Christ—not the pope—was the church's true head, and that Christ—not the church—was the agency of salvation. Hus removed the earthly church from any role in heavenly life and it responded in kind. The church removed Hus from his position of rector at the University of Prague, forbade him to preach, and finally excommunicated him for his views but initially allowed him to remain free. Under a guarantee of safe conduct from the Holy Roman Emperor, he traveled to Constance to defend his ideas. The emperor quickly withdrew his protection—Hus also committed the crime of urging Bohemian independence, a treason against secular authority—and the Council of Constance had Hus burned at the stake for heresy in 1415.

The Council of Constance produced another notable decree in 1415. As part of its deliberations to seal the Great Schism, it demanded that John Wycliffe, now dead for over 30 years, be disinterred, quartered, and burned at the stake. This sentence was carried out some 13 years later. Wycliffe in 1428 suffered the then common penalty for treason. And indeed he had committed treason, but not against a secular power or even god. He was a traitor to the church—the community whose members claimed sole authority to guard the entrance to heaven—and Pope Martin V ensured that he was duly punished.

Varieties of the Catholic Experience

The Wycliffian and Husian heresies revealed a willingness to seek salvation outside official church auspices. Increasingly, men and women sought personal communion with the deity as a means to achieve eternal life. These movements were emotional, not rational, but they nonetheless reflected the human-centered ideology of humankind's age. The simple assumption that humankind did not need a mediator to become one with god—or in the Platonic sense, the One—proved a particular hubris, but common to the period. Humankind could rely on itself to achieve virtually any end.

Associations of religious persons operated without respect to church sanction. Cults of saints and cults of relics became popular obsessions as persons repudiated the church by seeking direct union with someone or something god had touched. Others asked if the church's core was ritual or Christ. Those who found Christ at the church's heart often emphasized his humanity, especially his suffering, not his royalty. His all too human wounds were the gateway to heaven. Eternal salvation depended on personal contemplation, not reason nor church dogma and ritual. Individuals must "contemplate the drops of blood, the blows in the face, the persistence of the whip, the crown of thorns, the derision and spitting, the hammering of the nails into the palms and the feet, the raising of the cross, the twisted face, the discolored mouth, the bitterness of the sponge, the head hanging with all its weight, the atrocious death."

Yet another group concentrated on Christ, but as a classical hero, accentuating the way he lived rather than the way he suffered and died. This heroic vision stressed Christ's ability to find a virtuous Christian life no matter the earthly temptations. To these men and women, the church's presentation of Christianity was at fault. Scholasticism was and had been an unmitigated tragedy: Its proponents were neither wise nor eloquent but presumptuous as they boosted cool, dispassionate logic. Logic was amoral, inhuman, and the church suffered from the rejection of its historical roots. Morality—humanity—needed to be restored as Christianity's fundamental basis. Ignorance of history, grammar, painting, architecture, sculpture, and music prohibited the church from developing among its parishioners morality, a quality necessary for human society and heavenly salvation; human knowledge generally, including the Greco-Roman classics and explorations of humankind's terrestrial realm, could not corrupt or undermine Christianity but purify belief and thus uplift the church.

This optimistic Christian Humanism program proved especially potent in the Germanic principalities, particularly Basel and Wittenberg, but Rotterdam's Erasmus (1466–1536) emerged as its most celebrated advocate. He traveled through Europe attacking Scholasticism and clerical abuse. His speeches and writings stressed the acquisition of knowledge as a first step in developing a Christian morality and he located the appropriate moral sense in the classical and early church past. Centuries (and the Scholastic tradition) had distorted and perverted this material. Erasmus maintained that scholars of Hebrew, Latin, and Greek needed to complete modern retranslations of these important documents and then to render them into the vernacular to give persons access to their insights. He saw true religiosity not in dogma or ritual but in the Bible, especially the recounting of Christ's life, and argued that every person could learn from its passages. Erasmus rejected the premises that

Erasmus of Rotterdam. Working within the church to increase its members' appreciation of the holy scriptures, Erasmus retranslated the Bible from Greek. He maintained that each Christian should read the Bible, confident that all would understand it similarly.

"Christ had taught such subtleties that they can scarcely be understood even by a few theologians, or [that] the strength of the Christian religion consisted in men's ignorance of [Christ's earthly existence]." Erasmus undertook his own translation of the New Testament from the original Greek for the masses but he viewed neither the Bible nor Christ's life as open to interpretation. A humane perspective, a shared morality, enabled *each* individual to understand the Bible *and all* individuals to understand it similarly.

Other Christians working outside church auspices found salvation even more firmly rooted in the here and now. Pious individuals formed themselves into the Brethren of the Common Life. This association's members dedicated themselves to each other and, through that dedication, to eternal salvation. Brethren aimed directly to inspire and encourage each other to approach a state of divine goodness, which would produce an almost mythical communion with god. Their inspiration included their mode of living—a good Christian life, including attending to and establishing schools for the poor. The more general Devotio Moderna, which originated in the late fourteenth century, accentuated acting in a pious manner and demonstrating good character rather than ritual devotion or theological analysis. The Devotio more nearly equated acting holy with becoming holy. Still others went beyond the Devotio and the Brethren and focused on the millennial aspects of Christ's message. They professed that Christ would condemn the rich on his return and establish a society ruled by the poor for a thousand years. Such a radical difference from the then present church suggested that the person heading it, the pope, was not doing god's work but was in fact the Antichrist.

The papacy certainly gave its antagonists reason to reach that conclusion. Schism continued to ravage it, although not to the degree of the Great Schism. Nor would observers mistake the popes of the late fifteenth and early sixteenth centuries for paragons of virtue. Alexander VI (1492–1503) reflected the worst in the papacy of the age of humankind. Alexander worried only about his family's interests in Italy. He was the archtypical earthly pope, totally without concern about spiritual matters, interested solely in family aggrandizement and political power. Trained as a lawyer, Alexander made inroads in the papal bureaucracy when, in the mid-fifteenth century, his uncle, Calixtus III, became pope. Alexander cravenly used his series of positions to gain wealth and women, which drew a severe papal reprimand from Pope Pius II, Calixtus's successor. Alexander fathered children from his numerous mistresses, including seven from one mistress alone. Alexander generally acknowledged parentage and throughout his life showered high church offices—bishoprics and cardinalships—on his sons. Alexander worked to arrange prominent marriages for his daughters but when a marriage failed to secure the anticipated political influence, he was quick to annul it and to betroth his daughter to a different party. On at least one occasion, he made his daughter Regent of the Holy See while he was away from Rome. True to form, his election to the papacy had been marked by three candidates attempting to purchase votes; Alexander simply offered the best deal. During his papacy, he formed military leagues against Naples, Venice, France, Pisa, and Spain as well as alliances with most of those geopolitical units. Sometimes he did both at once. On at least two instances, he invested numerous new cardinals, which enabled him to place his supporters in power and to generate the revenue necessary for his profligate lifestyle. Both his 18-year-old son and the husband of one of his mistresses became cardinals in that fashion. Such voracious appetites required almost limitless funds and Alexander instituted a confiscation policy to feed his habits. A wealthy person was charged with some offense, taken to prison where he met an untimely demise—poison was favored—and had his property confiscated. Alexander regularly sold church offices and, toward the end of his reign, was accused of blatantly poisoning several opponents.

Julius II (1503–1513) had somewhat higher scruples but he, too, was no stranger to earthly temptation. Before Julius became pope, he held six bishoprics and was a cardinal at four locations. He had unsuccessfully led a movement to depose Alexander VI and was forced into exile in France. Upon his investiture as pontiff, he repudiated nepotism generally and simony in papal elections. He then set about to consolidate church holdings and power. This warrior pope pacified Rome and its environs, entered alliances with France and Germany, and used their might to reduce Venice's Italian influence. He also freed Bologna and concluded an agreement with Spain. The last endeavor included a papal ban on France, whose bishops responded by renouncing papal obedience and calling for Julius's ouster. The pope quickly allied himself with Venice, Germany, Spain, and England and drove the French out of Italy. He also called the Fifth Lateran Council, which condemned the French for renouncing papal obedience and urged a holy war against the Turkish threat in the East.

Julius's military adventures required money and he reinstituted simony and the selling of indulgences to replenish the papal treasury.

Leo X continued Julius's policy of simony and indulgence-selling and also reversed his antinepotism sanctions. Leo had become a priest at age 7 and a cardinal at age 14. A member of the Medici family, Leo learned from Pico and Ficino and was well versed in classical literature. As a cardinal, he avidly supported Julius and led the papal army on his Florentine home when it chose to side with the French against Julius's authority. As pontiff, he devoted himself to maintaining papal possessions, which meant fomenting and cementing alliances with the great powers and city-states. In at least one instance, Leo was accused of having "hitherto played a double game," pledging one thing to one power and delivering something else to another. His earthly ambitions forced him to reconcile with France and establish a tithing schedule to bankroll the war with the Turks. Yet before beginning the fight, he purposefully destroyed his carefully crafted solid European front by taking England's tithe and using it to wage war against France in Italy. Leo hoped to defeat France and force it to withdraw, which would allow him to carve out several rich duchies for his relatives. These and like maneuvers caused several cardinals to plot to poison Leo, who had the conspirators arrested. All were imprisoned and at least one was executed. Leo completely undercut the conspirators' base of power by investing 31 new cardinals, an unprecedented number, to dominate the college of cardinals.

Leo X received an estimated one-half million ducats per year through the sale of over 2,000 clerical offices. He also raised significant funds by providing papal dispensations to closely related persons wishing to marry. To be fair, Leo was simply continuing policies established by his predecessors. Some of those policies had been set hundreds of years earlier and the church bureaucracy was rife with their effects. Bishops had long paid a portion of first-year receipts to the power who appointed them, often served more than one bishopric—some never set foot in bishoprics that they "oversaw"—and continually tried to enhance church revenues. Concubinage and promiscuity remained rampant among the clergy, whose sexual peccadilloes had become so commonplace that the ribald priest had as early as Chaucer become a stock literary device. Excommunication persisted as a weapon to secure temporal rather than religious ends. These material, terrestrial concerns ran so deeply that the most respected priests appeared to act as if legal and financial considerations, rather than spiritual matters, defined the Christian religion.

Nor would it be correct to believe that all within the church bureaucracy condoned these behaviors. The Franciscan and Dominican orders worked to correct many of these abuses within the church generally, while the bishop of Canterbury instituted a strict moral behavioral code to uplift and regulate the clerics within his bishopric. Others, not affiliated with any order, established themselves into an informal group, known as the Oratory of Divine Love. Operating outside of papal or ecclesiastic sanction, these clergymen vowed to each other to reform the church in the areas they supervised, and they met occasionally to consider means to achieve that end. The Fifth Lateran Council (1512–1517) inspired by Pope Julius II legislated against simony, concubinage, and blasphemy in hope of returning the church's lost luster.

Martin Luther: His Humanity

In 1517, Martin Luther, an Ockhamist-trained Augustinian monk who served as professor of theology at the humanistic hotbed of the University of Wittenberg, seized upon the nearby presence of a papal-sponsored seller of indulgences to launch an attack on what he considered that nefarious practice. Luther drew attention to his cause by selecting All Saints' Day, a period when most of the city's population would attend church, to nail his objections on the church door for all to see. He offered his Ninety-five Theses or propositions for discussion and debate in established scholastic tradition but with an eye to capturing public appreciation. Yet Luther could not have anticipated the popularity his positions would command. The university press failed to keep up with demand for copies of the document, which was quickly translated from Latin to German. Within two weeks Luther's theses had spread across Germany. Western and southern Europe were scrutinizing them within a month.

The heart of Luther's attack on indulgences was the church's contention that they removed sin. One type of indulgence, that to reduce church penalties, met with Luther's approval because "the church can remit what the church has imposed." But he strenuously objected to the idea that the church could "remit what God has imposed." These god-imposed penalties or sanctions included guilt, divine punishment for sin, and perpetuation of souls in purgatory. The practice by which the church claimed to bank the excess good works and holy acts of pious Christians, who had used but a portion of them to achieve salvation, only to have the pope offer the remainder for sale to absolve others, drew special condemnation. Luther argued that the church only dealt with the living; its jurisdiction ended with death. The pope can pray for souls but he had neither the dominion nor the keys to release these tortured beings from their god-imposed scrutiny or torment.

The immediate effect of Luther's attack was a steep decline in the sale of indulgences, which caused great consternation among the papal representative in Germany, who sent a copy of Luther's work to Rome. Embroiled in Italian affairs, Leo X dismissed the matter as a dispute among monks. A pamphlet war raged between Luther and his detractors, which further depressed indulgences in Germany, and the pope finally grew concerned enough to command Luther to come to Rome and explain why his views did not constitute heresy. The emperor and Frederick of Saxony, the two civil authorities overseeing the part of Germany in which Luther preached, took the papal summons not as simply an attempt to deal with a heretic but, because it required the University of Wittenberg professor to appear at Rome, as a threat directed at their university—their earthly property and authority—and thus at their temporal power. When they made their protests known to Leo, he quickly relented and sent a legate to meet with Luther near Wittenberg.

Luther wrote an immensely popular account of that meeting for the German public, and it served to humanize him. Luther addressed the people of the German states as contemporaries, capable of understanding and treating crucial issues. Conversely, his touching and passionate rendition of his plight demonstrated to his audience the author's piety, torment, and confusion, experiences that characterized and defined humanity. In his public writings, Luther portrayed himself as characteristically

Martin Luther. Luther proved especially adept at arguing his case. Christ's sacrifice was humankind's sole salvation. Both the church and individuals could not achieve it. Since the church argued otherwise, then the church must be false. In public debates and in pamphlet wars, Luther capitalized on his humanness; he showed his humanity both by expressing the anguish his decision had caused him and by claiming that his contemporaries were capable of arriving at a similar conclusion.

human and acknowledged his contemporaries' humanness; they were all members of the same group. This deft touch converted an issue of authority between the church and god—indulgences—into a human question—humankind's ability to adjudicate that dispute (and to deal with religious matters generally)—as well as a contest between the heavenly church and the terrestrial state in earthly matters.

By November 1518, Luther had begun to reconsider the basis of his objections to indulgences. He quickly recognized that to attack the buying and selling of indulgences was to attack the power of the pope. But Luther also understood that church doctrine maintained that the pope was infallible. And if the pope were wrong in this instance, then the foundation of the church must be in error. An attack on indulgences, then, was tantamount to an attack on the church. That was the essence of heresy but Luther felt he could do nothing else nor come to any other conclusion. He examined and reexamined the indulgence question and could find no rationalist religious justification for the practice. If the pope erred in this circumstance, then the church lacked substantive moorings and Luther's subsequent investigations led him to believe that the indulgence question was only one of many fraudulent doctrines.

Luther developed his critique of the universal church over the course of the next several years. He looked backward to find material bearing on the present and hoped to restore what he considered early Christianity's objectives. St. Paul's admonition that good works under Jewish law did not save people and the saint's corresponding counsel that humans were saved only through faith in Christ struck Luther as especially pertinent. Unlike many of his contemporaries, Luther did not reject the church because its clergy lived badly but because they believed badly. His rejection stemmed from what was believed and from what was practiced because of those beliefs, not what was done. In that sense, Luther's critique was rational; his human reason led him to cast off church doctrine and ultimately to refuse to grant the universal church any role in salvation. Luther's use of human reason to settle this matter was entirely consistent—it was possible if somewhat tautological—because the church was to Luther a human institution, a product of humankind's reason, and therefore able to be proved or demonstrated to be unreasonable. If the church were truly a divine creation, Luther's Ockhamist training would not have permitted him to employ his human reason on what must constitute a matter of faith. In this context, the church's folly about indulgences undermined the institution's entire validity. It proved that the church was not the gateway to heaven and that god did not operate through its agencies, such as the sacraments. If god did not work through church sacraments and if the deity did not act through the intermediary of the church, then church officials—clergymen—had no special standing. That they claimed special purview smacked of charlatanism, perhaps worse. Luther sought not the reformation of this false church but its destruction. It was the "most lawless den of robbers, the most shameless of all brothels, the very kingdom of sin, death and Hell." The pope was himself the Antichrist.

Heavenly salvation came from god alone, not from a god-mediating bureaucracy. Holy Scripture, the divine Bible, showed god as just and merciful, willing to save humans from eternal damnation. Humans needed to believe that god's word meant what it said; they needed faith in god's promise because they could not prove it through human reason nor did they possess the power to effect their own salvation. Nothing humankind did or could do, including good works, would contribute to its being saved. Only god's grace made a difference.

Luther demanded that Christians read Holy Scripture and he translated the Bible into German to assist them. Urging that each individual read Scripture and deliberate about its message reflected Luther's contention that no clergyman was necessary to intercede between the individual and god. This "Priesthood of all Believers" did not individualize biblical interpretation. When asked if each person remained free to interpret Scripture as he or she wished, Luther simply said, "God forbid." Nor was the act of Bible contemplation something upon which human reason might come to bear. God, in the form of the Holy Spirit, guided individual biblical contemplation and ensured that all individuals who truly believed in the deity would interpret the word similarly. When coupled with belief, god's word interacted with and transformed the reader. In that sense, contemplation of Holy Spirit–directed Holy Scripture was reminiscent of achieving a sort of congress with god as in the Platonic One, Christian Kabbalism, or Hermeticism. An individual might achieve that union but all who achieve it must achieve it identically.

Luther's priesthood of all believers changed the Christian sacraments. Some, such as ordination, now seemed ludicrous but baptism to remove original sin and celebration of the Eucharist both remained vital parts of Luther's theology. He maintained that god acted through the faith of believers and, during Communion, transformed wine and bread into Christ's blood and body. And Luther was not reticent about sharing his views. When asked to disavow his heretical positions, Luther responded in a way that reflected his tortured humanity. "Unless I am convinced of error by the testimony of Scripture or by clear reason," he maintained, "I cannot and will not recant anything, for it is neither safe nor honest to act against one's conscience. God help me, Amen." In the 5 years after 1518, Luther continually pressed his case publicly and reached out to the German community for support. He engaged in public debates with high representatives of the papacy and published any number of personal laments and disputations. By 1520, over 300,000 copies of Luther's works had been disseminated in Germany. Luther publicly burned a papal bull excommunicating him from the church and made a stirring appearance at the first German diet in 1521. Whenever forces mounted to threaten him, Luther watched German crowds rise and protect him.

Luther's poignant and popular crusade against the Catholic church focused on the individual and his or her relationship with god. It dispensed with religious mediation, nurturing instead an incipient self-sufficiency—even as he supposed that each individual saw the question in the identical way. Bolstered by his reliance on his conscience and his intransigence, others were encouraged by Luther's personal search to reassess human possibilities, especially their particular earthly station, and to transfer the unnecessariness of heavenly mediation over to the terrestrial world. These men and women questioned the role of intermediaries in contemporary life. Peasants objected to landlords, journeymen to masters, masters to merchants, and landless knights to landed nobility. Luther-like, they issued their Twelve Articles in early 1525, which demanded modification of current practice. Provisions included the right to choose their own clergy to preach the gospel "without any human addition, doctrine or commandment"—an obvious attack on the pope—and an end to serfdom. "Christ has redeemed and bought us all with the precious shedding of His blood," the Articles recounted. Its framers maintained that they had "no doubt that, as true and real Christians," their lords would "gladly release us from serfdom, or show us from the Gospel" where serfdom was condoned for persons "who will be free, and will to be so." If serfdom was abolished, the peasants swore to obey their legitimate rulers as the nobility lived in accordance with Scripture.

Luther had long advocated living earthly life by divine law. He had railed against usury and those persons who made their livelihood off the sweat of others. Luther expected Christians to engage in good works and to serve others. These works were not traded for salvation, but fulfilled Christian love obligations, to live as Christ lived. But Luther proved adamantly opposed to the sentiments expressed in the Articles. He especially abhorred the use of his religious arguments to suit earthly ends. He thought the Articles an abomination, violating the commandments by condoning robbery. Scripture tolerated slaves as property as "Abraham and the other patriarchs and prophets [had] slaves." Each person seeking an end to divinely countenanced serfdom simply sought to steal his or her body from its owner; the serf's body was nothing more than the "lord's property." Luther concerned himself instead with the spirit, claiming that those seeking the abolition of serfdom denigrated and debased "Christian liberty" by reducing it to "an utterly carnal thing." These materialistic rebels would "turn the spiritual kingdom of Christ into a worldly external kingdom," which would degrade Christ's gift of eternal life. A Christian slave had "Christian liberty," Luther asserted, because of Christ's sacrifice. But that liberty was otherworldly, not earthly. Luther was no friend of the ruling classes, referring to them as "furious, raving, senseless tyrants." Yet he expected individuals to remain deferent to their earthly rulers. Luther recognized humankind's worldly lot as patiently suffering degradation and repeated indignities as humans waited for the time that salvation might replace earthly misery.

By May 1525, the rebels, now some 300,000 strong, were engaged in a full-fledged violent uprising. Luther's treatise, "Against the Robbing and Murdering Hordes of Peasants," claimed that the rebels' application of religious principles to earthly matters constituted blasphemy and treason. God reigned in heaven. To degrade god to the earthly sphere was an abomination. Luther called on secular authorities to act dramatically to end the debasement and to preserve the social order, urging them to "smite, slay, and stab, secretly or openly" all rebels. These "poisonous, hurtful or devilish" individuals were like "a mad dog," which must be struck down immediately or it "will strike you, and a whole land with you." Luther issued his pronouncement on the eve of his marriage to an escaped nun. As the bride and groom set up house in a seized Augustinian convent, the persons to whom Luther addressed the "Murdering Hordes" followed his advice and attacked the rebels. They slaughtered nearly 100,000 persons in two years as they demonstrated in no uncertain terms that the heavenly and terrestrial worlds had two separate and separable masters.

Broadening the Net: Reform and Reformation

Luther's religious message struck a responsive chord with broad sections of European society. Its adoption reflected spiritual concerns, not earthly matters. That various groups benefited from Luther's program did not mean that crass self-interest caused them to accept his views and discard those of the Roman church. Concern for the immortal soul was not something cast off lightly, especially when persons seemed to have the unprecedented ability to choose which way to proceed. Nor did Luther appeal to only one social group. Virtually every segment of society could find something in Luther's message. Townspeople, particularly merchants, appreciated the end to sending money to Rome. Noble men and women could reduce if not eliminate church taxes and confiscate church lands. Luther's triumphing the plight of the poor certainly resonated with those unfortunates.

But Luther was not alone in claiming guidance of the Holy Spirit and a monopoly of Christian truth. Many others also threw off the yoke of Roman Christendom and erected their own alternatives to that universal religion. Local and national congregations and religions resulted. Heinrich Zwingli was among the first to embrace and then split with Luther. By 1520, Zwingli had accepted many essentials of Luther's program: the authority of Scripture; justification by faith, not works; and denial of human free will. Yet he broke with Luther over religious ceremony and material manifestations of religiosity. Zwinglians thought religion a purely emotional, ethereal matter. God remained sovereign in heaven, but since the earth proved so materialistic and debased, the deity granted humankind considerable sovereignty on the corrupt, contemptible earth, an idea that permeated their entire program including their interpretation of the Eucharist. Luther believed that individual faith transformed wine and bread into Christ's blood and body; Zwinglians argued no such physical transformation occurred. To even suggest an earthly transformation struck them as tantamount to heresy. The terrestrial bread and wine remained bread and wine, only representing Christ's blood and body. Similarly Zwinglians abhorred complicated religious ritual and worked to simplify the liturgy. But they reserved special scorn for attempts to reduce heavenly faith into earthly structural manifestations. Church decorations aroused their special ire and in the Zwinglian center of Zurich, mobs destroyed stained-glass church windows and smashed religious statuary. They even went so far as to invade these buildings and whitewash their walls to remove all hint of the reduction of spiritual essences into material terms.

Zwinglians went much further than Luther but the Anabaptists thought them far too conservative. Anabaptists viewed Jesus' Sermon on the Mount as creating a new ethical/moralistic covenant between the deity and earthly believers and among earthly believers. Adult rebaptism formalized the new covenant. Anabaptists carried the notion of a priesthood of all believers to the social sphere. Within their community of believers they were strictly egalitarian in all matters. The 1525 rebaptism of a former priest by a lay person symbolized their rigid egalitarianism and has served as the putative origin of the Zurich-based, Zwingli-descended movement. Anabaptists also rejected the physical world. In that respect they agreed with others outside the Roman church who believed the earthly world corrupted, beneath god's glory. But Anabaptists sought to separate themselves from it, not to improve or reform it. Rejection of earthly life contributed to their refusal to swear oaths. Like some other Christians, Anabaptists refused to take god's name in vain, as in swearing an oath. But Anabaptists also adamantly refused to swear allegiance to any earthly leader, even the officers of municipal corporations. For similar reasons, Anabaptists neither testified in court nor participated in legal proceedings. They refused to hold civil office and to bear arms.

Anabaptist egalitarianism surfaced in other ways. Dressing similarly in coarse cloth and broad hats, they broke door locks to facilitate sharing goods among each other. Their emphasis on good works was not to enter heaven but to comply with Jesus' Sermon, to order human life according to his words, and to demonstrate their faith. Anabaptists believed the world evil and their choice of Christ required them to live virtuously apart from it. Ability to choose Christ was an important part of Anabaptist theology. Individuals possessed a will sufficiently unencumbered to choose virtue or evil, just as they chose adult baptism rather than have infant baptism forced upon them.

Anabaptists proved among the most hated European religious groups. Governments identified them as rebels or traitors because they refused to participate in civil society, grounds for persecution. Religious sects despised them for their religious beliefs. Their accentuation of human free will marked them as unusual as only a few non-Catholic sects after Luther held free will doctrines.

The Frenchman John Calvin (1509–1564) led a Geneva-based sect that maintained that only god's will was free; humanity's remained bound. Calvinists claimed humanity was depraved and loathsome. Only the Holy Spirit, infused throughout the words of Holy Scripture, illuminated the soul of humanity. But human illumination would have had little consequence had it not been for Christ's sacrifice. Christ's sacrifice showed Calvin's god to be truly merciful: The deity not only had offered humanity Holy Scripture, but had sent the Son to earthly humiliation, an act that provided for the redemption of a segment of humanity. The eternal salvation of this small part of humankind rested on union with Christ and becoming part of his body. Faith offered that union. Sincere belief in Christ justified the sinner, which led inevitably among true believers to repentance, regeneration, and sanctification. The Holy Spirit provided the believer assurance of salvation, which resulted in the manifold blessings of inner peace.

Humanity could do nothing to achieve salvation. Merciful god did grant some persons eternal salvation, but not because of their inherent goodness or good works. It simply pleased god to save some humans. The decree was "totally irrespective of human merit." Individuals were powerless to alter their divine destiny. God had decided each person's eternal fate at birth; predestination of some persons to eternal life remained god's sovereign purpose.

Calvinist theology presumed its church the agency through which god joined the elect to Christ and two sacraments sustained the saved. Baptism marked church initiation, while the Eucharist constituted a spiritual—not corporeal—transfusion of Christ into the individual. The church also served to awaken those not yet aware of their heavenly election. Provision of Holy Scripture and preaching of the gospel stirred and provided the first inkling of god's divine plan to the saved.

Church governance was a divided affair. Preachers preached the gospel, delivered the sacraments, and administered and executed church policies. Others, more

Calvinists. The Calvinist theocracy at Geneva closely regulated public and religious behavior. Its attempt to translate heavenly precepts into earthly existence emphasized good works, a just society, and humility and deference before god.

scholarly, continuously examined and judged church doctrine to ensure its purity and wholesomeness. A legislative-like body, comprised of the holiest and gravest lay congregants, joined these permanent officers. Church members selected these church senators by ballot and also voted for deacons to care for the poor.

Extending voting privileges to all congregants did not signal a belief that the entire congregation was saved. Each man and woman understood that god saved only a small portion of humankind. Yet each exalted in that fact. God saved some humans and Calvinists believed that god's act was cause for all humanity to celebrate. Each church member thanked god for salvation—the deity's "gratuitous mercy"—even when the thankful individual was not elected to eternal life. In thanks for what god would do for some humans, all humankind—at least all believers—needed to demonstrate its profound appreciation and awe. As Calvin put it, humankind's chief end was "to know and do the will of god." This corporate view of humankind suggested that humanity possessed a common mind—one objective, one aim, and one interpretation. Calvin's collective humanity lived according to the gospel and strict moral strictures not to achieve salvation but to glorify god. Its sole purpose in doing good works remained to demonstrate its profound gratitude for god's decision to save some of humankind.

Calvinist philosophy made no distinction between church and state. But Calvin's church did not overwhelm his state. Humankind's earthly existence remained critical: Humanity needed to erect a society reflective of the marvel and spectacle of god's greatest gift, salvation. Like Luther, Calvin had studied law, philosophy, and theology, but unlike Luther, he received extensive schooling in Greek and Roman literature and the entire humanistic program. A humanistic society constituted humankind's creation for god as it strove to do the deity's will. Humanity had the power to engage in good works, establish a just society, and manufacture beautiful productions, tempered by the understanding that humanity, corrupt and unworthy, needed to express its essential humility and deference before god.

Regulation of public and personal life were one consequence of the Calvinist theocracy. Transgressors were identified and warned. Repeated violation of church sanction led to their dismissal from the community. Reportable offenses included loud noise or talking in church, card playing, dancing, accepting the Catholic mass, and speaking well of the pope, known to Calvinists as the Antichrist. But with the rigorous discipline also went a desire and propensity for social experiment. Calvinists began by rejecting the status quo. They then attempted to take divine and heavenly precepts and to reduce them to human and earthly scale. Calvin's Academy, for example, was composed of arts, law, theology, and medical schools. It attracted people from across Europe, spreading Calvinism first to France and Scotland but then to England, Netherlands, Germany, Bohemia, and even North America.

Catholics Counter

Even before Luther posted his theses, the Catholic church had taken steps to redefine its earthly mandate. However, certain fundamental premises could not be abandoned: The pope's primacy and the church alone possessing the keys to heaven stood as nonnegotiable sections of Catholic theology. Luther's critique speeded efforts already under way and provided pressure for their extension. Neither Leo nor his successor Clement VII embraced reform, choosing instead to continue the papacy as a personal Italian fiefdom. Not until Paul III (reigned 1534–1549) did the papacy attempt to delineate and clarify Catholicism and show its distinctiveness from Luther's and the other reformers' positions.

Active suppression of heretical doctrine had long been the way of the church and it stepped up efforts after Luther. The Inquisition, which had been reintroduced into Spain prior to 1480, made its way to the Netherlands in the early 1520s and to Italy two decades later. The Spanish and later Inquisitions aimed to save the heretics' souls but demanded that they renounce their heresies in public. Recanting as part of a large public spectacle served as a cautionary tale; it alerted citizens that there were dangers afoot. But readmission to the church, which possessed the keys to heaven, came only with penance, sincere contrition followed by public displays of that contrition. These public, physical displays—pilgrimages, flogging, and the like—demonstrated god's mercy through the deity's willingness to reintegrate the heretics into the church as well as the virtues of the church itself.

Not all heretics rejoined the church. Those obstinate persons who refused to recant were remanded to secular authorities for burning. In essence, these persons died because their heresy threatened the Catholic community; they were traitors to it and to god. They had followed their individual proclivities rather than church dictates—individual standards over community values and standards—a sin of tremendous proportion.

Other early forms of suppression included burning the words of heretics and other blasphemers and dangerous people. Consigning these unholy doctrines to flames was not simply an attempt to deny access to the ideas in these written works; burning books, pamphlets, and tracts prevented instead the mystical union of readers with the words, joining the text and being transformed by it. Mystical transformations, organic unions with other entities, and the power of words to transform remained compelling facets of the age of humankind both inside and outside the church. As early as 1526, Henry VIII of England, proclaimed Defender of the Faith by Leo X in 1521, constructed a list of prohibited books and banned them from his kingdom. The church as a whole followed suit three decades later when it instituted the *Roman Index of Prohibited Books*.

The church also established a number of new clerical orders to beat back the Protestant assault. Among the most famous and productive was that formed by Ignatius of Loyola, who parlayed his military experience into founding an order of Christ's knights. Loyola's Company of Jesus (later renamed Society of Jesus) received papal sanction in 1540 as the "order of the church militant." Jesuits quickly became known for their tenacity. Wearing no distinctive clothing and swearing an oath of allegiance to the pope, the Jesuits undertook the church's most difficult and dangerous jobs, including infiltrating Protestant regions. Their efforts to reconvert Protestants and to convert heathens combined monastic discipline with passion for teaching and preaching. They attacked the idea of salvation in the religions of Luther and Calvin as restrictive, as open only to a segment of humanity. The Catholic church through its ceremonies, traditions, and priestly powers held that it offered the keys to heaven to all humankind and pressed this potent argument at every instance.

Council of Trent. Convened in 1545, the council condemned the Protestant heresy. It reaffirmed the papacy, maintained that the church held the keys to heaven, and contended that humankind through faith could effect its salvation.

Jesuits especially carried that message to earthly priests and encouraged them to strengthen the church in their territories. At the same time, Jesuits railed against many of those very same abuses that Luther and others detected. Although they remained loyal to the papacy, they did condemn corruption among local churchmen, a maneuver that displeased bishops and priests but fortified secular authorities, delighted the citizenry, and provided the Jesuits immediate credibility.

The Council of Trent (1545–1563) reaffirmed the Jesuitical commitment to purify the church of the Protestant heresy but the genesis of this grand conclave was quite different. From at least 1530, Charles V, Holy Roman Emperor, had pressed to reunite Christendom. Charles sought a doctrinal synthesis that would reintegrate Protestants into the Catholic church. Of special consideration to Charles were those practices that had initially engendered the split. Perhaps with an eye to what it might do to his secular power, Charles argued that removing the original causes of friction would resolve the problems that undergird them. These tension-generating practices included papal nepotism, papal indulgence selling, and the whole question of the secular papacy. Pope Paul III repeatedly refused the emperor's requests, viewing the questioning of the efficacy or propriety of these practices as an attack on papal preeminence. Moneys formerly sent to Rome would remain in the kingdom and a legislative council would supplant papal infallibility. Both would reduce the pope to a supplicant.

Paul finally agreed to the council but on his terms. Paul wanted a simple condemnation of the Protestant heresy at Trent, while Charles sought church reform. Location of the meeting and the decision to permit each cleric a vote gave the papacy-backing Italians a numerical majority and the council quickly approved the pope's agenda. It reaffirmed that only the Catholic church possessed the keys to heaven. On the most crucial question of biblical interpretation, the council maintained that the church held the sole right to interpret the Bible and that church traditions were equal to the Bible as a source of spiritual knowledge. There were seven sacraments rather than the Protestant two, priests alone could transform bread and wine into Christ's body and blood, and good works as well as faith marked individuals for salvation. The council sanctioned monasticism as an important part of the church hierarchy, the veneration of the Virgin Mary and saints, and the efficacy of relics and indulgences. It also stipulated that clerics must remain celibate.

These fundamental positions established Catholicism not as humanistic in the sense of the humanities but as human and human-oriented. Through worshipping saints and relics, selling indulgences, swearing vows, and believing in the reality of purgatory, the church accentuated human actions and the ability of humankind to effect its fate. Enthusiastic religion—praying, weeping, and other mystical emotionalism—and sincere contemplation seemed the means by which humans with the church's assistance could put themselves in union with god. Humanity could participate in its own salvation.

The council devoted its final years to reforming practice. It maintained supremacy of the papacy over the clerical councils, issued decrees requiring bishops to reside in their dioceses, and banned multiple office holding. It also demanded that priests receive a certain, precise training for the priesthood and created seminaries in each diocese to enable them to attain it. The council concluded by approving the *Index of Banned Books*, which until that time had had only papal sanction.

Religion and Great Geopolitical Entities

The post-Luther emphasis among Protestants on divorcing earthly life from salvation did not sever the connection between religion and politics. Calvin's Geneva demonstrated that the two might remain united. As it had for over a millennium, religion in the age of humankind often affected daily political and social existence. Yet integration of the politics of statecraft and religion was not always at the expense of earthly concerns; terrestrial issues were not necessarily subordinated to a divine purpose. The religion of a state's or principality's ruler commonly became that state's or principality's religion. Publicly at least, individual freedom of religion hardly existed. A social entity's official beliefs were the beliefs of the potentate that headed it.

The Peace of Augsburg, concluded in 1555, provided the characteristic expression of this idea. That peace, which formalized the right of each prince in Germany to set the religion for his principality, followed 8 years of prolonged warfare and three decades of rabid dispute. It had pitted the Catholic Charles V and his princely supporters against the Protestant princes, who dominated the northern, heavily urban provinces.

Both in the abstract and in fact, individuals could and did disagree with their ruler's designation, of course. But these public disagreements opened their proponents to charges of treason to the state or made them liable to be marked and treated in some way as outside the community. Protestants no less than Catholics embraced this concept. It was Calvin who had the Genevan civil authorities burn Michael Servetus (1511–1553) at the stake for attacking the Trinity and promoting adult baptism, two doctrines not approved in the city-state. Freedom of religious practice—as compared to freedom of belief—was rarely tolerated. Religious practice and ritual was so integrated with social practice and custom that to be out-of-step with one meant to fail at the other. To violate custom, to act in a manner contrary to custom, seemed to weaken the whole, to divide it into factions, which would compete with one another rather than promote the common good. In that sense, to be a traitor to society appeared more reprehensible than to be a traitor to god or Christ or the church. Maintenance and persistence of civil society was more critical than church ritual, a fact already in place prior to the Reformation. Without such sentiments there could not have been a reformation.

Protestantism had emerged as the religion of protest. The disenfranchised, unempowered, and discontented initially flocked to its banner as a means of protesting the status quo. But as anti-Catholic religions became firmly entrenched and intermeshed within civil society, they stopped offering that outlet and attraction. After that point, whatever religion did not receive official sanction in a place—including Catholicism—became the religion of protest in that place and drew to it those on society's margins. Religion became the way to mobilize the outs to get rid of the ins and, for much of the century after Luther, each conflict tended to include a "religious" dimension of this type.

It need be stated that all upstanding persons were not expected to believe what their ruler believed, but they were expected to practice what their ruler believed. Their own individual beliefs remained private, not part of the social discourse. Although clerics sometimes promoted the notion that rebellion might be justified on grounds of religion—something Luther refused to approve—political sovereignty became increasingly secularized. By the end of the sixteenth century, French political theorists had divorced religion from the idea of government. Jean Bodin (1530–1596) maintained that citizens needed to consider properly constituted civil authority without appealing to religion or religious questions. Michel de Montaigne (1533–1592) went further, dismissing religion from politics because religion was a matter of faith but its articulation was the product of reason. Frail human reason could never do faith justice and therefore the relative merits of competing religious ideas could not be known with certainty. Christianity should be believed, but religious and doctrinal differences tolerated and all civil law obeyed. Only those persons asserting religious dogma and demanding conformity deserved condemnation and then only because of their self-righteousness; they put themselves and their frail reason ahead of the common good.

Absolute monarchies continued to flourish in this intellectual milieu and what commonly became known as the divine right of kings served as powerful justification. In the age of humankind, the monarch represented society and ideally acted like a patriarch/matriarch who ensured that the greatest good prevailed. It was the whole's perseverance, it was the whole's furtherance, that proved divine. The monarch's ability to help society—not the individual—achieve that aim became a matter of faith, not the product of human reason. Human reason held a crucial place in social thought but only in positing the kind of social structure and measuring social determination; society judged whether the monarch was in fact working to secure the whole's best collective interests.

Divine right granted monarchs incredible latitude. England's Henry VIII severed connections with Rome in his attempt to establish a credible male line. Henry had proven himself an age-of-humankind monarch; he had brought humanistic learning to England and renovated the English common law. The pope's refusal to annul Henry's long marriage to Catherine of Aragon constituted to Henry and other English people a treason against the state. A stability-ensuring successor was imperative. Henry's sole daughter, Mary, did not seem likely to assume the throne as no queen had ever ruled England. Several potential female monarchs had been passed over for

Henry VIII. The pope initially declared Henry "Defender of the Faith." But after the pope refused to grant Henry a divorce and to ensure that his heirs would continue to govern England, Henry withdrew England from Catholicism and established the separate Church of England.

male relatives earlier and by Henry's day most English believed women were prohibited from the monarchy. That did not mean the field was devoid of potential successors. More than a handful of distant relatives and other claimants stood poised to begin what promised to be an extensive civil war for the crown at Henry's demise. The papacy's unwillingness to bend to these issues seemed deliberate provocation. By turning down the generally granted request, the papacy willfully interfered in the earthly statecraft matter and threatened social stability. The matter was cleanly drawn. A pope worried about French influence in Italy turned to Charles V, Holy Roman Emperor and king of Spain. As part of the price for his assistance, Charles demanded that the pope reject Henry's annulment plea; Henry's son-less death might position a relative of Charles as a prime claimant to the English throne. Proclaimed by the pope "the defender of the faith" only a few short years earlier, Henry used the pope's usurpation as justification for creation of a monarch-headed English Church in 1534. This church remained free of papal influence and two years later Henry even dissolved Catholic monasteries and seized their properties. That Parliament endorsed Henry's initiatives, including creation of an English clergy headed by the archbishop of Canterbury and an English-language prayer book that showed exquisite sensitivity to Catholic traditions in hope of reuniting English Anglicans and Catholics, testified to how critical it seemed to maintain social stability.

Decisions to challenge a ruler's sovereignty and therefore to redraw social boundaries hardly ever went unquestioned. Those in power often objected to the contentions of those out of power and these disagreements frequently broke down by religion. Armed conflict was sometimes the result. Such was the case in France. The Calvinist Huguenots had by 1559 become powerful and organized enough to mount a military challenge to their Catholic persecutor, King Henry II. Headed by disgruntled and provincial nobility, the Huguenots engaged in a decade-long civil war and an uncivil peace for some two decades after. Not until the Huguenot Henry Navarre came to the throne as Henry IV in 1589 was stability restored. His initial acts gave his co-religionists no joy. Henry quickly renounced Protestantism and converted to Catholicism to eliminate the menace to his authority posed by French Catholics and their potent Spanish supporters. But Henry recognized that he was merely playing a part in a social drama and so did not consider vanquishing the Huguenots. Instead of fighting them, he worked to reintegrate them into the social fabric. The Edict of Nantes (1598) marked the culmination of the reintegration effort. Protestants anywhere in France now gained full civil rights, including owning property, trading freely, and holding public office. They could establish houses of worship and worship publicly in only 200 places but the state paid their clergy as it paid the Catholic clergy. The edict also established 100 safe garrisons for Protestants in France and paid for forces assigned there to protect these men and women.

Although solution to the statecraft question in France took on a specific tinge, the themes outlined were typical. Public religion, not necessarily private faith, took a secondary position to statecraft; persons assumed roles in the play of society. England after Henry VIII demonstrated the same phenomenon. Henry's young Protestant son succeeded him upon the great monarch's death and moved the state more firmly into the Protestant camp but he died a few years later. Henry's daughter Mary (Bloody Mary) then came to the throne. Her claim stemmed from Henry's marriage to Catherine, the abolition of which led to formation of the Anglican church. Mary necessarily disavowed the dissolution of her mother's marriage, which would undercut her legitimacy and therefore her right to be queen, and her father's act that precipitated it; Mary worked to merge Anglicanism back into the Roman church. She needed to undo nearly a quarter-century of institution building, which she did with dispatch. Mary abolished antipapal legislation, burned over 300 Protestants as heretics, including the archbishop of Canterbury, and purged the Anglican church of the archbishop's supporters. Mary then established political ties to Catholic Spain by marrying Philip II, the Spanish royal heir apparent.

Mary's short reign ended with her death in 1558 and Elizabeth I succeeded her half sister to the throne. As daughter of Henry's second wife, Elizabeth's royal claims depended upon the validity of her father's annulment. Since the annulment was not possible in the Roman church, Elizabeth moved English Anglicanism squarely toward Protestantism, an act for which the pope excommunicated her. Elizabeth sought to keep England strong, stable, and independent and recognized that an all-out assault on Roman Catholicism would not achieve her goal. Instead of disenfranchising Catholics, she tried to steer a middle course and had *The Book of Common Prayer* revised to make its sections even more palatable to Catholics as an enticement to join the Anglican church.

But Elizabeth's most important tactic was to refuse to try "to make windows into men's souls." She would not penalize anyone for his or her religious beliefs nor would she attempt to determine exactly what those beliefs were. Elizabeth concerned herself with a person's outwardness—her or his acts—and rejected any attempt to determine his or her inwardness—an individual's faith. The queen delivered retribution only for actions and limited her vengeance to those persons who had persistently opposed her policies. As long as persons played their roles in the theater of society, Elizabeth found no offense. But those persons who warped the social fabric suffered royal wrath. Rabid Catholics most commonly crossed the line between thought and treason but radical Protestants demanding (and more) that the Anglican church be cleansed of all Catholic influences and customs also were persecuted for failing to play their social parts.

Statecraft, Sin, and Witchcraft

Statecraft and witchcraft in the age of humankind were virtually inseparable. As early as the late fourteenth century, men and women began to complain about pervasive moral decline and decay and maintained that it characterized then contemporary life. They often attributed the decline to the failure of the clergy, whose inability to live morally set the tone for a decadent society. As one commentator noted, the slackening of "ecclesiastical discipline" had transformed "the holiness of the Christian community" into "a dream." Discipline could only be "re-established if we" outside the church took the matter into hand. Society through use of civil authority must "abolish leniency toward vice, the person's reputation and the outrage of dispensation by payment of money." Sin was everywhere. Hedonism, sex, and avarice seemed to prevail.

The persistent claims to restore society to its former luster ignored the fact that sin in the age of humankind differed markedly from its medieval precursor. Medieval

Witchcraft. The Age of Humankind was rife with accusations of witchcraft. The vast majority of those charged were women, especially elderly women. Their crime was against society; they consorted with the devil and shunned civil society.

sin was the sin of pride, the sin of offending god through thought or thought and action. Sin was a state of mind, a conscious disregard of divine rule à la Abelard. Sin in the age of humankind was public, generally of the body, and certainly required an act or statement. It was not something inward but an outward deed. Sin was committed or performed. It threatened society by weakening social cohesion; it set the well-being, happiness, or prosperity of the sinner above social custom or civil law. Sin was against the body politic, against the social whole, not against the heavenly deity.

Transfer of punishment for major sins from the church to civil government reflected the shift in definition of sin. Governments, not the church, established supervision of and punishments for adultery, sodomy, infanticide, and prostitution, just as they had for the ultimate crime against society—treason. Society also erected punishments for witchcraft. Luther identified witches as "the Devil's whores" and claimed that they "steal milk, raise storms, ride goats or broomsticks, lame or maim people, torture babies in their cradles, change things into different shapes so that a human being seems to be a cow or an ox, and force people into love and immorality." Witches were the consummate societal abrogators. They shunned Christian society to join in league with the devil (and therefore to create a society dedicated to competing with and harming Christian civil society). Their motivation was simple. Avarice and cupidity led them to reject civil society for a selfish, vainglorious existence outside its boundaries. Their union with the devil mimicked that proposed in the Platonic One in the case of Hermeticism, Kabbalism, and astrology. Witches created an organic affiliation with the devil through "a thousand damnable sorceries, . . . printing the words, invocations, figures, circles and letters used by the greatest sorcerers who ever lived." Their union with the devil granted them the power to change their outwardnesses. Witches could assume different shapes and masquerade as different forms of life, especially animals. This devil magic was not natural, not derived from god's nature. It was black or bad magic in contrast to white or good magic.

Society punished witches and suspected witches the way it punished traitors. The mildest penalties sought to mark the witch as separate from society. These punishments included sitting in specially designated public places reserved for witches, branding the arm, hand, or face, wearing special clothing, or carrying a huge rosary. Demands that the witch recant always accompanied the public punishment. Those witches whose crimes to society were the greatest suffered the greatest punishments. Witches responsible for murder, poison brewing, or some other ghastly crime were drowned, buried alive, or burnt. As in the case of treason, heinous witchcraft required society to destroy the corpse of the guilty perpetrator.

Over 100,000 persons were accused of being witches in fifteenth- and sixteenth-century Europe. Roughly 75 percent of the witches whose cases went to trial were women. Contemporaries explained the tendency for women rather than men to join the devil as a consequence of their anatomies. Pregnancy was the woman's natural state, they argued. Women acted rationally only when pregnant, when their filled wombs balanced their delicate systems. When not pregnant, women were subject to hysteria and bouts of irrationality. Marriage and family mitigated these tendencies. Husbands headed the society-like family, ruling as absolute monarchs. Their discipline and order forced wives to behave appropriately and to remain in line. But when that miniature society fractured, as in the case of widowhood or spinsterhood, women reverted to their naturally unbalanced state. They sought instead another form of societal life and often found it by joining the devil.

For Further Reading

[See the end of Chapter 11]

CHAPTER 11

Keeping Everything in Perspective: Exploring, Defining, Representing and Manipulating Humankind's Realm

Age of Humankind men and women concentrated attention on the earthly realm. This human-centered focus was no mere intellectual exercise. It was expressed in virtually everything that these people attempted. Things as diverse as printing and handguns reflected this new human emphasis.

Printing

By 1250, Europeans had adopted the eighth- or ninth-century Chinese practice of carving impressions, on wood blocks, inking those impressions and then placing the blocks against sheets of paper. Somewhat later they affixed the paper to a frame and employed a beam press—by now a papermaking staple—to make contact between block and paper more regular. Europeans printed a few books by this time-consuming block method, but used it most commonly after 1300 to print cards. Holy cards provided graphic representations of heavenly figures—saints, martyrs, and the Blessed Virgin—while playing cards, sometimes known ironically as "Tickets to the Devil," were used in games of chance and other forms of gambling. Adoption of oil-based inks, adapted by early-fifteenth-century Flemish artists from their canvas varnish, produced clearer, more realistic pictures. Sometime before mid-century, several goldsmiths, silversmiths, and other fine metalworkers in what are now the Netherlands, Germany, and France independently began to produce metallic type. Adapting fine decorative metalworking techniques to printing, these highly skilled craftsmen focused on text rather than pictures and divided the text into a series of letters. They made a punch for each letter of the alphabet, used the punch to make type-molds, filled the molds with a tin-based alloy, and finally carved away the undesired metallic residues. Design of type molds itself was a prodigious intellectual event. Fine metalsmiths/printers needed to think multidimensionally; they needed to structure molds to produce type to operate in conjunction with then contemporary beam presses.

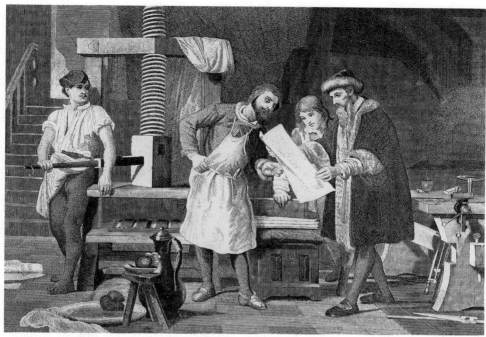

Johann Gutenberg and His Printing Press. A goldsmith by trade, Gutenberg was only one of a handful of gold- and silversmiths who, in the mid-fifteenth century, attended to the possibilities of movable-type printing. Creation of a three-piece mold for type manufacture was a key invention.

This type needed to be structured in some way so that when the beam pressed down flat on a piece of paper, the type would remain immobile and at the proper depth. Their ingenious solution—Johann Gutenberg, a German goldsmith, likely was the first to devise this form—was to create three-piece molds that produced type shaped like a three-dimensional capital "I." After they had produced a large stock of letters, they then set them for printing. The "I" shape of the finished type enabled printers to establish a set of adjustable rails called composing sticks and then to slide the thinnest part of the type into place where it would remain fixed. Each line of type was carefully crafted as these nascent printers placed letters in the appropriate order on these composing sticks. An entire page of type lined up in this manner and pressed against a series of sheets of paper could make any number of similar pages for any number of books.

Advent of movable type printing has long been hailed as a major milestone in the development of Western civilization. Printing made accessible information long held by only a few; it also enabled many who had not been able to share their thoughts and perspectives with others to do so, although only a small part of the population was able to avail itself of the new technology. Printing also speeded the pace of communication. An astonishing 9 million metal type books and over 40,000 editions were printed before 1500. But while scholars have accentuated its possible contributions to building Western civilization, few have considered movable type printing as a reflection of Western civilization in the Age of Humankind. The history of its invention, adoption, and adaptation reveal those critical assumptions that provided the period coherence. Printing was a creature of its time.

The simple fact that metallic movable type printing made sense only if volume of printed texts was to be exceedingly high testified to the widespread faith in humankind's ability to use the new technique and to benefit from it. Human reason enabled humankind to read and understand, and readers endowed with human reason would read the same works and understand them in the same ways or develop the same learning. Nor were topics restricted to religious tracts or texts. A wide variety of volumes appeared as Age of Humankind men and women wrote about their daily activities, theories of social organization, and crafts so that others could share their experiences; reading provided experience, almost the same as firsthand observation. This experience-based literature evinced a human centeredness unheard of since the Greeks and Romans. Age of Humankind authors wrote dictionaries, grammars, and encyclopedias in the vernacular, gathering and summarizing human language, the rules for human language, and human knowledge. Astrological, mathematical, medical, and legal texts were produced in great numbers as were local and universal histories. More new titles were offered in the half-century after 1450 than there had been in the millennium since the Fall of Rome.

Desire to provide a common, accurate human experience may have led at least one group to express unhappiness about the quality of printed matter before movable type. Several churchmen before 1400 complained about the quality of holy card pictures and maintained that these blurry and indistinct representations failed to capture the clarity of the immortal mortals. Use of water-based ink had permitted the image to run on the rag paper, ruining any prospect of a crisp picture. The Flemish artists' linseed oil, mixed with ground charcoal, significantly reduced running, which allowed later cards to have accurate, fully focused images—images with the sharpness of Greco-Roman statuary and images that provided the experience their advocates demanded.

The vast cost to establish and maintain a metallic type printing operation spoke to the potential demand for numerous copies of the same work. Goldsmiths and silversmiths did not need to invest much in printing equipment. Their many small anvils and furnaces were easily adapted to typemaking. But that these most highly paid craftsmen abandoned or downplayed their smithing work to take up printing indicated just how lucrative they anticipated printing to be. Extraordinary quantities of time were required to establish and continue a printing concern. Making a single punch took many days. Molded letters needed extensive trimming and filing. Setting one page of type was a several-day process for two or more craftsmen. The choice to engage in printing at the expense of fine metal smithing suggested a solid awareness of the widespread distribution possibilities of metallic type set publications.

Almost from the start, printers and others self-consciously concerned themselves with the outward appearance of printed works. The earliest printers mimicked the hand of late medieval manuscripts. This heavy, bulky Gothic typeface quickly fell into disfavor as Age of Humankind men and women rejected their immediate past for kinship with their reputed, humankind-focused Greco-Roman ancestors. Assuming that the outwardness of written works revealed much about the composer, they shunned Gothic typeface and adopted instead a thin, graceful typeface reminiscent of

Roman documents penned during the early Empire and copied during the ninth-century Carolingian Renaissance. Introduction of italics as a conscious refinement and as an extension of Greco-Roman fluidity and grace to this already balanced, well-proportioned typeface followed around 1500.

Printers quickly referred to type in terms of the human body. "Typeface" constituted a clear example of personification and the surface upon which the face rests was known as the "head." The "typefoot" corresponded to the other end of the "type body." Nor was the idea of typeface simply a coincidence. Printers demanded a human-scale type and, as had their Greco-Roman ancestors in the case of architecture, they turned to the human face as offering nearly perfect proportions. The shape of the face—its ovalness or circularity—was adapted to form the letter "O," while a line bisecting the "O" served as the "right" shape and proportion for the crucial "I." Like the Greeks and Romans, metallic type printers presumed that the straight line and circle—in this case perhaps more nearly an oval—stood as the two forms from which all other shapes (letters) could be derived. All letters thus formed would remain in true proportion to each other and to humankind generally.

Guns

Contrast metallic movable type with another major invention of the fifteenth century, the individually held firearm. It too took on a human cast, although few heralded its introduction. "Would to God that this unhappy weapon had never been invented," complained one man of the arquebus, a mobile, primitive gun. Without the arquebus, "I myself would not bear the scars [that] still cripple me today." Warfare as he knew it in his youth was now passé. "Cowards and shirkers who would not dare to look in the face" of "brave and valiant men" now "bring [them] down from a distance with their wretched bullets." Others agreed but extended the indictment of the gun. "Hardly a man and bravery in matters of war are of use any longer," decried one person. "Guile, betrayal, treachery together with gruesome artillery pieces have taken over so much that fencing, fighting, hitting and armor, weapons, physical strength or courage" have become all but obsolete. "Often and frequently . . . a virile bravo hero is killed by some forsaken knave with a gun."

These and numerous other commentators recognized in the emergence of the gunpowder-powered mobile gun a much larger phenomenon—the breakdown of established military practice and ideals and, by extension, of social regulations. These men, like most of their predecessors, had considered warfare a noble, religious undertaking. Christian knights fought in Christ's service according to universally held rules, which highlighted pomp and circumstance, honor, man-to-man combat, open battlefields with set formations, and assaults of walled structures. Rule violators were designated heathens, infidels, bad persons, persons outside the Christian community and were spurned. Rewards for holy or just wars—wars to god's ends—were measured not in material goods but in terms of salvation or credits on that path. Success suggested god's favor, a further reflection of the righteousness of the cause. Those most distinguished in the skills of warfare, which included the moral trappings and Christian purpose as well as physical talents, seemed likely to triumph.

The Handgun. This drawing from 1468 is the earliest drawing in Europe of a handgun. This individually held weapon was very heavy and unreliable. Newer, lighter, and more potent forms of handguns quickly followed.

To these commentators the gun ushered in a profound decline in social morals. Rewards of war shifted from the ethereal to the earthly and material. Gain and loss, life and death, victor and vanquished—human, terrestrial-centered concepts—now dislodged heavenly salvation as warfare's objective. Power, glory, money, and ownership, rewards in consonance with the Age of Humankind, replaced god's work as the justification for warfare. The glory of god through warfare ceased to command immediate obedience; decline in support for new Crusades and the abject disillusionment greeting the rise of the papal monarchy testified to the new earthly focus. Increasing reliance on mercenaries seemed the archetypal manifestation of war in the Age of Humankind. Mercenaries fought simply for money, without commitment to a cause other than the cause of oneself. They constituted a group outside of and antagonistic to society and therefore appeared as social abrogators even when they fought in society's defense. Kings, princes, and other nobles employing mercenaries generally escaped similar stigma. Their turn to mercenaries appeared an attempt to protect the interests of the social unit that these potentates were charged with administrating.

A Human-Centered Focus

Rejection of previously held social conventions during warfare constituted only a relatively minor part of a much larger phenomenon. Virtually every sphere of human activity changed to accommodate the notions that comprised the Age of Humankind and its earthly, human-centered focus. From the middle of the fourteenth century through the first three decades of the seventeenth century, European men and women labored to explore, define, represent, and ultimately manipulate their new, human-based realm. They dispensed with established conventions and identified new ones. They overthrew old institutional structures and created others to replace them. In many cases, customs and conventions seemed to remain the same, yet were really changed. The matter rested in explication. Age of Humankind men and women explored and explained extant customs and conventions in a way different from that of their predecessors. This change was not a change of form but of substance. Established customs and institutions came to be understood in new ways. Little truly remained untouched.

At the heart of the human-centered shift lay a fundamental transformation in perception. Europeans seemed to perceive things as much more complex and intertwined than had their immediate predecessors and incorporated a profound conception of multidimensionality into their thinking. Three-dimensionality and physical space, ways of conceiving things strikingly reminiscent of the Greeks in their concern for shape and the occupation of physical reality, emerged as essential elements of Age of Humankind thought in Europe and through that thought, action. The idea of virtuosos, of totally whole (or multidimensional) humans adept in virtually every human and humane activity—the genesis of the modern term "Renaissance man"—depended on this multidimensional view. So too did their rejection of the medieval Great Chain of Being and their development and embrace of a reconceptualization of the earth, earthly space, and the heavenly bodies. It also produced the persistent sense of wonder and passion for exploration and explication that characterized this period in European history. Age of Humankind men and women became convinced that their perspectives required attention and remained adamant that they demanded exposition. These people depended on and explored use of human senses as well as the senses themselves. For example, community-supported bathhouses and other means to reduce bodily odors were created as personal cleanliness assumed new importance. People also took great care to rid population centers of noxious smells by flushing urinals into waterways and by emptying privies of human wastes. Age of Humankind Europeans cherished human experience, but not in terms of personal or individual experience. They celebrated what was human and sought to learn how humanity would characteristically respond to particularistic situations and conditions.

Humankind's Realm: Society and Wealth

Emphasis on the material world gave the government in the Age of Humankind the task of increasing its society's total wealth. Strategies included providing for the common defense and permitting the government to act as if it were a single individual in the pursuit of wealth. Government undertook either high-risk activities or those that no human could achieve individually as it labored to increase its citizens' common wealth. This wealth-enhancing strategy prized social stability within the geopolitical entity but rewarded creativity. Citizens within states engaged in numerous wealth-creating activities as they produced goods far in excess of what was needed within the state. These production economies depended on markets outside the immediate geopolitical entity. But desire to export goods and therefore to increase a society's wealth was matched by an equally strong disinclination against importing others' finished goods in return for wealth. European entities were thus placed in direct economic competition with each other and sometimes warfare erupted.

The Art of Field Warfare

The Second Lateran Council (1139) outlawed one weapon as too gruesome and ghastly for use by Christians against Christians. This weapon could pierce a knight's armor from considerable distance and seemed to violate all sense of chivalric fair play. That weapon was not the handgun but the crossbow, the first weapon that Europeans maintained offended the laws of civility. Europeans infrequently used crossbows for about 150 years after the ban. But that weapon's vast potential and its ability to permit even semi-skilled archers to act as an effective artillery proved too seductive to resist forever. Crossbows and longbows appeared with increasing regularity in Christian versus Christian military engagements after 1300. The Battle of Crecy in 1346 has been referred to as a turning point in aerial weaponry: 15,000 English bowmen nearly wiped out over 60,000 mounted French knights. By the 1350s, crossbows had become well-established and well-integrated military weaponry. Steel arches replaced wood and enhanced the crossbow's destructive power. A windlass was added two decades later. Addition of the windlass to pull back the bowstring further reduced whatever skill, size, and physical dexterity had been necessary to function as a bowman.

Pikes began to make a significant impact on warfare a bit before crossbows gained currency. Foot soldiers carried these 10-foot-long wooden shafts (some were nearly 18 feet long) with sharp iron heads first as a defensive measure to ward off charges from armored horsemen. Standing still with the base of their poles dug into the ground and with their pikes crossed, pikemen served as an almost impenetrable shield. To attempt to assault the pike defensive formation, armored knights had to dismount, making them easy prey for swordsmen and halberdiers. By the mid-fourteenth century, the Swiss had neatly integrated the pike into their offensive as well as defensive formulations. The Swiss military took as its new formation a dynamic, mobile multidimensional shape that organized pikemen into compact, 6,000-men squares and gave them extensive training in precise and rapid movement. Pikemen thus arranged provided multidirectional offensive and defensive capabilities; the square shape eliminated vulnerable sides or exposed flanks as carefully choreographed infantrymen learned to mount (and withstand) charge after charge while retaining the integrity of their formations. Like the phalanx of the Greek past, Swiss pikemen aimed to overrun their enemies. Only after the pike square proved its mettle did the Swiss integrate other forms. Use of bowmen, who could attack at long distance, balanced the intensely immediate pikemen and provided the square considerable flexibility. Again coordination among square members was paramount.

The adept Swiss achieved their independence from the Habsburg monarchy in the later fourteenth century and were hired by the French and Italians as mercenaries soon after. The Swiss pikemen-dominated phalanx had spread throughout the continent by the mid-fifteenth century. As the phalanx pervaded Europe, the Swiss continued their innovation: They added firearm-bearing foot soldiers to support pikemen.

Early handguns were rude affairs. Little more than iron bars crudely welded around mandrels to form tubes and attached to wooden stocks because the tubes proved much too hot to touch, the first guns measured less than 10 inches in length. These and all subsequent early guns were loaded through their muzzles. The gunman first introduced a charge of fine gunpowder and then followed the powder with a wad of material, which was rammed down the barrel to seal the chamber in order to utilize the full force of the rapid gaseous expansion caused by gunpowder ignition. The projectile came next and a barrel-sealing wad finished the loading operation. A gunman fired his weapon by taking the smoldering cloth held in one hand and touching it to the firearm's touchhole to ignite the gunpowder charge.

Europeans tried numerous permutations of this basic firearm design and by 1500 had settled on the arquebus. These stock-fitted guns had 50-inch-long barrels, which gave the gun increased power and accuracy. Whenever the gunman engaged the trigger, an affixed smoldering match reached the touchhole and detonated the powder, which eliminated the need for soldiers to handlight each charge. The Spanish refined the gun a bit further in the early sixteenth century by creating the musket, a 6-foot-long, 15-pound device that could hurl lead bullets up to 200 yards. Not until about 1590 did a flint-steel firing mechanism replace earlier ignition systems. Pistols, simply smaller versions of the arquebus, emerged with that gun but offered no military advantage. Pistols were difficult to use on horseback. Loading and firing generally required horsemen to dismount. The short barrel made pistols much less accurate than the longer-barreled muskets.

Introduction of the handgun, proliferation and improvement of the crossbow, and the establishment of pike squares as the central defensive and offensive formation doomed the cavalry. As early as 1530, only 9 percent of French and about 8 percent of Spanish armies rode horses. What remained of the cavalry existed generally to pursue and capture fleeing foes.

Siege Warfare

By 1630, handguns had become a central feature of each state's military efforts. But handguns were not the first gunpowder weapons to influence military affairs. Nor were they always the most significant. Threatened infantry often withdrew behind fortifications rather than risk a losing battle. Weapons to breach fortified areas were crucial and cannons emerged as the earliest successful use of gunpowder technology. Cannons existed in Europe from the mid-fourteenth century (if not earlier) and were commonplace after 1400.

Medieval Europeans constructed castle and city walls to withstand boring, ramming, and scaling, but not to bear up to massive aerial bombardment. The earliest gunpowder bombards ironically could not significantly damage the structures; these weapons mostly made noise and only occasionally produced injury. Early cannons fired arrows, were shaped like vases, and were composed of iron strips welded and held together with thick iron rings. An old-fashioned catapult or trebuchet packed a greater wallop. Not until about 1430 did cannons begin to achieve superiority over traditional siege devices. The new cannons were marked by spherical shot (and,

Cannon. Cannons replaced traditional siege weapons by the 1430s. Within one-half century, a more radical transformation had taken place. Smaller, mobile cannons gained use as field artillery. These multipurpose cannons were lighter than earlier field weapons and easily adjustable.

within a half-century, 30-pound iron cannonballs), tubular barrels to maximize the impact of gaseous expansion, and bronze or brass cast bodies to prohibit seepage, to allow for greater explosion, and to provide a smooth, consistent bore. Replacement of finely ground gunpowder by corned gunpowder enabled cannoneers to reduce the amount of powder per charge and greatly to increase cannon capacity. Fine gunpowder tended to clump or consolidate when rammed into a cannon's mouth. The surface of the gunpowder mass would ignite but the flame could not pass through the charge's heart until the projectile had been expelled and oxygen introduced; only a small part of the charge would power the object. As significant, fine powder often separated during long, bumpy journeys, and the saltpeter and sulfur gravitated to the bottom. Only a thorough reintegration of its elements at the site of battle restored the powder to its earlier proportions. Unlike fine powder, corned powder was mixed when wet. The paste was then spread and allowed to dry into cake, which was finally crumbled into granular form. Each grain now contained the same proportion of sulfur, charcoal, and saltpeter—cannoneers did not have to remix corned powder at the site of the siege—while the granules resisted every attempt to pack them too tightly for complete and proper ignition.

These cannons were extremely effective. One breached Constantinople's mighty walls in 1453. For nearly a century after their introduction, no means existed to defend against them. Nor did cannoneers stop trying to improve their machines. Early attempts focused on making cannons larger but military men quickly learned that bigger was not necessarily better or even more powerful. These behemoths, some of which weighed over 35,000 pounds, were almost impossible to move—the Constantinople cannon was cast on the spot rather than transported from a distant place—and proved sitting targets for defensive weapons. In the 1460s and 1470s, a radical change took place. Cannoneers abandoned their dream of bigger cannons for weapons that would be mobile on the battlefield and therefore have several uses. These multipurpose cannons measured only 8 feet in length, threw iron cannonballs of between 20 and 30 pounds, and were mounted on horse-drawn carriages. Trunnions located near the carriage's center enabled cannoneers to adjust the firing angle of this combination field and siege artillery. Movement of the carriage after firing dissipated the force of recoil.

Flemish and French military technicians had pioneered development of the multipurpose cannon. Rulers of other European governments quickly labored to catch up, hiring skilled workers from other lands to build these new cannons. Cannon mercenaries often surreptitiously brought crucial plans and models with them when crossing borders. Cannoning became so important to state success that governments from the late fifteenth century established arsenals and gun foundries—wealthy Spain was among the first—to manufacture these and other weapons and to devise innovations.

England initially lagged behind. Only when cannoneers near Sussex began in the 1540s to fashion cannons out of cast iron did the state catch up and then quickly surpass others in Europe. Sussex ironmen were not the first Europeans to experiment with cast iron, but they were the first to make an effective cast iron cannon. They took advantage of the nearby high-phosphorous iron and coupled casting that iron with a new slow cooling process they developed. Unlike previous cast irons, the Sussex iron thus prepared was not brittle and likely to crack under pressure. Sussex techniques reduced cannon manufacturing costs by nearly three-quarters over brass cannons. The British technique soon became known throughout Europe and Sussex ironmen quickly entered the world of cannon mercenaries. Britain kept its cannon lead but cannoneers enticed from their native Sussex enabled the Swiss and Dutch to seize the cannon export market.

Rising to the Defense

The cannon menace terrified Europe; little seemed to protect against these hideous monsters. From at least the mid-fifteenth century, Europeans tried to modify castle and wall design to counter them. The Italians were among the first and devoted a substantial amount of money to the cause. It is perhaps a misnomer to refer to the Italians collectively for the city-states worked in competition with each other. Competition to find a fortification able to withstand cannon fire was no gentlemanly

quest. City-states hired fortification builders away from each other and these mercenaries carried their knowledge from place to place. But while city-states took advantage of each other's insights, they most expressly did not work in tandem. To the Italians wanting new fortifications as well as those hoping to formulate them, the whole
cannon fortification issue was purely a matter of design. What shape or series of
shapes would negate the authority of cannons? That definition of the question circumscribed the field of likely candidates. Those experienced with design—any type
of design—or design techniques took up the challenge. They included jewelers and
goldsmiths as well as painters, sculptors, and architects. It remained a matter for
designers, not builders.

From the beginning, these designers conceived of the design question not simply
in terms of length and width but also depth and height; they examined the question
multidimensionally and on several geometric planes. They also adopted the perspective of the cannoneer, seeking to learn what situations and conditions hampered or
destroyed his ability to wreak havoc. That perspective led the designers to observe
that although solid masonry or rock crumbled when struck by a cannonball, loosely
heaped earth merely absorbed the blow and suffered no significant malformation or
damage. They also realized that cannons shot in a moderately straight line and were
most effective attacking structures that stood high on the horizon. Italian designers

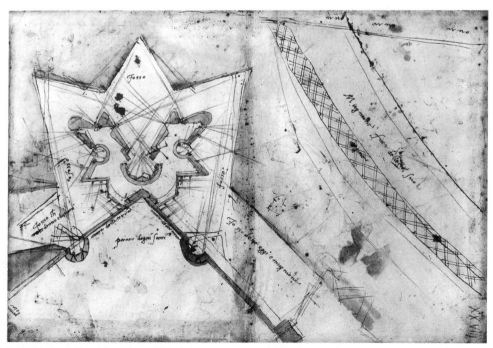

Renaissance Fortifications. The vast majority of noted Renaissance artists also designed
fortifications. Shape, depth, texture, and other three-dimensional concerns dominated their
plans. Star-shaped fortifications proved especially popular, because they enabled defenders to
focus the fire of two bastions on any attacker.

understood that a point was less likely to be hit from afar by cannon fire than a broad flat or semicircular protuberance.

The Italians combined these structural and substantive insights to create a new fortification in the half century after 1470. Rather than situate the place to be protected on a bluff, as was the case with Constantinople's citadel, the Italians chose to locate their town, castle, or fort in a humanmade depression. Thus they dug a huge ditch and placed an earthen wall—really piles of dirt removed to make the ditch—around the entire ditch. While the earthen wall rested at the ditch edge, the fort itself was centered in the middle of the ditch, somewhat distant from the earth barrier. The walls of this middle structure tended to be significantly higher than the surrounding earthen facade but to appear much lower; they were in the ditch while the other walls were outside it. As a matter of course, no siege machine could send a straight-line projectile from the higher ground to the center structure. Cannonballs would harmlessly land in the dirt wall.

Italians took precautions to defend the inner fort when the earthen barriers were breached. Wedge-shaped protuberances, known as bastions, jutted out from fort walls. Loaded with cannon and other firearms, bastions served to defend the walls proper. Any enemy seeking to lay siege to the wall from the ditch would immediately be attacked by two bastions' batteries. The closer the enemy and their cannon came to the wall the greater the benefits of the crossfire. Bastions not only guarded the walls but also each other. Regularly positioned bastions placed around the fort at blunt, outward angles offered complete protection.

Inner fortifications designed in this manner were symmetrical and resembled stars of five or more sides. The elegance and regularity of this structure pleased the Italians, who quickly accepted Vitruvius as their spiritual forebear. A dozen editions of the classic appeared in Italy before 1560. Several Italians published their own treatises in homage to that great author. Like Vitruvius, they acknowledged the centrality of mathematics to architecture as enabling builders to calculate costs as well as elevations. But their real focus in the fortification chapters was on explaining the virtuousness of these new structures. This analysis was pursued in characteristic Age of Humankind terms. The purpose of fortifications was "to stymie one's enemies . . . and to render the world more beautiful and enjoyable." Their beauty should "disarm [the enemy's] anger"; the structures "ought to look fierce, terrible, rugged, dangerous and unconquerable." Their dignity came from their harmony and their beauty stemmed from their geometrical form. These divinely harmonious ratios, proportions, and shapes were taken from humankind. Humanity remained the measure as proper "proportions, qualities . . . the square and every other measure is derived from man." Humankind even provided a model of the parts of the fortification itself. Bastions were likened to arms and batteries to eyes. The Italians also made analogies between fortifications and human ears, shoulders, noses, and testicles. Michelangelo, who like many Italian artists and sculptors, found his earliest employment as a fortifications designer, maintained as did his numerous colleagues that "there is no question that architectural members reflect the members of man."

By 1520, the new Italian fortifications had proved their ability to withstand even the most potent assaults. Within a decade, they spread from Italy across Europe. Although new fortifications were built according to these plans, it was unrealistic to destroy and reconfigure large cities. Yet these places too were infused with the

Italian scheme. Earthen barriers in front of stone walls and bastions extending around and beyond city walls became commonplace.

Wealth: Africa and the New World

Another strategy to increase the wealth of a society lessened chances of immediate conflict and protected traditional sources of state wealth. Most wealth had been generated by cannibalizing the natural resources within a state's borders and converting them into marketable goods. After about 1400, states increasingly looked beyond their geopolitical boundaries (and the boundaries of their European neighbors) to seize untapped resources in new or less frequented venues.

Portugal: Gold and Spices

Africa became the initial target. Europeans coveted African gold as a means to African wealth. Muslim traders had purchased substantial quantities of gold from Africans as early as the tenth century, carried it across the Sahara to the Mediterranean, and sold it to Italian merchants dominating the Mediterranean trade. The Italians then reaped huge profits in Europe. By the later-fourteenth century, the wealth of African leaders had assumed mythical proportions and the Atlantic-bound, gold-poor Portuguese saw an opportunity to circumvent both the Italians and Muslims and to seize African gold themselves. Led by Prince Henry the Navigator, son of King John I, the Portuguese hired intellectual and sailing mercenaries; Henry employed men of foreign origin because of their reputed knowledge of the most modern sailing technique or their familiarity with African geography and the location of prolific gold deposits. Henry incorporated their fund of knowledge and experience in his plans. He outfitted ship after ship and proceeded to send them ever farther down the West African coast. Never venturing beyond sight of land, Henry's mercenaries made their initial voyage in 1415 and arrived at the Gold Coast in 1455. They erected fortifications at each stop down the coast and took great pains to learn about the inhabitants there. Henry, in fact, became obsessed with the Africans and had several carried back to Lisbon to serve as part of his household. Beginning about the time of Henry's death in 1460, the Portuguese consolidated, expanded, and exploited their new African holdings. Military outposts now also served as trading posts as the Portuguese swapped colorful trinkets and fabrics for first gold and ivory and then slaves. At least 1,000 slaves reached the Portuguese capital every year after 1450.

The vast majority of slaves went not to Portugal but to sugar and pepper growers on Portuguese-colonized islands off the African coast. Portuguese use of Africans as slaves was a first for a European power. It stemmed from factors similar to Portugal's decision to establish its own African connection. Portugal's isolation from the Mediterranean made it nearly impossible for Portugal to secure slaves from the Middle East to work these new island agricultural plantations. Forcing Muslims from their final European strongholds and converting many East European Slavs to Christianity had removed two other potential slave sources. Africans emerged as a likely alternative, in part because they generally were not Christians; forcing them into

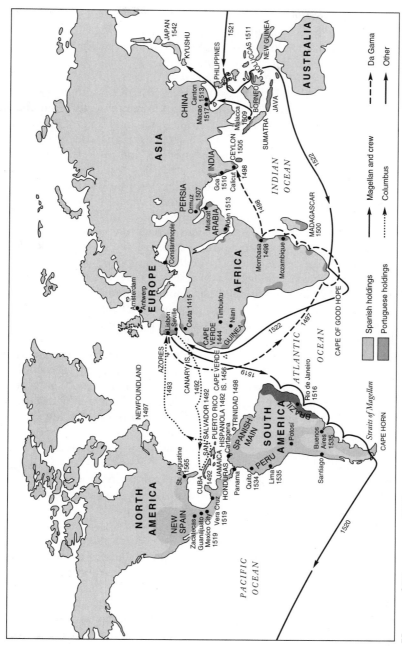

Voyages of Discovery to 1522

slavery did not violate church pronouncements. As important, slavery in sub-Saharan Africa was a long-standing institution. Chieftains had long sold tribal members and reduced captured enemies to slavery.

But slavery was a consequence of African exploration, not its cause. Gold had been its intended goal, only to be supplanted by sugar and the more dear pepper. Securing pepper from these "lands of many strange races, where marvels abounded" joined the premier commodity of the Far East spice trade with a rationale for African exploitation and perhaps refocused Portuguese ambitions. As with the gold and slave trades, Venetian, Genoan, and other Italian city-states long had a monopoly on the spice trade. They exchanged gold for spices with Muslim traders directly connected to the Orient at Alexandria, Algiers, Tunis, and Beirut; India and China wanted little that was European other than precious metals. The Italians then brought their valuable cargoes of pepper, nutmeg, cloves, cinnamon, ginger, and other exotic spices overland to sell in Western Europe.

Prior to the mid-fourteenth century, only the wealthiest Europeans chose to indulge themselves with spices. But demand for these expensive commodities gained new immediacy after about 1350. The heightened appeal of spices corresponded to an increased emphasis on human emotions and perceptions—those senses common to all humans. Europeans desired and concerned themselves with defining and developing a full sensory experience, a well-rounded if not complete sampling of the senses as partial demarcation of humankind's realm. Taste proved no exception. Culinary pleasure was at a premium but emphasis on taste cannot be correlated to a dramatic change in the European diet. For most common Europeans, diet remained as it had been. Fourteenth-century Europeans had no rice, corn, or potatoes and little cheese or butter. Fresh fruits and vegetables were eaten only in season. Fresh meat consumption was limited to the late fall when a mass slaughtering of animals, generally old, retired work animals, occurred. If Europeans consumed meat at all during the rest of the year, it was dried and salted. A coarse-ground bread and a thin gruel made of meal boiled in water were staples and were supplemented with pickled cabbage, turnips, peas, lentils, and onions. Rather than the product of a new dietary reality, accentuation of taste stemmed from new expectations. Material pleasures were not necessarily to be denied nor were they necessarily to be restricted to a very small segment of humanity.

Creation of a myriad of sauces to color or transform the outwardness—the taste—of the mundane diet became high art. As early as the 1390s, cookbooks appeared to assist those less adept in masking or transmuting the taste of everyday foods. The almost alchemical art of disguise depended on spices, and states bordering the Atlantic Ocean quickly realized that conventional trade with the Orient required them to pass great wealth to the Italian and Muslim traders as well as to India and China. Blocked from direct access to the Mediterranean or an overland route to the Orient, Atlantic states, led by Portugal, put into practice the idea, long held by educated Europeans, that the world was spherical; on this three-dimensional world, travel south permitted the voyager to reach the north and voyages west would ultimately enable the traveler to reach east. Europeans employed intellectual and sailing mercenaries, who, based on Greco-Roman writings and their experiences, including stories told them by others, estimated the size of the earth and the extent of Africa as far smaller than they actually are. These men, often Genoans—Genoa itself was facing stiff competition for the Asian trade—could not refer to maps drawn in the Middle Ages or before for confirmation. These earlier, two-dimensional maps were either of the known world, which generally meant the Mediterranean basin, and oriented by the twelve winds, or of specific ports and harbors. In both cases, they offered no rectification.

These bold prospects, coupled with the new emphasis on exploring humankind's realm, encouraged first the Portuguese and then the Spanish. The English, French and Dutch followed later still. Portugal cautiously but progressively continued down the west coast of Africa, going south to get north. They reached the Cape of Good Hope in 1489 and India in 1497. Forty-nine of 50 Portuguese expeditions returned safely. By 1500, the Portuguese had secured most of the trade once monopolized by African Muslims and in 1509 defeated a Muslim fleet sent to dislodge them from the Indian Ocean. By 1515, Portuguese domination was so complete that it forced the Venetians to get their pepper from Lisbon.

Spain: Gold and Silver

The Portuguese did not sponsor all persons seeking to discover a sea route to the Orient. The Genoan Christopher Columbus sailed for Portugal in 1482 but the king denied his 1484 request for support to find a route to India. The Spanish monarchs Ferdinand and Isabella proved more receptive and Columbus received his Spanish commission in January 1492. Rather than attempt to circumnavigate Africa to get to Asia, Columbus went west to get east. He reached the Bahamas in October and met with the islands' inhabitants, the "Indians," to celebrate his triumphant voyage. Columbus made three subsequent trips but died without recognizing that he had not found a western route to India. Others confirmed that Columbus had discovered a continent unknown to Europeans resting between Europe and Asia. The Spanish explorer Vasco Núñez de Balboa was the first European to set sight on the Pacific Ocean and ships under the command of Ferdinand Magellan circumnavigated the world between 1519 and 1522.

The "Indians" that populated this "New World" that the Spanish had uncovered were victimized by disease and European weaponry and could provide only minimal resistance. Hernando Cortez landed in Mexico in 1519 and within two years had conquered the great Aztec empire. Francisco Pizarro experienced similar success a decade later against the Incas of Peru. The indigenous population of Mexico fell from 25 million in 1492 to 6 million in 1540 and to a scant 1.5 million in 1650. The New World quickly paid culinary and monetary dividends. Corn, peanuts, pumpkins, papayas, pineapples, tomatoes, cocoa, chili peppers, potatoes, sweet potatoes, tapioca, squashes, and avocados all came to Europe from the New World and offered new and exciting tastes. Aztec chocolate became a European health food after about 1520 and, by 1560, tobacco grown in the New World had become a European staple. Nor were they only sensory experiences that resulted from exploration. Ethiopian coffee reached Europe about 1450 and coffeehouses soon followed. Japanese tea gave rise to Western European teahouses.

The Spanish New World also became a feedlot for livestock. In 1550, there were a half million goats, sheep, and cattle there; by 1600, it held over 8 million. The Spanish also carried copper, sugar, and indigo back to the old world—they quickly introduced enslaved Africans into the Caribbean to grow the sugar and indigo—but precious metals constituted the single greatest source of New World wealth. The earliest Spaniards simply raided the Aztec and Inca hoards but these extensive repositories quickly ran dry and mining made up the slack. The Spanish converted many of the surviving Aztecs and Incas into mining slaves and hired German metallurgists as early as the 1530s to supervise the extraction process. These metallurgic mercenaries adapted to the New World a silver ore purification process first used in Venetian mines some half-century earlier. The mercury-amalgamation process enabled miners to quadruple output as lower-grade silver ores were tapped for their precious material. Still other veins were discovered and mined. These New World mines grew so productive that the main Spanish New World business became silver mining. From 1564, no less than 20 and sometimes as many as 60 ships yearly left the New World for Spain packed with silver and gold bullion.

The tremendous increase in wealth brought to the old world spawned unprecedented inflation. For example, Spanish prices more than doubled by 1560 and doubled again before 1630. Nor was Spain unique. In some parts of Europe cereal prices were eight times higher in 1620 than they had been a century earlier. An unprecedented population boom exacerbated the situation as the number of Europeans doubled between 1460 and 1620. Cobbled together by the marriage of Ferdinand and Isabella in the late fifteenth century, Spain by the mid-sixteenth century emerged as the wealthiest, most powerful European state. Monarchical policy to step up production helped achieve that end. For example, Ferdinand and Isabella provided economic incentives for the shepherds' guild to extend its operations over an area much larger than before. Royal policy not only fostered production agriculture and a well-paying cash crop but also transformed what had been cropland into pasture, freeing up labor and creating a ready supply of army recruits. Yet the rapid inflation, coupled by the demands of an overseas empire, led Spain's rulers to repudiate the state debt five times in the 70 years after 1557, placing Spain at a marked disadvantage in international markets. Merchants demanded cash and refused to accept credit, a move which forced Spain to rely more heavily on New World bullion. As long as the supply held out, Spain could sustain its European prominence. Portugal had experienced a somewhat similar debt problem a bit earlier. Its explorations and the need to defend itself against the ever mightier Spain forced the Portuguese to accept loans from German and other bankers. Economic restrictions accompanied the loans, rendering the state less able to compete with its neighbors. By 1580, Portugal had fallen under Spain's grip.

The plight of Portugal and Spain exposed the centrality of sixteenth-century merchants to the new production economy. Merchants placed their wealth in many ventures to cut the risk from any one investment. The Florentine Medici, for example, bought and sold raw wool and woolen cloth as well as silk and raw cotton. They specialized in alum and other dyestuffs. But they also invested in spices, olive oil, and citrus fruits. The Medici traded without regard to state borders and transported goods across them, changed money, served as bankers, insurance brokers, and industrialists, and speculated in urban and rural real estate. The patriarch of the House of Fugger, Jakob Fugger, parlayed early-sixteenth-century loans to Charles V and Emperor Maximilian I to become the world's leading copper and silver merchant. Fugger controlled copper from production to distribution; he owned Hungarian copper mines, refineries, foundries, and forges. Fugger became the papal banker—the papal monarchy depended on his business acumen to stretch its resources—and, as a reward for his efforts, managed the sale of papal indulgences in Germany.

Inflation raised prices and generated additional revenue to invest in trading and production of goods. Although this wealth was disproportionately distributed among the population, much of it went into increasing the supply of woolen textiles. From the thirteenth century, textiles had been the surest way to wealth, but the market for heavy woolens skyrocketed when Scandinavian demand was realized. Manufacture of these goods had moved westward by the sixteenth century. Florence left wool for silk and was joined by France, which also produced linens. The Netherlands gravitated to light woolens. England, formerly merely a wool producer, much more than made up the slack by becoming the leading woolen manufacturer. English manors emerged as sites both of wool production and of woolen cloth manufacture. Enclosed manors pastured sheep. Those serfs not displaced from the land either tended the sheep or made wool. Rural manufactories sought to supplant urban guilds, which increasingly seemed expensive and contrary. Tensions between masters and journeymen erupted into disputes over wages, hours, holidays, and food. In the new, extensive rural putting out system, guild controls over wages and quality of merchandise were absent and several stages of production occurred under a single roof. Sometimes several hundred operators worked in the same multifaceted and multitasked facility.

Ships

The fully rigged ship became the vessel upon which most Age of Humankind sea trade and exploration occurred. The ship itself was new, replacing the two major varieties of ships that had been the backbone of the Mediterranean trade: round cargo ships and war galleys. The lateen-sailed, single-masted, flat-bottomed round ships were relatively slow, cumbersome, and awkward, but their design facilitated transport of large amounts of goods. Galleys accompanied round ships and provided defense. These narrow, highly maneuverable, oared vessels were around 120 feet in length, usually had 24 benches on each side, and seated three men per oar. A single mast carrying a lateen sail rose above the deck. A catapult-like device rested at the bow, but boarding the enemy's vessel and then winning at hand-to-hand combat with the oarsmen remained the main source of victory at sea. Crossbow-bearing archers situated in the crow's nest provided aerial defense against boarding.

Oar-powered galleys offered maneuverability unmatched by early sailships and, therefore, only other galleys could contest them. Their military superiority commended them to northern Europeans, who used galleys to patrol the coasts and inland waterways. Many of these ships had been built by Italian-trained ship carpenters, who, beginning in the very late thirteenth century, began a practice that would persist for several hundred years—selling their skills and the latest knowledge of ship design to northern Europeans. Introduction of shipboard cannon in the late fifteenth century made galley prospects somewhat less certain. Shipbuilders initially replaced the galley's catapult with a single cannon, but Mediterranean states soon turned to making larger, bigger galleys with several guns. More massive cannon-carrying

The Galley. Under oar or sail power, the galley had dominated Mediterranean trade since Greco-Roman time. Gradually, its catapults gave way to a single cannon and then batteries of cannon. This floating gun platform would prove no match for the fully rigged ship in the open seas.

galleys required more oarsmen to retain maneuverability. A variant of the galley popular in the early sixteenth century, the galeass, had more guns than the galley and as many as 700 men on board. Expansion of the number of oarsmen per vessel, coupled with the casting of guns, caused galley operation costs to skyrocket. Despite exorbitant costs, these floating gun platforms proved effective striking forces. Armies no longer needed to board vessels to defeat enemies or to defend merchant ships.

The Portuguese and later the Spanish voyages of discovery had no use for galleys, which held too few provisions and required too many men for long, open-sea travel. Henry the Navigator's Genoan shipbuilding mercenaries led him to adopt the caravel, a small, two-masted, lateen-sailed ship of southern European origin. The caravel handled excellently—the Portuguese sailed near the coast in frequently

uncharted waters so split-second maneuverability was essential—but spatial requirements of long-distance travel led designers to increase the ship's width. That
expanded its carrying capacity so designers added a third mast as compensation.

The caravel was a single-purpose vessel. It worked well as an explorer but it lacked
other attributes. It could not carry large quantities of gold and slaves or function as
a successful cannon platform; the caravel was neither a cargo carrier nor a fighting
ship, two activities required after initial exploration. Portugal's early Atlantic interest
stimulated the Basque in what is now northern Spain, who also hoped to circumvent
Italian merchants. But unlike the Portuguese, the Basque during the first half of the
fifteenth century—Spain did not become a meaningful geopolitical unit until the
union of Ferdinand and Isabella late in the century—did not seek a direct link to Asia
or to capitalize on African gold. The Basque focused instead on establishing direct
trade routes with northern European and Mediterranean trading partners, thus
bypassing the Italians. This trade objective ended any thought of using the small,
swift caravel. But the Basque familiarity with the North Atlantic and North Sea also
led them to dismiss Mediterranean vessels as much too flimsy to bear up in the
strong storms and choppy waters. What Basque designers did was fashion a boat that
could achieve their purposes and meet the environmental conditions. This multipurpose vessel needed to hold up in rough seas, maneuver smartly in rough, calm, and
uncharted waters, possess a large cargo capacity, and defend itself against small pirate
vessels and great galleys. The Basque ship, the fully rigged ship, incorporated a delicate balance of technologies to permit the vessel to navigate in extraordinarily different situations. The ship was a matter of design. Designers needed to confront two
multidimensional problems. They needed to design a configuration that would
enable ships to cut into the wind in almost any way ship captains would want, regard-
less of the direction and speed of the wind. In addition, they needed to locate shipboard space for the many masts, sails, and other navigational devices that such a multidimensional perspective entailed. Basque designers greatly expanded the number of
sails and masts, incorporated several different sail shapes and designs, and pioneered
the division of square sails. They carefully placed the sails and masts in precise relation to one another—fore, aft, and offset as well as at different heights and on different planes—and to the rudder, varied the height of castles on deck and the ship's
length-to-beam ratio, and joined the sternrudder to the keel. Introduction of cannon,
first on the deck and then beneath it, completed the design process. Gunports with
waterproof covers were cut near the waterline to increase ship stability. Recoil would
bring the barrels into the ship, which would ease reloading. The guns were then
pushed forward to fire.

The fully rigged ship dominated European waters until the nineteenth century. It
was the kind of vessel that Columbus sailed to the New World. These ships conquered the Muslim fleets in the South Seas. Rather than ramming and boarding, fully
rigged ships attempted to move to the wind and broadside the enemy with cannons.
Asian and New World natives had no defense for shipboard artillery. The Spanish
galleon, which comprised the backbone of the dreaded Armada, was a less castled and
rounded variant of the fully rigged ship as were its nemeses, the smaller, quicker
English craft led by Francis Drake. The Dutch vessels used to help block the Spanish at the English Channel and thus to secure and preserve the Netherlands's independence from that economic giant were also fully rigged. These ships would also

carry the Dutch to European trade domination in the next century. The Dutch built more fully rigged ships yearly in the early seventeenth century than the other European nations combined. Dutch sea superiority gave rise to Amsterdam and let the country control much of the spice trade and a considerable part of the New World in the early 1600s.

Representing Humankind and Its Realm

Civic Architecture

Three-dimensional space played a prominent role in naval and military architectural design. That three-dimensionality also was an important part of Age of Humankind civic architecture ought not to surprise. Many military architects also were civic architects. These civic designers turned to military architecture and from military to civic architecture because they followed the money. They earned their livelihoods as mercenaries, designing structures for either military or civic patrons. But the three-dimensional considerations that proved critical to both military and civic designers often differed somewhat. For example, ship designers examined means to interact with the wind and the ocean current as well as shipboard space requirements to achieve maximum flexibility. Fortification designers dealt with planes, with ways of intervening between a projectile and its target, and with establishing configurations that provided maximum firepower as well as defensive capabilities. Rarely were explicitly epistemological concerns addressed. Some historians have suggested that the star-like shape of late-fifteenth- and sixteenth-century fortifications testified to the Age of Humankind's belief in the harmonic relationship between heaven and earth, but few contemporary documents directly support that contention.

When architects designed Age of Humankind civic structures they were not reticent about explaining the philosophical underpinnings of their designs. Italian civic architects consciously looked and pointed to their Roman forebears for inspiration and Vitruvius emerged as a civic architectural patron saint. The oneness and indivisibility of the universe provided the basis of design and the harmony of the human body its earthly reflection and application. "Because from the human body derive all measures and their important denominations," then in the body "is to be found all and every ratio and proportion by which God reveals the innermost secrets of nature." The prominent early-fifteenth-century Florentine architect, Leone Battista Alberti, extended the analysis. Alberti explained that since humanity was made in god's image and since a spread-eagled human fit neatly within a circle, then the sphere (a circle rotated through three-dimensional space) was the perfect shape and the basis of divine harmony. This divine harmony Alberti and other early Italian civic designers reserved for the church. To these Age of Humankind men, the church was the institution that god gave humanity, the creature god created in god's image, and its design justifiably was to portray god and humankind's intimate relation to its creator. A church was to be a sublimely beautiful, geometrically perfect, circular building that stood alone in the center of a city, rising from a pedestal in the middle of a spacious piazza. Andrea Palladio, the great mid-sixteenth-century Venetian civic architect and author of the *Four Books on Architecture*—an obvious homage to Vitruvius—explained the majesty of the circular church as a consequence of its form. A circular church, Palladio argued, "is enclosed by one circumference only, in which is to be found neither beginning nor end, and the one is indistinguishable from the other; its parts correspond to each other and all of them participate in the shape of the whole; and moreover every part being equally distant from the center, such a building demonstrates extremely well the unity, the infinite essence, the uniformity and the justice of God."

Architects placed the altar in the exact center of their symmetrical church, equidistant from all points on the circumference. Humanity then accepted god at the focus of the circle, a fit place for god's special creation. Atop the entire church rested a dome, which gave the circular building a spherical appearance. Italians chained their domes in place with iron bands buried in upper walls. Even those churches that were simply remodeled or expanded during the later fifteenth and sixteenth centuries exhibited the emphasis on the unity of humankind and the One. Semicircular arches and vaults as well as domes spread from Italy to France before 1500 and to Spain and England in the mid-1500s.

A few designers decided against circular churches and used other shapes for religious structures. Despite the differences in shape, the same tenets remained vital. Square churches, churches shaped like a Greek cross with four equal arms, or octagonal churches, which could be circumscribed within a circle, each drew attention to the exact center, to humanity as a crucial aspect of the divine One.

Northern Europeans devoted less attention to building churches than did their southern counterparts. Much of the northern civic architecture was royal and mercantile, not religious. Yet like civic religious architecture, secular architecture in the Age of Humankind was regular, stately, and substantive, not soaring and ethereal like its Gothic predecessors. It too depended heavily on Greece and Rome.

Painting and Sculpture

Painting and sculpture in the Age of Humankind were also a matter of design. Artists in conjunction with their patrons needed to determine what they would represent and how they would represent it. Both issues apparently changed over time. Art historians and other scholars have identified these changes serially as Renaissance, Mannerist and Baroque art. To be sure, the subject matter differed. Renaissance art was oriented toward the past—specifically, the Greco-Roman past—while Baroque art was oriented toward the human senses. Styles also varied. Renaissance art highlighted perspective, Mannerist art accentuated emotions, and Baroque art paid special attention to creating a feeling of timelessness and spacelessness. Despite these stylistic variants, however, fundamental similarities persist among these styles. Each incorporated multidimensionality—not necessarily multiple perspective—into its vision; each painter attempted to fashion three-dimensional images on a two-dimensional medium. Humanity and humanity's realm persisted as the focus and different perspectives on those subjects were the central stylistic themes. Whether attempting to create a universal perspective or an individual perspective or to explore the idea of an infinity of perspectives, Age of Humankind artists and painters devised any number of new techniques to provide the visual representation that they sought. These

Albrecht Dürer's *Knight of Death*. Accompanied by Sin and Death as footman and squire, respectively, Dürer's knight travels to the wars. This potent image addresses the seeming lack of clear moral purpose to Renaissance warfare. Also, note Dürer's technique. This engraving leaps off the page. Its attention to detail is striking, as is its concern for shape and shading.

outwardnesses were visual understandings of the appearance of things. Their inwardnesses remained disguised and constant, ultimately part of the divine One.

Age of Humankind artists and sculptors realized that they were presenting visions, outwardnesses, not reality or inwardnesses. Leonardo da Vinci said it simply: "The good painter must paint principally two things: man and the ideas on man's mind." Representing these "divine proportions" required great skill and Albrecht Dürer, a German contemporary of Leonardo, provided Leonardo's description substance. He explained representation as geometry, the "foundation of the whole graphic art." Without "a great and true understanding" of the compass and the rule, Dürer argued, "no one can either be or become an absolute artist." Artists must see "not only by simple straight lines, but by straight lines of sight, by reflected lines of sight . . . or refracted lines of sight." Artists must process and draw this multidimensional perspective of "all seen things into one cone towards the eye, whose point is in the eye and whose base or foundation is the seen thing." What artists painted was not reality or true beauty, things known only to god, but human representations—regular geometric shapes—of those things. "For what the world prizes as right we hold to be right, so that all the world esteems beautiful that we also hold for beautiful and ourselves strive to produce the like." In his two classic texts, *Instruction in Measurement* and *Four Books of Human Proportion*, Dürer established that the important geometric shapes had a divine basis and joined heaven and earth. Geometry was derived from the proportions of the human body, which reflected the laws governing the heavens as established by god, the architect of the universe. In yet another way, humanity served as the measure.

The early Age of Humankind artists rediscovered the Greco-Roman past and portrayed classical themes in classical, not Christian, terms and contexts. They also painted frescoes and numerous portraits. These artists integrated the background with the subject of the picture to create a kind of organic unity. Placing their subjects in context, including scenes from everyday life, permitted them to show the diversity and multiplicity of the human experience; it also helped portray physical size, distance, and depth as it provided any number of reference points on any number of presumed planes. Almost always persons were engaged in some activity. Motion and dynamism seemed inseparable parts of the human life.

These early artists achieved three-dimensionality and perspective by alternating light and shade through their egg-based paints, by foreshortening, and by arranging physical space on the canvas to tell a story and to suggest directional movement. Proportion, balance, and harmony were important from the beginning in portraying heroic humankind, but not until the early fifteenth century did artists, particularly in Italy, reduce perspective to a series of mathematical equivalents. The human body, especially the unadorned nude, symbolized that mathematical precision. Artists and sculptors recognized in humanity the divine proportions and studied human anatomy to achieve them. Through use of human models, artists fashioned an extraordinary number of studies of the human body. Freestanding nude sculptures, reintroduced in the early fifteenth century for the first time since Greco-Roman antiquity, emerged as a common expression of humankind's dominion in this world and as testament to humankind's relationship to its creator.

Northern European artists introduced oil-based paints into their craft because these paints provided a more lifelike appearance. By the later fifteenth century that technological innovation led Italian artists to revisit the conflicting demands of three-dimensional expression on a two-dimensional surface. Perspective conveyed depth and distance. Composition gave the appearance of either enhancing or minimizing but it had a three-dimensional reality; paint on canvas rests on several different planes. Harmonizing actual representations with idealized images was an early casualty. Geometric preciseness came at a cost of solidity and anatomical correctness as artists substituted grace and flowing lines, especially of necks and shoulders, for actual proportions. They also left outlines of body parts a bit vague and shadowy, which created a softening atmosphere and enabled artists to reconcile reality, design, and perspective. Leonardo's *Mona Lisa* exemplified that technique. Late fifteenth- and early sixteenth-century artists also used color for composition to achieve a sense of unity and harmony. In portraiture, background achieved new immediacy. Some artists used landscapes, especially rich or colorful landscapes, to give their works emotive force. Others simplified backgrounds, reducing them simply to shades of black, brown, or gray. Shading gave the paintings direction and movement and conveyed a potent sense of the multidimensionality of human emotions. The vast storehouse of humanity's emotions was also explored, unlocked and represented by backgrounds that were simply gradations of colors, especially earth tones. A rich burnt orange appeared frequently. Artists often set their works near open fires or hearths to use the color and shape of flames and their reflections on human visages to achieve

Sistine Chapel. Humans abound in Michelangelo's paintings of the Sistine Chapel, the symbolic home of the papacy and Catholicism, generally. Even the deity takes on human appearance as the ceiling mural has a grandfatherly god touch Adam to life.

dynamic emotions. The Mannerists used shape to suggest emotional power, deliberately rejecting graceful lines for tortured forms. Sixteenth-century brushstrokes were accentuated and many artists refused to harmonize them. These new brushstroke styles provided depth, movement, and a profound sense of emotionalism. Yet masters, such as Titian, created in their brushstrokes a new kind of dynamic balance, playing off these strokes by incorporating unbalanced sets of figures and reconciling the dissonance through combinations of color and light. Others deliberately rejected graceful lines in favor of tortured shapes to suggest great emotional power. Stock techniques and conventions also provided perspective and holism. Placing open doors, steps, windows, or passageways in a work of art provided depth and demonstrated the relativity of space and distance. So too did the representation of mirrors, which not only provided the possibility of infinite reflection but also permitted artists to fashion both the observed and the observers.

Humankind regularly appeared in almost every painting. The rebirth of portraiture was one manifestation but even paintings focusing on divine creatures were done in human terms and displayed human emotions. The numerous representations of the Madonna and Child, for example, ran the gamut of human emotions—tenderness, love, suffering, and grief. Life and death had fewer moral overtones than during the Gothic period as artists represented them as times of great human emotion, even when drawing the holiest of icons. Rarely were heavenly figures portrayed in the absence of humanity. Michelangelo's fatherly god stretching out to touch and give life to a filial Adam, the central feature in the ceiling of the Sistine Chapel, is perhaps the best known example but even most representations of Christ's crucifixion emphasize the crowd of onlookers as well as Christ's human suffering. The human nude became the central object of art in the early sixteenth century but artists did not restrict their study to anatomy—dissection of the condemned apparently sometimes occurred—or rules of spatial perspective. They also studied human behavior to assist them in placing humankind in the context of the events they depicted as well as in showing humanity's full expressive range.

Machine Design

Similarities embodied in conceptions of fortifications, civic structures, and artistic works also extended to design of machines and explanation of mechanical force. On one level, that was not surprising. Many of the same people engaged in several of those tasks. But the heart of the question went far beyond a small coterie of designers. The vision was not the product of a small design community but of the culture at large. Machine designers talked of employing "the forms and proportions of force and body found in nature" to make mechanical contrivances. To these men, force had shape and relationship to other forces and material forms. Linear and circular force proved much too two-dimensional to capture the complexity, and Age of Humankind machinists talked of cones of power and cones of force. Like the Greeks before them, these people hypothesized three-dimensional fulcrums and continuously acting levers spinning through space. The resulting spiral shape emerged as an Age of Humankind fascination. Screw-cutting machines, multidimensional gearing, cycloid gears, toothed wheels, and various planes of intersection were little more than physical and graphic representations of this mode of thought. Wood screws and threaded bolts with matching nuts, the former used in about 1400 for the first time since Imperial Rome while the latter was first introduced to Europe in around 1450, both incorporated the idea of a three-dimensional spiral in their design. Their form provided unprecedented power to manipulate humankind's realm.

Springs and Clocks

The spring stood within this context as the most important manifestation because it combined form *and* force. Leonardo explained the spring in a way characteristic of the Age of Humankind. Its power "is in the nature of the cone, since its beginning is

Leonardo's Stone-Lifting Machine. In his notebooks, Leonardo sketched hundreds of machines. Yet this passion for machine design did not mark him as unique. Many of his artistic peers drew machinery and often put their drawings into practice by building the devices. Machinery based on the spring or the screw incorporated their multidimensional perspective.

great and it ends in nothing." To balance "such a conical power" required "another conical power." This three-dimensional explanation of a three-dimensional force and body had found utility well before Leonardo's birth. As early as 1410, the great Florentine jeweler, architect, and mechanic Filippo Brunelleschi had begun to construct spring-driven clocks instead of the medieval weight-driven mechanisms. Spring-driven clocks became popular after about 1450. Substitution of a spring, regulated by a fusee opposed at relatively constant torque throughout the spring's unwinding, for a weight-driven escapement permitted clockmakers to make smaller, portable clocks.

Spring clocks proved immensely popular. Some 20-odd master clockmakers worked in Paris in 1550. Over 60 labored in London 70 years later. Guilds took great care in making multipurpose devices for individual use. In Augsburg, for example, guild regulations in 1577 required an artisan to demonstrate his proficiency in spring clock design before he could become a master. This test, which had to be completed within a 6-month period, concentrated on multipurpose design and convertibility. It asked the candidate to make an apple-sized clock to hang around a person's neck and, as the historian of technology Otto Mayr has noted, a clock of from 7 to 8 inches tall that performed the following functions: "hour and quarter-hour striking; alarm; an astrolabe dial showing the position of the fixed stars in the zodiac; an automatic indicator for the length of the day and night; a calendar dial; and indications adjustable for 12- to 24-hour cycles."

The clock proved the archtypical machine. Early clocks measured earthly time and showed astronomical movement, symbolically linking heaven and earth. Nicole Oresme, a French bishop, capitalized on the idea of a heaven/earth linkage to argue in about 1400 that clocks proved the existence of god; just as there was no clock without a clockmaker, there could be no earth without a god to form and maintain it. In the fifteenth century, clockmakers began to discontinue astronomical representations and the clock began to assume its modern shape. Clocks harmonized the circle and the straight line. The two major parts of the clock dial were named after parts of the human body—the clock had a face and hands. Introduction of a minute hand to accompany the long-established hour hand produced a series of geometrically precise angles. But the clock itself was a totality, self-contained. Its internal mechanisms moved regularly and it measured discrete, regular intervals. Revolution of the clock hands marked changes in time but in a curiously endless way; each day marked the same passage and was repeated on the following day.

Mechanical Magus

Clocks were not the only captivating machines. Nor were Age of Humankind machinists reticent about sharing their insights. Any number of men wrote books explaining machine fundamentals and how their efforts took advantage of and reflected those fundamentals. In every case, the machinist was the designer who took universal design and organizational principles—principles often drawn in the heavens—and filtered them to come to bear on and resolve a practical issue. Machinists composed these books for one simple reason. They knew that any human could manipulate the principles to his or her end once he or she learned and understood them; each book accentuated humankind's ability to use divinely offered knowledge to human mechanical ends. In that sense, machinists acted as maguses and engaged in white magic, the kind of magic that unlocked universal secrets for noble purposes. *Various and Ingenious Machines* (1588) by the obscure Italian Agostino Ramelli stood as just one example. Ramelli, who worked for a time in service to Henry III of France, set out any number of complicated mechanical devices to lift water, power mills, and the like. He found the origin of these mechanisms in mathematics, which he argued was necessary for "fully investigating the truth and revealing it to the world." Truth was of divine origin and mathematics the key to disclosing it. According to Ramelli, mathematics came to humanity from god. He gave it to Adam and Eve (and thus to humankind) to take care of earthly necessities once they fell from grace. Mathematics, especially "the kind of mathematics which deals with palpable things"—geometric forms—enabled humanity to take advantage of the laws of the universe to modify outwardnesses. When this shape-oriented mathematics was initially applied, it became mechanics, "which first began to reveal to the world how to cultivate the fields and how to subject the horse and the ox to the yoke for plowing the earth" and then the mechanic arts, the design of machines. Ramelli's magus, then, used the mathematics of forms to devise numerous novel machines—which were applications of the forms—to undertake a wide assortment of tasks.

Discussions of form were not the product of some convenient communal convention adopted by these men. Form represented their reality. Their books even provided plates of their inventions drawn with exquisite concern for perspective and for faithfully representing action that took place on different planes. Machines as simple and unexceptional as reverberatory furnaces were explored and explained in terms of three-dimensional forms. Such furnaces needed to be "of such a shape that the force of fire may operate better," an assumption that focused consideration on understanding why and how fire had force. Its heat was not the answer. Fire's shape gave it its abilities. Fire, the power inside the furnace, "penetrated metallic ore." "Splitting, dividing or cutting the metal with fire" was the furnace's role and the "virtues of fire" stemmed from its pyramidal shape. It then stood to reason that furnace design must capitalize on fire's physical form. Vannoccio Birrunguccio, an early-sixteenth-century fortress designer, arms maker, mine owner, and architect, summed up the then contemporary design debate. Some machinists favored a funnel-like, pyramidal vault "so that as the flames are forced in they may go forward and, deflected by the vault and the arrangement of the walls, they may unitedly enter the place of the bronze." Others argued for egg-shaped furnaces because "this shape contains a greater quantity of flames united in themselves and unbroken, and that the force of the fire is where its greatest quantity is." Adherents of spherical furnaces claimed that "all lines tend toward a center and that the fire enclosed in that concave acts no differently than does the sun in a concave mirror. This does not happen in any other shapes."

The Macrocosm as Model

The designers' repeated assertion that they merely sought to apply god-derived, heavenly manifested principles to earthly tasks suggested that those qualities they recognized as deterministic on earth—shape, form, harmony, and proportion—could be identified as fundamental to and in the heavens, the macrocosm. These men looked to the heavens for potential insights to terrestrial questions, but few actually attempted to study its operation. Those others who did in fact try to correlate observations of heavenly movement with theories of heavenly composition and operation found without exception shape and form to be telling features. These students of the cosmos generally first turned to the ancients—the Greco-Roman past—and immediately saw explanations of heavenly activity cast in terms of form and shape. Aristotelian crystalline spheres comprised the immutable heavens, and the various heavenly bodies revolved around the centrally located earth in orbits described in circles. These orbits included several cycles and epicycles, which enabled these men to harmonize their belief that the motion of the heavens needed to be in pure circles with measurements that indicated that heavenly bodies traveled in patterns more complicated than simple circles. Astrologers turned to the zodiac, the division of the spherical heavens into 12 quadrants, each of which had identifiable characteristics, "a shape that nature depicted," and affected life on earth depending on its position to

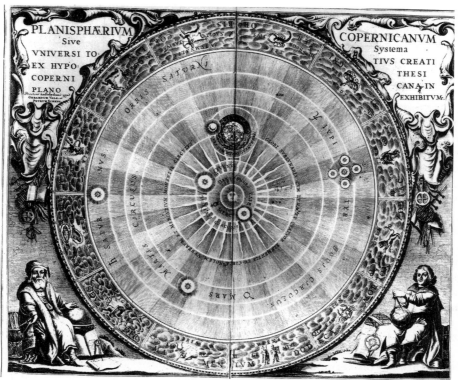

Copernican Astronomy. Copernicus's positioning of the sun at the center of the universe reduced the number of epicycles necessary to account for the motion of the heavens. But his planetary system was not immediatley accepted. Many feared that it gave humankind, tainted by original sin, a much too prominent place in the divine plan.

the stationary earth. Even those who in the twentieth century are given credit for demolishing these classical frameworks did their work with no less reliance on form and shape than did their ancient predecessors. The sixteenth-century cleric Nicholas Copernicus, for instance, generally receives credit for establishing the sun at the center of the universe. Copernicus justified this radical reorganization, which lessened the number of epicycles necessary to describe heavenly motion from 80 to 34 and simplified the geometry, in terms characteristic of the Age of Humankind—as the One from which all originate. "In the center of all resides the Sun. Who, indeed, in this most magnificent temple would put the light in another or in a better place than that one wherefrom it could at the same time illuminate the whole of it?" asked Copernicus. "Therefore it is not improperly that some people call it the lamp of the world, others its ruler. Trismegistus [calls it] the visible God, Sophocles' Electra, the All-Seeing. Thus, assuredly, as residing in the royal see the Sun governs the surrounding family of stars." Copernicus's radical cosmology did not cause him to do away with concerns of shape and form. Rather than jettison them, he embraced them as partial explanation for his cosmology. Copernicus was adamant that "the universe is spherical; partly because this form, being a complete whole, needing no joints, is the most perfect of all; partly because it constitutes the most spacious form which is thus best suited to contain and retain all things; or also because all discrete parts of the world, I mean the sun, the moon and the planets, appear as spheres."

Copernicus's removal of earth from the center of the universe elevated humanity, a fit project in the Age of Humankind. To the medieval mind, the center of the universe was the basest place, just as Dante reserved the worst circle of hell for the center. Medieval men and women considered the earth rightly "situated in the center, which is the worst place" because it "consists of a more sordid and base matter" than any other place and deserved to be placed "at the greatest distance from those purer incorruptible bodies, the heavens." Copernicus's heliocentric world raised humanity but he worried that it redeemed humankind too much. That fear had given Copernicus cause to hesitate about publicizing his astronomical conclusions but he assuaged his conscience by cautioning his readers not to assume that humanity merited a place on par with the quintessential heavens. Others took exception and argued that a central sun lifted humankind precisely because earth now attained star status. With the universe composed of many stars and with earth now assuming its rightful place as a heavenly body, humankind seemed no longer a creature unique to earth but instead master and mistress of almost too many places to imagine. Such a view would have dramatically altered the god-humankind relationship and would especially have many repercussions for established religions, especially the then dominant Catholic church. It was not surprising therefore that for over a century the church disclaimed as heresy the Copernican hypothesis.

The other major figure of this astronomical revolution, Johannes Kepler, relied at least as heavily on shape and form as had Copernicus. Each discovery for which Kepler is known to twentieth-century men and women depended on three-dimensional, shape-oriented thinking: that planets travel around the sun in ellipses (which are conic sections) with the sun as one focus; that planets, with reference to the sun and in the planes of their elliptical orbits, sweep out equal areas in equal times during their travels around the sun; and that the squares of the time it takes any two planets to revolve around the sun were proportional to the cubes of their mean distances from the sun. And Kepler arrived at these determinations in ways characteristic to the Age of Humankind. He began with the premise that "God has established nothing without geometrical beauty" and that god provided humankind the power to know. "Just as the eye was made to see colors, and the ear to hear sounds," Kepler maintained, "the human mind was made to understand" shape, form, proportion, ratios, which Kepler called "quantity." Kepler called the sun "the most excellent" body in the universe, claimed that it "alone appears by virtue of its dignity and power, suited . . . to become the home of God himself," and set out to discover "why the number, the size, and the motions of the orbits [of the planets] are as they are and not otherwise." He quickly deduced "the cause for the planets being six in number." "God, in creating the universe and regulating the order of the cosmos, had in view the five regular bodies of geometry [Platonic solids] and He has fixed, according to these dimensions, the number of heavens, their proportions, and the relations of their movements."

For over a decade Kepler persisted in arguing that the orbit of each heavenly body rested within the confines of one of the nested Platonic solids—cube, tetrahedron, octahedron, dodecahedron, and icosahedron. But when he recognized that astronomical measurements indicated that some planets would have to travel through the solids, he abandoned his theory but not a shape-based explanation for planetary motion. Realizing that planets travel in ellipses was the fruit of his continuing search. Kepler's long adherence to the Platonic solids stemmed from the mistaken belief that planets traveled in circles—perfect forms. He incorrectly thought of god as a sculptor and expected god to pick the most "elegant form." But Kepler admitted that he forgot that perfect shapes do not reflect an imperfect solar system; when representing imperfection, perfection remained a "rough-hewn mass." The divine sculptor chose to "fashion [his stones] in the very articulate image of the animated body"—in human terms—something much more detailed as it was marked by "eccentricities." God "made the nose, eyes, and remaining limbs a part of the statue" and so selected the shape of the ellipse. To Kepler and others, the ellipse–humankind identification demonstrated the "harmonies in natural things," or "consonances." The human mind "seizes upon these forms and, whether by instinct or by astronomical or harmonic ratiocination, discerns the cordant from the discordant." Humankind's mind, then, was tuned to resonate with the One, who created and governed the universe and established consonances for humankind to experience and use as it sought to explore and master its realm.

From Macrocosm to Microcosm

Scrutinizing the heavens also played a central role in the new Age of Humankind medicine. Gothic medieval physicians had depended on the corpus of two classical medical authorities, Aristotle (via his Islamic commentator Avicenna) and Galen, and established schools to train physicians in that joint method. Although these schools continued after 1350 and Galenic and Aristotelian medicine remained important, increasing numbers of medical men and others objected to reliance on these authorities. They maintained that these authorities were not authorities at all but dogmatists. Their theories failed to correlate with material gathered by the human senses. Rather than defer to persons long dead and to restrict schools simply to perpetuating these untruths, they urged their contemporaries to use their own experiences to forge a new, greater understanding. God, these persons argued, gave humankind two great books: the book of divine revelation (Scriptures) and the book of creation (nature, including the heavens). It was within those two books that humankind could find medical answers.

An extensive investigation within the human body resulted as physicians turned to the book of nature and dissected (and sometimes vivisected) condemned criminals and others in front of attentive medical students. These efforts differed considerably from earlier dissections, which sought only to demonstrate Galenic wisdom. Age of Humankind dissections also often were undertaken before medical students but as voyages of exploration. These inquiries into how the human body was structured usually incorporated three-dimensional mapping of sorts to represent the complicated three-dimensional human form. Anatomists employed artists to draw parts of human anatomy, especially the systems—skeletal, cardiovascular, and musculature—

in consonance with each other to represent the "true" physical relationships. These drawings reflected the fruits of human anatomical investigation and provided those not able to attend dissections the experience of "observing" them and learning from those observations. Publication of Andreas Vesalius's *De Humani Corporis Fabrica* in 1543 marked the zenith of this three-dimensional, human anatomical mapping effort.

Physicians also employed the book of nature to explain human physiology. William Harvey's insistence in the 1610s and 1620s that the heart circulated blood through the human body stemmed from this new Age of Humankind medicine. Harvey saw the center as the necessary director of activities and maintained that a functional similarity existed between the heart and the sun. The heart, "like the sun in the greater world," which sent "forth the essential beams circularly from [its] center," was, according to Harvey, "the principle part because [it resided] in the principle place, in the center of a circle, the middle of the necessary body." It became conceivable to claim that blood revolved around the heart (to our mind, circulated in the body) the way the heavenly orbs revolved around the sun.

Magus as Medicine Man

Other physicians concentrated on healing. They too turned to the book of nature but not exclusively as they used all faculties and abilities god gave humankind to cure disease. Implicit in their utilization of the book of nature was rejection of classical medicine, especially within medical schools. These new Age of Humankind physicians adapted alchemy and astrology to medicine. They joined the book of divine revelation and the book of nature and found correspondences in god's two books and between the heavens and the earth.

Philippus Aureolus Theophrastus Bombastus von Hohenheim, commonly known as Paracelsus, emerged as leader of this movement at least as much because of his personality as his intellect. Trained in chemistry and mining but not medicine, he toured Europe for a dozen years to learn the secrets of nature and the healing arts. Paracelsus's reputation as healer led the great theologian Erasmus to select him as his personal physician and enabled the medical man to secure a position at the University of Basel in 1527. He immediately attacked his new colleagues and all Galenic medical practitioners as fools. Maintaining that "my shoe buckles are more learned than your Galen and Avicenna," he termed their defense of classical authorities as "belly-crawling and flattery." Instead of trusting to authorities, Paracelsus challenged them to learn from the book of nature as had "old women, Egyptians, and such-like persons; for they have greater experience in such things than all the academians." He further argued that his medical colleagues were not "experienced enough to refute even one word of mine," and Paracelsus mused that "I wish I could protect my bald head against the flies as effectively."

Paracelsus, which in Latin meant "greater than the Roman physician Celsus," publicly burned volumes of Hippocrates, Galen, and Avicenna and asserted that from then on he would only lecture from his experience. He was soon chased from Basel and his house was firebombed. Paracelsus spent much of his remaining years fleeing his foes and their supporters, never staying in any one place for as much as 12 months. He died in 1541 at about age 50.

Paracelsian experience demanded that physicians consult the macrocosm—the heavens—to understand the cause of and cure for a person's ailment. The position of heavenly bodies emitted resonances, which harmonized in some individuals and caused them to become ill—the orientation of the heavens at a person's birth often explained why he or she later took sick at a particular confluence of the planets. Only a specific locality in the body responded negatively to the astral influence. This was because the human body resembled the heavens; each organ corresponded to a heavenly body. Paracelsians carried this understanding throughout their medicine. To Paracelsus, for example, it was no accident that the face contained seven orifices, one for each of the seven heavenly orbs—the five (then known) planets, the moon, and the sun.

Alchemical physicians likened astral influence on the human body to planting a seed in the earth and having it grow into a vein of iron or coal. The particular area around which the seed was planted became the site of the vein or of the disease. Disease arose in the locality when the human body's main archeus—located in the stomach—stopped separating earthly matter—food, air, or drink—into its constituents and selecting the useful while discarding the rest. When this personified function failed to operate properly, poison accumulated in the body at the site predicted by astral influence and allowed the seed of disease to take root in that organ. The seed grew and disease resulted. Physicians needed to counteract the poison, to restore balance to cure disease.

By examining the heavens, physicians learned what astral influences generated the illness. But god in creating a microcosm that mimicked the macrocosm provided humanity the means to cure every malady. He imprinted the signatures of the heavenly orbs upon everything; god inscribed each earthly thing with marks correlating with one or more heavenly body. Humanity was not excluded. Each person's body carried the signatures of the heavens; each human contained "the stars within himself" and so bore the heavens "with all its influences." Correspondences were crucial as Paracelsians believed that the earthly correlate of a disease-producing heavenly configuration—a substance that bore its signature—also held the power to heal that disease. "By signs and outward correspondences," argued Paracelsus, "we men discover all that is hidden." There existed "nothing in the depths of the sea, nothing in the heights of the firmament that man is not capable of discovering." Nothing, he maintained, "can hide from the gaze of man what is within it; it is revealed to him by corresponding signs."

This prescription held a practical translation: Metallic compounds, plants, or minerals that when ingested produced symptoms similar to those of the particular disease had the appropriate signature of and contained curative properties for that disease. Put baldly, they possessed the poison and its antithesis or antidote. The terrestrial physicians' task was to identify those astral influences, to locate their earthly representatives or manifestations, and to use their essences to cure the archeus and to restore balance for resumption of proper functioning of the affected part. Chemical manipulation enabled physicians to remove the substance's outwardnesses and to separate its true "virtues," necessary in compounding what was useful for curing this disease and removing what was not. Each substance's virtues or essence was inherent within it but was masked; the alchemical physician knew the signatures to identify the virtuous material and techniques to separate what was needed from what was not. Dosage remained critical. Disease resulted from the master archeus's inability to maintain balance. To add too much corrective quality would cause an overreaction, destroy pretenses of balance, and generate yet another disease.

Alchemical medicine placed humankind at the crux of medicine. Disease originated in planetary confluences, but human activity could provide remedies. Humanity held the power to cure disease by consulting the books of creation and nature. But medicine also required physicians to possess perspective. They needed to use reason tempered by observation. The heavens yielded the disease-producing resonance, but its outwardness—disease symptoms—differed; disease was always imbalance but what was imbalanced and how it was imbalanced varied. Cure also necessitated perspective. Physicians had to find exactly which plant corresponded to that particular disease, to strip away the plant's outward disguise, and to reduce it to its critical constituent. Only then could physicians use that constituent to restore harmony to the affected part and by extension to the entire body. In that sense, medical alchemy was a microcosm of the macrocosm of Age of Humankind thought.

For Further Reading (Chapters 9–11)

Bellamy, John. *The Tudor Law of Treason.* London: Routledge & Kegan Paul, 1979.

Braudel, Fernand. *The Structures of Everyday Life.* Translated by Sian Reynolds. London: Collins, 1981.

Brown, Lloyd A. *The Story of Maps.* New York: Dover, 1979.

Chambers, E. K. *The Medieval Stage.* 2 vols. Oxford: Oxford University Press, 1903.

Cipolla, Carlo M. *Clocks and Culture, 1300–1700.* New York: Norton, 1978.

Cipolla, Carlo M. *Guns, Sails and Empires.* New York: Minerva Press, 1965.

Conway, William Martin, trans. *The Writings of Albrecht Dürer.* New York: Philosophical Library, 1958.

Crosby, Alfred W., Jr. *The Columbian Exchange. Biological and Cultural Consequences of 1492.* Westport, Conn.: Greenwood, 1972.

Cutter, S. H. *The Law of Treason and Treason Trials in Later Medieval France.* Cambridge: Cambridge University Press, 1981.

Davis, David Brion. *The Problem of Slavery in Western Culture.* Ithaca: Cornell University Press, 1966.

Davis, Natalie Zemon. *Society and Culture in Early Modern France.* Stanford: Stanford University Press, 1975.

Debus, Allen G. *The English Paracelsians.* London: Oldbourne, 1965.

Debus, Allen G. *Man and Nature in the Renaissance.* New York: Cambridge University Press, 1978.

Dickens, A. G. *Reformation and Society in Sixteenth-Century Europe.* London: Thames and Hudson, 1966.

Dulmen, Richard van. *Theatre of Horror: Crime and Punishment in Early Modern Germany.* Translated by Elisabeth Neu. Cambridge: Basil Blackwell, 1990.

Elias, Norbert. *Time: An Essay.* Oxford: Blackwells, 1992.

Gardiner, Robert, ed. *Cogs, Caravels and Galleons. The Sailing Ship 1000–1650.* London: Conway Maritime Press, 1994.

Giedion, Siegfried. *Mechanization Takes Command.* New York: Oxford University Press, 1948.

Gille, Bertrand. *The Renaissance Engineers.* London: Lund Humphries, 1966.

Gilmore, Myron P. *The World of Humanism, 1453–1517.* New York: Harper & Row, 1962.

Ginzburg, Carlo. *The Cheese and the Worms: The Cosmos of a Sixteenth-Century Miller.* Translated by John and Anne Tedeschi. Baltimore: Johns Hopkins University Press, 1980.

Hale, J. R. *Renaissance Fortification: Art or Engineering.* London: Thames and Hudson, 1977.

Huizinga, J. *The Waning of the Middle Ages.* 1949; Garden City, N.Y.: Doubleday, 1954.

Jeanneret, Michel. *A Feast of Words: Banquets and Table Talk in the Renaissance.* Translated by Jeremy Whiteley and Emma Hughes. Chicago: University of Chicago Press, 1991.

Jordan, R. Furneaux. *A Concise History of Western Architecture*. London: Thames, 1971.

Keller, A. G. *A Theatre of Machines*. New York: MacMillan, 1964.

Koyre, Alexandre. *From the Closed World to the Infinite Universe*. Baltimore: Johns Hopkins University Press, 1957.

Kristeller, Paul Oskar. *Renaissance Thought II: Papers on Humanism and the Arts*. New York: Harper Torchbooks, 1965.

McNeill, William H. *The Pursuit of Power. Technology, Armed Force, and Society Since A.D. 1000*. Chicago: University of Chicago Press, 1982.

Monter, E. William, ed. *European Witchcraft*. New York: John Wiley and Sons, 1969.

Parsons, William B. *Engineers and Engineering in the Renaissance*. Cambridge, Mass.: MIT Press, 1976.

Rice, Eugene F., Jr. *The Foundations of Early Modern Europe, 1460–1559*. New York: Norton, 1970.

Unger, Richard W. *The Ship in the Medieval Economy 600–1600*. London: Croom Helm, 1980.

Van Creveld, Martin. *Technology and War: From 2000 B.C. to the Present*. New York: Free Press, 1989.

Yates, Frances A. *Giordano Bruno and the Hermetic Tradition*. Chicago: University of Chicago Press, 1964.

Yates, Frances A. *The Occult Philosophy in the Elizabethan Age*. London: Routledge and Kegan Paul, 1979.

CHAPTER 12

A World of Boundaries: Later Baroque Europe, 1630–1715

In 1711, the famous English poet Alexander Pope spoke for his generation when he wrote the following couplets.

> Those rules of old discovered, not devised,
>
> Are Nature still, but Nature methodized,
>
> Nature, like liberty, is but restrained,
>
> By the same laws which first herself ordained.

Pope's words addressed several fundamental tenets of his age. He recalled natural law, the law of nature, and maintained that this law (really a series of laws) was a divine creation—not devised by humankind. Natural law had existed and operated long before humans had recognized it. Reason had enabled humankind to uncover these laws. Laws of nature described the natural world and were natural in that they were real, and true and could be represented. Their human recognition had changed humanity's understanding of nature itself. Nature no longer seemed wild, capricious, or unruly but confined, regular, and conforming. Rather than a patternless, truly random creation, Pope's nature hewed to and obeyed specific rules and regulations that operated without respect to time or place.

Pope then joined humanity's social world with the natural world by equating nature with liberty. Neither was absolute, completely free, or untamed but rather bounded, limited by particularistic natural rules that preceded its identification by humankind. Liberty, Pope claimed, resulted from the application of the natural laws governing social interactions. Liberty could never be absolute but humanity could achieve the maximum quantity of liberty permitted humankind by establishing an artificial set of relationships that adhered to the appropriate natural laws of social organization.

These sentiments characterized later Baroque Europe. On one hand, they promised humankind the ability to learn nature's laws and then to fashion productions in accordance with those laws. But they also suggested that possibilities were not unlimited. Existence of laws—even laws not precisely or completely derived and even "laws" lacking agreed upon parameters—placed palpable boundaries, limits, on humanity and humankind's abilities. Humankind remained master of its own earthly fate and now would have better tools with which to fashion that fate but the human prospect appeared less ambitious, less expansive, less limitless than it had in Renaissance Europe. A dichotomous situation resulted. Europeans experienced an optimism based on the idea of discovery and manipulation of natural laws and a pessimism, often subsequent, stemming from the realization that the existence of these laws was in fact in some sense restrictive, bounding human ability.

A rather bleaker view of human nature, the nature that each individual received at birth, accompanied the circumscription of human potential. This Baroque world of limits, however, retained its emphasis on studying humanity. As Pope pithily put it,

> Know then thyself, presume not God to scan;
> The proper study of mankind is man.

But now humankind's flaws became clear and its limits more discernible. John Milton in his classic *Paradise Lost* has Satan, who serves as the characteristic human, argue that

> To reign is worth ambition though in hell:
> Better to reign in hell than serve in heav'n.

Milton's very human Satan was limited to a subordinate position in the heavenly world and his greedy, corrupt nature seized at any avenue that helped him break out of these restrictive confines and achieve a virtually limitless, free state. Success was ultimately impossible, of course, and Satan's attempt had its price. It cost Satan his immortal soul.

Milton's use of Satan was allegorical. He represented humankind generally; Satan and Satan's momentous decision exemplified the strivings and urgings of humankind as well as its limitations. To Milton and his contemporaries, humankind seemed an apt collective noun because each human seemed essentially the same at birth. Each human newborn possessed two identical things: reason and human nature. Differences among humans, then, occurred after birth and were therefore relatively minor and artificial. Each human was as alike at birth as matchsticks or pins. The universality of humankind, not the after-birth-distinctions, riveted later Baroque Europeans. These men and women almost always addressed humankind's fundamental similarities when they pondered the condition and status of humanity.

Creating an Artificial Humanity: Society

That government depended upon the consent of the governed was a statement that would have met with overwhelming assent by late Baroque Europeans. Yet that ought not to be construed as a dramatic move to democracy or modern representative government or even a rejection of the divine right of kings. No such rejection or movement occurred. Sentiment for the consensual nature of government simply reflected resignation, an acknowledgment that government was a lesser evil than a lack of government, a statement consistent with a profoundly questionable view of human nature that dominated the seventeenth century. Europeans found humankind reasonable enough to be able to give its consent and fashion workable government yet sufficiently depraved to have that government erect rigid boundaries to check humanity's nature.

Government required individuals to agree to place a portion of their authority in the hands of others. It also demanded recognition that any one person might not benefit from this agreement but that collective, coordinated, and centrally generated activity would reap greater general well-being and prosperity.

The State as Theorized: Hobbes and Locke

Thomas Hobbes and John Locke, two English gentlemen writing some 40 years apart, have come to symbolize the opposite extremes of a great philosophical debate on the nature of and raison d'être for society and government that is said to have rocked Baroque Europe. To be sure, discussion of and interest in questions of society, government, and sovereignty captivated the seventeenth century. Yet theoreticians held more in common with each other than it has appeared. Even Hobbes and Locke were in essential concordance, although they suggested differing applications.

Hobbes justified and explained society and government by looking first to nature, the collection of principles by which "god hath made and governs the world," and claiming that humankind regularly imitated those principles to create machinery, artificial beasts of burden. In this Hobbesian "artificial animal," mechanical springs mimicked living hearts, gears and pulleys replaced joints, and strings were reminiscent of nerves. Hobbes, an English intellectual patronized by a noble family, contended that humans took imitation a step further and copied humanity itself, "that Rational and most excellent work of nature." This "artificial man," or state, acted as an artificial animal did, easing humankind's burden. Hobbes's state, or Leviathan, was to protect and defend humanity from human nature. It was to protect a collection of humans from the selfish, destructive machinations of any single human. Humanity granted its artificial man a soul by granting the state sovereignty, provided it joints through creation of magistrates, and furnished it nerves through a system of rewards and punishments.

Dependence on creation of an artificial man stemmed from Hobbes's understanding of humanity. He maintained that humankind was similar in three ways. Each human shared with all other human beings a "similitude of thoughts and passions," including "desire, fear [and] hope," similar intelligence—"faculties of mind" and similar physical attributes—"faculties of body." This "greater equality amongst men," this "equality of ability," produced an "equality of hope in the attaining" of the same goals. Seeking similar goals meant that unsuccessful parties would be jealous of those who were successful and become their mortal enemies. Constant disappointment would ultimately produce "a time of war, where every man is Enemy to every man" and all humans would have only that security that "their own strength" and ingenuity could furnish. Such a condition would, according to Hobbes, doom agriculture, sea trade, monumental architecture, machine making, arts and letters, and social intercourse. It would "worst of all" bring "continual fear and danger of violent death." Life of humans in this arena would be marked by "war of every man against every man." It would be "solitary, poor, nasty, brutish and short."

Only collective action could free humanity from certain catastrophe. A "Law of Nature" gave each human "the liberty . . . to use his own power," "his own judgment and reason," "for the preservation of his own . . . life." Each human could transfer liberty "or renounce it . . . in consideration of some right reciprocally transferred to himself." The reciprocal transfer of rights willingly placed each participant's personal sovereignty into the communal sovereignty of an artificial man—a Leviathan—and created a consensual, contractual bond among humans. In any particular instance, an individual might suffer because of the transfer. But the nature of humanity indicated that without the transfer all would repeatedly and continually

Leviathan. Thomas Hobbes's *Leviathan* was based upon the notion that humankind was selfish, and that humanity's natural state was a war of all against all. Only an artificial human, a strong, powerful government, could hope to keep human passions in check. Without a Leviathan, life would be "solitary, poor, nasty, brutish and short."

fail. Only through agreement for the common good could each person achieve a part of the common wealth.

Although Hobbes argued that humans had similar merits and abilities, his commonwealth made no pretense of establishing equal statuses. Humankind's innate selfishness required drastic, even draconian, efforts, including creation of artificial hierarchies and artificial decision-making mechanisms. Hobbes sought to minimize friction among members of a commonwealth by minimizing competition among them, not by granting each equal access or even equal success. His Leviathan, his state, was to compel all individual interests to submit for the common good. Nor were all to benefit equally. The state's economic benefits were expected to be at least as stratified and as unequal as its social hierarchy. Yet the Leviathan seemed compelling because of its fundamental premise: that any person would achieve a greater degree of well-being as part of the Leviathan than those individuals who chose to remain in a state of nature, where "the condition of man is a condition of war of every one against every one."

The notion of boundedness, that resources were limited and that humankind would destroy those precious commodities if not restrained, fueled virtually all late Baroque justifications for state creation. Writing some 40 years after Hobbes, John Locke agreed with his countryman that persons in the state of nature—before creation of the State—had several natural rights, which he identified as the right to life, liberty, and property. Protection of these fundamental rights provided the raison d'être for the state. Locke's social theories stemmed from his understanding of humanity's nature. Like Hobbes, Locke, who was also dependent for his livelihood on the good offices of a noble family, maintained that each human possessed equal abilities and that distinctions among them were artificial, not ability-based. Locke's analysis began at birth and claimed that each person was like a blank slate, imbued only with reason. Differences among humans came after birth and were merely the consequence of experience. Locke asserted that experience—what an individual read, how one was reared, what one had seen—was received by the human faculties or senses and produced distinctions among persons by almost mechanical means. It was as if each particular experience etched itself into the blank slate that made up each person. Only in that way did artificial distinctions emerge in humankind.

Hobbes's Leviathan demanded complete and abject submission to the central authority. Human nature seemed so debased that humanity had no choice but to agree to submit. No matter how later generations would interpret him, Locke held no higher opinion of human nature. Like his Baroque contemporaries, Locke maintained human nature depraved. He claimed that in the state of nature a law of nature suggested that all persons had the "perfect freedom to order their actions . . . as they think fit" and that each human ought to be "equal one amongst another without subordination or subjection." But Locke found the reality of human nature fostering a quite different situation. Rather than idyllic, life in the state of nature was "uncertain and constantly exposed to the invasion of others," a product of humanity's seriously flawed nature. This "very unsafe, very insecure" environment was marked by the "corruption and viciousness of degenerate men," by "bias," "passion," and "revenge." Humankind was "full of fears and continual dangers" and for the "mutual preservation of life, liberty and [property]," humans left the state of nature to grant "dominion and control" to others. But unlike Hobbes and others, Locke worried not just about the miserable nature of the governed but especially about the abuses of the persons doing the governing. He found individuals, when imbued with the power of the Leviathan, more threatening to the common wealth than a war of all against all. Ironically, those tenets that commended the State to Hobbes seemed to Locke to be the very tenets against which to guard. Locke checked human nature by checking the power of its creation, artificial humanity, the state. Locke's government stressed checks and balances, refusing to cede even the slightest authority without some mechanism to hold unbridled selfishness in tow. He prohibited legislatures from delegating powers or raising taxes without direct permission. He forced them to apply laws to all groups and classes so as not to allow one faction to gain at the expense of the others. Locke also divided authority into the legislative, executive, and federative (diplomatic) and refused all attempts to join the legislative and executive under one banner.

Statecraft as Practiced

Government in which each social order received a proportionate share of power had no place in later Baroque Europe. This medieval conception considered government the sum of the elements or stations of society and proved antithetical to ideas that humans began life essentially at the same point and that the social divisions that emerged were merely artificial. Theoretically, each and any person could represent the interests of all persons, a fundamentally different assumption than had marked Gothic Europe. Not surprisingly, representative assemblies first created centuries earlier declined during the seventeenth century; their control of the public purse, their key to power, loosened as later Baroque Europeans rejected the basis on which they were created.

An autocracy, an absolute monarchy, stood as the most common type of consensual government after 1600. In effect, a state's citizens contracted among themselves and with an absolute monarch, who promised to reduce waste. In Hobbesian terms, a single mighty ruler could set a single statewide policy and centralize authority; he or she did away with destructive competition within the realm and enabled the state to conduct its affairs with an unchallenged voice. Through creation of a centralized bureaucracy and dynamic military, an autocratic state could maximize its ability to accumulate a great portion of the world's limited wealth. Additional wealth could come only from outside the state "for whatsoever is somewhere gotten is somewhere lost." An increase in its citizens' well-being was the anticipated consequence of this mercantilist policy and citizens would use this liberty to pursue the arts and other higher forms, activities that the great Dutch philosopher Baruch Spinoza deemed made life worth living.

Absolutism offered efficiency but other forms seemed to some even more advantageous. Persons throughout Europe recognized the first purpose of the state as wealth accretion, but only a relative few sought to fashion a government that would explicitly use the experience of its citizens to further that aim. This form of government enabled those individuals with the greatest experience in wealth capturing to make most of the crucial wealth-acquiring decisions. These governments proved no more representative than absolute monarchies, and no less autocratic. They simply adopted a different approach to absolutism, one that sought to benefit from the corporate experience of those persons adept at securing wealth.

Both types of government provided later Baroque Europeans with a sense of stability. The widespread acknowledgment that absolute monarchs reigned by "divine right" implied several things. First, by transferring the explanation for absolutism to the heavenly realm, people overcame the question of its arbitrariness; if humanity approached equality at birth, on what human basis could one individual be selected to rule? But in addition to offering legitimacy to a head of state, divine right also reined in its recipient. Divine right stemmed from god, as did divine law on earth, or natural law. Adherence to natural law constituted the terms of a monarch's contract to head a state and to receive divine sanction. God-given natural law was anything but arbitrary and its definitive terms severely circumscribed a monarch's authority. To violate natural law was to relinquish or abdicate one's divine right to rule. And while debate might occur in any instance over whether an individual so massively ignored natural law that he or she abdicated her or his divine right to rule, the ability of a population to declare an agreement between a ruler and citizens of the state abrogated when an insufferable outrage went unquestioned. The right to rule was divine as were the rules but members of the compact—humans—were the judges.

No less an authority on the divine right of rulers than France's Louis XIV sounded these views. The monarch who in his time seemed most to embody the divine right concept, Louis recognized that "the deference and the respect" received from subjects was "not a free gift from them." Instead, it constituted "payment for the justice and the protection that they expect to receive from us." Homage required the monarch to conform to natural laws of justice—a sense of consistency tempered with fairness but not equality—and to provide protection, which meant not only military defense but also the defense of state wealth. Together these mercantilist activities formed the basis of the agreement for social organization. "Our debts toward [the people of France] are even more binding than theirs to us," Louis admitted, because his responsibilities and powers were truly awesome. He argued baldly that the perpetuation of the state of France as a successful venture depended on its absolute ruler's ability to provide consistent and firm direction. If a French citizen failed in an endeavor, "a thousand others come in a crowd to fill his post." But "the position of sovereign can be properly filled only by" one person at a time, "the sovereign himself." If he failed to provide his contractual duties, the state would lack basis for its existence. "I am the State," Louis was thought to have said, a statement that neatly captured the representative nature of the monarchy as well as the ruler's centrality.

Yet it would be a mistake to think that the dependence on an absolute monarch, coupled with the ability to abrogate governments, was seen as creating instability within Baroque Europe. Just the opposite was the case. Divine right, absolutism, autocracy, and natural law each separately and together conspired to provide stability through the preservation of normality. Stability—normality—meant that change— significant deviations from normality—was intolerable. The status quo needed always to prevail. Rulers were neatly limited in their abilities to foment radically different policies. Efforts to implement fundamental change were often greeted with calls to political and ultimately military action in protest precisely because introduction of new factors apparently violated natural law. The ability of a populace to abrogate a "divine right" provided a dramatic reason for a ruler not to appear to provoke change but it also made revolts seem not revolutionary. Political uprisings were always cast as restorations. Rather than a sense of newness, broad-based political action, even military action, seemed a reflection and an announcement of communitywide stability. Humankind's nature opened the likelihood of repeated usurpation of power and authority. The consensual nature of the state, coupled with the concept of natural law, controlled usurpers by authorizing community members to render usurpation untenable. In this context, the concept "revolution," as in the case of the English Revolution of 1688, did not signify a fundamental rejection of established frames of reference; it was not revolutionary. Instead, revolution was akin to revolving, like the revolution of the earth, for example. Revolutions were not radical events but essentially cyclical. The act of revolution, of restoring things, was to repeat itself ad infinitum.

Achievement of stability through regularization and routinization—normalcy— infiltrated every sphere of politico-economic activity. Something as mundane as the supplanting of fairs by regularized markets and merchants' exchanges testified to its cross-cutting nature. Fairs had made commodity exchange into a spectacle. They had disrupted establishment of normal trade patterns and partners and encouraged the purchase of commodities made or secured outside the commonwealth. The tremendous seventeenth-century proliferation of laws and lawyers also demonstrated the profound integration of the idea of natural law as basis for human social action and as the raison d'être for social stability. By establishing rules for eventualities, governments could constrain behavior and channel action into regular, consistent modes.

France

Louis XIV did not initiate French absolutism. His father, Louis XIII, and especially his father's advisor, Armand Cardinal Richelieu, had shaped absolutism in France decades earlier. Richelieu explained absolutism as the king's obligation to do whatever furthered the collective interest of the states' citizens even if individuals suffered. The state's responsibility for the common good made it "essential to banish pity." Each human "is immortal," argued the Christian cleric. Its "salvation is hereafter." The state, however, "has no immortality; its salvation is now or never." A ruler needed to recognize threats to the common weal and crush them at any price.

As threats to the French state, Richelieu identified the Protestant Huguenots, who by the Edict of Nantes were permitted to maintain fortified cities within Catholic France; the great nobility, who refused to abide by the central authority of the state; and the Habsburg family, branches of which controlled much of Spain and Germany and therefore menaced France militarily. He showed these enemies of the state no mercy and condemned to death even men innocent of any crime as a way to stamp out dissent and possible insurrection. The Richelieu-controlled military attacked the Huguenots and destroyed their autonomy and did repeated and prolonged battle with the Habsburgs. The cardinal also instituted a special tribunal to punish nobles, a group previously outside the conventional justice system, to signify their deference to and dependence upon the state. The epidemic of peasant and urban revolts that accompanied his policies did not dissuade Richelieu. Nor did these policies end with Richelieu's death in 1642. His hand-picked successor, Cardinal Mazarin, persisted even as he fled France twice to escape the nobility's wrath. Mazarin's perseverance

Revocation of the Edict of Nantes. Abandoning that edict ended the special protection given the Huguenots and what the Catholic French complained had been a state within the State.

helped defeat the Spanish Habsburgs and, when the cardinal died in 1661, Louis XIV adopted similar policies.

Louis XIV reigned until 1715 and implemented virtually any policy that promised to increase the wealth of the French state. His finance minister, Jean-Baptiste Colbert, embarked upon an ambitious program to extract duties from foreign shipping to render imports to France unprofitable. Believing that state wealth was measured by the greatest quantity of precious metals within its boundaries, Colbert sought both to prevent gold and silver from leaving the state as payment for foreign goods and to transform raw materials into exportable and therefore precious metal–generating commodities. He placed high duties on foreign ships in 1664 and 1667 and during the next decade founded several industries to compete for lucrative foreign markets. He spent large sums of money to seduce Dutch artisans to emigrate to France where they established manufactories to compete with those of their native land. Colbert granted these guilds unprecedented authority and privileges as incentives to generate higher quality, more uniform products than the Dutch competition.

Further anti-Dutch tariffs created a potent trade war and cost the Netherlands an impressive share of its foreign markets.

Louis XIV approved Colbert's program and concentrated his personal attention on military and domestic policy. Louis's application of later Baroque mercantilist assumptions meant that France remained at war for most of his reign. France allied itself with other states in the late 1660s and 1670s but thought itself strong enough to take on the Western world in the 1690s and the first 15 years of the eighteenth century. Louis also attempted to get France to act collectively not through negotiations or concessions but rather through brute authority. He revoked the Edict of Nantes, which forced nearly 200,000 Protestants to leave the overwhelmingly Catholic country, and imposed his will by decree. To administer France more efficiently, he established a chain of command within the bureaucracy. A series of king-appointed secretaries headed executive departments and reported directly to him. Louis institutionalized an elaborate etiquette and ceremony and surrounded himself with it. Courtly manners, grand gestures, huge palaces, and the like were august symbols of the state. Artificial patterns of deference and magnificent physical structures offered the state's citizens a graphic demonstration of their responsibilities to and their dependence upon it.

Louis met protests against royally proclaimed state policies forcefully. Mass hangings quickly dispatched tax revolts. Refusal of the French to pay the share of taxes that the state demanded particularly galled the king. Louis claimed that in the name of the state he "alone should have sovereign direction" over state finances and financial requirements because only the king was not subject to the petty interests and selfishness that characterized Baroque humanity. Only the king addressed the commonweal exclusively "because he alone has no fortune to establish but that of the state."

Despite Louis XIV's considerable power and broad popularity, he was forced at least twice to flee from Paris to protect himself. In that sense, he merely followed in what had become a European tradition of persistent examination of social contracts. New states often emerged from the reconsideration. For example, in 1648 the Peace of Westphalia ended 30 years of European warfare. It reaffirmed the idea of sovereignty, especially the humanistic construct of the sovereign state. The Holy Roman Empire survived scrutiny but in name only. Its sovereignty was undercut when the treaty recognized the rights of each of the 300 German principalities to negotiate alliances and to wage war; each of these now sovereign states could institute its own mercantilist policies. European recognition of the sovereignty of Switzerland and Netherlands also emerged from Westphalia, the latter at the expense of once mighty Spain. Portugal had declared its freedom from the Spanish in 1640 and Catalonia revolted 14 years later. Spain's inability to retain control of these two places was compounded by the marked reduction in New World gold and silver arriving in the mid-seventeenth century in Spain. The dramatic decrease in wealth ended the Spanish Habsburg's pretensions of European dominance.

England

The English proved no less fractious than the Spanish or the Germans but like the French managed to persist as a single state. For nearly the entire seventeenth century, the English repeatedly fought over what form their commonwealth should take.

Proponents ranged from Hobbesian sentiments to Lockian ones as the English argued whether a single ruler or a group of rulers could best secure the commonwealth's interests.

Part of England's unique problem came from the nature of its representative institution, Parliament. That representative assembly had not proportioned power in some time-honored fashion. Its members did not reflect the vestiges of traditional medieval orders but instead the wealthy, influential, and dynamic elements of seventeenth-century English commercial society. Composition of Parliament placed its members as those most likely and able to challenge a failed mercantilist policy. Their persistent willingness to interject themselves galvanized advocates of an absolute monarchy to resist even calling Parliament into session. But since members of Parliament and those they represented comprised the wealthiest British subjects, the king's ability to raise moneys through increases in taxation was severely circumscribed without Parliament's consent.

Both James I, who died in 1625, and his successor, Charles I, tried to effect absolute monarchies. Both instituted regal trappings, centralized the state bureaucracy, and appointed to high office only those persons known to support their rule. Charles failed to call Parliament into session after 1629. Only a Scottish invasion of England over a decade later ended Charles's absolute reign. It placed great financial strains on Charles and his demands for increased taxes fell on deaf ears. England's moneyed interests—those interests represented in Parliament—refused to support higher taxes unless Parliament granted its consent and Charles was forced to call Parliament into session in 1640. It then attacked Charles's absolutism, maintaining that to get its approval, the king must cede additional, permanent authority to Parliament. The king refused and Parliament outlawed many crown practices.

A civil war ensued in 1642. The Parliament-funded army defeated Charles, who was beheaded by parliamentary edict in 1649. Numerous replacements for the monarchy were suggested but a parliamentary system not unlike that proposed by Locke some 40 years later emerged. Various parliamentary bureaucracies checked and balanced each other as they attempted to formulate an efficient mercantilist policy. The Navigation Acts, acts that mandated that only English ships and crews carry certain articles bound for English markets, were the primary legacy of that effort. But in 1653, Oliver Cromwell, a former member of Parliament and leader of the army, demonstrated the human nature that Locke would come to fear. He forcibly dissolved Parliament and appointed 156 persons to serve as the new body. Many of Cromwell's appointees returned their authority to him and he declared himself "Lord Protector" with supreme legislative power. Cromwell thanked the Parliament for its brief service and prepared a written document from which to govern, but its legislative branch—a single-house Parliament—was not scheduled to convene for nearly a year. In the interim, Cromwell and a hand-picked council reigned. Cromwell used his absolute power to establish monarchical pomp and circumstance. In fact, his pronouncements and procedures so far exceeded those instituted by the despised Charles I that several persons tried to kill the Lord Protector.

Cromwell's carefully selected single-house Parliament later met, but its questioning of Cromwell caused him to stop it from reconvening until it declared his actions legal. Nearly one-third refused to sign such a pledge and Cromwell dissolved the entire body. He established an iron rule more draconian than anything that Charles had contemplated, punishing opponents swiftly and finally. In 1656, Cromwell held parliamentary elections but excluded over one-quarter of the victors. The others refused to accept Cromwell's decision and he dismissed Parliament with the admonition "Let God judge between me and you." He then restored tyrannical absolutist rule.

Cromwell died in 1658 but the absolutism that he implemented continued. In 1660, Charles II, son of Charles I, was invited to England to become king. His brother, James, who had converted to Roman Catholicism some years earlier, succeeded him in 1685. James labored to make England Catholic, violating law and appointing co-religionists to critical positions. Birth of a male heir to the throne in 1688 terrified many English mercantilists, especially in the wake of the mass migration caused by the revocation of the Edict of Nantes in France. They summoned James's Dutch Protestant nephew and son-in-law, William of Orange (William's mother was James's sister), to England to depose the king and assume the crown. After a bloodless coup, William reigned with his wife, Mary, James's daughter.

The country that William and Mary inherited forced them to accept a Lockian government. William could use the English military to fight the French, but had to declare a Bill of Rights, limiting his powers. The bill forbade William from suspending Parliament or from interfering with the courts. William did retain considerable authority and formed a Bank of England to fight France's commercial power. Its considerable funds purchased stock in collective endeavors of individual citizens and thereby helped capitalize mercantilist ventures aimed at seizing some French wealth. The bank also lent the state money in anticipation of tax revenues, which enabled William to spend money on military and commercial adventures before tax collection. But the bank's benefits to William marked the extent of parliament's willingness to rest power in a single person. Numerous subsequent acts enhanced parliamentary authority, and Mary's sister, Queen Anne (1702–1714), presided over a much-diminished court. A prime minister, who administered a cabinet in which each minister guided an executive department, maintained the ship of state. Checks existed on executive as well as legislative actions.

The Military

An effective state mercantilist policy depended on the army: The army often subdued hostile forces to permit colonization, which became in the seventeenth century a major way to increase state wealth. Colonists created goods or grew commodities not available or easily accessible within state boundaries. In addition to turning raw materials into finished products, colonies provided new markets for the state. The military also protected state trade and stopped other states from making incursions against state territories and possessions.

Warfare itself changed after 1630. Few open field, pitched battles occurred. Protracted siege warfare became increasingly common as armies tried to surmount elaborate fortifications. The increased duration of military adventures placed a premium on dependability; assaults might take years. Armies found that the changed nature of warfare made it inconvenient to sell their services from monarch to monarch. States claimed it inconceivable not to have a powerful military at their full-time, regular disposal. Monarchs changed but states persisted, and control of the military and contracts between the military and the monarch devolved to the state. State armies received regular pay from tax revenues and military bureaucracies were streamlined to offer enhanced integration of the infantry, cavalry, and artillery. States standardized their military supplies, services, and equipment. By the 1670s military conscription—the draft and routine impressment of the urban and rural troubled and poor—became normal; state citizens needed to join armies to protect the state's collective interest when threatened. Introduction of the gun-mounted socket or ring bayonet about 1680 ended reliance on pikemen. A full-time, regular army became the single most expensive state activity. In 1690, for instance, the military expenses comprised over 75 percent of the French state budget.

These massive military changes actually had begun soon after 1600. A pervasive sense of palpable limits—on manpower, funds, and equipment—struck European military men. Each leader desired to maximize his forces' prowess and labored to do so within the context of finite resources. Rather than seek additional funds to purchase more men and equipment, each attempted to extract the maximum out of what he had. Each aimed to eliminate waste.

Early seventeenth-century Netherlands was the site of the earliest significant attempts to extract additional benefit from military forces. Commanders there, especially Maurice of Nassau, looked to the Roman military for ideas and discovered that the legions productively used the time when not fighting to prepare for an engagement and to practice military techniques. Roman generals had their forces build ramparts and dig ditches whenever possible. These techniques enabled soldiers to burrow closer and closer for a final assault, while at the same time keeping out of harm's way. Dutch commanders found that digging in decreased casualties markedly. It also helped curtail desertion and disobedience. Soldiers engaged in work had less time to get into trouble or to flee their unit.

Digging in improved military performance but institution of regular, systematic drill had a greater effect. Military practice had been haphazard. Firing of weaponry had not been coordinated and, even more significantly, soldiers often forgot important steps in weapon loading. Maurice worked to simplify and systematize weapon firing by reducing it to its component parts. He then had his forces practice in succession each of those activities according to specific verbal commands. Maurice divided gun loading and firing into 42 separate steps, each identifiable by command. He trained his troops to act in unison, to do each task at the same time, and therefore to be able to fire simultaneously and dependably. The Dutch also pioneered regular marching. Troops were taught to keep in step and to move in prescribed patterns. In addition to marching back and forth and left and right, they also learned to countermarch. One group of soldiers would move back and load, while another group would step forward and fire. The second group would then recede as the first group moved ahead and discharged their weapons. The process would continue indefinitely.

Division of the army into smaller units also maximized efficiency. Tactical units could come to bear on special tasks; only a handful of persons might be committed at one time and at the direction of their tactical commander work alone or in coordination at lightning speed. But the actual ties that developed among soldiers and between the troops and their immediate commander furthered group identification and subconsciously led each person to achieve maximum productivity. Soldiers refused to let their units down. They strived to best typify this new military man.

Such a profound set of ideas could not long remain the province of the Dutch. A military drill book first appeared in German in the 1630s. By 1649 it had been translated into as esoteric a language as Russian. Europeans also created schools to train officers in these new military arts. The Netherlands formed its first such academy in 1619 and by the end of the century similar schools could be found in virtually every country. But the transformation of the military encompassed far more than introducing these practices and procedures. As one historian has written, "The dexterity and resolution of individual infantrymen scarcely mattered any more. Prowess and personal courage all but disappeared beneath an armor-plated routine." Persons never considered desirable for military service, such as the urban and rural poor, now seemed more than suitable for the army. The universal humans could be tempered by their experience. The poor could be made into new men, soldiers, by drilling, by repetition and rote. Armies had become self-perpetuating training institutions, in which recruits were drilled until they became interchangeable, quite different from their former selves. But the new dimensions of soldiering and the new reality of army life had an even more penetrating metamorphosis. "Military units became a specialized sort of community, within which new, standardized face-to-face relations . . . did very swiftly replace the customary hierarchies of prowess and status." A "few weeks of drill created sentiments of solidarity, even among previously isolated individuals." The new military had become a tiny leviathan, the state wrought small or in miniature.

Each of these measures served to increase military productivity through elimination of waste. But this neat military choreography assumed not only soldiers standardized by training but also standardized equipment and supplies. Without those latter standards, drill would fail. But establishing a single type of military equipment or supplies for a state's entire armed forces promised further to reduce expense. Manufacturers worked continually; they always knew what type of equipment or supplies were to be used and they always knew that demand for them would continue to exist. Standardization of equipment, supplies, and soldiers made reinforcement easy. Each soldier, supply, and type of equipment was interchangeable, ideally as alike as matchsticks or pins.

State Culture

Hobbes argued that the arts, literature, and music depended on the existence of the state. An all-consuming war of all against all would prevent the time or resources necessary for cultural creations. A proliferation of cultural forms then proved the efficacy of the state, that a truce in the war had been declared. But the idea of the state, the collective representative of humanity in a particular location, itself deserved celebration. Seventeenth-century Europeans recognized the state as a triumphant product of human ingenuity. Confronted by its own inferior nature, humankind fashioned a mechanism by which to mitigate, if not overcome, those deficiencies. The state seemed the appropriate body to support and finance the celebration, which was always conducted in very human terms. Artists, litterateurs, composers, architects, and other humanists created monuments to human ingenuity, its creation—the state—and humanity itself.

Empirical evidence would suggest that Hobbesian analysis was correct. An unprecedented number of new cultural endeavors swept Europe in the decades after 1650 after conclusion of the wars that rocked the early seventeenth century. Also unprecedented was the pace at which the state employed artists, musicians, composers, poets, sculptors, and others. The state, not the individual noble, became the single most important grantor of cultural largess as the state was celebrated, commemorated, or enhanced. Royalty mattered only because it represented the state.

Creation of the Academie de Peinture et de Sculpture in 1648 to organize French art for the glory of the state provided a potent demonstration of the new patronage. A state-run academy for art guaranteed that art would exist within the state. Colbert, the great architect of French mercantilist policy under Louis XIV, soon recruited artists, especially sculptors and architects, from Italy. These Italians had a two-fold purpose: to teach the French and to create monumental architecture and other works to celebrate the power and authority of the French state.

The French decision to solicit Italians to make monuments to the French state was not unusual. Increasingly after about 1630, Italian and Spanish artists left their native countries and brought their cultural wares to the northern states. In impressive numbers, these men found employment in the northern capitals and major cities, such as Vienna, Paris, Dresden, and London. Their work in these places was to a large degree secular. Instead of glorifying god, which had captivated Vatican-dominated Italy, they adopted and expanded on the secular theme of the state.

As Italian artists moved north they carried the Italian style with them. This style, the later Baroque, permeated Europe. Tension and conflict were its dominant themes. It mixed the grandiose and the dramatic as it portrayed humanity torn between two elemental forces. Humankind was juxtaposed with the universe or other humans or inwardly conflicted. Duty versus pleasure emerged as a common subject as did excess versus authority and power versus frailty. So too did humankind's efforts to control or even subjugate nature. Contrasting or merging the natural with the artificial became one way to resolve this fundamental tension. Artists used distinct contrasts as well as attempts to create the appearance of seamlessness to symbolize these elemental battles. Intensity of color, complexity of pattern, rhythm broken or enhanced by flow, light contrasted with darkness, and even the radical disruption of patterns provided onlookers with the artists' sense of humankind's cruel fate.

But it would be wrong to suggest that a single, neatly defined pan-European style resulted. Artists in each state modified the basic formulation to suit that state's preferences and experiences. The French, for instance, gravitated to an understated harmony and balance with fewer flourishes but emphasized power and awe. Precision marked their work as an almost mathematically calculated symmetry and proportion arose. In contrast, the Italian style was recognized for its boldness—bright colors, loudness, and daring. Great flourishes and an attempt to shock helped provide the Italianate its characteristic forms. The English more nearly incorporated the Italian than the French and its artists shunned mathematical certitude for passion.

Yet within each state considerable differences among artists were tolerated, even cherished. Artists were part of the artistic process; they brought their experience to bear on the question that they sought to expose. The situation was most clear in music. Composers wrote relatively simple lines and left directions for musicians on how to embellish those lines. They did not seek to write exactly what type of embellishments each musician should add; they only set boundaries. Musicians used their virtuosity, their unique skill produced by years of practice and study, to enhance the music. They became part of the creative process. Composers and musicians together produced later Baroque music.

Similar corporate technique marked painting. Artists organized the canvas, picked the colors, and sketched the piece's outline. But these selections and markings served as boundaries, circumscribing possibilities, for those who would finish painting the work. The result was a collaboration in which the designer and the colorist together achieved a painting.

Interaction of designer and colorist to yield art and composer and musician to produce music are suggestive. Although the parallels to the collective action of the state itself are obvious, it also helps indicate how these men and women expected their contemporaries to view and evaluate their art, music, and poetry. It gave hints about how space was organized and the emphasis on conflict and tension and served as an analogy for the way the work itself needed to be understood. Its creators viewed their artistic production as an integrated whole, not a series of reducible parts. Its boundaries merged as if one. The ostensible focus of a work was inseparable from the forms, colors, decorations, and other embellishments, modifiers, unifiers, or enhancers. As one historian argued, the later Baroque vision yielded "the castle, within its setting of a great park, adorned with statuary and fountains; the city, laid out according to an over-all plan, a comprehensive conception which blended all works of art, architecture and nature in accordance with a rational design; and finally the opera as drammadi musica with its combination of song, dance, instrument music, elaborate stage decorations, conceived in the spirit of baroque architecture, sculpture and painting."

Architects used several unifying techniques. Ornate facades and balustrades implied the rhythmic movement of waves, and magnificent flowing stone staircases swept observers into, around, or through structures or interiors. Castle and palace settings, whether carved into a great ornamental garden or park or abutting open alleys to refocus eyes and to point to repetitions in theme, conveyed not a sense of balance but an overall expression of power. The tasteful but static balance of the Renaissance was replaced by the flow or dynamism of the Baroque. The result was a kind of balanced movement, which carried the eye through the piece or structure and conveyed a potent sense of power or grandeur. Mass and size were sometimes emphasized as was artificiality, which provided a sense of boundedness. Extravagant colors, striking plaster and stone designs, and grandiose patterns symbolized domination and power.

Louis XIV's great palace at Versailles exemplified Baroque architectural technique as well as the period's emphasis on state magnificence. Begun in 1661 but built primarily between 1675 and 1685, Versailles was undertaken without consideration of cost. The French army provided the labor. Over 90 sculptors worked on the project. Nearly 5,000 orange trees were imported, 3,000 from Italy alone. The kitchen garden extended over 20 acres. Coffee trees, pineapples, and asparagus were some of its fare. When the main structure was completed—it had been Louis XIII's hunting lodge—it could house 5,000 persons. Palace elements were neatly constrained.

Versailles. Louis XIV's great palace glorified the state as it set about to improve on nature. Each structure was laid out for its site lines. Trees were manicured to portray a certain image. Orange trees, not native to the area, were imported in great number. Water spurted from fountains, giving the appearance of the sea.

Shrubs, bushes, and hedges all were drastically clipped to look identical. Gardens were extremely formal as were trees, each of which was to look like all the others. The structures exhibited a similar discipline and formalism. No odd stone, glass, or plaster edges or unexpected turns were permitted in either the exterior or interior.

Three artists joined to plan and build Versailles. Le Vau laid out the structures, Le Nôtre controlled the grounds, and Le Brun oversaw the decorations. The palace itself was organized around two sight lines: east-west and north-south. West of the palace, an archlike opening led to a palace-dependent town where the myriad courtiers lived. Numerous basins of water were juxtaposed with pools, fountains, fountains on several levels, different shaped fountains, different shaped fountains on various levels, and spuming water. Roads leading to and from Versailles were straight. At right angles, elements of interest and portent intervened: sloping pathways, marble sculptures, sculpted rows of trees, meticulously manicured hedges, topiary art, gravel walks, statuary in basins, patterns of flowers as color and decoration, and trees in tubs. (Versailles-contrived nature palled, however, when compared with that of the Dutch. Topiary art provided fanciful interest without requiring large areas.)

Painting

Incorporating the whole was no less important in painting than in architecture. Later Baroque artists used the entire canvas to make their points. Artists shunned the

Renaissance's vivid pastels for murkier colors—intermediate shades of gray, brown, and green. Extensive use of these colors, especially their tonal gradations, enabled artists gradually to eliminate distinct outlines and to merge objects into the surrounding backgrounds.

Light and shadow provided focus as well as subtlety. Stark contrast captured the eye and often provided drama. That remained true whether bathing a figure in light or setting it in the dark and having it float through space. Artists used landscapes and human faces to create finer distinctions. Late Baroque painters regularly applied large quantities of pigment to their works. Visible brushstrokes resulted. Brushstrokes conveyed a sense of movement and depth but since each ridge and furrow reflected light differently, they also yielded different colors, which augmented and refined shading. It is no exaggeration to state that later Baroque artists used color and light in a manner radically different than had their Renaissance counterparts. Renaissance artists used light and pastels to bring the eye out, to expand or push the horizons of onlookers. Later Baroque men and women employed light and murky colors to create boundaries, to limit, focus, circumscribe, or constrain the eye and to illuminate the subject of the painting.

States patronized the vast majority of great seventeenth-century painters. Paintings done by state artists often reflected state themes and members of the court and their families frequently commissioned their portraits. But a considerable amount of artistic labor went to painting the more common people in their natural settings. Work and household dominated this portraiture, which intended to expose a full range of human experience.

Despite these similarities, significant difference existed between countries. Italian painting was the least secular and also used the most vibrant colors. The French most closely approximated the Italian tradition, while the Spanish proved more somber. The Dutch used darkness most effectively. But even within countries significant distinctions held true. For example, the contemporary Spaniards, El Greco and Diego Velásquez, seemed to have less common techniques than Velásquez and the Dutch master, Franz Hals. Yet Jan Vermeer and Rembrandt Van Rijn, two Dutch contemporaries of Hals, clearly shared less technique with each other than with Hals.

Music

Late Baroque assumptions transformed virtually every aspect of European music. The state assumed a prominent role in music creation as its magnificence demanded music at every public occasion. Producers of music, composers, became an important part of courtly society. Performers also found themselves increasingly bound to the state. Stable groups of musicians in state service replaced the wandering minstrels and musicians of earlier times. These musicians, often Italian trained, signed contracts to play certain instruments for specified periods and only to play in conjunction with this single group. As virtuosos—and they needed to be virtuosos because the absence or primitive form of keys made playing instruments far more difficult than it is today—they had developed the individual skills necessary to do justice to a state composition. By keeping them together, the state guaranteed that their collective skill would exceed their individual talents. Choral music also was reformulated. Polyphony, the verbally indistinct harmonizing of several relatively equal voices, gave way to the monodic style, in which one voice dominated and the others enhanced or accompanied it. Language in singing took on meaning. What a vocalist said became at least as important as the instrumental melodies themselves. But later Baroque composers went further. Rather than simple music-heightened speech, their music intensified the sense of the speech. Emotions were expressed through words; even the recitative seemed inseparable from and even dictated instrumental music. These sentiments found expression in two newly popular musical forms—cantatas and oratorios. Oratorios were longer and more complex than cantatas and often lacked the poetic nature of these smaller compositions. Both accentuated tension and boundaries as both surveyed the scope of human emotions to frame their stories. Both used repetition and pattern to reinforce their sentiments and to suggest that those sentiments were eternal, confining and defining, undeniable facets of human nature.

At this time popular musical instruments were not structured for this emphasis on voice, word and conflict. The viol, lute, virginals, and clavichord proved adept for melodious harmonizing and for supporting choral harmonies, but none was strong or distinct enough to play against the others. Only brass instruments possessed the necessary vigor to counter and contrast the others. Earlier composers had faced this limitation as their contrapuntal music was restricted to using dramatic, uncontested opening chords to provide a clear, startling counterpoint to what followed. Development of powerful new instruments to play against the brass or to work in conjunction with each other permitted composers to extend their emotional range. Violins, perfected under Stradivari, made possible the nonbrass concerto. In Germany, the organ emerged as an important orchestral instrument. The oboe and, after about 1690, the clarinet enabled woodwind and string instruments to combine to form an impressive musical force. The sonata capitalized on these new instruments. It produced musical unity by setting boundaries; the sonata's three different instrumental movements varied by pace, mood, and rhythm, the juxtaposition of which formed a coherent whole. Orchestras became large—positioning the instruments to play off each other and to produce a unified sound itself was an art—and their power enhanced as these musical leviathans reflected their patron, the state. At the orchestra's head rested the conductor, who served his orchestra the way a sovereign served the state. The maestro kept the competing instruments and virtuosos toward the same goal. He ensured that grandeur and flourishes would enhance the composition, not simply showcase the player's virtuosity.

States quickly published their composers' music. Compositions—and by implication state glory—quickly spread across Europe as musicians greedily played the latest creations. Churches became important consumers of the new music. The Catholic church tended to prefer ornate instrumental compositions, concertos and sonatas. Protestant denominations favored choral music—oratorios and cantatas.

Opera

Opera marked the culmination of later Baroque musical reorganization as it combined the new choral music and orchestral arrangements. But opera did more than link musical forms. In the careful hands of Claudio Monteverdi and his spiritual descendants, opera in the seventeenth century became the ultimate expression of later Baroque humanism. Monteverdi and others used elaborate scenery and costuming to join the visual with the auditory and to make opera a festival for the human eye and ear. But the new opera transcended the mere integration of the eye and ear—and through its music human emotions. It also incorporated reason. Operas had plots; they were literature. Opera did for the humanities what the state did for humankind. Literature, art, and music were joined and tamed. Just as the state bent nature to its will in the form of palaces and topiary art, opera took artificial conventions and situations to new heights. Widespread use of castrati to sing duets with coronets reflected this thrust. Castrating young boys for brief operatic careers demonstrated the extent to which the state felt it possible to shape its human boundaries.

The Written Word

The play and the poem stand above all other forms of Baroque literature. Drama and comedy almost always came from the pen of the same author. Each reinforced the other; comedy made drama more dramatic. Heroes became more resolute when their weaknesses were exposed and then overcome. Excessive habits, libidiousness juxtaposed with chastity, for instance, or even love and duty highlighted the human struggle between passion and control. The plays of the French dramatist Molière, for example, established comedic situations by presenting a foil—the miser, the doctor, the bureaucrat—and then letting the very human characters play off the foil and reveal human expression.

Boundaries of humanity and the human experience were explored by poets as well as playwrights. The couplet, heroic and otherwise, provided the archtypical forum in which to express and to juxtapose human dilemmas and to expose and explore the parameters of human experience. Poetry proved every bit as contrived as opera and topiary art. Poets hewed to a mechanical set of rules; couplets must rhyme and be metrically precise. Yet authors wanted energy and movement within their symmetrical, harmonious form but not at the expense of restricting the full range of human emotion, including human power and potentialities. The last criteria sometimes led poets to draw their characters with almost superhuman powers, a technique that permitted them to draw more sharply the boundaries of human endeavor. Milton's Satan, almost a match for god, was perhaps the best known of these poetic creations.

Hope and Fear in an Age of Boundaries

Creation of the state was an act of desperation. An idea of limits, both in terms of resources and of human nature, made it acceptable. The state at once symbolized and institutionalized the two-pronged possibilities of later Baroque Europe. A sense of limits generated fear but also promise. It channeled thought and made achieving consensus far easier. At the same time, it encouraged daring experiments to maximize those limited resources. Innovation became both critical and desirable. The seventeenth century was a heady time, albeit a fearful time. To be sure, Europeans formed the state to reduce those fears and to increase promise. But states attempted to achieve these goals in numerous ways, some not readily apparent. States confronted limited water, wood, coal, and minerals. They dealt with famine, war, inflation, and economic stagnation. They confronted the question of human nature.

Seeking refuge in the state was not the only fear-driven initiative. Some Europeans sought solace and certainty in religion. Although long-established religions—Catholicism, Calvinism, and Lutheranism—had developed ties intertwining them with the state, new religious groups emerged in the seventeenth century, especially during particularly anxious times. All were similar in postulating a Christian community rather than a civil one. They mimicked the state and competed with it, sometimes seeking to replace, undermine, or subvert that institution. In its place, they would erect a Christian state; they emphasized both the terrestrial and humanity in their formulations.

New religious groups often placed themselves in opposition to more established and generally state-linked religions. For example, George Fox's Quakers actively promoted civil disobedience. Touched by an "inner light," Quakers railed against dogma, yet dressed, spoke, and behaved unconventionally but similarly to one another. Their anti-dogma dogma set them apart from normal society but provided them group identity and coherence. Others also staked out separate identities based upon some sort of uniquely unifying experience. The Pietists sang together, did social projects together, and believed in communal transformation. The Quietists, Jansenists, and Deists each maintained a separate organizational structure based upon their particular experiences.

The State and Agriculture

Even those who hoped to erect a more Christian community to compete with or replace the state often turned to the state as a matter of course. Until a replacement could be fashioned, the state remained the only institution capable of approaching peak efficiency. Agriculture proved no exception. States embarked upon conscious policies to expand agricultural production, sometimes assisting private enterprise directly. Nowhere had pressure been more intense to increase agricultural productivity than in the Netherlands. Farmers there desperately tried to capitalize on every acre of arable land that they had reclaimed from the sea. An assault on fallow land became the newest Dutch initiative. Small farmers, operating closest to the margin, took the greatest chances. They understood that soil needed rest but acted to make that rest productive. Growing turnips and parsnips on fallow land enabled them to produce fodder for wintering animals. These penned animals generated huge quantities of manure, which, when applied to fields, increased soil fertility. A refined convertible agriculture soon began to supplant turniping. To virtually eliminate fallowing, farmers converted pasture into cropland and vice versa. They grew cereals for two years and then pastured animals there for the next three. Growing clover on pasture restored soil nitrogen and provided good forage for cattle. A year of turnips or a completely fallow year capped the 6-year cycle.

Redoubled animal agriculture proved more profitable than grain agriculture. Sheep and cattle maintained their value more consistently than grains and the Dutch found it worthwhile to produce meat for export and import grains for human consumption. The Dutch also began a large dairy export industry. But animal agriculture was not the only market-oriented initiative. The Dutch readily grew industrial crops—hemp, madder, woad, flax, and cole seed for oil. Each crop had a high market value, more than enough to justify importation of human foodstuffs. The Dutch also produced specialty crops for export. Their famous tulips were a large enough cash crop to make it profitable to import staples.

Both tulips and industrial crops required heavy manuring. The Dutch supplemented animal manure with human and chemical fertilizers. They capitalized on the proximity of large cities and towns to ship night soil from privies to the countryside, applying the noxious material to the fields. The Dutch also used lime and peat to enhance soil fertility and tried as best as possible to drain farmland.

In the seventeenth century, other Europeans studied Dutch techniques and brought them back to their native lands. France adopted many of the new practices and England carried on the innovation. By the early eighteenth century, a form of four-crop rotation emerged in some parts of England. In the first year of the rotation, farmers grew turnips to feed penned cattle. Barley or wheat was planted the next year. Landowners sold the crop at market but kept the straw for their animals. A year of clover revitalized the soil and provided pasture, while in the final year of the rotation wheat and barley were again planted. In the British four-crop system, fallow had been eliminated as had distinctions between soil use for cropping and animals.

Not all places immediately accepted Dutch or English methods. Some Spanish farmers adopted clover and other aspects of Dutch practice but many gravitated to the easily cultivated maize, a product of Spain's New World conquests. Italian agriculturists also grew the marketable maize in great quantities. Eastern Europeans retained more of traditional agriculture. Large grain-producing landowners—wheat and barley had become export market crops—increasingly tried to reinstitute a form of serfdom on their tenant farmers, while maintaining the peasants that were never freed. Local differences prevailed in the East as they had in the West. Yet it would be wrong to suggest that the Dutch and English methods did not yield a kind of standardized agricultural practice, at least in theory. The simple agricultural calendars of the Renaissance gave way to sophisticated discussions of farm management in the seventeenth century. Rather than a string of aphorisms aimed at providing memorable jingles as guides to action, the new literature spoke to farmers as reasoning persons and took into account the entire farm, seeking to integrate its many activities throughout the year into a rational whole. The prolific Gervase Markham was a master of the new agricultural literature. His several volumes in English spread the latest agricultural practice and ideas, including the importance of tile drainage on frequently wet lands and the advantages of mechanical seed drills.

The state took a more visible hand in the barren land question. Barren lands constituted waste, pure and simple, and their transformation into productive agricultural lands was a challenge outside the scope of any individual. What made certain lands barren was the first question asked. Framing the question in that fashion and assuming it could be resolved almost certainly indicated an inquiry of significant proportions and a 1665 Commission on Agriculture looked at the entire English state to generate answers. This commission provided a model of state efforts. It canvassed the entire kingdom to determine what was known, decided what techniques could be tried, and finally communicated its findings to English agriculturists generally. It used respondents' observations to find what crops grew best where and to deduce by what rules they grew. A neat classification of English agricultural practice resulted. It began with soils as the committee divided English soils by type (essentially particle size) and then divided those types by products and by techniques of preparation. It also identified and cataloged what kinds of plows and other agricultural implements farmers used, even considering relationships between type of crop and depth and length of furrow. Every step of the investigation proceeded in this manner. A portrait of what was known of English agriculture and what seemed to work best where was the final product.

The State, Knowledge, and Mastery

The British agricultural investigative committee was not an isolated creation. It was part of a far larger state effort, the Royal Society of London . . . for the Propagation and Dissemination of Useful Knowledge. Mimicked in state after state in the later seventeenth and early eighteenth centuries, the Royal Society and its imitators capitalized on later Baroque ideas of knowledge, especially its limited character, the state's role in revealing that knowledge, and humankind's ability to use that knowledge to master its realm. Two persons, Francis Bacon in England and René Descartes in France, best expressed the basic philosophy that found institutionalization in these new state mechanisms. Although each approached the knowledge question somewhat differently, both Bacon and Descartes reached similar conclusions. Seventeenth-century Europeans needed to formulate a philosophy that would maximize the present, one that operated according to Baroque notions, and one explicitly different from those of the past. Both demanded certainty in an uncertain world, where a sense of limits and boundaries produced uneasiness but also promise. This new philosophy targeted the relativism and perspective of the Renaissance, which Bacon and Descartes saw as a continuation of classical thought, as the problem. A new humankind-focused philosophy capitalizing on what humankind held in common, its reason and senses, held the potential to dominate the natural world.

Bacon was 35 years Descartes's senior and, for a time, a barrister at the royal court. His critique of the past was two-fold and very Hobbesian, even as he wrote decades before Hobbes. Bacon's ancient Greeks, the group he railed against, had presented humankind nothing more than "brain-creations and idle displays of power." In the past "everyone philosophizes out of the cells of his own imagination." The result was catastrophic. As we followed that "folly," all things in the world became what "we think [they] should be," rather than what we have "found [them] to be in fact." Our purpose has become "to overcome an opponent in argument" when it should be "to command nature to action." Bacon sought "the better and more perfect use of human reason in the inquisition of things" and urged his contemporaries "to try the whole thing anew upon a better plan, [to embark upon] a total reconstruction" of "all human knowledge, raised upon proper foundations." We must seek "invention not of arguments but of arts; not of things in accordance with principles, but of principles themselves." Bacon called for a rejection of past practice and theory and a reconstitution based upon observation. But he also understood that observation when conducted individually would soon replicate what he sought to replace. In his scheme, each human mind "at the very outset [would] not be left to take its own course but

René Descartes. Here portrayed by the famous Dutch artist Franz Hals, Descartes understood the difficulties of operating without agreed-upon parameters and so thought to establish mathematics as a useful but artificial frame of reference. Together with Francis Bacon, Descartes is often credited as a molder of modern science.

guided at every step . . . as if done by machinery." The quest for the laws of nature required a collective mechanism to organize and systematize that pursuit. Just as the artificial creation of the state stopped a war of all against all, an organization dedicated to working collectively to discover the laws of nature would end "volatile and preposterous philosophies, which have preferred theses over hypotheses."

Descartes was no less blunt in his call for "an absolutely new science." The Jesuit-trained soldier came to this position when he realized that although "reason is naturally equal in all" humans, numerous differences afflict humankind. That could only have arisen by "conducting our thoughts along different lines and not examining the same things" and he warned that "nothing solid could [be] built on such shifting foundations." The then favored decentralized, relativistic, individualistic approach enabled its practitioners only to "win the admiration of the less learned." Descartes saw the problem as similar to the one faced by artists puzzled about how to represent a three-dimensional object in a two-dimensional painting. To Descartes, artists resolved their problem not by attempting to replicate nature but by developing an agreement among themselves about how to represent nature. They chose to place in the light "one of the principal" faces and left "the others in the shade, let[ting] them appear only in so far as they can be seen while one is looking at the principal one." That act provided artists certainty; it established the boundaries of what they deemed artistically acceptable.

Descartes challenged his contemporaries to reject the "speculative philosophy taught in schools" and to create instead "a practical philosophy" to "procure . . . the general good of all men." This new philosophy would enable humankind to employ "the power and effects of fire, water, air, the stars, the heavens and all other bodies which surround us" for "all the uses for which they are appropriate and thereby make ourselves, as it were, masters and possessors of nature." The "invention of an infinity of devices by which we might enjoy, without any effort, the fruits of the earth and all its commodities" would be the natural consequence.

Descartes's practical philosophy owed much to "mathematics, because of its certainty and self-evidence of its reasonings." His method required him to "never accept anything as true" that he "did not know to be evidently so," to divide questions into as many simple facets as possible, and to think "in an orderly way, beginning with the simplest objects and the easiest to know, in order to climb gradually, as by degrees." In this fashion, "each truth" would become a tool that "served afterwards to find other" truths. A mind channeled to this type of reasoning would accustom "itself little by little to conceive its objects more clearly and distinctly," which would accelerate the quest for more truths.

The genius of Descartes's method lay in providing practitioners a consistent frame of reference. Rather than establish a formal institution through which to work on mutually agreed-upon problems, Descartes offered a "normal" method to unite humankind as if it were one investigator. Each person applying the same method would arrive at information that would further the interests of the whole. Bacon wanted humankind to create an institutional mechanism to achieve consistency. Descartes demanded that humanity adopt an approach to nature that enforced consistency. The end in both cases was the same. Humankind systematically worked to uncover laws of nature, laws that could be used to maximize humanity's grasp of the natural world. Humankind could use the laws of nature in unnatural ways.

The Cartesian emphasis on mathematics led to introduction of several techniques to establish consistency of effort and expression in the quest to more closely approximate certainty. Descartes himself proposed what we call today Cartesian coordinates, a union of geometry and algebra that arbitrarily created and fixed certainty, but invention of decimals to represent fractions and a well-defined understanding of probability as statistical certainty were also significant. So too was the pendulum clock, which enabled later Baroque men and women to approximate time more closely. Calculus, used to determine areas under curves that asymptotically approached straight lines, provided mathematically useful boundaries, the limits of which replaced attempts to develop the "true" values of those areas. Calculus transformed something infinite into something that could be manipulated.

Mathematical/geometrical measurement became increasingly important in the search for natural law but Bacon's proposal itself was memorialized in the Royal Society and similar institutions. Granted special powers by the crown to own property, raise and expend funds, limit and select members, and publish their deliberations, these organizations operated as de facto state waste-reducing monopolies. They sought to gather observations from all over the globe, to bring them to a central place and examine them in conjunction with other material, and then to subject them to human reason. They encouraged correspondents in distant places and paid some a regular wage to send biological, geological, and other specimens to the group. In all cases, the organizations set agendas for action. They awarded prizes for persons answering specific institution-dictated questions, and established other competitions to direct inquiry into particular areas. They determined what met organizational scrutiny, if it merited dissemination, and in what form it would be disseminated.

These organizations generally pledged to steer clear of theological or political discussions or speculations. They chose to ignore the ultimate or first cause of things—god—and concentrated on the question how. By what principle does something operate? In what order is living nature? How best to achieve a certain objective? Members of these groups and others interested in natural phenomena explained physical properties as mechanisms, products that could be quantified or measured. Each particle of a certain category of material was just like every other particle of that material. For example, the relationship between gaseous pressure and volume was explained in quantifiable terms as if each gaseous particle was like an identically acting spring; as it was wound up, it got increasingly smaller but exerted an inversely proportional force on the object compressing it.

The inverse pressure-volume relationship constituted a law of nature, the revelation of which demonstrated to contemporaries the efficacy of their program. In this context, Isaac Newton's discovery of the law of universal gravitation in 1687 approached mythic status. The law, which described in mathematical terms the rules by which bodies attract and thus permitted humankind to reduce the motion of the heavens to a series of timeless quantifiable expressions, captured a prize for that feat that the Royal Society had long offered. Newton's discovery and by extension humankind generally now seemed to approach the divine. It had revealed one of god's most masterful secrets. Alexander Pope hailed the Newtonian revelation in a heroic couplet:

> Nature and nature's law lay hid in night;
> God said, "Let Newton be," and all was light.

Newton's law of universal gravitation demonstrated that god ran the heavens as if by clockwork, like a great machine. That view profoundly affected many persons' understanding of god. But discovery of such a momentous natural law, a mechanical law, further held the promise of other seminal laws and not just for the natural world. Natural laws governing life, society, and politics, including the natural way to organize society, seemed possible, even imminent, as later Baroque Europeans began to identify persons in stereotypical terms: noble savages, wise Egyptians, and Chinese philosophers, for instance. The antiquity of a people seemed the product of experience, which gave them cachet, and served as a clue upon which to develop laws of human societies.

The State, Commerce, and Manufacturing

The state's commitment to maximizing the collective wealth of its citizens led to numerous state-sponsored or -supported enterprises. It also produced several new

Isaac Newton. Newton's law of universal gravitation regularized the motion of the heavens. Contemporaries looked on Newton's law as a natural outcome of their quest for natural laws to govern all mechanical and human activity and as a goad to further efforts.

experiments. In the Holy Roman Empire, for example, alchemy became official court policy. Unable to achieve economic dominance by traditional means, the state sought to discover the philosophers' stone and thereby solve the empire's economic troubles by turning base metals into gold and silver. But direct intervention by the state in economic enterprise was not the sole means of proceeding. The state was not responsible for initiating all commercial or manufacturing activities but for providing and maintaining an environment favorable to commerce and manufacturing.

Transoceanic activities fell in that category. Earlier Europeans had embarked on voyages of discovery and in the process explored, plundered, and traded. Seventeenth-century Europeans rarely sought new lands. Humankind had learned the extent of its world. In fact, the noted Danish geographer who settled in England, Herman Moll, in *The Compleat Geographer* (1709) assured his readers that his maps would not become obsolete; geographic knowledge approached completeness. Similar sentiments were reflected in the proliferation of encyclopedias, places where all knowledge was categorized and tabulated. What remained for later Baroque Europeans was to achieve maximum economic benefit from what the previous voyages of discovery had revealed. The long-standing extraction of precious metals, especially

Mexican silver, had virtually run its course and trade with the natives of these foreign lands netted only marginal gain. Establishing settlements in newly discovered places became the preferred Baroque method of wealth enhancement. Colonists oversaw slaves growing coffee, sugar, tea, spices, tobacco, or cotton, highly profitable crops in great demand in Europe. Other colonies produced primarily raw materials. These substances were scarce in the colonizing state but not necessarily in Europe as a whole. Generating wealth from colonies was a two-fold benison. A state's total wealth would increase and it would not have to squander moneys by importing a scarce material from a competitor state. States sometimes provided colonists economic incentives—monetary, land, or tax bounties—to mine, plant, or produce substances, such as iron or trees, that would further the state's interests. Forcing specific goods to travel to Europe only on a state's vessels manufactured additional wealth from the colonial relationship.

The state sometimes used bounties and other incentives to produce much-desired agricultural commodities in Europe but as a rule it was much less directly intrusive in the rural nonagricultural economy. This was especially the case in textile manufacture, where the Netherlands-originated "putting out" system spread throughout rural Europe. It reduced entrepreneurial risk markedly. Entrepreneurs paid employees by the piece, not regular wages. These wealthy persons needed only to secure the raw materials necessary for production to respond to market expansion or contraction. Yet its rapid proliferation throughout Europe had its costs. In the Netherlands and England, places of initial enterprise, textile manufacture stagnated after about 1650.

The scale of enterprise was among the most striking features of the Baroque economy. Printing, sugar refining, distilling, chemicals manufacturing, dyeing, mining, and metal refining achieved unprecedented scale. Introduction of new technological processes or inventions did not fuel the expansion of scale. The seventeenth century was a particularly desultory time for new technologies. Etched glass and fire hoses were cutting-edge inventions, neither of which spawned a potent industry. Glass window panes became common but they did not amount to a huge new manufacture. Scale stemmed in part from the idea of the state as a single entity. State policies also helped foster large-scale manufacturing. Grants of exclusivity—monopolies and patents—permitted manufacturers to achieve whatever size the market would bear without fearing or responding to domestic competition. State grants came to another end. They freed nascent and other industries receiving them from commercial interests, who had long dominated the economy, and thus diversified economic power within the state. The state itself even began to compete with commercial financial houses and family partnerships. Its great potential wealth made it a likely source of credit and at a scale that could eclipse smaller partnerships. That states operated so close to the margin proved the major check in their ability to manage (and dominate) the domestic economy.

The state's economic emergence led to great growth among state capitals. For example, the population of London tripled to about 600,000 in less than 100 years. The state's dramatic introduction into enterprise also produced a new kind of city, the great financial city. London and Amsterdam, the leading cities of the Baroque's two economic giants, received that mantle and assumed a magnificent presence. The two cities were long experienced with joint-stock companies and other complex forms of generating significant amounts of capital while limiting partnership liability and easily became lending's twin European focuses. Their extensive lending activities also converted both into de facto stock markets. Depersonalizing investment and extending it beyond friends, coreligionists, and family had brought new perspective to borrowing. Rather than perpetuate marginal, undercapitalized firms and concentrate therefore on profit or loss of any single venture or handful of ventures, persons adopted an outlook far less immediate. The nature of risk changed. Greater capital reserves granted investors considerable latitude to speculate, to wait for initial losses to turn into long-range profits. The great number of persons and states interested in these financial undertakings produced a surplus of investors looking for good investments and competition for shares of stock in promising companies. A market sprung up for these stock transfers and Amsterdam and London became the primary financial centers in which stocks were exchanged. Investors successively sold promissory notes or assigned them to any number of persons, many of whom lived far from the financial center. De facto state sanction of these economic transactions, which included offering written checks for debt payment and more complicated credit transfers, regularized the process and secured Amsterdam's and London's ascendancy.

Urban Life and Living

Urban life replicated the state in miniature. Securing economic success was its reason for being and so everything was structured to best achieve that goal. Those with the greatest experience and stake in the urban economy received predominant authority. Social distinctions—status, wealth, influence, nobility—all mattered. Cities controlled themselves and their religious, judicial, and economic institutions, often exerting considerable power over their hinterlands. Like states, not all cities were equally successful. Seaports grew faster than nonseaport cities of comparable size and larger cities grew quicker than smaller places. Cities dedicated to long-distance or sea trade or industrial production increased in population the quickest. Participating in the economic life of a city required persons to become city citizens, a status not unlike being a joint-stock company member. Citizenship depended upon several things: property ownership, wealth, residence, reputation, and skill. Citizenship was often a necessary prerequisite for guild membership, voting, and serving in city government. Many cities allowed wives of deceased guild members to become members of the guild themselves, even take apprentices. But only textile groups regularly granted women guild membership. In Holland, citizenship restrictions were eased somewhat. Those hardworking and with exceptional skills were admitted as citizens no matter their personal views or religious practices. Some worked in textiles but most congregated in printing, mapmaking, and ceramics. The Dutch citizenship practices helped explain that state's dramatic seventeenth-century rise. Yet so too did heavy use of wind-powered sawmills and water-driven power hammers to produce standardized goods as well as Dutch merchants' adoption of the fluit, an easily handled, large-capacity cargo ship operated by a skeleton crew. But even in a tolerant, relatively open state, such as Holland, an estimated 10 percent of the urban population in the smallest cities failed to meet citizenship requirements. The percentage was doubtless much greater in larger Dutch cities and in the cities of other states, especially state capitals and metropolises.

Acknowledgment that a percentage of the population lived in urban places but were not citizens weighed heavily on city residents. Violent crime seemed everywhere and vagrancy was deemed the problem. As explained in the seventeenth century, vagrancy was a conscious choice, a rejection of the state by ill-designing persons. Persons chose to live by their wits outside of society and to prey on society to achieve wealth. Vagrants were not considered isolated persons but rather a permanent feature of the urban environment. More important, European city residents claimed that vagrants organized themselves to attack society more effectively. These rebels formed gangs to better extract society's riches. Baroque Europeans sometimes called them gypsies or an international brotherhood of thieves and pickpockets. Other times they explained vagrants as strangers from rural regions, vagabonds, or deserting soldiers. But while their origin and identification differed from place to place, each place saw them as similar threats to society. These people not only refused to add to society's well-being but actively drained off society's resources by competing with society. Rather than work for a livelihood, these people labored to trick society and to achieve wealth dishonestly at the expense of others.

The understanding that a permanent class existed in cities dedicated to the destruction of urban institutions forced cities to act to control these criminals. Imprisonment, flogging, impressment in the military, and forced labor proved the most popular methods but creation of workhouses best captured the Baroque spirit. Physical facilities separated from society, workhouses kept vagrants and their ilk from wreaking their havoc on society. To maximize resources, workhouses needed to be as inexpensive as possible. But instead of trying to reduce costs, Baroque Europeans demanded that workhouses make money. Inmates needed to produce something marketable, such as brooms, that would more than pay for the cost of their institutionalization. Cities and states cracked down on vagrancy in one final way. Some cities in England, France, and Sweden required passports or testimonials for even local travel. Afraid that some vagabonds would move en masse from place to place, these cities prohibited entrance to anyone not able to prove himself or herself a citizen of another place or possessing an unimpeachable reputation. To be sure, seventeenth-century men and women understood that war, pestilence, famine, or religious intolerance—revocation of the Edict of Nantes, for example, spread the Huguenots throughout Europe—could dramatically affect a person's socioeconomic situation. And they erected mechanisms to cater to these deserving poor. Churches and guild organizations gave alms and established almshouses to shelter unfortunates. But they considered the deserving poor small in number compared to the catastrophic influx of vagrants that seemed to prey on society.

Paralleling concern about vagrants was concern over Satanism. Epidemics of bubonic plague and smallpox, periodic famines marked by a rapidly deteriorating climate—some historians have called the period from the early seventeenth century to about 1740 a mini ice age—fires that devastated entire cities of wood-framed buildings, and the seemingly endless wars appeared to some religious Europeans as early signs of the millennium. Especially in cities, churchgoing, god-fearing Europeans noted a sharp upturn in Satan worship. These men and women feared the mischief Satan's forces might unleash. But they seemed to fear in at least equal measure the abandonment of god and, by extension, of Christian civil society or the compactual or contractual state. Not surprisingly, church and state, including city governments, worked hand in glove to rid themselves of this social plague. No one church performed the crusade alone. Whatever church received state sanction worked diligently with the state to regulate expression and to weed out deviations to the socio-religious norm. Satanism now seemed a rebuff of secular society.

Raw Material Shortages: Iron, Wood, and Coal

Tremendous urban growth and extension of large-scale manufacturing enterprises were based on iron and wood. So too was the almost constant state of war that characterized much of the seventeenth century. Yet from the sixteenth century, Western Europeans regularly faced an impending wood shortage. The thriving Venetian shipbuilding industry first noted a timber shortage and prepared to import that precious commodity from northern Europe, but the situation was most acute in the Netherlands and England, two relatively small countries. In both places, desire to maximize agricultural production had led entrepreneurs to destroy woodlands as they transformed forests into cultivated land. Unavailability of wood directly affected both states' ability to produce iron. Charcoal, wood heated in a deficiency of oxygen, burned much hotter than wood and its use in iron smelting and refining was required to produce truly adequate iron. Europeans also employed this valuable wood-derived commodity to refine other ores. Wood's prohibitively high cost in Western Europe virtually doomed ore mining there. Western European states found agricultural exports more profitable even when balanced against importation of iron, copper, and tin.

The Case of England

The spectacular growth of England in the seventeenth century rivaled that of Holland, the other major state not blessed with an abundance of resources. Both grew to dominate the Baroque economy. The Dutch specialized in trade and manufacture of a limited range of goods. England achieved its prominence by adapting many industries to a new fuel source, coal. Struck by the impending wood shortage, the English as early as the late sixteenth century began to convert to coal. In 1560 the state used 35,000 tons of the material. It burnt more than six times as much a scant 40 years later. In 1700, England would consume over 2.5 million tons of coal. The English ruthlessly took advantage of economies of scale as they changed to coal. By the early seventeenth century, glassmaking, brewing, brick making, saltpeter refining, alum manufacture, seawater evaporation for salt, textile dye production, and sugar refineries were all coal-powered enterprises. Coal also became a predominant household heating source as English ships carried the material from coal fields to London and other major cities. It would not be incorrect to claim that coal fueled the state's great late-sixteenth-century expansion. Population grew by 60 percent and agricultural incomes, including incomes of small free and bound farmers, skyrocketed as these relatively well-to-do agriculturists became a ready market for England's new industrial output.

Iron manufacture was one area in which coal could not be substituted for wood-based charcoal since coal was not hot enough to replace charcoal in smelting nor pure enough to replace it in refining. Ore smelted at too low a temperature or metal refined with high-sulfur-content coal proved brittle, unsuitable for industrial, military, and other applications. English entrepreneurs desperately tried to increase the

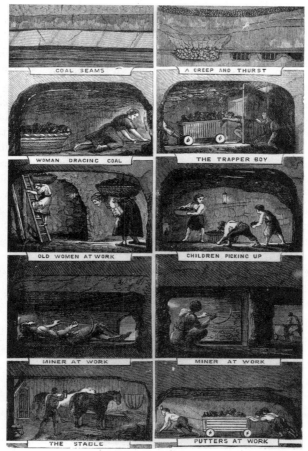

English Coal Mining. Coal use rose spectacularly in seventeenth-century England as the English feared that its nation was on the verge of deforestation. The land possessed plentiful coal resources, but much of it rested hundreds of feet beneath the surface. England's high water table filled these underground mines with water and made mining exceedingly difficult.

state's supply of trees. They planted coppices, dense thickets of seedling trees, near smelting furnaces and systematically harvested the immature plants after about 15 years to maximize wood production per unit time. Others sought a wood substitute. Peat among other materials was tried but none of these potential replacements proved hot enough to supplant charcoal.

Even without new smelting or refining fuels, the English managed to maintain iron production nearly sufficient for their needs. But the coal situation turned desperate after about 1640. Surface and shallow coal deposits seemed to be on the verge of exhaustion. Sinking shafts and lifting coal from deeper in the earth posed no technical problem but high water tables in coastal Europe and in England, Italy, and the Netherlands did. Water needed to be drained from the mines before miners could extract the coal. They could not work under, or even waist deep in, water.

The Age of Steam: Its Origins

Invention of the first workable steam engine by Thomas Newcomen and John Calley, two English ironmongers, would be an act of fundamental importance in human history. This mechanical leviathan was the progenitor of a class of devices and means to achieve work that would permit humankind to accomplish unheard-of tasks. Its descendants would enable humanity to work at a scope unfathomable to the seventeenth-century mind. But while the steam engine would hold a myriad of both positive and negative implications for the late eighteenth, nineteenth, and twentieth centuries and beyond, the Newcomen engine, its genesis and application were very much creatures of their time. Embedded in the engine's invention and utilization was the web of ideas fundamental to and defining of Baroque Europe. The state was involved in many ways: through the patent grant of exclusivity; sanction of joint-stock companies; interest of the sovereign; and creation of institutions that gathered and disseminated knowledge. A potent sense of limits, especially the desire to squeeze the maximum out of every endeavor, permeated the search for an engine as well as its design. Those both achieving success and failure cleaved to contemporary ideas of natural law, human reason, observation, and use of the human senses. They

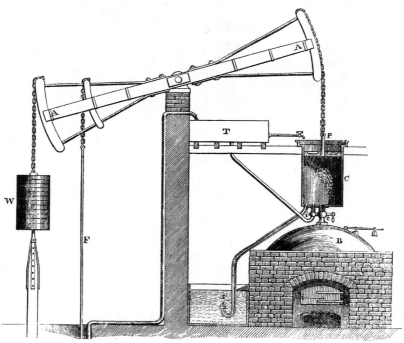

Newcomen Engine. The world's first successful steam engine, the Newcomen engine, used the weight of the atmosphere to force down a piston to do work. It proved especially adept at raising water from coal mines where the tremendous inefficiencies of the engine did not matter.

also held to the ideas that through the application of these notions humankind could harness, tame, or dominate nature and make it conform on a regular basis to what humanity wanted to do.

The Engine

The problem of water in coal mines inspired the steam engine. Prior to the seventeenth century, several entrepreneurs designed mine drains or pumps, or sought workable systems of manual water haulage. For example, Agricola's late sixteenth-century *De Re Metalica* devoted several chapters to that question. His most elaborate device required extremely wide shafts and thousands of pounds of iron just to lift water some 100 feet. All this metal was necessary because Agricola encountered one problem, confirmed by the observations of numerous others: Water could not be raised by suction more than about 30 feet. This apparent limitation confounded inventors, who, by the early seventeenth century, had abandoned suction pumps to seek other water-raising methods. These ingenious persons often sought to force water from mines rather than lift it and claimed the "impellent force of fire" as the means. Nowhere was the quest for a fire-propelled mechanism for thrusting water from mines more passionately pursued than in England. Men there tried to capitalize on the Statute of Monopoly of 1624, which regularized the process of patenting, a technique used sporadically for over a century. This procedure offered inventors unilateral protection to share their discovery with their countrymen. When a person "by his own wit" invented something that led "to the furtherance of a trade," the sovereign could grant him a patent—an exclusive right to manufacture or sell the patented object—for a reasonable period "in consideration of the good that he doth bring by his invention to the Commonwealth." When this period of exclusivity expired, the patented invention became commonwealth property.

Seventeenth-century patent specifications were very slim. Noted persons requested the privilege of exclusivity for an idea, not a finished product. Such a vague description as "raising water from low pits by the impellent force of fire" constituted a full patent description. The English state, like the other states of Europe, recognized the dilemma inherent in granting a broad charge of exclusivity on such unspecific grounds, but a world potentially marked by a war of all against all refused to compel its citizens to reveal detailed plans or inventions in patent petitions. Instead, in 1639 England required patent grantees to develop their devices within 3 years of the initial grant. If they failed to produce the promised article, the patent returned to the state to be granted to some other ingenious person.

More than a handful of patents were awarded for fire-driven water-raising devices in England alone in the half-century after 1639. As best as can be determined, all attempted to use steam produced from boiling water to lift a piston, which would push water up a considerable length. None of the patent recipients produced a workable device. Baroque methods could not be marshaled nor then contemporary materials fashioned to produce a mechanism forceful and sturdy enough to press up water any considerable distance. But while forcing water by fire was apparently proving fruitless, several persons examined the anomaly that helped generate that investigative line: the inability of humans to lift water by suction more than about 30 feet.

The mines of Grand Duke Ferdinand II of Tuscany were among those affected by standing water, and Evangelista Torricelli, the court philosopher-mathematician, turned to the water question in 1641. He thought that the level to which water ascended by suction pump must be balanced by another force and presumed that particles of something—earth-surrounding air—pressed down. These air particles exerted a mechanical force as if by unfolding springs or by sheer weight. He then postulated in 1644 that we "live submerged at the bottom of an ocean of elementary air" and that the "heaviest part [is] near the surface of the earth." He recreated in miniature the water-level problem with a tube of mercury, a very heavy liquid, and found that the mercury too "rises to the point at which it is in balance with the weight of the external air that is pushing it."

Torricelli died before he was able to determine "when the air is coarser and heavier and when more subtle and light." In 1648, Blaise Pascal put the theory to a test. He carried a mercury air-measuring device not unlike that used by Torricelli up a mile-high slope near his birthplace in France, stopping periodically to take readings. As expected, the higher that Pascal went, the less high the mercury rose, indicating that something approaching an inverse relationship between height in the air and in the column existed.

The weight or force of air also was reflected in the studies of Otto von Guerricke in the late 1640s and early 1650s. He demonstrated that an evacuated copper sphere would implode as the weight of the air pressed on it; the weight of the air could be used to accomplish physical labor. Von Guerricke gave a series of public demonstrations and trials before the Holy Roman Emperor in 1654, and his work and techniques soon became standard fare for the cadre of investigators seeking to discover natural law. Among those most impressed was Robert Boyle, a future founder of the Royal Society, and several persons who would participate in creation of the Academie des Sciences, the French equivalent of the Royal Society. Boyle's exposition in England of von Guerricke's, Pascal's, and Torricelli's studies inspired Sir Samuel Morland to seek a patent to raise water from mines "by the force of Aire and Powder conjointly." Morland apparently never produced such a device but even his brief patent application suggested the line of effort he sought to pursue. Morland hoped to force the air out of a cylinder by gunpowder explosion and use the weight of the atmosphere to press a piston down. The atmosphere would provide the work. A similar strategy was undertaken in France by Christian Huygens and Denis Papin in the early 1670s. Their Academie des Sciences–sponsored water-raising device would have aided the French state but not by clearing mines. It would supply water to the fountains at Louis XIV's palace at Versailles.

Gunpowder proved difficult to work with and the French experiments ended in 1675 when Papin, a Huguenot, fled to England. The Royal Society welcomed him and he shared his labors with his new colleagues, but Papin soon turned away from water raising. Not until the late 1690s was the subject broached again in a major way. Thomas Savery, descendant of a prominent English merchant family, participant in numerous joint-stock adventures, and a leading inventor, designed a water-raising machine he called "The Miner's Friend."

Savery, who had labored as a military and mining engineer, received his patent in 1698 "for raising water by the impellent force of fire." But his actual device, completed soon thereafter, used both a vacuum to raise water about 30 feet and then steam to force it up an additional small distance. Savery's device worked poorly—it could raise water about 50 feet—but was important because it condensed steam to create a vacuum. Savery communicated his findings to the Royal Society and became a fellow in 1705.

Newcomen began his steam engine work at about that time and probably knew of the labors of his predecessors. He certainly combined many of their insights in his deceptively simple device. Rather than force a piston and water up, he permitted the atmosphere to force a piston down. A boiler produced steam, which was injected into a cylinder, and cold water was applied. The ensuing vacuum caused the piston to plummet. A rocker arm attached to a rod running from the piston took that power-ful working stroke and used it to lift a column of water a specific height—a bicycle valve, a leather flap, provided easy entrance of the water but prohibited egress. The arm then rocked back and forced the piston down and the condensed steam out of the cylinder. The process could continue uninterrupted.

Newcomen's steam engine violated the Savery patent and the interests combined to form a joint-stock company to shepherd the device. The first Newcomen engines successfully pumped water up well over 100 feet. By the mid-eighteenth century, miners sunk shafts over 600 feet deep and Newcomen engines kept them dry. In 1729, Newcomen engines pumped water from over 100 coal mines throughout East-ern and Western Europe. Shortly thereafter the initial patent for the engine expired. By 1770, at least 1,500 Newcomen engines were in use in the European world. Eng-land alone produced over 8 million tons of coal.

The State, the Steam Engine, and the Modern World

The steam engine's invention and adoption provided the second of the two major pil-lars of the modern industrial state. With creation of the state itself, humanity now possessed both the means and mechanisms—it long had the hubris—to create what later observers have called the modern world. Humankind brought the steam engine out of the mine and applied it to work generally. Humanity then produced other mechanical prime movers to labor ever more efficiently. In that sense, the electric motor and even nuclear energy are descendants of Newcomen's engine. Humankind also took the state itself through several transformations. Formation of the nation-state, joining ethnic identity and geography and combining them with sociopolitical considerations, proved a particularly potent mix.

That these twin pillars of modernity sprung from the Baroque is highly ironic. The Baroque concern over limits, over boundedness, yielded a mechanism that pow-ered, mined, and milked production and expansion, colonialism, and the factory. It opened in the West a world of unprecedented plenty, including a higher standard of living, democracy, and ethnic hatred. The state and the steam engine proved exceed-ingly secular, effectively ending concepts of Christendom or even pan-Europeanism, except as a consumer market.

Yet it would be a mistake to claim that modernity simply evolved out of Baroque Europe. Humanity's relationship with its past has been much more complicated and complex. At least since the advent of writing, each time in the human past has entered into its own relationship with its past. It has selected what parts of its past it wanted to retain and ignored those parts it found not germane. It has decided if there even was a past as well as what that past meant. What has been considerably more revealing and more fruitful is the relationship among the ideas of a past and what is selected in the past. These ideas as well as many others are found throughout a wide range of human endeavors at the same time. They infuse an extraordinary scope of enterprises and structures—intellectual, social, and physical. It is upon these and other ideas that Western civilization has been built.

For Further Reading

Braudel, Fernand. *The Wheels of Commerce*. London: Collins, 1982.

Dijksterhuis, E. J. *The Mechanization of the World Picture*. Translated by C. Dikshoorn. London: Oxford University Press, 1961.

Foucault, Michel. *The Order of Things: An Archaeology of the Human Sciences*. New York: Random House, 1970.

Laslett, Peter. *The World We Have Lost*. New York: Charles Scribner's Sons, 1965.

Middleton, W. E. Knowles. *The Experimenters: A Study of the Accademia del Cimento*. Baltimore: Johns Hopkins University Press, 1971.

Munck, Thomas. *Seventeenth-Century Europe: State, Conflict and the Social Order in Europe 1598–1700*. London: Macmillan, 1990.

Newton, Norman T. *Design on the Land: The Development of Landscape Architecture*. Cambridge: Harvard University Press, 1971.

Nussbaum, Frederick L. *The Triumph of Science and Reason, 1660–1685*. New York: Harper & Row, 1953.

Pennington, D. H. *Europe in the Seventeenth Century*, 2d ed. London: Longman, 1989.

Rolt, L. T. C., and J. S., Allen. *The Steam Engine of Thomas Newcomen*. New York: Science History Publications, 1977.

Shapin, Steven, and Simon Schaffer. *Leviathan and the Air-Pump*. Princeton: Princeton University Press, 1985.

Smith, Pamela H. *The Business of Alchemy: Science and Culture in the Holy Roman Empire*. Princeton: Princeton University Press, 1994.

Stoye, John. *Europe Unfolding, 1648–1688*. New York: Harper & Row, 1969.

Willey, Basil. *The Seventeenth Century Background*. Garden City, N.Y.: Doubleday, 1934.

Wilson, Catherine. *The Invisible World*. Princeton: Princeton University Press, 1994.

Wilson, Charles. *The Dutch Republic*. New York: McGraw-Hill, 1968.

Wolf, John B. *The Emergence of the Great Powers, 1685–1715*. New York: Harper & Row, 1951.

Photo Credits

1.1 ©Erich Lessing/Art Resource; 1.2 ©Erich Lessing/Art Resource; 1.3 ©Photo Researchers, Inc.; 1.4 UPI/Corbis-Bettmann; 1.5 ©Photograph by Erich Lessing/Art Resource; 1.6 ©Photograph by Erich Lessing/Art Resource; 2.1 Corbis-Bettmann; 2.2 North Wind Picture Archives; 2.3 Art Resource; 2.4 Scala/Art Resource; 2.5 North Wind Picture Archives; 2.6 North Wind Picture Archives; 2.7 North Wind Picture Archives; 3.1 ©Photograph by Erich Lessing/Art Resource; 3.3 ©Copyright 1994 George Haling. All Rights Reserved. Photo Researchers, Inc.; 3.4 ©Archivi Alinari 1990. All Rights Reserved. Art Resource; 3.5 North Wind Picture Archives; 4.1 Corbis-Bettmann; 4.2 Corbis-Bettmann; 4.3 Corbis-Bettmann; 4.4 North Wind Picture Archives; 4.5 Archive Photos; 4.6 North Wind Picture Archives; 5.1 Corbis-Bettmann; 5.2 ©Erich Lessing/Art Resource; 5.3 ©Bridgeman/Art Resource; 5.4 North Wind Picture Archives; 5.5 Culver Pictures, Inc.; 5.6 Giraudon/Art Resource; 6.1 North Wind Picture Archives; 6.2 Corbis-Bettmann; 6.3 North Wind Picture Archives; 6.4 Corbis-Bettmann; 6.5 UPI/Bettmann; 6.6 The Bettmann Archive; 7.1 Corbis-Bettmann; 7.2 Giraudon/Art Resource; 7.3 The Bettmann Archive; 7.4 North Wind Picture Archive; 7.5 Corbis-Bettmann; 7.6 Culver Pictures, Inc.; 7.7 North Wind Picture Archives; 8.1 North Wind Picture Archives; 8.2 Culver Pictures, Inc.; 8.3 North Wind Picture Archive; 8.4 ©Archivi Alinari 1990. All Rights Reserved. Art Resource; 8.5 Giraudon/Art Resource; 8.6 Corbis-Bettmann; 9.1 Corbis-Bettmann; 9.2 Foto Marburg/Art Resource; 9.3 Corbis-Bettmann; 9.5 Corbis-Bettmann; 10.1 North Wind Picture Archives; 10.2 North Wind Picture Archives; 10.3 North Wind Picture Archives; 10.4 North Wind Picture Archives; 10.5 North Wind Picture Archives; 10.6 Corbis-Bettmann; 10.7 North Wind Picture Archives; 11.1 North Wind Picture Archives; 11.2 North Wind Picture Archives; 11.3 ©Photograph by Erich Lessing/Art Resource; 11.4 Alinari-Scala. Art Resource; 11.5 North Wind Picture Archives; 11.6 North Wind Picture Archives; 11.7 Fratelli Alinari 1993. Art Resource; 11.8 North Wind Picture Archives; 11.9 Corbis-Bettmann; 12.1 North Wind Picture Archives; 12.2 Corbis-Bettmann; 12.3 Corbis-Bettmann; 12.4 North Wind Picture Archives; 12.5 Giraudon/Art Resource; 12.6 Corbis-Bettmann; 12.7 The Bettmann Archive

Index